John

ABOUT THE AUTHORS

General editor

Clinton E. Arnold (PhD, University of Aberdeen), professor and chairman, department of New Testament, Talbot School of Theology, Biola University, Los Angeles, California

Gospel of John:

Andreas J. Köstenberger (PhD, Trinity Evangelical Divinity School; Dr. rer. soc. oec., Vienna University of Economics), professor of New Testament and Greek, director of PhD/ThM studies, Southeastern Baptist Theological Seminary, Wake Forest, North Carolina

Zondervan Illustrated Bible Backgrounds Commentary

John

Andreas J. Köstenberger

Clinton E. Arnold *general editor*

Zondervan Illustrated Bible Backgrounds Commentary: John

Requests for information should be addressed to:

Zondervan, *Grand Rapids, Michigan 49530*

Library of Congress Cataloging-in-Publication Data

Zondervan illustrated Bible backgrounds commentary / Clinton E. Arnold, general editor.
p.cm.
Includes bibliographical references.
ISBN-10: 0-310-27828-7
ISBN-13: 978-0-310-27828-3
1. Bible. N.T.—Commentaries. I. Arnold, Clinton E.
BS2341.52.Z66 2001
225.7—dc21 2001046801

Printed in China

Interior design by Sherri L. Hoffman

07 08 09 10 11 12 13 • 12 11 10 9 8 7 6 5 4 3 2 1

CONTENTS

INTRODUCTION

All readers of the Bible have a tendency to view what it says it through their own culture and life circumstances. This can happen almost subconsiously as we read the pages of the text.

When most people in the church read about the thief on the cross, for instance, they immediately think of a burglar that held up a store or broke into a home. They may be rather shocked to find out that the guy was actually a Jewish revolutionary figure who was part of a growing movement in Palestine eager to throw off Roman rule.

It also comes as something of a surprise to contemporary Christians that "cursing" in the New Testament era had little or nothing to do with cussing somebody out. It had far more to do with the invocation of spirits to cause someone harm.

No doubt there is a need in the church for learning more about the world of the New Testament to avoid erroneous interpretations of the text of Scripture. But relevant historical and cultural insights also provide an added dimension of perspective to the words of the Bible. This kind of information often functions in the same way as watching a movie in color rather than in black and white. Finding out, for instance, how Paul compared Christ's victory on the cross to a joyous celebration parade in honor of a Roman general after winning an extraordinary battle brings does indeed magnify the profundity and implications of Jesus' work on the cross. Discovering that the factions at Corinth ("I follow Paul . . . I follow Apollos . . .") had plenty of precedent in the local cults ("I follow Aphrodite; I follow Apollo . . .") helps us understand the "why" of a particular problem. Learning about the water supply from the springs of Hierapolis that flowed into Laodicea as "lukewarm" water enables us to appreciate the relevance of the metaphor Jesus used when he addressed the spiritual laxity of this church.

My sense is that most Christians are eager to learn more about the real life setting of the New Testament. In the preaching and teaching of the Bible in the church, congregants are always grateful when they learn something of the background and historical context of the text. It not only helps them understand the text more accurately, but often enables them to identify with the people and circumstances of the Bible. I have been asked on countless occasions by Christians, "Where can I get access to good historical background information about this passage?" Earnest Christians are hungry for information that makes their Bibles come alive.

The stimulus for this commentary came from the church and the aim is to serve the church. The contributors to this series have sought to provide illuminating and interesting historical/cultural background information. The intent was to draw upon relevant papyri, inscriptions, archaeological discoveries, and the numerous studies of Judaism, Roman culture, Hellenism, and other features of the world of the New Testament and to make the results accessible to people in the church. We recognize that some readers of the commentary will want to go further, and so the sources of the information have been carefully documented in endnotes.

The written information has been supplemented with hundreds of photographs, maps, charts, artwork, and other graphics that help the reader better understand the world of the New Testament. Each of the writers was given an opportunity to dream up a "wish list" of illustrations that he thought would help to illustrate the passages in the New Testament book for which he was writing commentary. Although we were not able to obtain everything they were looking for, we came close.

The team of commentators are writing for the benefit of the broad array of Christians who simply want to better understand their Bibles from the vantage point of the historical context. This is an installment in a new genre of "Bible background" commentaries that was kicked off by Craig Keener's fine volume. Consequently, this is not an "exegetical" commentary that provides linguistic insight and background into Greek constructions and verb tenses. Neither is this work an "expository" commentary that provides a verse-by-verse exposition of the text; for in-depth philological or theological insight, readers will need to have other more specialized or comprehensive commentaries available. Nor is this an "historical-critical" commentary, although the contributors are all scholars and have already made substantial academic contributions on the New Testament books they are writing on for this set. The team intentionally does not engage all of the issues that are discussed in the scholarly guild.

Rather, our goal is to offer a reading and interpretation of the text informed by what we regard as the most relevant historical information. For many in the church, this commentary will serve as an important entry point into the interpretation and appreciation of the text. For other more serious students of the Word, these volumes will provide an important supplement to many of the fine exegetical, expository, and critical available.

The contributors represent a group of scholars who embrace the Bible as the Word of God and believe that the message of its pages has life-changing relevance for faith and practice today. Accordingly, we offer "Reflections" on the relevance of the Scripture to life for every chapter of the New Testament.

I pray that this commentary brings you both delight and insight in digging deeper into the Word of God.

Clinton E. Arnold
General Editor

LIST OF SIDEBARS

John

LIST OF CHARTS

INDEX OF PHOTOS AND MAPS

ABBREVIATIONS

1. Books of the Bible and Apocrypha

1 Chron.	1 Chronicles
2 Chron.	2 Chronicles
1 Cor.	1 Corinthians
2 Cor.	2 Corinthians
1 Esd.	1 Esdras
2 Esd.	2 Esdras
1 John	1 John
2 John	2 John
3 John	3 John
1 Kings	1 Kings
2 Kings	2 Kings
1 Macc.	1 Maccabees
2 Macc.	2 Maccabees
1 Peter	1 Peter
2 Peter	2 Peter
1 Sam.	1 Samuel
2 Sam.	2 Samuel
1 Thess.	1 Thessalonians
2 Thess.	2 Thessalonians
1 Tim.	1 Timothy
2 Tim.	2 Timothy
Acts	Acts
Amos	Amos
Bar.	Baruch
Bel	Bel and the Dragon
Col.	Colossians
Dan.	Daniel
Deut.	Deuteronomy
Eccl.	Ecclesiastes
Ep. Jer.	Epistle of Jeremiah
Eph.	Ephesians
Est.	Esther
Ezek.	Ezekiel
Ex.	Exodus
Ezra	Ezra
Gal.	Galatians
Gen.	Genesis
Hab.	Habakkuk
Hag.	Haggai
Heb.	Hebrews
Hos.	Hosea
Isa.	Isaiah
James	James
Jer.	Jeremiah
Job	Job
Joel	Joel
John	John
Jonah	Jonah
Josh.	Joshua
Jude	Jude
Judg.	Judges
Judith	Judith
Lam.	Lamentations
Lev.	Leviticus
Luke	Luke
Mal.	Malachi
Mark	Mark
Matt.	Matthew
Mic.	Micah
Nah.	Nahum
Neh.	Nehemiah
Num.	Numbers
Obad.	Obadiah
Phil.	Philippians
Philem.	Philemon
Pr. Man.	Prayer of Manassah
Prov.	Proverbs
Ps.	Psalm
Rest. of Est.	The Rest of Esther
Rev.	Revelation
Rom.	Romans
Ruth	Ruth
S. of III Ch.	The Song of the Three Holy Children
Sir.	Sirach/Ecclesiasticus
Song	Song of Songs
Sus.	Susanna
Titus	Titus
Tobit	Tobit
Wisd. Sol.	The Wisdom of Solomon
Zech.	Zechariah
Zeph.	Zephaniah

2. Old and New Testament Pseudepigrapha and Rabbinic Literature

Individual tractates of rabbinic literature follow the abbreviations of the *SBL Handbook of Style*, pp. 79–80. Qumran documents follow standard Dead Sea Scroll conventions.

2 Bar.	*2 Baruch*
3 Bar.	*3 Baruch*
4 Bar.	*4 Baruch*
1 En.	*1 Enoch*
2 En.	*2 Enoch*
3 En.	*3 Enoch*
4 Ezra	*4 Ezra*

3 Macc.	*3 Maccabees*
4 Macc.	*4 Maccabees*
5 Macc.	*5 Maccabees*
Acts Phil.	*Acts of Philip*
Acts Pet.	*Acts of Peter and the 12 Apostles*
Apoc. Elijah	*Apocalypse of Elijah*
As. Mos.	*Assumption of Moses*
b.	*Babylonian Talmud* (+ tractate)
Gos. Thom.	*Gospel of Thomas*
Jos. Asen.	*Joseph and Aseneth*
Jub.	*Jubilees*
Let. Aris.	*Letter of Aristeas*
m.	*Mishnah* (+ tractate)
Mek.	*Mekilta*
Midr.	*Midrash I* (+ biblical book)
Odes Sol.	*Odes of Solomon*
Pesiq. Rab.	*Pesiqta Rabbati*
Pirqe. R. El.	*Pirqe Rabbi Eliezer*
Pss. Sol.	*Psalms of Solomon*
Rab.	*Rabbah* (+biblical book); (e.g., *Gen. Rab.=Genesis Rabbah)*
S. ʿOlam Rab.	*Seder ʿOlam Rabbah*
Sem.	*Semahot*
Sib. Or.	*Sibylline Oracles*
T. Ab.	*Testament of Abraham*
T. Adam	*Testament of Adam*
T. Ash.	*Testament of Asher*
T. Benj.	*Testament of Benjamin*
T. Dan	*Testament of Dan*
T. Gad	*Testament of Gad*
T. Hez.	*Testament of Hezekiah*
T. Isaac	*Testament of Isaac*
T. Iss.	*Testament of Issachar*
T. Jac.	*Testament of Jacob*
T. Job	*Testament of Job*
T. Jos.	*Testament of Joseph*
T. Jud.	*Testament of Judah*
T. Levi	*Testament of Levi*
T. Mos.	*Testament of Moses*
T. Naph.	*Testament of Naphtali*
T. Reu.	*Testament of Reuben*
T. Sim.	*Testament of Simeon*
T. Sol.	*Testament of Solomon*
T. Zeb.	*Testament of Zebulum*
Tanh.	*Tanhuma*
Tg. Isa.	*Targum of Isaiah*
Tg. Lam.	*Targum of Lamentations*
Tg. Neof.	*Targum Neofiti*
Tg. Onq.	*Targum Onqelos*
Tg. Ps.-J	*Targum Pseudo-Jonathan*
y.	*Jerusalem Talmud* (+ tractate)

3. Classical Historians

For an extended list of classical historians and church fathers, see *SBL Handbook of Style*, pp. 84–87. For many works of classical antiquity, the abbreviations have been subjected to the author's discretion; the names of these works should be obvious upon consulting entries of the classical writers in classical dictionaries or encyclopedias.

Eusebius

Eccl. Hist.	*Ecclesiastical History*

Josephus

Ag. Ap.	*Against Apion*
Ant.	*Jewish Antiquities*
J.W.	*Jewish War*
Life	*The Life*

Philo

Abraham	On the Life of Abraham
Agriculture	On Agriculture
Alleg. Interp	*Allegorical Interpretation*
Animals	*Whether Animals Have Reason*
Cherubim	*On the Cherubim*
Confusion	*On the Confusion of Thomas*
Contempl. Life	*On the Contemplative Life*
Creation	*On the Creation of the World*
Curses	*On Curses*
Decalogue	*On the Decalogue*
Dreams	*On Dreams*
Drunkenness	*On Drunkenness*
Embassy	*On the Embassy to Gaius*
Eternity	*On the Eternity of the World*
Flaccus	*Against Flaccus*
Flight	*On Flight and Finding*
Giants	*On Giants*
God	*On God*
Heir	*Who Is the Heir?*
Hypothetica	*Hypothetica*
Joseph	*On the Life of Joseph*
Migration	*On the Migration of Abraham*
Moses	*On the Life of Moses*
Names	*On the Change of Names*
Person	*That Every Good Person Is Free*
Planting	*On Planting*
Posterity	*On the Posterity of Cain*
Prelim. Studies	*On the Preliminary Studies*
Providence	*On Providence*
QE	*Questions and Answers on Exodus*
QG	*Questions and Answers on Genesis*
Rewards	*On Rewards and Punishments*
Sacrifices	*On the Sacrifices of Cain and Abel*
Sobriety	*On Sobriety*
Spec. Laws	*On the Special Laws*
Unchangeable	*That God Is Unchangeable*
Virtues	*On the Virtues*

Worse	*That the Worse Attacks the Better*

Apostolic Fathers

1 Clem.	*First Letter of Clement*
Barn.	*Epistle of Barnabas*
Clem. Hom.	*Ancient Homily of Clement* (also called *2 Clement*)
Did.	*Didache*
Herm. Vis.; Sim.	*Shepherd of Hermas, Visions; Similitudes*
Ignatius	*Epistles of Ignatius* (followed by the letter's name)
Mart. Pol.	*Martyrdom of Polycarp*

4. Modern Abbreviations

AASOR	Annual of the American Schools of Oriental Research
AB	Anchor Bible
ABD	*Anchor Bible Dictionary*
ABRL	Anchor Bible Reference Library
AGJU	Arbeiten zur Geschichte des antiken Judentums und des Urchristentums
AH	*Agricultural History*
ALGHJ	Arbeiten zur Literatur und Geschichte des Hellenistischen Judentums
AnBib	Analecta biblica
ANRW	*Aufstieg und Niedergang der römischen Welt*
ANTC	Abingdon New Testament Commentaries
BAGD	Bauer, W., W. F. Arndt, F. W. Gingrich, and F. W. Danker. *Greek-English Lexicon of the New Testament and Other Early Christina Literature* (2d. ed.)
BA	*Biblical Archaeologist*
BAFCS	Book of Acts in Its First Century Setting
BAR	*Biblical Archaeology Review*
BASOR	*Bulletin of the American Schools of Oriental Research*
BBC	*Bible Background Commentary*
BBR	*Bulletin for Biblical Research*
BDB	Brown, F., S. R. Driver, and C. A. Briggs. *A Hebrew and English Lexicon of the Old Testament*
BDF	Blass, F., A. Debrunner, and R. W. Funk. *A Greek Grammar of the New Testament and Other Early Christian Literature*
BECNT	Baker Exegetical Commentary on the New Testament
BI	*Biblical Illustrator*
Bib	*Biblica*
BibSac	*Bibliotheca Sacra*
BLT	Brethren Life and Thought
BNTC	Black's New Testament Commentary
BRev	*Bible Review*
BSHJ	Baltimore Studies in the History of Judaism
BST	The Bible Speaks Today
BSV	Biblical Social Values
BT	*The Bible Translator*
BTB	*Biblical Theology Bulletin*
BZ	*Biblische Zeitschrift*
CBQ	*Catholic Biblical Quarterly*
CBTJ	*Calvary Baptist Theological Journal*
CGTC	Cambridge Greek Testament Commentary
CH	*Church History*
CIL	*Corpus inscriptionum latinarum*
CPJ	*Corpus papyrorum judaicorum*
CRINT	*Compendia rerum iudaicarum ad Novum Testamentum*
CTJ	*Calvin Theological Journal*
CTM	*Concordia Theological Monthly*
CTT	Contours of Christian Theology
DBI	*Dictionary of Biblical Imagery*
DCM	*Dictionary of Classical Mythology.*
DDD	*Dictionary of Deities and Demons in the Bible*
DJBP	*Dictionary of Judaism in the Biblical Period*
DJG	*Dictionary of Jesus and the Gospels*
DLNT	*Dictionary of the Later New Testament and Its Developments*
DNTB	*Dictionary of New Testament Background*
DPL	*Dictionary of Paul and His Letters*
EBC	*Expositor's Bible Commentary*
EDBT	*Evangelical Dictionary of Biblical Theology*
EDNT	*Exegetical Dictionary of the New Testament*
EJR	*Encyclopedia of the Jewish Religion*
EPRO	Études préliminaires aux religions orientales dans l'empire romain
EvQ	*Evangelical Quarterly*
ExpTim	*Expository Times*
FRLANT	Forsuchungen zur Religion und Literatur des Alten und Neuen Testament
GNC	Good News Commentary
GNS	Good News Studies
HCNT	*Hellenistic Commentary to the New Testament*
HDB	*Hastings Dictionary of the Bible*

HJP	*History of the Jewish People in the Age of Jesus Christ*, by E. Schürer
HTR	*Harvard Theological Review*
HTS	Harvard Theological Studies
HUCA	*Hebrew Union College Annual*
IBD	*Illustrated Bible Dictionary*
IBS	*Irish Biblical Studies*
ICC	International Critical Commentary
IDB	*The Interpreter's Dictionary of the Bible*
IEJ	*Israel Exploration Journal*
IG	*Inscriptiones graecae*
IGRR	*Inscriptiones graecae ad res romanas pertinentes*
ILS	*Inscriptiones Latinae Selectae*
Imm	*Immanuel*
ISBE	*International Standard Bible Encyclopedia*
Int	*Interpretation*
IvE	*Inschriften von Ephesos*
IVPNTC	InterVarsity Press New Testament Commentary
JAC	*Jahrbuch fur Antike und Christentum*
JBL	*Journal of Biblical Literature*
JETS	*Journal of the Evangelical Theological Society*
JHS	*Journal of Hellenic Studies*
JJS	*Journal of Jewish Studies*
JOAIW	*Jahreshefte des Osterreeichischen Archaologischen Instites in Wien*
JSJ	*Journal for the Study of Judaism in the Persian, Hellenistic, and Roman Periods*
JRS	*Journal of Roman Studies*
JSNT	*Journal for the Study of the New Testament*
JSNTSup	Journal for the Study of the New Testament: Supplement Series
JSOT	*Journal for the Study of the Old Testament*
JSOTSup	Journal for the Study of the Old Testament: Supplement Series
JTS	*Journal of Theological Studies*
KTR	*Kings Theological Review*
LCL	Loeb Classical Library
LEC	Library of Early Christianity
LSJ	Liddell, H. G., R. Scott, H. S. Jones. *A Greek-English Lexicon*
MM	Moulton, J. H., and G. Milligan. *The Vocabulary of the Greek Testament*
MNTC	Moffatt New Testament Commentary
NBD	*New Bible Dictionary*
NC	Narrative Commentaries
NCBC	New Century Bible Commentary Eerdmans
NEAE	*New Encyclopedia of Archaeological Excavations in the Holy Land*
NEASB	*Near East Archaeological Society Bulletin*
New Docs	*New Documents Illustrating Early Christianity*
NIBC	New International Biblical Commentary
NICNT	New International Commentary on the New Testament
NIDNTT	*New International Dictionary of New Testament Theology*
NIGTC	New International Greek Testament Commentary
NIVAC	NIV Application Commentary
NorTT	*Norsk Teologisk Tidsskrift*
NoT	*Notes on Translation*
NovT	*Novum Testamentum*
NovTSup	Novum Testamentum Supplements
NTAbh	Neutestamentliche Abhandlungen
NTS	*New Testament Studies*
NTT	New Testament Theology
NTTS	New Testament Tools and Studies
OAG	*Oxford Archaeological Guides*
OCCC	*Oxford Companion to Classical Civilization*
OCD	*Oxford Classical Dictionary*
ODCC	*The Oxford Dictionary of the Christian Church*
OGIS	*Orientis graeci inscriptiones selectae*
OHCW	*The Oxford History of the Classical World*
OHRW	*Oxford History of the Roman World*
OTP	*Old Testament Pseudepigrapha*, ed. by J. H. Charlesworth
PEQ	*Palestine Exploration Quarterly*
PG	*Patrologia graeca*
PGM	*Papyri graecae magicae: Die griechischen Zauberpapyri*
PL	*Patrologia latina*
PNTC	Pelican New Testament Commentaries
Rb	*Revista biblica*
RB	*Revue biblique*
RivB	*Rivista biblica italiana*
RTR	*Reformed Theological Review*
SB	Sources bibliques
SBL	Society of Biblical Literature
SBLDS	Society of Biblical Literature Dissertation Series

SBLMS	Society of Biblical Literature Monograph Series
SBLSP	*Society of Biblical Literature Seminar Papers*
SBS	Stuttgarter Bibelstudien
SBT	Studies in Biblical Theology
SCJ	*Stone-Campbell Journal*
Scr	*Scripture*
SE	*Studia Evangelica*
SEG	*Supplementum epigraphicum graecum*
SJLA	Studies in Judaism in Late Antiquity
SJT	*Scottish Journal of Theology*
SNTSMS	Society for New Testament Studies Monograph Series
SSC	Social Science Commentary
SSCSSG	Social-Science Commentary on the Synoptic Gospels
Str-B	Strack, H. L., and P. Billerbeck. *Kommentar zum Neuen Testament aus Talmud und Midrasch*
TC	Thornapple Commentaries
TDNT	*Theological Dictionary of the New Testament*
TDOT	*Theological Dictionary of the Old Testament*
TLNT	*Theological Lexicon of the New Testament*
TLZ	*Theologische Literaturzeitung*
TNTC	Tyndale New Testament Commentary
TrinJ	*Trinity Journal*
TS	*Theological Studies*
TSAJ	Texte und Studien zum antiken Judentum
TWNT	*Theologische Wörterbuch zum Neuen Testament*
TynBul	*Tyndale Bulletin*
WBC	Word Biblical Commentary Waco: Word, 1982
WMANT	Wissenschaftliche Monographien zum Alten und Neuen Testament
WUNT	Wissenschaftliche Untersuchungen zum Neuen Testament
YJS	Yale Judaica Series
ZNW	*Zeitschrift fur die neutestamentliche Wissenschaft und die Junde der alteren Kirche*
ZPE	*Zeischrift der Papyrolgie und Epigraphkik*
ZPEB	*Zondervan Pictorial Encyclopedia of the Bible*

5. General Abbreviations

ad. loc.	in the place cited
b.	born
c., ca.	circa
cf.	compare
d.	died
ed(s).	editors(s), edited by
e.g.	for example
ET	English translation
frg.	fragment
i.e.	that is
ibid.	in the same place
idem	the same (author)
lit.	literally
l(l)	line(s)
MSS	manuscripts
n.d.	no date
NS	New Series
par.	parallel
passim	here and there
repr.	reprint
ser.	series
s.v.	*sub verbo*, under the word
trans.	translator, translated by; transitive

Zondervan Illustrated Bible Backgrounds Commentary

JOHN

by Andreas J. Köstenberger

Who Wrote the Gospel?

The Gospel itself claims to have been written by a member of Jesus' inner circle, an apostle, one of the Twelve. Since the apostolic office was foundational and unrepeatable in the history of the church (Acts 2:42; Eph. 2:20), their message, the gospel, has special authority. As an apostle (i.e., one specially commissioned by Jesus Christ), John was given a mission to testify to what he had seen and heard (John 15:27; 1 John 1:1–4). In fact, being an eyewitness of Jesus' ministry was an indispensable requirement for apostleship (Acts 1:21–22; cf. John 1:14).

Implicit in John is also the claim of having been written by the disciple who was closest to Jesus during his earthly ministry. All the Gospel writers concur that John's relationship with Jesus was particularly close. In the present Gospel, the apostle conceals himself behind the

THE SEA OF GALILEE

John IMPORTANT FACTS:

- **AUTHOR:** The apostle John, the son of Zebedee.
- **DATE:** A.D. 80–90.
- **OCCASION AND PURPOSE:**
  - To demonstrate that Jesus is the Messiah, the Son of God, by presenting and commenting on seven selected messianic signs.
  - To show that the Christian faith is universal, applying to Jews and non-Jews alike, and the only way to God.
  - To equip believers for mission.
  - To evangelize unbelievers by equipping believers to share the good news.
- **KEY THEMES:**
  1. Jesus as the preexistent, incarnate Word, the fully divine and human Messiah, the crucified and risen Savior of the world.
  2. The Jewish rejection of Jesus the Messiah and the universal offer of salvation to everyone who believes.
  3. Believers' need to follow Jesus through obedient, committed, and faithful discipleship, realized through love and unity in the Christian community and dependence on the Holy Spirit.

expression "the disciple whom Jesus loved" (13:23; 19:26; 20:2; 21:20). As an apostolic eyewitness, John is uniquely qualified to write an authoritative account of Jesus' life: "The man who saw it has given testimony, and his testimony is true" (19:35; cf. 21:24).

Where and Why Was the Gospel Written?

John's purpose is bound up with believing in Jesus and having life in his name (20:30–31). By presenting certain startling events in Jesus' ministry as evidence that Jesus is the long-awaited Messiah, John seeks to lead his readers to place their faith in Jesus. In the aftermath of the destruction of Jerusalem and the temple in A.D. 70, John shows Jesus to be the fulfillment of Jewish as well as universal human aspirations.

While ancient tradition places the writing of John's Gospel at Ephesus (Irenaeus, *Haer.* 3.1.2), the work ultimately transcends any one historical setting and applies to the entire church of John's as well as our day. Some of the material incorporated in this Gospel probably grew over years of preaching and teaching. John's awareness of the contents of the other canonical gospels may also have influenced his final selection of material.

Together with Rome, Corinth, Antioch, and Alexandria, Ephesus ranked among the most important urban centers of the Roman empire. Located at the intersection of major trade routes, Ephesus was the largest and most well-known city of Asia Minor (modern Turkey).

In an important development, Emperor Augustus declared Ephesus as capital of the province of Asia in place of Pergamum. The Ephesian temple of Artemis was one of the seven wonders of the ancient world, and its theater could seat 25,000 people. Ephesus acquired its first imperial temple (attaining to the status of *neokoros*, "temple warden") during the latter years of Domitian's reign (A.D. 81–96).

A Gospel of Decision

John's Gospel has rightly been called "a Gospel of decision." Every person must choose between light or darkness, faith or unbelief, life or death. Light, life, and salvation, in turn, can be attained only by faith in the crucified and risen Messiah, Jesus.

RUINS AT EPHESUS

(left) The town council building (the *prytaneion).*

(right) Columns of the mercantile agora.

The Word's Eternal Preexistence (1:1–2)

Like the other evangelists, John gives an account of the life and ministry of Jesus. But he does so differently from the start. Matthew and Luke begin their Gospels with Jesus' family tree and an account of his birth. Mark jumps immediately to the ministry of John the Baptist, Jesus' forerunner. But John begins his account by showing Jesus embarking on a journey—not from Galilee to Jerusalem, but from existing eternally with God to becoming a human being like us. Thus we start in 1:1 in eternity past and arrive in 1:6 around A.D. 29 in the land of Palestine. Jesus' ministry is about to begin.

In the beginning (1:1). When hearing the phrase "in the beginning," any person in John's day familiar with the Scriptures would immediately think of the opening verse of Genesis: "In the beginning God created the heavens and the earth." John reaches back even farther into eternity past. His point is that in the beginning, even prior to creation, someone already existed along with the Father: the Word (cf. 1 John 1:1).

Was the Word (1:1). Echoes of the creation account continue here with allusion to the powerful and effective word of God ("And God said, 'Let there be light,' and there was light"; Gen. 1:3). The psalmists and prophets alike portray God's word (*logos*) in almost personal terms (e.g., Ps. 33:6; 107:20; 147:15, 18; Isa. 55:10–11). Isaiah, for instance, describes God's "word" as coming down from heaven and returning to him after achieving the purpose for which it was sent (Isa. 55:10–11). John takes the prophetic depiction of God's word in the Old Testament one decisive step further. No longer is God's word merely spoken of in personal terms; it now has appeared as a real person, the Lord Jesus Christ (cf. 1 John 1:1; Rev. 19:13).

While the primary source of John's depiction of Jesus as the Word is the Old Testament, his opening lines would resonate with his Greek-speaking audience. In Stoic philosophy, for instance, *logos* was used to refer to the impersonal principle of Reason, which was thought to govern the universe. It is a mark of John's considerable theological genius that he is able to find a term ("the Word") that is at the same time thoroughly biblical—that is, rooted in Old Testament teaching—and highly relevant for his present audience.[1]

The Word was with God (1:1). The term "God" (*theos*) is familiar to John's readers since it refers to the God revealed in the Old Testament. This word occurs in Genesis 1:1 (LXX) with reference to the Creator. The same expression is also used for "god" in the Greco-Roman world whose pantheon was made up of dozens of deities. In contrast, the Jews believed in only one God (Deut. 6:4).

The Word was God (1:1). Having distinguished the Word (i.e., Jesus) from God, John now shows what both have in common: They are God.[2] From the patristic era (Arius) to the present (Jehovah's Witnesses), it has been argued that this verse merely identifies Jesus as *a* god rather than as God, because there is no definite article in front of the word *theos*. But John, as a monotheistic Jew, would hardly have referred to another person as "a god." Also, if he had placed a definite article before *theos*, this would have so equated God and the Word that the distinction established between the two persons in the previous clause ("the Word was *with* God") would have been all but obliterated. Clearly calling Jesus God stretched the boundaries of first-century Jewish monotheism.[3]

Moreover, in Greek syntax it is common for a definite nominative predicate noun preceding the verb *einai* (to be) not to have the article,[4] so that it is illegitimate to infer indefiniteness from the lack of the article in the present passage. If, in fact, John had merely wanted to affirm that Jesus was divine, there was a perfectly proper Greek word for that concept (the adjective *theios*).

The Word's Involvement in Creation (1:3–5)

Through him all things were made (1:3). The affirmation that all things were made through *wisdom* or through God's *Word* is thoroughly in keeping with Jewish belief. John's contention, however, that everything came into being through "him"—that is, *Jesus*, God-become-flesh—is startling indeed. Nevertheless, this notion is in no way unique to John; it pervades much of the New Testament. Paul speaks of Jesus as the image of the invisible God, through whom and for whom all things were created (Col. 1:16). Jesus is the "one Lord . . . through whom all things came and through whom we live" (1 Cor. 8:6). Hebrews refers to Jesus as God's Son through whom he made the universe (Heb. 1:2). The Aramaic Targum refers to the "word" (*memra*) of the Lord as an agent of creation.[5] Greco-Roman parallels likewise portray various intermediaries as instrumental in creation (e.g., Lucretius, *Rer. Nat.* 1:4–5, 21–23 [first cent. B.C.]), as does Philo, the Hellenistic Jewish philosopher, who identifies wisdom and the Word (*Alleg. Interp.* 1.65; *Heir* 191; *Dreams* 2.242–45) and portrays the latter as the instrument through which the universe was created (*Cherubim* 127).[6]

Life . . . light (1:4). Both "life" and "light" are universal religious terms,[7] but John's teaching is deeply rooted in the Old Testament. At creation, calling forth "light" was God's first creative act (Gen. 1:3–5). Later, God placed lights in the sky to separate between light and darkness (1:14–18). Light, in turn, makes it possible for "life" to exist. Thus on the fifth and sixth days of creation, God makes animate life to populate both the waters and dry land, culminating in his creation of humankind (1:20–31; 2:7; 3:20).

Now, according to John, life was "in him," Jesus. Jesus is the source of life, including both physical and spiritual ("eternal") life. He also is the source of

The Stoic Understanding of "the Word"

In Stoic thought, which drew on ideas attributed to the pre-Socratic philosopher Heraclitus (c. 500 B.C.), Logos was Reason, the impersonal rational principle governing the universe. Zeno, the founder of this school of thought (c. 336–263 B.C.), believed that "the General Law, which is Right Reason, pervading everything, is the same as Zeus, the Supreme Head of the government of the universe" (*Fragm.* 162). People were to live in keeping with Reason, whose spark was thought to reside within them, or at least with the wisest and best of them. Stoic teaching on the Logos may have constituted common ground between John and some of his readers but hardly represents the major source of John's teaching regarding "the Word."

light, since only those who possess spiritual, eternal life have within themselves the capacity to "walk in the light," that is, to make moral decisions that are in accordance with the revealed will of God.

This again shows John's knack for contextualization. While drawing on solidly Old Testament concepts, he employs these universal terms to engage adherents of other religions and worldviews. For some, light was wisdom (or wisdom was even superior to light; cf. Wisd. Sol. 7:26–30); for others, light was given by the Mosaic law (*2 Bar.* 59:2) or Scripture (Ps. 19:8; 119:105, 130; Prov. 6:23); still others looked for enlightenment in philosophy, morality, or a simple lifestyle. Into this religious pluralism of his day, John proclaims Jesus as the supreme Light, who is both eternal and universal and yet personal.

Light . . . darkness (1:5). Beneath this contrast between light and darkness lies a significant cluster of Old Testament passages. Most interesting in this regard are several instances in Isaiah that depict the coming Messiah as a light entering the darkness. In Isaiah 9:2, we read that "the people walking in darkness have seen a great light; on those living in the land of the shadow of death a light has dawned." In Isaiah 60:1–5, a time is envisioned when the nations will walk in God's light and the glory of the Lord will shine brightly.[8]

Some believe John is here alluding to the Greek dualism between light and darkness. Rather than affirming belief in a personal God who is sovereign, all-powerful, and good, the Greeks viewed reality in terms of polar opposites, such as light and darkness or good and evil. John, however, refutes this kind of thinking in his first letter, where he states emphatically, "God is light; in him there is no darkness at all" (1 John 1:5). Another kind of light/darkness dualism is found in the Dead Sea Scrolls, particularly in the so-called "War Scroll" (1QM) depicting the battle between the "sons of light" and the "sons of darkness." But because of the sectarian nature of the Qumran community, light is never offered to those who live in darkness (cf. 1QS 3:21; 4:9–14).[9]

MENORAH

The seven-branched Jewish candelabrum.

In John, however, Jesus urges his listeners to "put your trust in the light while you have it, so that you may become sons of light" (John 12:36; cf. 8:12; 9:5). Light and darkness are no equally matched duality, but in the titanic battle between Jesus and Satan, Jesus, "the light," emerges as the overwhelming victor. Regarding this final outcome, John's readers are never left in suspense. Rather, the evangelist announces at the outset that the darkness has not overcome the light (1:5).[10] To be sure, at the cross, the forces of evil appear to have gained the upper hand; but this is followed by the resurrection.

John the Witness to the Light (1:6–8)

A man . . . sent from God (1:6). The evangelist now moves on to anchor Jesus' ministry firmly in salvation history. This phrase is reminiscent of the Old Testament description of a prophet whose role was to function as a spokesman for God (e.g., Ezek. 2:3).

His name was John (1:6). The name "John," a common name in the Hellenistic world of that day, occurred frequently among the members of the Jewish priesthood, which included John's father Zechariah (Luke 1:5).[11] "John" in this Gospel always means "John the Baptist." The "other John" known from Matthew, Mark, and Luke—that is, John the apostle, the son of Zebedee—is not referred to by name in this Gospel. It is likely that he, as the author of the present gospel, conceals himself behind the phrase "the disciple whom Jesus loved" (first used in 13:23; see comments there).

All . . . might believe (1:7). The desired (though not actual) result of John's ministry is that "all might believe" in Jesus (cf. comments on 1:9). The expression "believe" is found frequently in the Old Testament to describe the trust God desires from his people. Abraham "believed the LORD" and thus became the father, not just of the Jewish nation, but of all believers (Gen. 15:6).[12] Israel as a nation, on the other hand, is known in the Old Testament not so much for her faith in God as for her unbelief (John 12:38; cf. Isa. 53:1). While John is not averse to "believing" as the affirmation of certain religious truths, he is much more concerned about active, relational trust in Jesus Christ.

JUDEAN WILDERNESS

Jebel Quruntul, a mountain in the desert near Jericho associated with the temptation of Jesus.

The World's Rejection of the Light (1:9–11)

The true light (1:9). The coming of the Messiah is frequently depicted in the Old Testament in terms of light.[13] An important oracle, picked up also by Qumran, envisions the coming of "a star" out of Jacob (Num. 24:17). Isaiah, too, describes the coming of the Messiah as "a light" shining in darkness (Isa. 9:2; cf. 42:6–7; see comments on John 1:5). Malachi announces that "the sun of righteousness will rise with healing in its wings" (Mal. 4:2). Echoing these words, Zechariah (father of John the Baptist) says about Jesus that "the rising sun will come to us from heaven to shine on those living in darkness" (Luke 1:78–79). By affirming that Jesus is the "true light"—just as he is the "true bread from heaven" (John 6:32) and the "true vine" (15:1)—John indicates that Jesus is the fulfillment of Old Testament hopes and expectations.

Some have suggested that John is here engaging the Greek dualism between shadow and reality, contending that the expression "true light" is better rendered "*real* light" (in distinction to a mere resemblance). Perhaps some of John's Greek-speaking readers took it that way. But the primary contrast seems to be, not between real over against ideal in the Greek sense, but between earlier manifestations of God in Old Testament times through the law or various prophets and God's final, definitive revelation through Jesus Christ (cf. 1:17; 5:39; 12:38; cf. Heb.

1:1–3). In that sense, previous manifestations of God were merely "foreshadowing" the coming of the fulfillment, Jesus, who is the very essence to which the entire Old Testament symbolism points (see also John's portrayal of certain of Jesus' acts as "signs").

The true light . . . was coming into the world (1:9). This is a subtle way to convey the Christian gospel to Hellenistic ears. There also may be an implied contrast with Hellenistic religions that offered false "light."

Believing in His Name (1:12–13)

Received him . . . believed in his name (1:12). On one level, believing in "the name" of Jesus is nothing other than to believe in Jesus (3:18). Yet the phrase "believe *in the name* of Jesus" places particular emphasis on the fact that in order to believe in Jesus one must believe that he bears the divine name, the name of God. In the early church, the name of Jesus could simply be called "the Name" (Acts 5:40–41; 3 John 7).

Gave the right to become children of God (1:12). The expression translated "right" (*exousia*; cf. 5:27; 10:18; 17:2; 19:10) refers to the authorization or legitimate claim of becoming God's children, which has now been made available to all who believe in Jesus as Messiah. This assumes that in one sense sinful people are not God's children (even though they are created by God) unless and until they believe in Jesus Christ. John is careful to distinguish believers as children (*tekna*) of God from Jesus, who is the unique Son (*huios*) of God. In the Old Testament, the Hebrews are called God's children (Deut. 14:1), even God's son and firstborn (Ex. 4:22). Yet Old Testament saints did not call God "Father" or "Abba"; this constitutes a later development.

Not of natural descent, nor of human decision or a husband's will (1:13). "Natural descent" renders the phrase *ex haimatōn* (lit., "out of bloods"); it denotes a blood relationship, on the basis of the belief that natural procreation entails the intermingling of bloods (cf. Ezek. 16:6; Wisd. Sol. 7:1–2). Descent from the patriarchs was vital in the Jews' understanding of their divine sonship (cf. esp. John 8:31–41). The phrase "a husband's will" implies the Old Testament concept of male headship.

But born of God (1:13). In the Old Testament, God is said to have given birth to his people Israel (Deut. 32:18). See comments on John 3.

The Incarnation of the Word (1:14)

The Word became flesh (1:14). Rather than using the term "(hu)man (being)" (*anthrōpos*) or "body" (*sōma*), John here employs the almost crude term "flesh" (*sarx*; cf. Rom. 8:3). The affirmation that "the Word became flesh" takes the opening statement ("in the beginning was the Word") one step further: That same Word has now taken on human nature. While John does not elaborate on the precise way in which Jesus did so, his contention that deity assumed human nature in Jesus would have been anathema for Greeks, who held to a spirit-matter dualism and could hardly have imagined immaterial Reason becoming a physical being. The idea of gods appearing in human form in itself was not uncommon to the ancients. But John makes clear that the Word did not merely manifest itself as an apparition—as was alleged by the Docetists (from *dokeō*, "seem")—but that it literally became flesh.[14]

And made his dwelling among us (1:14). The Greek word for "made his dwelling" (*skēnoō*) literally means "to tabernacle" (from the word for "tent"). This rare term, which is used elsewhere in the New Testament only in the book of Revelation (Rev. 7:15; 12:12; 13:6; 21:3), suggests that in Jesus, God has come to take up residence among his people once again, in a way even more intimate than when he dwelt in the midst of Israel in the tabernacle (Ex. 40:34–35; see further the chart below). Jesus' "making his dwelling among us" is here related to the Incarnation, that is, his assumption of human flesh. In a slightly different application, both Paul and Peter refer to the human body as a "tent" (cf. 2 Cor. 5:1, 4; 2 Peter 1:13–14). The Matthean equivalent is Jesus as Isaiah's Immanuel, "God with us" (Matt. 1:23; cf. Isa. 7:14; 8:8, 10; Matt. 18:20; 28:20).

His glory (1:14). In the Old Testament, God's glory was said to dwell first in the tabernacle and later in the temple.[15] The intertestamental period was marked by the absence of God's revelation in light of Israel's apostasy. Now, in Jesus, God's glory has taken up residence in the midst of his people once again.

THE TABERNACLE

A model of the courtyard and structure.

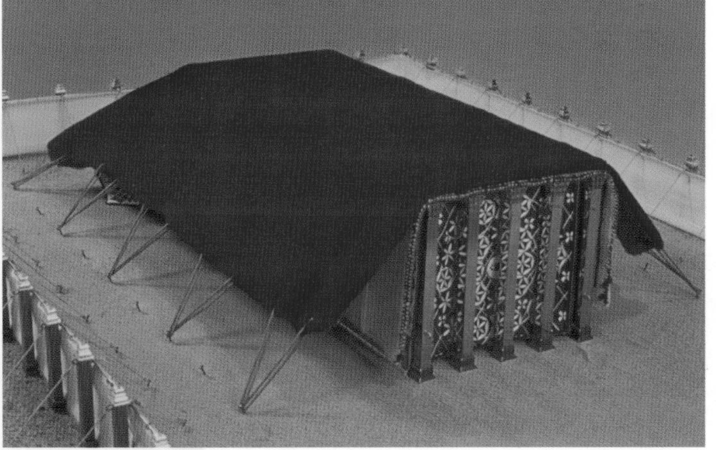

The One and Only (1:14). In Genesis 22:2, Isaac is called Abraham's "only" son, even though the patriarch had earlier fathered Ishmael. "Only" son therefore means "unique" son (in Isaac's case, son of promise). In both the Old Testament and intertestamental literature, the Son of David as well as Israel are called God's "firstborn" or even "only" son (cf. Ps. 89:27; *4 Ezra* 6:58; *Pss. Sol.* 18:4). In a decisive step, John applies the designation "One and Only" (*monogenēs*) to God's unique Son par excellence, Jesus (cf. 1:18; 3:16, 18; 1 John 4:9).

The Father (1:14). The word "Father" is more personal than the term "God" (*theos*; see comments on 1:1). It is Jesus' favorite way of referring to God in John. While Jesus taught his disciples to call God "Father" as well (Matt. 6:9 par.), his divine sonship remains unique. Thus, shortly after his resurrection, Jesus tells Mary to tell his disciples, "I am returning to *my* Father and *your* Father, to *my* God and *your* God" (John 20:17). The relationship Christians are able to enjoy with God their "Father" is unique among the world's religions, many of which portray God as remote, stern, impersonal, or mystical. The special fatherhood of God for believers is already implied in the reference to the "children of God" who are "born of God" (see 1:12–13 above).

Full of grace and truth (1:14). "Grace" occurs in John's Gospel only in 1:14–17 in the phrase "grace and truth." In distinction from the Pauline writings (where it denotes God's unmerited favor; see Eph. 2:8–9), "grace" in this

Gospel, in conjunction with "truth," alludes to the Old Testament phrase "lovingkindness and truth" (cf. Ps. 25:10; 26:3; 40:10; Prov. 16:6; see also Ps. 83:12 LXX = Ps. 84:11). The word "truth" refers to God's covenant faithfulness to his people Israel. According to John, this faithfulness found ultimate expression in God's sending of Jesus, his unique Son.

John's Witness (1:15–16)

He . . . has surpassed me because he was before me (1:15). John the Baptist was six months older than Jesus (Luke 1:24, 26) and began his ministry before Jesus did (3:1–20). The Old Testament generally (though not without exception) supports the notion that rank and honor are directly tied to one's age (Gen. 49:3; Prov. 16:31). Thus priority in time (such as being the firstborn) implied preeminence (Deut. 21:17; Isa. 61:7). In the context of John's openings words (where Jesus is portrayed as having existed with God from eternity), the Baptist's personal confession also points to Jesus' eternal origin (John 1:14; cf. 8:58; 12:41) and thus his preeminence.

Fullness of his grace (1:16). The term "fullness" occupied an important place in Gnosticism, the first major Christian heresy, which began to germinate in the second half of the first century (1 Tim. 6:21). For John, fullness can be found in one thing only: the grace of God displayed in Jesus, whose purpose was to bring "life . . . to the full" (10:10). When John attributes "fullness of grace" to Jesus, he evokes parallels with similar descriptions of God in the Old Testament.[16]

The Superior Revelation Brought by Jesus (1:17–18)

The law was given through Moses; grace and truth came through Jesus Christ (1:17). The law is seen as the gracious gift of God, albeit a gift that has now been superseded by God's gracious giving of his Son.[17] Note that what is referred to here is the event of the giving of the law, not later abuses (including legalism) by the Jews (cf. Paul).

No one has ever seen God (1:18). In the Old Testament, God had stated clearly that no one could see his face and live (Ex. 33:20). Moses received a glimpse of God's "back" (33:23), as did Hagar (metaphorically; Gen. 16:13). Old Testament saints were usually terrified of seeing God (Ex. 3:6b; Judg. 13:21–22;

Parallels Between John 1:14–18 and Exodus 33–40 [A-1]

John 1:14–18	Exodus 33–34
The Word "tented" among the disciples (1:14)	God gloriously dwelt in a tent (33:7; 40:34–35)
The disciples saw the Word's glory (1:14)	God's glory passes by Moses (33:18–23; 34:6–7)
Jesus is full of grace and truth (1:14, 17)	God abounds in lovingkindness and truth (34:6)
Disciples receive (lit.) "grace instead of grace" (1:16)	Israel finds grace in God's sight (33:14)
The law was given through Moses (1:17)	Moses was given the law (34:27–28)
Jesus is mediator between God and humanity (1:17–18)	Moses is mediator between God and Israel (34:32–35)
No one has ever seen God (1:18)	No one can see God's face and live (33:20)

Chronology of Jesus' Ministry in John's Gospel[A-2]

TIME	LOCATION/EVENT	PASSAGE IN JOHN
Origin (1:1–18)		
Eternity Past	The Word was with God	1:1–18
Initial ministry (1:19–2:12; A.D. 29–30)		
Summer/fall 29	John the Baptist near the Jordan	1:19–34
Subsequently	Jesus' calling of his first disciples	1:35–51
Winter/spring 30	The wedding at Cana of Galilee	2:1–12
First Passover and first full year of ministry (2:13–4:54; A.D. 30–31)		
April 7, 30	Jesus' first Passover (Jerusalem)	2:13–3:21
Spring/summer 30	John the Baptist near the Jordan	3:22–36
Dec./Jan./Feb. 30/31?	Jesus' ministry in Samaria	4:1–45
Subsequently	The healing at Cana of Galilee	4:46–54
Second year of ministry (ch. 5; A.D. 31–32)		
March 27, 31	Passover not recorded in John	Matt. 12:1 par.?
Oct. 21–28, 31?	The Sabbath controversy (Jerusalem)	5:1–47
Second Passover recorded in John and third year of ministry (6:1–11:54; A.D. 32–33)		
April 13 or 14, 32	Jesus' second Passover recorded in John (Galilee)	6:1–21
Subsequently	Jesus' teaching in the synagogue of Capernaum	6:22–71
Sept. 10–17, 32	Jesus at the Feast of Tabernacles (Jerusalem)	7:1–52; 8:12–59
Oct./Nov. 32?	Healing of blind man, good shepherd discourse	9:1–10:21
Dec. 18–25, 32	Jesus at the Feast of Dedication (Jerusalem)	10:22–39
Jan./Feb. 33?	Jesus' withdrawal to the area near the Jordan	10:40–42
March 33?	The raising of Lazarus (Bethany near Jerusalem)	11:1–53
March 33?	Jesus' withdrawal to Ephraim	11:54
Third Passover in John, passion week, resurrection appearances (11:55–21:25; A.D. 33)		
Friday, March 27, 33	Jesus arrives at Bethany	11:55–12:1
Saturday, March 28, 33	Dinner with Lazarus and his sisters	12:2–11
Sunday, March 29, 33	"Triumphal entry" into Jerusalem	12:12–50
Monday–Wednesday, March 30–April 1, 33	Cursing of fig tree, temple cleansing, temple controversy, Olivet discourse	Synoptics
Thursday, April 2, 33	Jesus' third Passover recorded in John (Jerusalem), betrayal, arrest	13:1–18:11
Friday, April 3, 33	Jewish and Roman trials, crucifixion, burial	18:12–19:42
Sunday, April 5, 33	The empty tomb, first resurrection appearance	20:1–25
Sunday, April 12, 33	Second resurrection appearance recorded in John	20:26–31
Prior to May 14, 33	Third resurrection appearance recorded in John	21[A-3]

Job 13:11; Isa. 6:5). The reason for humanity's inability to see God is twofold: (1) God is spirit (John 4:24); (2) mankind fell into sin and was expelled from God's presence (Gen. 3; Isa. 59:2). Jesus surmounted both obstacles: (1) He who is himself God became a human being so that others could see God in him (John 14:9–10); (2) he who was without sin died for us sinners, so that our sinfulness no longer keeps us from entering into fellowship with God (Rom. 5:1–2, 6–11).

But God the One and Only (1:18). The phrase "God the One and Only," which John here uses with reference to Jesus, is both striking and unusual (though note the equally clear ascriptions of deity to Jesus in 1:1 and 20:28). Some manuscripts, apparently in an effort to soften this statement, read "one and only Son" in keeping with 3:16, 18. If "God the One and Only" is what John actually wrote, this would identify Jesus even more closely as God than the phrase "one and only Son." Judaism believed that there is only one God (Deut. 6:4). As John shows later in his Gospel, Jesus' claims of deity bring him into increasing conflict with the Jewish authorities. In the end, the primary charge leading to his crucifixion is blasphemy (John 19:7; cf. 10:33).

At the Father's side (1:18). Literally, John here says that Jesus is "in the Father's lap," an idiom for greatest possible intimacy. This is the way the term is used in the Old Testament, where it portrays the devoted care of a mother for her children (Num. 11:12; Ruth 4:16; Lam. 2:12). The most pertinent New Testament instance of the expression is the reference to "Abraham's side" in Luke 16:22. These parallels show just how intimate John considered Jesus' relationship with the Father to be. Access to divine revelation was also prized in the pagan mystery religions and Jewish apocalypticism and mysticism. But John here claims that Jesus' access to God far exceeds that claimed by other religions.

John's Witness to the Priests and Levites (1:19–28)

John the Baptist is at this time baptizing at the Jordan (see 1:28). Luke (Luke 3:1) informs us that it was the fifteenth year of the reign of Tiberius Caesar (A.D. 14–37), which brings us up to A.D. 29.[18] Pontius Pilate (A.D. 26–36) is governor of Judea, Herod Antipas tetrarch of Galilee (4 B.C.–A.D. 39), and Herod Philip II tetrarch of Iturea and Traconitis (4 B.C.–A.D. 34). In light of the information provided by Luke that Jesus is "about thirty years old" when he starts his ministry (3:23; about thirty-three years to be precise; see introduction

JUDEA, SAMARIA, AND GALILEE

The region of Batanea is east of the Sea of Galilee.

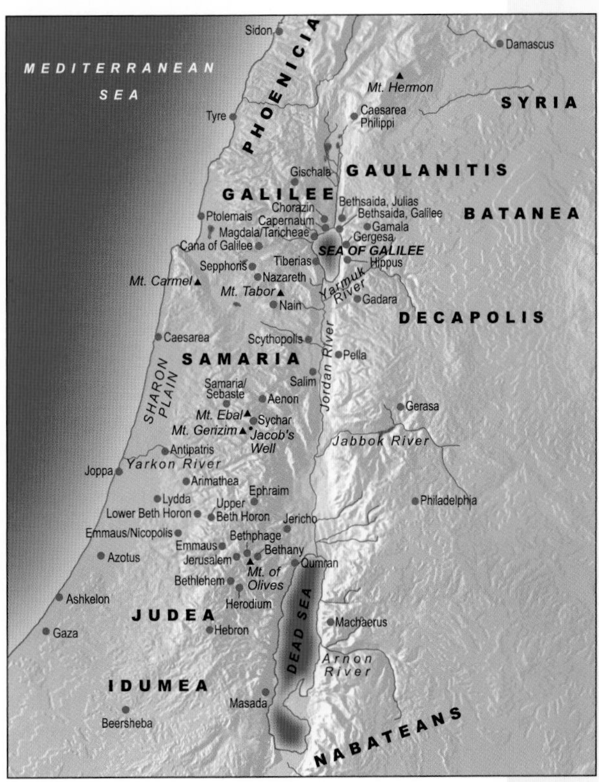

to John 1:35–42 below), John the Baptist, six months Jesus' elder (Luke 1:26), is about thirty-three and a half years old at this time.

The Jews of Jerusalem sent priests and Levites (1:19). Ministering mainly in and around the temple area in Jerusalem, these priests and Levites are specialists in ritual purification, an important issue in John the Baptist's and other baptizers' ministries (see 3:25). According to Luke, crowds come to John from all different walks of life (Luke 3:7–14). Matthew refers to both Pharisees and Sadducees (3:7); Pharisees lived scattered all over Palestine as local interpreters of the law while Sadducees were mainly stationed near the temple. It seems that everyone in that day wants to see what John the Baptist is up to.

I am not the Christ (1:20). As in 1:15, John the Baptist disavows being the expected deliverer/Messiah. Rather, he professes to be the voice of one calling in the desert, "Make straight the way for the Lord" (1:23 citing Isa. 40:3; cf. Matt. 3:1 par.). Messianic hopes were at a fever pitch in early first-century Palestine.[19] Many Jews waited for the coming greater Son of David predicted in the Old Testament (cf. 2 Sam. 7:11b–16; Hos. 3:5; cf. Matt. 1:1, 6, 17; Luke 3:31; Rom. 1:3). This does not mean, however, that these Jews are united in their expectations of what the Messiah will be, nor does it mean that their expectations are necessarily in accordance with scriptural predictions. John gathers many of the messianic expectations of Jesus' day in John 7.

"Are you Elijah?" He said, "I am not" (1:21). See also comments on 5:35. In addition to the Messiah, first-century Jews were looking for Elijah.[20] Elijah, who never died (2 Kings 2:11), was to come "before that great and dreadful day of the LORD" (Mal. 4:5). Some expected him to settle rabbinic disputes, others thought he would perform great miracles or introduce the Messiah (e.g., *4 Ezra* 6:26–27). In any case, he would "restore all things" (Matt. 17:11), turning the hearts of the fathers to their children and vice versa (Mal. 4:6; cf. Luke 1:17; Sir. 48:10).

John denies literally being the returning prophet Elijah. Nevertheless, Jesus clearly states that John the Baptist was Elijah (Matt. 11:14; 17:12; Mark 9:13), since his ministry constituted the typological fulfillment of the prophecy of Malachi 4:5 (cf. Luke 1:17). As the Synoptic Gospels make clear, the Baptist indeed resembled Elijah in his rugged lifestyle (Matt. 3:4; cf. 2 Kings 1:8) and powerful message of judgment (cf. Matt. 3:7–12; Luke 3:7–17). Even before the Baptist's birth, an angel prophesied to his father Zechariah that John would "go on before the Lord *in the spirit and power of Elijah*" (Luke 1:17, italics added).[21]

Are you the Prophet? (1:21). "The Prophet" was yet a third end-time figure expected by the Jews (cf. 6:14; 7:40). The coming of this individual was predicted by Moses in Deuteronomy 18:15, 18.[22] Samaritans had a similar expectation.[23] The Qumran community likewise was committed to waiting "until the prophet comes, and the Messiahs of Aaron and Israel" (1QS 9:11; see also the collection of messianic passages in 4QTest 5–8, citing Deut. 18:18–19). According to *4 Ezra* 2:18, God would also send his servants Isaiah and Jeremiah (cf. 2 Macc. 15:13–16; Matt. 16:14). Again, John denies being this expected end-time figure.

I am the voice of one calling in the desert (1:23). By applying the words of Isaiah 40:3 to himself, John presents himself as "the herald of a new exodus, announcing that God is about to redeem his people from captivity, as he had in the days of Moses."[24] The desert had been the place of God's gathering and deliverance of his people from slavery in Egypt. Many leaders in the history of Israel, from Moses to Paul, were equipped for their divinely appointed task in the desert. The Baptist's statement makes clear that, rather than being a messianic figure himself, his ministry is preparatory, yet in keeping with Old Testament prophecy. Interestingly, the Qumran community applied the same passage from Isaiah to itself (1QS 8:12–14).[25]

Some Pharisees (1:24). see comments on 3:1.

Why then do you baptize? . . . I baptize with water (1:25–26). There is no clear indication in the Hebrew Scriptures that the coming of the Messiah to Israel would be preceded by a baptism of repentance for the Jews. Hence the questioning of the Jewish delegation seems legitimate. However, the Old Testament does use water as a symbol for cleansing and renewal (Ps. 51:2, 7; Ezek. 36:25–26; Zech. 13:1; cf. 1QS 4:20–21).

Various forms of baptism and ritual purification were practiced in the first century—most notably proselyte baptism, which marked a Gentile's conversion to Judaism. Yet John is baptizing not *Gentiles*, but *fellow Jews*. Some Jewish communities practiced *self-immersion*, citing Ezekial 36:25; John is baptizing *other Jews*, for which we have no other evidence. At times Jews might *rebaptize* themselves as they felt the need to be cleansed; John's baptism is *once-and-for-all*. Only a figure such as the Christ, Elijah, or the Prophet (who John the Baptist denies being) can, in the religious leaders' minds, assume such authority.

JORDAN RIVER

This location is just south of the Sea of Galilee.

He is the one who comes after me (1:27). See the Baptist's explanation at 1:15; see also 8:56–58.

The thongs of whose sandals I am not worthy to untie (1:27). R. Joshua b. Levi (A.D. 250) taught that "all manner of service that a slave must render to his master, the pupil must render to his teacher—except that of taking off his shoe" (*b. Ketub.* 96a). But the Baptist acknowledged that he is unworthy to untie Jesus' shoelaces, a task judged too menial even for a disciple![26] This is a telling statement of just how great the Baptist considers Jesus to be.

Bethany on the other side of the Jordan (1:28). John takes care to distinguish this "Bethany beyond the Jordan" (cf. 10:40) from "Bethany near Jerusalem," the village where Lazarus was raised from the dead (11:1, 18). The "Bethany" mentioned in the present passage, one of the places where John baptizes (note the later mention of Aenon near Salim in 3:23), is probably not a village but the region of Batanea in the northeast (called Bashan in the Old Testament). This is suggested by the fact that Jesus is said to leave from Bethany for Galilee in 1:43 and apparently calls Philip to follow him on the same day.

Hence Bethany must have been within a day's journey and thus closer to Galilee than to Judea.[27] If this reconstruction is correct, "Bethany" is a variant spelling of "Batanea," chosen by the evangelist to underscore that Jesus' ministry begins and ends in "Bethany." At Bethany in the (Galilean) north, John the Baptist confesses Jesus as "the Lamb of God"; at Bethany in the (Judean) south, Jesus nears his crucifixion. The mention of all four major regions of the Promised Land—Judea, Samaria, Galilee, and the Transjordan (of which Batanea was a part)—indicates that the sending of Jesus is for the whole of Israel.

LEATHER SANDALS

These well-preserved sandals were found at Masada and date to the first-century A.D.

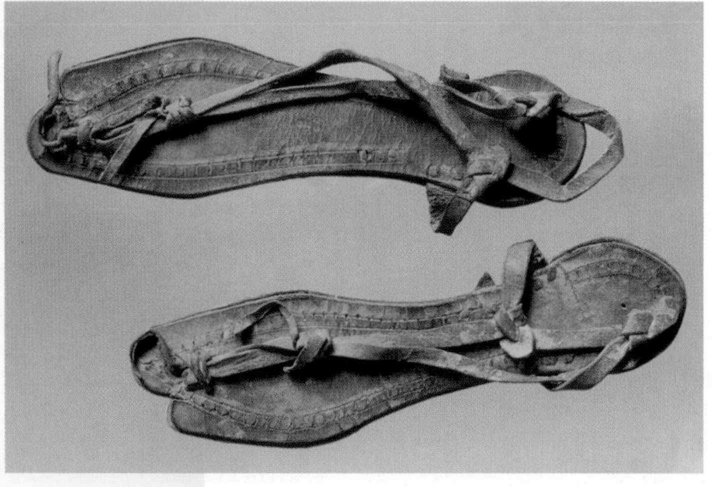

John's Witness at Christ's Baptism (1:29–34)

The Lamb of God (1:29). John says Jesus is "the," not just "a" lamb (*amnos*), of God; he is the Lamb par excellence. And he is the Lamb *of God*, that is, the lamb especially provided by God for the sins of the world.[28] As is common in John's Gospel (e.g., 11:49–52), the Baptist here speaks better than he knows. For he himself, it appears, merely thinks of the lamb referred to in Isaiah 53:7 (LXX *amnos*; cf. Acts 8:32; 1 Peter 2:21–25), which Judaism interpreted not in terms of a dying Messiah, but as substitutionary suffering for sin that fell short of actual death (cf. Matt. 11:2–3; Luke 7:18–20).[29]

The evangelist, however, places the Baptist's declaration into the wider context of his passion narrative, where Jesus is shown to be the ultimate fulfillment of the yearly Passover lamb (see Ex. 12) whose bones must not be broken (John 19:36; cf. 19:14). Paul makes the same point when he writes, "For Christ, our Passover lamb, has been sacrificed"

(1 Cor. 5:7). The expression "Lamb of God" would have acquainted a Hellenistic audience with the Jewish roots of Christianity. Yet the added phrase "who takes away the sin *of the world*" immediately points to the universal implications of the lamb's sacrifice.

Who takes away the sin of the world (1:29). The Lamb of God will *take away sin*. How? By means of a sacrificial, substitutionary death. According to the pattern set by the Old Testament sacrificial system, the shed blood of the substitute animal covers the sins of others and appeases the divine wrath by way of atonement (cf. 1 John 2:2; 4:10). As the book of Hebrews makes clear, however, the entire Old Testament sacrificial system was merely provisional until the coming of Christ. The idea that the Messiah would suffer for the sins of *the world* (rather than merely for Israel) was foreign to Jewish first-century ears. John makes clear that Jesus came to save the entire world (John 3:17) and that he is the Savior of the world, not just Israel (4:42).

I myself did not know him (1:31). John here acknowledges that he did not know that Jesus *was the Messiah* until he saw the sign referred to in 1:32–33.

◀ *left*

LAMB

I saw the Spirit come down from heaven as a dove and remain on him (1:32). The Spirit does not merely *descend* on Jesus but *remains* on him, a sign of his divine anointing. For while in Old Testament times the Holy Spirit came on certain individuals for a temporary enablement to a particular task,[30] Isaiah prophesied that the Messiah will be full of the Spirit at all times (Isa. 11:2; 61:1; cf. Luke 4:18).[31] Thus, the Baptist testifies later in John's Gospel that "God gives the Spirit without limit" (John 3:34).

Will baptize with the Holy Spirit (1:33). The Messiah's "baptism with the Holy Spirit" is in keeping with the Old Testament prediction that God will pour out his Spirit on all people in the last days.[32]

Son of God (1:34). While some early manuscripts read "Son of God" (NIV), others, including a recently published papyrus (P^{106}), have "the Chosen One of God." If "Chosen One of God" is what John wrote, this closely parallels the wording of Isaiah 42:1, where God promises to pour out his Spirit on his "chosen one." While Old Testament Israel was called God's "chosen people," and Jesus' disciples, too, are said to be "chosen" (e.g., John 6:70; 13:18; 15:16, 19), Jesus is "the Chosen One" par excellence. The expression "chosen one of God" also occurs in Qumran texts (4Q534), but its messianic nature is disputed.[33]

Andrew, Another Disciple, and Then Peter Follow Jesus (1:35–42)

Stepping out of the shadow of the Baptist, Jesus begins his own ministry by calling his first disciples. According to Luke 3:23, Jesus is "about thirty years old" at this time. If Jesus was born in 5 or 4 B.C.

Translations of Aramaic Terms in John's Gospel

1. Rabbi (which means Teacher; 1:38; 20:16)
2. The Messiah (that is, the Christ; 1:41; 4:25)
3. Cephas (which, when translated, is Peter; 1:42)
4. Siloam (this word meant Sent; 9:7)
5. Thomas (called Didymus [twin]; 11:16; 20:24; 21:2)
6. The place of the Skull (which in Aramaic is called Golgotha; 19:17)

(as is commonly held to be the most likely date for his birth) and if (as has been argued, see introduction to 1:19–28) the Baptist's ministry started in A.D. 29, Jesus would be about thirty-three years old at this point.[34] The events recorded in 1:35–4:42 apparently belong to the period between Jesus' baptism and temptation and the beginning of his Galilean ministry (see Mark 1:14–15).

When the two disciples heard him say this, they followed Jesus (1:37). Disciples in that day literally "followed" or walked behind the one they had chosen as their teacher (e.g., *y. Ḥag.* 2:1).[35] In John's Gospel, however, the term gradually moves from this literal to a more figurative sense to denote a "following" of Jesus' teaching (8:12; 10:4–5, 27; 12:26).

Rabbi (which means Teacher) (1:38). The Semitic term "rabbi" (lit., "my great one") was a common term of honor used by disciples to address their teacher. For the benefit of John's Greek-speaking readers, he here translates the term into Greek (*didaskalos*; cf. 20:16). By the end of the first century A.D., the expression had become a technical term for "ordained" teachers who had satisfied certain formal requirements of rabbinic training. At this point, however, the term is used more generally to refer to a respected Jewish religious teacher, such as Nicodemus (3:10), Jesus (1:38, 49; 3:2; 4:31; 6:25; 9:2; 11:8; 20:16), and even John the Baptist (3:26).

It was about the tenth hour (1:39). Starting to count, as was customary, from sunrise at around six A.M., "tenth hour" would mean about 4 P.M. Because daylight was going to run out before too long, people refrained from engaging in major outdoor activities past that hour and began to make preparations for lodging if necessary. This was not confined to the Jewish world: "Caesar, for two reasons, would not fight that day; partly because he had no soldiers in the ships, and *partly because it was after the tenth hour of the day*."[36] Since the main meal was usually taken in the late afternoon, "tenth hour" may also indicate that Jesus extended table fellowship to these two disciples of John the Baptist.[37]

right ▶

LARGE ROCK (CEPHAS)

A huge rock outcropping at Timnah.

Andrew, Simon Peter's brother (1:40). This statement seems to presuppose the readers' knowledge of Synoptic tradition (written or oral), since Simon Peter is not mentioned until the following verse. See also 3:24; 4:44; 6:67; 11:1–2. Andrew is mentioned elsewhere in this gospel only in 1:44; 6:8; 12:22.

Andrew . . . was one of the two (1:40). The name of the other disciple is not mentioned. This unusual omission can best be explained if the disciple is John the evangelist, since he never refers to himself by name in this Gospel (see comments on 1:6).

The Messiah (that is, the Christ) (1:41). The term "Messiah" is a transliteration of the Aramaic/Hebrew word meaning "the Anointed One" (see "Translations of Aramaic Terms in John's Gospel").[38] In the Old Testament, the term variously refers to the king of Israel (1 Sam. 16:6), the high priest (Lev. 4:3), or others set apart for a particular office.[39] Since John's readers are not necessarily expected to know Aramaic, the predominant language of first-century Palestine, John translates the term into the equivalent Greek expression (*Christos* also means "the Anointed One"). The term "Messiah" is also found in Jewish writings preceding or roughly contemporary with the New Testament, such as the Qumran scrolls[40] or other literature.[41]

Simon son of John (1:42). Last names as we use them today were not in existence in biblical times. Instead, a person would be known by who his father was (e.g., Simon, son of John) and/or by his origin (e.g., Jesus of Nazareth; Simon of Cyrene).

Cephas (1:42). Cephas is an Aramaic word meaning "rock" (cf. Matt. 16:16–18). In Old Testament times, God frequently changed people's names to indicate their special calling (e.g., Abraham, Israel). Rabbis in Jesus' day likewise occasionally gave characteristic names to their disciples. Jesus' "renaming" of Simon Peter is therefore in keeping with both biblical and rabbinic precedents.

(Which, when translated, is Peter) (1:42). "Peter" does not appear to have been a proper name in ancient times. It may have been used by Jesus as a nickname.[42]

References to Time in John's Gospel

Generally, people in the first century A.D. counted time from sunrise to sunset (c. 6 A.M.–6 P.M.). As Jesus himself says, "Are there not twelve hours of daylight?" (11:9). Thus "the fourth hour," for instance, would mean "about 10 A.M." In addition, the day was divided into three-hour intervals, and in this day before wristwatches, people often approximated the estimated time to the next full three-hour segment. "The sixth hour," then, may mean "roughly at 12 noon," which may span anywhere from 10:30 or 11 A.M. to 1 or 1:30 P.M.

John's Gospel contains the following four references to time:

1. *"about the tenth hour"* (1:39): Jesus' first followers opt to stay with him at about 4 P.M.
2. *"about the sixth hour"* (4:6): Jesus meets the Samaritan woman at the well at around noon.
3. *"yesterday at the seventh hour"* (4:52): Jesus healed the royal official's son at about 1 P.M.
4. *"about the sixth hour"* (19:14): Jesus' trial before Pilate ended at around noon.

Philip and Nathanael Follow Christ (1:43–51)

Finding Philip, he said to him, "Follow me" (1:43). Jesus' practice of calling his followers went counter to contemporary practice, where disciples opted to attach themselves to a rabbi of their choice (cf. 15:16).

Philip, like Andrew and Peter, was from the town of Bethsaida (1:44). Mark seems to indicate that Andrew and Peter were from Capernaum (Mark 1:29; cf. 1:21); here they are said to be from Bethsaida. Most likely, Andrew and Peter grew up in Bethsaida and subsequently moved to Capernaum (which is only a few miles directly west of Bethsaida). This is similar to Jesus, who is regularly said to be from Nazareth (John 1:45) although he had moved to Capernaum (Matt. 4:13).

Bethsaida (meaning "place of the fishery") is probably to be identified with the mound called et-Tell, located east of the Jordan River about one and a half miles before it enters the north shore of the Sea of Galilee. After Jerusalem and Capernaum, Bethsaida is the most frequently mentioned city in the Gospels (cf. Matt. 11:21 par.; Mark 6:45; 8:22; Luke 9:10; John 12:21).[43] Mark records that a blind man was healed in this city, and the feeding of the four thousand took place in a deserted place nearby. Tragically, the city was cursed by Jesus along with Chorazin and Capernaum because of its unbelief.

RUINS AT BETHSAIDA

Philip found Nathanael (1:45). Nathanael is also mentioned in 21:2 as one of the seven disciples to whom Jesus appears on the shore of the Sea of Galilee. There we learn that Nathanael came from Cana of Galilee, the site of two of Jesus' signs (cf. 2:1–11; 4:46–54). Since the name Nathanael is not mentioned in the Synoptic Gospels, it is likely that this is the personal name of Bartholomew (Bar-Tholomaios = son of

REFLECTIONS

IT IS STRIKING HOW JESUS' FIRST followers do not merely attach themselves to Jesus but immediately seek to bring others to him as well. The first thing Andrew did was to find his brother Simon, while Philip recruited Nathanael. This is where Old Testament Israel had gone astray: Rather than fulfilling her role as a channel of blessing to other nations, God's "chosen people" construed their election as ethnic privilege. Where they should have shared their joy and faith in God with those outside, their pride and presumption led the Jews jealously to guard their blessings and to keep them for themselves. It must be different with members of the new covenant community: Those who are called by Jesus must be willing to share the good news of salvation in Christ with others, what is more, to be driven by a passionate desire to see unbelievers come to faith.

Tholomaios), who is linked with Philip in all three Synoptic apostolic lists (Matt. 10:3; Mark 3:18; Luke 6:14).

The one Moses wrote about in the Law, and about whom the prophets also wrote (1:45). "The Law and the Prophets" was a common Jewish designation for the Hebrew Scriptures in their entirety. Philip has come to believe that Jesus is the Messiah foretold in the Scriptures, both in the Law (cf. Deut. 18:15, 18; see comments on "the Prophet" at John 1:21) and in the Prophets (e.g., Isa. 9:1–7; 11:1–5, 10–12; 52:13–53:12).

Jesus of Nazareth, the son of Joseph (1:45). While born in Bethlehem, Jesus grew up in Nazareth, so that he could properly be said to be "from Nazareth."

Nazareth! Can anything good come from there? (1:46). It is ironic that Nathanael, himself from the small village of Cana in Galilee (21:2; cf. 2:1–11), here displays prejudice against the relatively insignificant Galilean town of Nazareth (cf. later 7:41, 52). Mentioned neither in the Old Testament nor in Josephus, Nazareth was a small town of no more than two thousand people, located about three and a half miles southeast of the regional capital Sepphoris. The Nazarenes probably had relations with their more cosmopolitan neighbors and more than likely also came into contact with the Greek-speaking Gentile traders who passed through Sepphoris in the north or the Esdraelon Valley in the south.

True Israelite, in whom there is nothing false (1:47). The rendering "true Israelite" (NIV) is incorrect. Rather, Jesus says, "truly" here is an Israelite in whom there is nothing false (lit., "no deceit"; *dolos*). In this Nathanael differs from the original "Israel" (i.e., Jacob), who was deceitful (*dolos;* cf. Gen. 27:35–36 LXX). Nathanael is free from such duplicity of heart (cf. Ps. 32:2) and thus prepared to consider whether or not the claims regarding Jesus are true.[44] This attitude stands in sharp contrast not only with Jacob of old, but also with the hypocrisy of the Pharisees (Matt. 26:4 = Mark 14:1: *dolos*).

I saw you while you were still under the fig tree (1:48). In the Greco-Roman world, such knowledge was regularly

◀ *left*

GALILEE

Nazareth was located west of the Sea of Galilee near Sepphoris.

MODERN NAZARETH

attributed to magic or some other mysterious link to the gods. The Jews, however, considered access to divine revelation to be the mark of a true prophet. Yet Jesus was more than a prophet: he was the unique Son of God, whose place "at the Father's side" (1:18) provides him with an unlimited supply of divine insight. Nevertheless, Jesus does not display his supernatural knowledge to impress others but to identify himself as Messiah (1:49–51).

Fig tree (1:48). The fig tree is sometimes used in the Old Testament as a figure for home or prosperity, at times in an end-time or messianic context (1 Kings 4:25; Isa. 36:16; Mic. 4:4; Zech. 3:10). In rabbinic literature it is a place for meditation on the Scriptures and prayer (e.g., *Midr. Qoh.* 5:11 §2).

BRANCH OF A FIG TREE

Rabbi (1:49). See comments on 1:38.

Son of God . . . King of Israel (1:49). By calling Jesus "Son of God," Nathanael identifies him as the Messiah predicted in the Old Testament (cf. 2 Sam. 7:14; Ps. 2:7; see John 20:31 below). The term "Son [of God]" was also a current messianic title in Jesus' day.[45] "King of Israel," too, is a common designation for the Messiah (cf. 12:13; note also the phrase "king of the Jews" in chs. 18–19). Because of the expression's political overtones, however, Jesus is reluctant to identify himself in such terms (6:15), for his kingdom is "not of this world" (18:36).

I tell you the truth (1:51). This phrase renders the Greek transliteration of the Hebrew term *amēn* ("it is firm"). While the Synoptics feature a single *amēn,* John always uses the double expression *amēn, amēn,* perhaps in order to stress the authoritative nature of Jesus' pronouncements. In the Old Testament, the term confirms the truthfulness of someone else's statement. Jesus, by contrast, uses the expression to assert the veracity of *his own* sayings.[46]

Heaven open, and the angels of God ascending and descending (1:51). The imagery is drawn from Jacob's vision of the ladder "resting on the earth, with its top reaching to heaven, and *the angels of God* were *ascending and descending* on it [or: him, that is, Jacob, italics added]" (Gen. 28:12).[47] As the angels ascended and descended on Jacob (who was later renamed "Israel")—a sign of God's revelation—so the disciples are promised further divine confirmation of Jesus' messianic identity.

Son of Man (1:51). Apart from functioning (as in the Synoptics) as Jesus' favorite self-reference (6:27; 9:35; cf. Ezek.), the expression is fused in Johannine theology to denote both Jesus' heavenly origin and destination (John 1:51; 3:13; 6:62; cf. Dan. 7:13) and his "lifting up" (substitutionary sacrifice) on the cross (John 3:14; 6:53; 8:28; 12:23, 34; 13:31). The Son of Man is also presented as the end-time judge (5:27). Notably, the term is always found on Jesus' lips in John's Gospel (12:34 is no real exception).

The Wedding at Cana (2:1–11)

After calling his first disciples, Jesus takes them along to a wedding in Cana of Galilee, not far from his hometown, Nazareth. Jesus here performs the first of his startling signs, providing his followers with an initial glimpse of his messianic identity. In anticipation of that great messianic banquet at the end of time, Jesus is here shown to fill up the emptiness of Judaism. John's Ephesian audience may also have read the present account in light of the myth of Dionysius, the Greek god of wine and the most popular deity in the Hellenistic world.[48]

The Setting (2:1–2)

On the third day (2:1). "The third day" is to be counted from the last event narrated, Jesus' encounter with Nathanael. Including the first day in one's calculation, this means two days later. In conjunction with John's initial testimony to Jesus in 1:19–28 and the three references to "the next day" in 1:29, 35, and 43, this completes an entire week of activity.

Day 1: John the Baptist testifies concerning Jesus (1:19–28).

Day 2: John the Baptist's encounter with Jesus (1:29–34; "the next day").

Day 3: John the Baptist refers two of his disciples to Jesus (1:35–39; "the next day").

Day 4: Andrew introduces his brother Peter to Jesus (1:40–42).

Day 5: Philip and Nathanael follow Jesus (1:43–51; "the next day").

Day 6: No information is given (Sabbath?).

Day 7: Jesus attends the wedding at Cana (2:1–11; "on the third day").[49]

If no information is given regarding Day 6 because it was a Sabbath, the Cana wedding—or at least the day on which Jesus and his friends joined the wedding party—would have fallen on a Sunday. This may not have been the first day of the wedding, since weddings lasted for a whole week (cf. Judg. 14:12) and it is unlikely that wine ran out immediately.

A wedding (2:1). Jewish weddings were important and joyful occasions in the lives of the bride and the groom and their extended families, and the entire community joined in the celebration (see "Jewish Weddings"). Cana was not far

Jesus' Signs in John's Gospel

Event	Reference in John	Date
1. Changing water into wine	2:1–11	Winter/Spring, A.D. 30
2. Temple cleansing	2:13–22[A-4]	Spring, A.D. 30
3. Healing of nobleman's son	4:46–54	Spring, A.D. 31
4. Healing of lame man	5:1–15	Fall, A.D. 31
5. Feeding of multitude	6:1–15	Spring, A.D. 32
6. Healing of blind man	9:1–41	Fall, A.D. 32
7. Raising of Lazarus	11:1–44	Spring, A.D. 33

from Nazareth (less than ten miles), and the fact that the guest list includes Jesus and his disciples as well as his mother may indicate the wedding of a close family friend or relative. This may also explain why Jesus' mother feels responsible to help when the hosts run out of wine.

At Cana in Galilee (2:1). Despite its insignificance, Cana becomes the site of Jesus' first and third signs (cf. 4:54: the second sign *in Cana*). Several sites have been proposed for ancient Cana ("place of reeds"). Some older commentators suggest Kafr Kennamm, some four miles northeast of Nazareth on the road to Tiberias, but this is rendered unlikely by the doubling of the letter "n" in "Kafr Kennam."[50] The probable location is Khirbet Qânam in the Plain of Asochis, about eight miles northeast of Nazareth (cf. Josephus, *Life* 16, 41 §§86, 207).[51] Fittingly, Khirbet Qânam overlooks a marshy plain featuring plenty of reeds. To date, the site has not been excavated, but cisterns and the remains of buildings are visible and nearby tombs are cut into the rocks. Some first-century coins have also been found on the site. The plain where Cana was located was apparently part of the royal domain of the Herodians and was cultivated by their tenants under the supervision of royal officials (cf. 4:46).[52] John's mention of "Cana in Galilee" seems to presuppose another Cana (not in Galilee), perhaps in Lebanon (referred to in Josh. 19:28; cf. 16:8; 17:9).[53]

CANA

The area of Kafr Kennamm.

Jesus' mother . . . Jesus and his disciples . . . invited to the wedding (2:1–2). Mary may have been a friend of the family, helping behind the scenes.[54] Jesus may

Jewish weddings[A-5]

Marriage was the norm in Jewish life on the basis of Genesis 1:28. People generally married young (*b. Sanh.* 76b; cf. Tobit 4:13; Josephus, *Ag. Ap.* 2.25 §199–203), men between the ages of eighteen and twenty-four (*m. ʾAbot* 5:21), women as early as age thirteen or fourteen. Generally, it was considered important that bridegroom and bride come from similar social backgrounds, that the age difference between them not be too considerable, and that the bride be free from physical defects. Family background was also judged to be important; even compatibility in height is occasionally mentioned.

On the eve of the wedding day, the bride was brought from her father's home to that of her husband in joyful procession. Veiled by a bridal veil and surrounded by her bridesmaids, she was led by "the friends of the bridegroom" (often not found in Galilee) and the "children of the bridechamber." Upon arrival, the bride was led to her husband, and the couple was crowned with garlands. This was followed by the signing of the marriage contract (*ketubah*). After the marriage supper, which could last up to a full day, the "friends of the bridegroom" led the pair to the bridal chamber.

Jesus' Natural Family[A-6]

Jesus was miraculously conceived in the womb of his mother Mary by the Holy Spirit (Matt. 1:18–23; Luke 1:35). Mary's husband Joseph apparently died in Jesus' youth, for he is never mentioned in Scripture past the account of the twelve-year-old Jesus in the temple (Luke 2:41–52). The names of Jesus' brothers are given in Matthew 13:55 and Mark 6:3 as James, Joseph, Judas, and Simon.[A-7] No names are supplied for Jesus' sisters; the best attested names in post-canonical tradition are Salome and Mary.

Jesus is called "the carpenter's son" in Matthew 13:55 and "the carpenter" in Mark 6:3, indicating that he took up his father's trade, as was customary in Judaism (though *tektōn* probably means "craftsman, artisan, builder"—that is, someone who works in wood, stone, and metal). He met strong opposition within his own household (Mark 3:21, 31–34 par.). His own brothers did not believe in him as late as midway through his earthly ministry (John 7:1–9). Later, Jesus' mother and brothers are among those praying in the upper room prior to Pentecost (Acts 1:14). According to Paul, the risen Christ appeared to one of his brothers, James (1 Cor. 15:7).

have been invited because of a childhood association, because he was one of the distinguished people in the neighborhood, or both. The group of Jesus' disciples presumably included the five mentioned in 1:35–51.

Jesus Turns Water into Wine (2:3–11)

In Jewish thought, wine is a symbol of joy and celebration: "There is no rejoicing save with wine" (*b. Pesaḥ.* 109a). In John, running out of wine at the Cana wedding may be symbolic of the barrenness of Judaism. Prophetic expectation cast the messianic age as a time when wine would flow freely.[55] At a cultural level, running out of wine was considered to be a major social faux pas, since the host was responsible to provide the wedding guests with wine for seven days.

Jesus' mother said to him, "They have no more wine" (2:3). If women's quarters at ancient Jewish weddings were indeed near the place where the wine was stored, Mary may have learned of the shortage of wine before word reached Jesus and the other men.[56] In what may have constituted a breach of etiquette, Mary informs Jesus, in the process disturbing the male guests.

Dear woman (2:4). Jesus' address of his mother as "woman" sounds brusque; at the very least, it establishes polite distance.[57] Yet the expression, while not particularly endearing, need not be harsh.[58] The unusual nature of Jesus' use of this address for his own mother is underscored by the fact that this practice is without parallel in ancient Jewish or Greco-Roman literature.[59] Jesus' making provision for his mother at the foot of the cross indicates that this address does not show absence of filial affection (19:25–27).

Why do you involve me? (2:4). The underlying thrust of this phrase is: "What do you and I have in common (as far as the matter at hand is concerned)?" The implied answer: "Nothing." As Old Testament parallels make clear, the phrase always distances two parties and frequently carries a reproachful connotation.[60] Jesus is here issuing a fairly sharp rebuke to Mary (cf. Matt. 12:46–50), similar to his rebuke of Peter when he fails to understand the nature of Jesus' calling (cf. 16:23). Alternatively, Jesus may be advising his mother that he has already decided to help and that he will do so when he chooses to rather than in response to her prompting (cf. 2 Kings 3:13).[61]

Do whatever he tells you (2:5). The fact that she is able to give instructions to the servants may indicate that Mary is helping the bridegroom's mother with the preparation of dishes. The wording of Mary's instructions to the servants perhaps alludes to Pharaoh's words to the Egyptians to go to Joseph and to "do what he tells you" (Gen. 41:55).

WATER JARS

Large storage jars found in Ekron.

Nearby stood six stone water jars (2:6). The jars stood *nearby*—probably not in the dining room itself, but more likely in a passage near the courtyard near the well. There are *six* jars: In light of the significance the number seven has for John, the number six may connote imperfection as falling one short of the perfect number seven. The jars are made of *stone*, because stone was not itself considered to contract uncleanness.

The kind used by the Jews for ceremonial washing (2:6). This practice may have involved the washing of certain utensils used at the wedding and the washing of the guests' hands (cf. Mark 7:2–5; more broadly, John 3:25).

Each holding from twenty to thirty gallons (2:6). The original text reads "two to three *metrētēs*"; one *metrētēs* equals roughly ten gallons.[62] This adds up to a

Wine[A-8]

Scripture portrays wine both as a blessing, commended even by the example of Christ,[A-9] and as an emblem of violence, corruption, or wickedness incurring divine wrath.[A-10] In the Greco-Roman world, and presumably in the Palestine of Jesus' day, three kinds of wine were in use: fermented wines, which were usually mixed in the proportion of two or three parts of water to one of wine; new wine, made of grape juice (similar to cider, not fermented); and wines in which, by boiling the unfermented grape juice, the process of fermentation had been stopped and the formation of alcohol prevented.

Passages such as Matthew 11:19 clearly suggest that Jesus drank fermented wine; Mark 14:25 implies the same. Moreover, the latter passage intimates that wine will be drunk in heaven. Thus, neither Christ's teaching nor his example can be adduced in favor of advocating total abstinence from alcohol. Rather, proper use of wine must be distinguished from excessive consumption. Some may judge total abstinence to be expedient for personal or local reasons (cf. Rom. 14:21; 1 Cor. 6:12), but should not insist that this is the only biblical option.

REFLECTIONS

WE ALL HAVE HEARD STORIES OF now famous conductors or performers who, as virtual unknowns, were thrust into the limelight unexpectedly when the regular cast had to be replaced on short notice. It was their opportunity to prove themselves, and they seized it. Jesus, too, has such an experience when called on to help with the shortage of wine at the wedding of Cana—and he makes the most of it, revealing his glory to his disciples, who believe in him. He wants us likewise to stand ready to be used in case a sudden need arises. May we be alert and available whenever he needs us.

total of one hundred and twenty to one hundred and eighty gallons for all six jars combined. A large number of wedding guests must be accommodated for the course of an entire week of festivities.

The servants (2:7). "The fact that there were servants, and more than one, indicates that the family was in at least comfortable if not opulent circumstances."[63]

The master of the banquet (2:8). The role of "master of the banquet" (*architriklinos*; lit. "ruler of the table") is a position of honor, with one of the master's primary duties being the regulation of the distribution of wine. Sirach 32:1–2 (c. 180 B.C.) counsels, "If they make you master of the feast [*hēgoumenos*], do not exalt yourself; be among them as one of their number. Take care of them first and then sit down; when you have fulfilled all your duties, take your place, so that you may be merry along with them and receive a wreath for your excellent leadership." The position may represent an adaptation of the Greco-Roman "ruler of the feast" (called a *symposiarch*), even though differences may apply. Apparently, the "master of the banquet" did not join the wedding party at the table but, as a head waiter in charge of catering, supervised the serving of food and drink, with several servants under him carrying out his orders. He may also have served as "master of ceremonies."[64]

Return to Capernaum (2:12)

Went down (2:12). Jesus goes "down" from Cana to Capernaum, since Cana is located in the hill country while Capernaum is situated directly at the Sea of Galilee at a lower elevation (the site has been excavated: Tel-Hûm).

Capernaum (2:12). Capernaum, located on the northwest corner of the Sea of Galilee, is about fifteen miles to the northeast of Cana; it can easily be reached in a day's journey (about six to eight hours).[65] After the imprisonment of John the Baptist and after encountering strong opposition in his hometown of Nazareth, Jesus permanently moves to Capernaum (cf. Matt. 4:12–13; Luke 4:28–31). Matthew ties Jesus' taking up of residence

CAPERNAUM

An aerial view of the remains of the synagogue.

in Capernaum to the fulfillment of Old Testament prophecy, calling it "his own town," owing to the length and variety of his activities there (Matt. 9:1).

The Cleansing of the Temple (2:13–25)

Cleansing was an important part of Passover observance. Even today, observant Jews search their house prior to Passover in order to remove any vestiges of leavened bread. The "Feast of Unleavened Bread" began with the Passover meal and continued for seven days (14–21 Nisan; cf. Ex. 12:18–19; Mark 14:12). The major point of the temple cleansing in John is the fact that Jesus is presented as the replacement of the temple in the life of the messianic community. According to John, Jesus' mission is to cleanse the community of God from defilement and to restore the proper worship of God (this echoes Old Testament prophetic concerns: cf. Zech. 14:21; Mal. 3:1, 3). Ultimately, true cleansing is provided only by Christ's death on the cross on our behalf (cf. John 13:10–11; 15:3).[66]

Jewish Passover (2:13). The Passover was the most important Jewish feast, commemorating God's dramatic deliverance of the Jews from Egypt on the night of the Exodus, when the death angel "passed over" the firstborn in homes whose doorposts had been marked with blood (cf. Ex. 12, esp. vv. 14–16). It was celebrated on the fourteenth day of the lunar month Nisan (full moon at the end of March or the beginning of April), which marked the beginning of the festive calendar. The Passover was one of the three annual pilgrim feasts that all Jewish men were to celebrate in Jerusalem (cf. Deut. 16:16).[67] Large numbers of worshipers from the outlying provinces of Palestine (Luke 2:41–42) and the

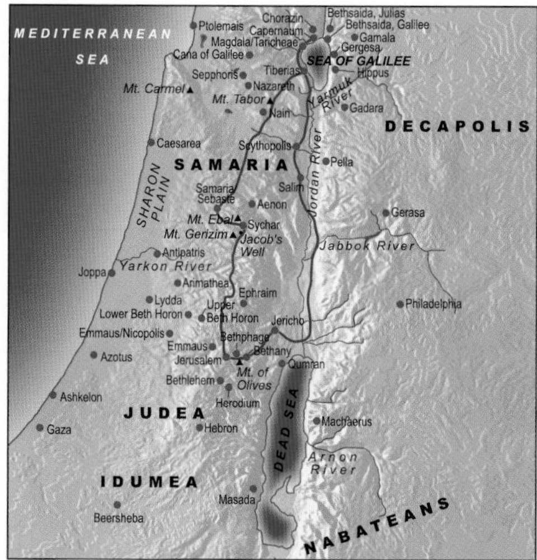

right ▶

GALILEE, SAMARIA, AND JUDEA

This map shows the routes from Capernaum to Jerusalem.

Jewish Festivals in John's Gospel[A-11]		
Name of Feast	**Reference in John**	**Time Celebrated**
Passover	2:13, 23	April 7, A.D. 30
"A feast of the Jews"	5:1	October 21–28, A.D. 31?
Passover	6:4	April 13/14, A.D. 32
Tabernacles (Booths)	7:2	September 10–17, A.D. 32
Dedication (Hanukkah)	10:22	December 18–25, A.D. 32
Passover	11:55; 12:1	April 3, A.D. 33

Diaspora (Acts 2:5) filled the capital city (cf. Josephus, *J.W.* 2.1.3 §10). The present Passover, the first during Jesus' public ministry, probably took place on April 7 in A.D. 30.[68]

Went up (2:13). People went "up" to Jerusalem because it was situated at a higher elevation than Galilee and because it was the capital city.

Temple courts (2:14). "Temple courts" (*hieron*), in distinction to the temple building proper (*naos*; see comments on 2:20 below), generally denotes the area surrounding the temple. In the present instance, this probably refers to the outermost court, the Court of the Gentiles. Gentiles were barred from entry into the inner court of the temple. A complete Greek inscription to this effect was discovered in 1870:

> *No foreigner shall enter within the*
> *balustrade of the temple,*
> *or within the precinct,*
> *and whosoever shall be caught shall*
> *be responsible for (his) death*
> *that will follow in consequence (of his*
> *trespassing)*.[69]

WARNING INSCRIPTION

A first-century inscription from the balustrade around the temple building warning Gentiles not to enter.

Men selling cattle, sheep and doves, and others sitting at tables exchanging money (2:14). The sale of sacrificial animals rendered a valuable service to those who travelled to the Passover from afar, enabling them to buy the animals on site rather than having to carry them for long distances. *Cattle* and *sheep* were needed for various kinds of offerings (e.g., Ex. 20:24; 22:30; 24:5; Lev. 1:3–9; 4:2–21; 8:2; 22:21). *Doves* were required for the purification of women (Lev. 12:6; Luke 2:22–24), especially if they were poor (Lev. 12:8), the cleansing of people with certain kinds of skin diseases (14:22), and other purposes (15:14, 29).

The *money-changers* likewise rendered a service: Visitors to Jerusalem needed their money changed into the local currency because the temple tax, paid by

TEMPLE MOUNT

Leen Ritmeyer's classic drawing of the Jerusalem temple mount.

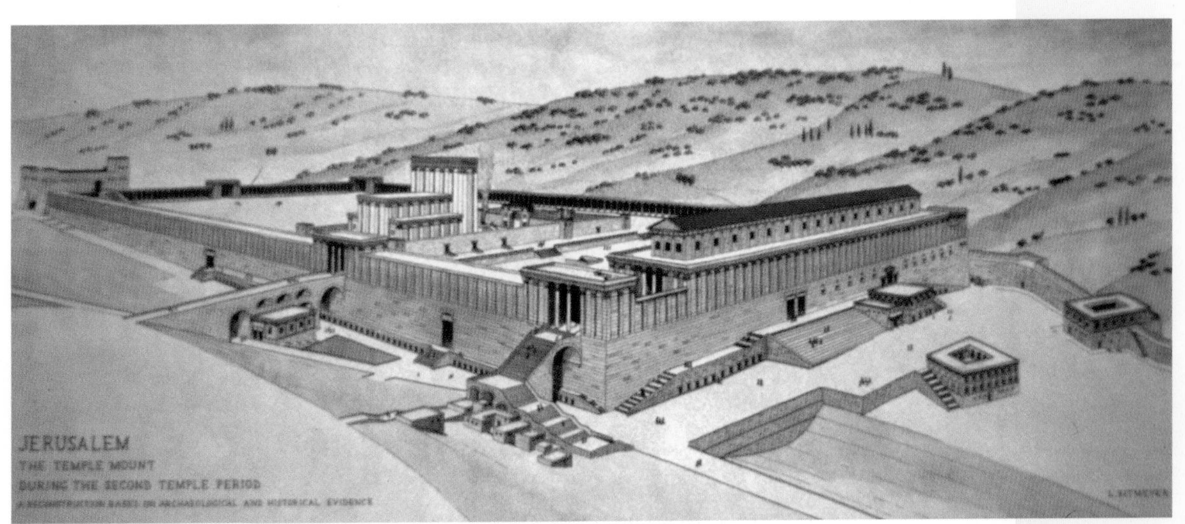

THE JERUSALEM TEMPLE

The model shows the temple proper and the courts.

The Jerusalem Temple

The Jerusalem temple was a symbol of Jewish national and religious identity. The original temple was built by Solomon. It was destroyed by the Babylonians in the sixth century B.C. and rebuilt by Zerubbabel (Ezra 3; Hag. 1–2; Zech. 4). Later renovated by Herod, the edifice was renowned for its magnificence. Josephus raved that "the exterior of the building wanted nothing that could astound either mind or eye. For, being covered on all sides with massive plates of gold, the sun was no sooner up than it radiated so fiery a flash that persons straining to look at it were compelled to avert their eyes, as from the solar rays. To approaching strangers it appeared from a distance like a snow-clad mountain; for all that was overlaid with gold was of purest white" (*J.W.* 5.5.6 §§222–24). Even the rabbis, who were no friends of Herod, had to admit that "he who has not seen the Temple of Herod has never seen a beautiful building" (*b. B. Bat.* 4a).

Surrounded by porticoes, the temple consisted of an Outer Court (the Court of the Gentiles) and an Inner Temple, made up of the Court of Women on the east and the Inner Court on the west. Behind these rose the temple itself, a huge edifice 300 feet wide, long, and high. In Jesus' day, the temple, once the glorious symbol of God's dwelling with his people, had degenerated into a place of commerce and perfunctory ritual (John 2:14–16). It was razed in A.D. 70 by the Romans, shortly after the restoration of the entire temple area had been completed. This destruction had been predicted by Jesus, who saw in it God's judgment of Israel on account of its rejection of the Messiah (Matt. 24:1–2 par.). John's Gospel, most likely written within a decade or two after the destruction of the temple, presents Jesus as the replacement of the temple and as people's new proper focus of worship (John 2:19–21; cf. 4:19–24).[A-12]

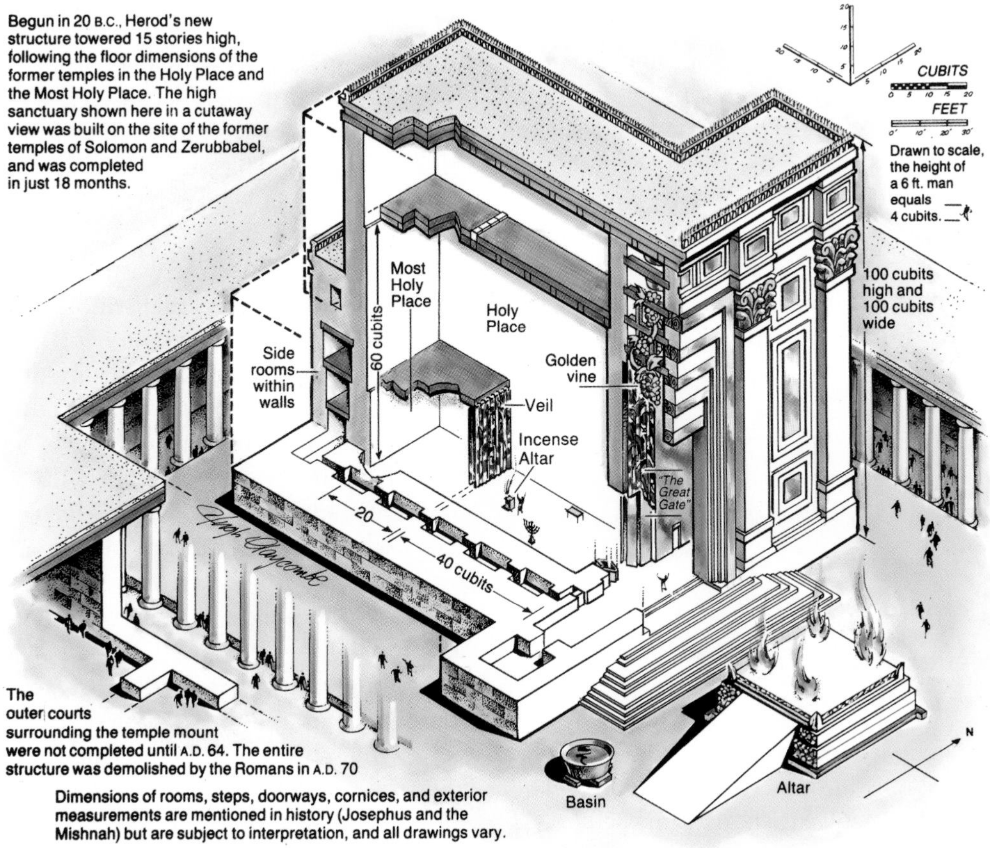

THE JERUSALEM TEMPLE

This cutaway reconstruction is based on testimony from Josephus and the Mishnah.

Begun in 20 B.C., Herod's new structure towered 15 stories high, following the floor dimensions of the former temples in the Holy Place and the Most Holy Place. The high sanctuary shown here in a cutaway view was built on the site of the former temples of Solomon and Zerubbabel, and was completed in just 18 months.

CUBITS
0 5 10 15 20
FEET
0' 10' 20' 30'

Drawn to scale, the height of a 6 ft. man equals  4 cubits.

100 cubits high and 100 cubits wide

Most Holy Place

Holy Place

60 cubits

Side rooms within walls

Golden vine

Veil

Incense Altar

"The Great Gate"

20

40 cubits

Basin

Altar

N

The outer courts surrounding the temple mount were not completed until A.D. 64. The entire structure was demolished by the Romans in A.D. 70

Dimensions of rooms, steps, doorways, cornices, and exterior measurements are mentioned in history (Josephus and the Mishnah) but are subject to interpretation, and all drawings vary.

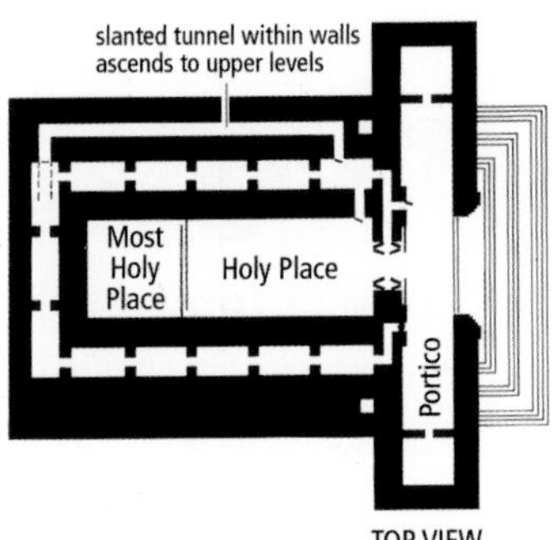

TOP VIEW

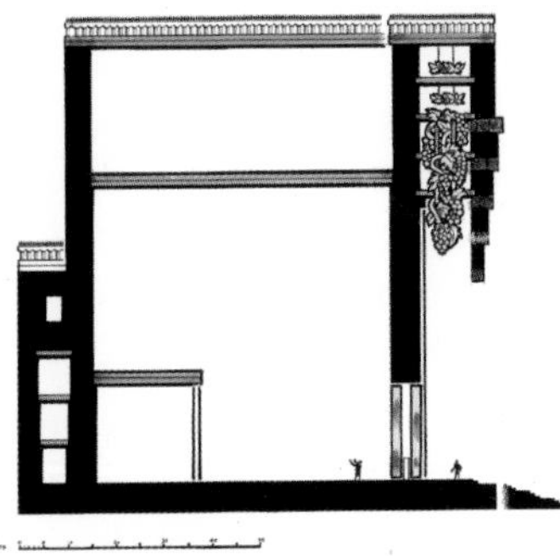

SIDE ELEVATION

Was the Ark still present during the Roman period? Josephus describes the Most Holy Place as having "nothing at all" which was accurate on the day he wrote it. Yet the Mishnah hints that the Ark was hidden (*Shekalim 6:12*).

Fearing Roman intervention, it could have been secretly moved into the Temple interior for use only on the Day of Atonement. It may be hidden underground to this day.

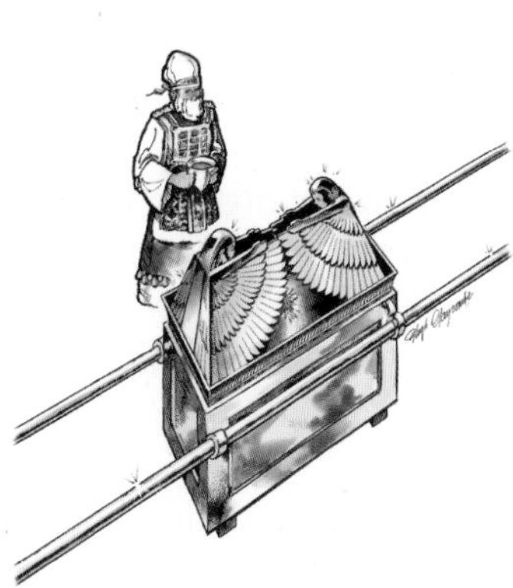

every conscientious Jewish male of twenty years or over, had to be paid in that currency. The coinage of choice was Tyrian, owing to its high silver content (*m. Bek.* 8:7).[70] The annual half-shekel equalled half a Tyrian stater or tetradrachma, so that two Jews often joined together to pay the tax in one coin (cf. Matt. 17:27). The temple tax was collected in Jerusalem from 25 Adar on, the lunar month preceding Nisan.[71]

TYRIAN SHEKELS

The smaller are half-shekel coins.

The merchants' primary offense was that of disrupting Gentile worship.[72] The temple establishment had amassed excessive wealth in Jesus' day, which made the merchants and money-changers part of a system that exploited the poor for the alleged purpose of beautifying and administering the affairs of the temple.[73] The sale of sacrificial animals and money exchange should have been facilitated near the temple rather than within its walls. This, incidentally, is exactly what had been the case earlier in Israel's history when the animal merchants had set up shop across the Kidron Valley on the slopes of the Mount of Olives.

Zeal . . . will consume me (2:17). Jesus' cleansing of the temple stirs in his disciples the memory of the righteous sufferer of Psalm 69:9 (cf. John 2:16: "my Father's *house*" with Ps. 69:9: "zeal for your *house*"). While God's people were warned against "zeal without knowledge" (Prov. 19:2; cf. Rom. 10:2), religious zeal was an important part of Jewish piety. In the Old Testament, Phinehas is promised a covenant of a lasting priesthood, "because he was zealous for the honor of his God" (Num. 25:13). In fact, God himself is shown to be zealous for his holy name (Isa. 59:17; Ezek. 39:25).

First-century Palestine was rife with religious as well as nationalistic zeal.[74] The Pharisees were concerned for the religious state of Judaism, while the Zealots played an important part in the rebellion against Rome in A.D. 66–70. Particularly notorious were the Sicarii (from Latin *sicae*, "dagger"), religious terrorists who murdered people in broad daylight in an effort to destabilize the political situation in Roman-occupied Palestine.[75] Jesus' zeal, righteous rather than blindly nationalistic, was so great it would "consume" him. This refers to his death, which brings life to the world (cf. John 6:51).

The Jews (2:18). See "'The Jews' in John's Gospel" at 5:10.

REFLECTIONS

WE ALL KNOW THE CLICHÉ OF "gentle Jesus, meek and mild." But when he cleanses the temple, Jesus, in truly prophetic style, does something highly courageous and startling. Sure enough, his authority is promptly challenged. But Jesus does not back down. He displays spiritual authority and confidence and is not afraid to take bold action where necessary. Of course, as the rest of this Gospel amply makes clear, Jesus' confidence is rooted in humility and dependence on God. In this, too, we must follow his example.

It has taken forty-six years to build this temple (2:20). The NIV rendering suggests, almost certainly incorrectly, that the temple building was still under reconstruction at the time of the temple cleansing. However, historical records indicate that Herod the Great (37–4 B.C.) began the project of restoring the temple building proper (*naos*, the term used here) in the eighteenth year of his reign, i.e., 20/19 B.C. (Josephus, *Ant.* 15.11.1 §380) with completion a year and a half later in 18/17 B.C. (*Ant.* 15.11.6 §421). Forty-six years later is A.D. 29/30, which places Jesus' first Passover in the spring of A.D. 30.[76] The restoration of the entire temple area (*hieron*, see comments on 2:14) was not completed until A.D. 63/64 under Herod Agrippa II and governor Albinus (*Ant.* 20.9.7 §219), shortly before its destruction by the Roman army in the Jewish war of A.D. 66–70.[77]

The Scripture and the words that Jesus had spoken (2:22). The Scripture may be Psalm 69:9 as in 2:17; "Jesus' word" probably refers to the saying in 2:19.

He knew all men (2:24). According to Jewish belief, God knows people's hearts and judges their motivations.[78] The present statement implies that Jesus is God or at least possesses a divine attribute. Jesus' knowledge of people's hearts is displayed in his encounters with Nicodemus and the Samaritan woman in the following two chapters.[79]

Jesus' Conversation with Nicodemus (3:1–21)

While still in Jerusalem, Jesus is paid a nightly visit by Nicodemus, a high-ranking Jewish rabbi. Later, on his way back from Judea to his native Galilee, Jesus encounters a Samaritan woman at a well. The contrast between these two individuals could hardly be more extreme. Nicodemus, the esteemed "teacher of Israel," is a wealthy member of the Sanhedrin, the Jewish ruling council, who comes to Jesus at night in order to avoid the crowds. The Samaritan is a nameless, immoral woman who meets Jesus in the heat of day, probably because she is too ashamed to draw water when other people are at the well. In both instances, Jesus directs the conversation to what he perceives to be the central issue: in Nicodemus's case, his need to be "born again," in the case of the Samaritan woman, her need to repent from her sinful lifestyle and to trust Jesus the Messiah.

Nicodemus (3:1). The name Nicodemus was common in first-century Palestine. The fact that a wealthy philanthropic Jew by the same name was living in Jerusalem around A.D. 70 adds historical plausibility to John's account (*b. Giṭ.* 56a; *b. Ketub.* 66b).[80] Apparently, Nicodemus represents a more open element among the Pharisees (cf. 12:42; Acts 5:34–39).

A member of the Jewish ruling council (3:1). "Jewish ruling council" (lit., "ruler," cf. 7:26, 48; 12:42) refers to the Sanhedrin (from *synedrion*, "gathering, assembly"), the highest national body in charge of Jewish affairs.[81] Headquartered in Jerusalem, it was composed of Pharisees and Sadducees. When Judea became a Roman province in A.D. 6, the Sanhedrin became even more autonomous in handling internal Jewish matters. As John's Gospel progresses, the Sanhedrin turns out to be the driving force in the plot against Jesus.

At night (3:2). First-century Judaism encouraged the study of Torah at night with reference to passages such as Joshua

1:8 or Psalm 42:8 (cf. 1QS 6:7). Nicodemus may have come to Jesus at night in order to avoid the crowds rather than out of fear. John later shows Nicodemus to be outspoken in his support of Jesus (John 7:50–52) and refers to his coming to Jesus at night without a hint of disparagement (19:39).

Rabbi (3:2). See comments on 1:38. It is remarkable that this highly respected Jewish teacher would honor the about thirty-year-old Jesus as a fellow rabbi, especially since Jesus was known to lack formal rabbinic training (7:15).

We know you are a teacher who has come from God (3:2). While doubtlessly intended as a compliment (contrast the categorical denial of Jesus' divine commission by other Pharisees in 7:15), Nicodemus still falls far short in understanding Jesus' true nature—for he is the heaven-sent Son of Man (3:13).

For no one could perform the miraculous signs you are doing (3:2). It was commonly held in Judaism that miracles attested to God's presence. References to "signs" in the Old Testament cluster around two major periods: the "signs and wonders" performed by Moses at the Exodus (Ex. 4:1–9; etc.); and the signs—with attendant symbolism, but not necessarily miraculous—performed by various Old Testament prophets (e.g., Isa. 20:3).[82] While Jesus discourages dependence on "signs and wonders" (cf. John 4:48), he does perform various signs, both miraculous (e.g., 2:1–11) and nonmiraculous (2:14–22). These signs show him to be not only a divine prophet (6:14; 7:40) but the God-sent Messiah (7:31; 20:30–31). The present statement probably refers primarily to Jesus' Jerusalem signs (cf. 2:23) rather than to his first sign in Cana of Galilee (2:11). For a similar acknowledgment, see 11:47.

If God were not with him (3:2). This is a common Jewish expression, used by Jesus himself (8:29; 16:32) and frequently found in the Old Testament (e.g., Gen. 21:20; 26:24; 28:15; 31:3; Deut.

▸ The Pharisees

The roots of this Jewish party can be traced to the Hasidim, a group of pious Jews in the second century B.C. The Pharisees, "a distinctive group of ostentatious religious pietists" (cf. Josephus, *J.W.* 1.5.2 §110), emphasized preserving the traditions of the fathers, which included both oral and written tradition in further development of the Old Testament Scriptures (Josephus, *Ant.* 13.10.6 §298, 13.16.2 §408; 17.2.4 §41; Hippolytus, *Haer.* 9.28.3).[A-13] Unlike the Sadducees (who only accepted the Pentateuch), the Pharisees believed in the resurrection (Josephus, *J.W.* 2.8.14 §§162–63; *Ant.* 18.1.3 §§12–14). They were a close-knit group (*J.W.* 2.8.14 §166) and avoided luxury (*Ant.* 18.1.3 §12).[A-14]

The Gospels portray the Pharisees as generally antagonistic toward Jesus (though there are exceptions such as Nicodemus or Joseph of Arimathea). Jesus, in turn, charged them with hypocrisy (e.g., Matt. 23:23–26; Luke 18:9–12). According to Josephus, the Pharisees had "the masses as their ally" (*Ant.* 13.10.6 §298), and their interpretation of Scripture had a reputation for accuracy (*Ant.* 17.2.4 §41; *J.W.* 1.5.2 §110; 2.8.14 §162; *Life* 38 §191) and set the standard for Jewish liturgy and ritual (*Ant.* 18.1.3 §15). In John's Gospel, the Pharisees are shown to mastermind the plot against Jesus in conjunction with the Sadducee-dominated high priests, who in turn controlled the Jewish supreme council, the Sanhedrin (John 7:32, 45; 11:47, 57; 12:42; 18:3).

31:23; Josh. 1:5; Jer. 1:19). Through his polite yet cautious introductory statement, Nicodemus tacitly inquires as to what new doctrine Jesus is propagating. John thus presents Nicodemus's conversation with Jesus as a typical encounter between a person interested primarily in orthodox doctrine and the One who has come to bring life itself.

Kingdom of God (3:3). The exact expression "kingdom of God" is, surprisingly, not found in the Old Testament. Yet Nicodemus has no difficulty understanding its meaning. The Hebrew Scriptures make clear that "the LORD is king" and that his sovereign reign extends to every creature (e.g., Ex. 15:18; Ps. 93:1; 103:19). Moreover, the Jews expected a future kingdom ruled by the Son of David (Isa. 9:1–7; 11:1–5, 10–11; Ezek. 34:23–24; Zech. 9:9–10), the Lord's Servant (Isa. 42:1–7; 49:1–7), indeed, the Lord himself (Ezek. 34:11–16; 36:22–32; Zech. 14:9). While not everyone was to be included in this kingdom, Jews in Jesus' day generally believed that all Israelites would have a share in the world to come, with the exception of those guilty of apostasy or some other blatant sin (*m. Sanh.* 10:1).

Born again (3:3). The notion of a new beginning and a decisive inner transformation of a person's life is also found in certain Old Testament prophetic passages (e.g., Jer. 31:33–34; Ezek. 11:19–20; 36:25–27; see comments on John 3:5). This concept of a new spiritual birth is similar to that of a "new creation" (cf. 2 Cor. 5:17; Gal. 6:15). The term *anōthen*, translated "again" in the NIV, can mean either "from above" (be it fig. [John 3:7, 31; 19:11; James 1:17; 3:15, 17] or lit. ["from top to bottom": Matt. 27:51 = Mark 15:38; John 19:23]) or "from the beginning" (Luke 1:3; Acts 26:5: "for a long time"; Gal. 4:9: "all over again" [with *palin*, "again"]). This potential ambiguity opens up the possibility of misunderstanding.

Born of water and the Spirit (3:5). The fact that "born of water and the Spirit" further develops "born again" in 3:3 suggests that one birth is in view rather than two. The closest Old Testament parallel is Ezekiel 36:25–27 which predicts God's cleansing of human hearts with water and their inner transformation by his Spirit (see also Isa. 44:3–5; *Jub.* 1:23–25).[83] The terminology may also be reminiscent of first-century proselyte baptism, where the Gentile convert to Judaism was compared to a newborn child. Thus R. Yose ben Ḥalafta (c. A.D. 130–160) said, "One who has become a proselyte is like a child newly born" (*b. Yebam.* 48b; cf. 22a; 62a; 97b; *b. Bek.* 47a).

Flesh gives birth to flesh, but the Spirit gives birth to spirit (3:6). Although the Old Testament does not literally refer to God's Spirit "giving birth" to spirit (cf. 6:63), it does hold out the vision that God, who is spirit (4:24), will "put a new spirit" in his people (Ezek. 36:26; cf. 37:5, 14).

You must be born again (3:7). "You" is in the plural, which shows that this requirement does not extend solely to Nicodemus but to the entire group he represents (cf. "anyone" in 3:3, 5; "we" in 3:2, 11). This includes the Pharisees and the Sanhedrin—and thus the entire Jewish religious leadership—but ultimately the entire nation.

The wind blows wherever it pleases . . . born of the Spirit (3:8). "Wind" and

"Spirit" translate the same Greek and Hebrew words (Gk. *pneuma*; Heb. *ruaḥ*). Both the Old Testament and Jewish literature contain numerous references to the mystery of the wind's origin (cf. Eccl. 8:8; 11:5; *1 En.* 41:3; 60:12; *2 Bar.* 48:3–4). In the present instance, the point of Jesus' analogy is that both wind and spiritual birth are mysterious in origin. Nevertheless, while they themselves are invisible, their effects can be observed. Despite its inscrutability, spiritual birth is nonetheless real, as real as the mysterious movements of the wind. Moreover, just as the wind blows "where it pleases," so the Spirit's operation is not subject to human control, eluding all efforts at manipulation.

You are Israel's teacher (3:10). Jesus may be returning Nicodemus's compliment in 3:2, where that rabbi had called Jesus "a teacher come from God" (cf. 3:11). The definite article before "teacher" in the original suggests that Nicodemus was an established, recognized teacher.[84]

Earthly . . . heavenly (3:12). "Earthly things" may refer to the elementary teaching on the necessity of a spiritual birth. If "Israel's teacher" stumbles over such a foundational truth, how can Jesus enlighten him on "heavenly things," such as the more advanced teachings of the kingdom? A similar sentiment is expressed in the Wisdom of Solomon (first century B.C.): "We can hardly guess at what is on the earth . . . but who has traced out what is in the heavens?" (Wisd. Sol. 9:16; cf. Judith 8:14).

The Talmud tells the story of Rabban Gamaliel (c. A.D. 90) conversing with the Roman emperor Nerva (A.D. 96–98) or Domitian (A.D. 81–96) at the occasion of a visit to Rome. When the emperor claims to know what Gamaliel's God is doing and where he is seated, the rabbi becomes distressed and, when asked for the reason, tells the emperor, "I have a son in one of the cities of the sea, and I yearn for him. Please tell me about him." When the emperor protests that he has no way of knowing where he is, Gamaliel replies, "You do not know what is on earth, and yet [claim to] know what is in heaven!" (*b. Sanh.* 39a).

No one has ever gone into heaven except the one who came from heaven—the Son of Man (3:13). The Old Testament identifies heaven as the place where God dwells.[85] John's Gospel refers several times to a descent *from* heaven, be it of the Spirit (1:32–33), angels (1:51), the Son of Man (3:13), or the "bread of life" (6:33, 38, 41, 42, 50, 51, 58). However, this is one of only three instances where it speaks of an ascent *into* heaven (angels: 1:51; the Son of Man: 3:13; the risen Lord: 20:17). Jesus here contrasts himself, the "Son of Man" (cf. Dan. 7:13), with other human figures who allegedly entered heaven, such as Enoch (Gen. 5:24; cf. Heb. 11:5), Elijah (2 Kings 2:1–12; cf. 2 Chron. 21:12–15), Moses (Ex. 24:9–11; 34:29–30), Isaiah (Isa. 6:1–3), or Ezekiel (Ezek. 1; 10). A whole cottage industry of intertestamental literature

REFLECTIONS

WE MUST CONSCIOUSLY CULTIVATE AN OPENNESS to new spiritual insights from God, even if this involves a radical change of life. Nicodemus, the revered "teacher of Israel," was confronted with his need to be "born from above." Would he be open to acknowledge his spiritual need and humble himself before God? Would he be receptive to that new revelation? The older we get, the harder it may be to retain such openness, but without it we will either suffer spiritual death altogether (if we are unbelievers) or cease to grow as a Christian.

revolved around such figures and their heavenly exploits (e.g., *1 En.*).[86] While believers can expect to join Christ in heaven one day (cf. John 14:1–3; 17:24), only Jesus came down from heaven as well as ascended back up to heaven (cf. Luke 24:51; Acts 1:9; though note the similar ascent-descent pattern by angels in John 1:51).

Just as Moses lifted up the snake in the desert (3:14). The allusion is plainly to Numbers 21:8–9, where God is shown to send poisonous snakes to judge rebellious Israel. When Moses intercedes for his people, God provides a way of salvation in the form of a raised bronze serpent, so that "when anyone was bitten by a snake and looked at the bronze snake, he lived" (Num. 21:9). But the primary analogy established in the present passage is not that of the raised bronze serpent and the lifted-up Son of Man. Rather, Jesus likens the restoration of people's physical lives as a result of looking at the bronze serpent with people's reception of eternal life as a result of "looking" in faith at the Son of Man (cf. John 3:15–18). Yet as in the case of desert Israel, it is ultimately not a person's faith but the God in whom the faith is placed who is the source of salvation: "[They] received a symbol of deliverance to remind them of your law's command. For the one who turned toward it was saved, not by the thing that was beheld, but by you, the Savior of all" (Wisd. Sol. 16:6–7).

Everyone who believes in him (3:15). This phrase strikes a markedly universal note. While looking at the bronze serpent in the desert restored life to believing Israelites, there are no such ethnic restrictions on believing in Jesus. *Everyone* who believes will receive eternal life (cf. 3:16–18 and comments on 1:4, 9, 12). God sent Jesus to save not just Israel, but the entire world (3:17).

Its insistence on the universality of the Christian message marks John's Gospel off from sects such as the Qumran community or the large number of mystery religions, all of which saw salvation limited to a select few. At the same time, however, John's Gospel does not teach universal*ism*, that is, the notion that all will eventually be saved. Rather, salvation is made contingent on *believing in him*, that is, Jesus (cf. 20:30–31).

Eternal life (3:15). See comments on "life" at 1:4.

For God so loved the world (3:16). The Old Testament makes abundantly clear that God loves all that he has made, especially his people (e.g., Ex. 34:6–7; Deut. 7:7–8; Hos. 11:1–4, 8–11). In the Mishnah, R. Aqiba (c. A.D. 135) is quoted as saying, "Beloved is man for he was created in the image [of God]. . . . Beloved are Israel for they were called children of God" (*m. ʾAbot* 3:15). In these last days, God has demonstrated his love for the world through the gift of his one and only Son. Significantly, God's love extends not merely to Israel but to "the world," that is, sinful humanity.[87] Just as God's love encompasses the entire world, so Jesus made atonement for the sins of the whole world (1 John 2:2).

That he gave his one and only Son (3:16). On the phrase "one and only," see comments on 1:14, 18. The next verse says that God *sent* his Son; here the term used is "he gave." This draws attention to the sacrifice involved for God the Father in sending his Son to save the world. Surely to see his son die in such a cruel fashion would break any father's heart, much more that of our heavenly Father.

In a similar Old Testament passage, Abraham was asked to give up his "only son," Isaac (Gen. 22). Unlike Jesus, however, Isaac was not offered up but spared when God provided a substitute. Note also the parallel wording in the messianic prophecy of Isaiah 9:6, that "to us a *son* is *given*."

Perish . . . eternal life (3:16). Already in the Old Testament, blessings for obedience correspond to curses for disobedience (Deut. 28–30). In John, likewise, there is no middle ground. Believing in the Son (with the result of eternal life) or refusing to believe (which results in destruction) are the only options. Since "perish" is contrasted with "*eternal* life," it stands to reason that perishing is eternal as well. Yet "perishing" does not mean annihilation in the sense of total destruction but spending eternity apart from God and from Jesus Christ, in whom alone is life (John 1:4).

God did not send his Son into the world to condemn the world, but to save the world through him (3:17). The Old Testament makes clear that God would rather save than judge (e.g., Ezek. 18:23). The Jews, however, believed that the coming Messiah would save Israel but judge the Gentiles. "In no time at all, with the coming of harvest, the straw is disposed of in the water, the chaff in the wind, and the weeds in flame, but the wheat is brought in for safe-keeping. . . . Likewise, the peoples of the earth . . . in the time-to-come, when the day of judgment arrives, will be dragged into the Valley of Hinnom. . . . Only Israel will remain in the time-to-come" (*Midr. Ps.* 2:14).

Isaiah's words "Morning is coming, but also the night" (Isa. 21:12) were taken to mean that when the Messiah, the Son of David, comes, "there will be morning for the righteous, and night for the wicked, morning for Israel, and night for idolaters [i.e., the nations]" (*y. Ta'an.* 1:1; cf. *Num. Rab.* 16:23). The Qumran sect maintained that only its own members would be saved while the rest of the world would perish: "There will follow a time of salvation for the people of God and a period of rule for all the men of his lot [i.e., the Qumran covenanters], and of everlasting destruction for all the lot of Belial" (1QM 1:5). The adherents of mystery religions likewise believed that only they were the initiated. Contrary to these expectations, John affirms that the Messiah's coming manifested God's saving will for all, not just Jews.

Light . . . darkness (3:19). For general remarks, see comments on 1:4–5. In the present passage, "light" and "darkness" have clear moral connotations, grounding the world's rejection of Jesus in human depravity, which is the result of the Fall (Gen. 3; Rom. 1:18–32). In the ultimate analysis, sin (including people's failure to recognize God's Messiah) is irrational and self-destructive. Notably, and contrary to Jewish self-perception, the Jews are not exempt from this pattern; they are shown to be in bondage to sin and spiritual blindness, refusing to face their guilt and preferring to suppress the truth instead (John 8:31–59; 9:39–41; cf. Matt. 21:33–46 par.; Acts 7).

In the Hellenistic world, Plato's well-known "Allegory of the Cave" (*Republic* 7.1–11; c. 390 B.C.), provided a partial analogy to John 3:19–21. According to this myth, human beings live from birth in a cave, a world of shadows. Only those who dare step out of this dark existence can experience the light, but many prefer to stay in the darkness. However, in

Plato's allegory, the person who has seen the light is the philosopher who is cognizant of the world of ideas and thus is able better to explain reality; in Jesus' teaching, the light is himself (cf. 1:4–5; 8:12; 9:5), and people's main problem is not ignorance but sin.[88]

For fear that his deeds will be exposed (3:20). The verb "exposed" points further to the shame that comes through such exposure (cf. 16:8). An interesting parallel is found in the *Damascus Document* of the Qumran sect: "And so is the judgment of everyone who enters the congregation of the men of perfect holiness and is slack in the fulfillment of the instructions of the upright. . . . When *his deeds are evident*, he shall be expelled from the congregation" (CD 20:1–3).

Lives by the truth (3:21). Similar is 5:29: "those who have done good." "Lives by the truth" contrasts with "does evil" in the preceding verse. The literal rendering of the phrase is "does the truth," a typical Jewish expression meaning "acts faithfully." It is found in the Old Testament (Neh. 9:33 LXX; Isa. 26:10 LXX), apocryphal literature (Tobit 4:6; 13:6), and the Qumran scrolls (1QS 1:5; 5:3).

Done through God (3:21). This unique phrase literally means "accomplished *in* God" (cf. Mark 14:6), that is, through God rather than by one's own strength. This excludes human pride (see Jer. 9:23–24). For not just salvation, but also subsequent works are, properly understood, works "done through God."

John the Baptist's Witness Concerning Christ (3:22–36)

Judean countryside (3:22). The Greek word *gē* usually means "land" or "region." However, this rendering seems to be excluded here, for Jesus has been in *the land of* Judea ever since attending the Passover (i.e., from 2:23–3:21). Thus, the word likely means "countryside" (cf. Mark 1:5: *chōra*) here. If so, Jesus leaves the vicinity of Jerusalem and heads north. The next verse places him with John the Baptist at Aenon near Salim (see comments on John 3:23), while 4:3 indicates that Jesus leaves Judea altogether, returning to Galilee (cf. 2:12) via Samaria.

JUDEA AND SAMARIA

Spent some time (3:22). As in 11:54, this refers to an indefinite period of time Jesus spends with his disciples. In Acts, the only other place where this word (*diatribō*) occurs in the New Testament, the stay may be longer but need not extend for more than "seven days" (Acts 20:6) or "eight or ten days" (25:6).

Aenon near Salim, because there was plenty of water (3:23). "Aenon" is a Semitic term meaning "springs"—hence the mention of "plenty of water" (lit., "many waters," i.e., springs), an ideal site for John's (and Jesus') baptismal preaching. "Salim" comes from the Hebrew word for "peace." The location of this place is disputed. The two primary sites that have been suggested both lie in Samaria: One possibility is the Salim eight miles southeast of Beth Shean (Scythopolis), the other the Salim four miles southeast of Shechem further south.[89] The presence of a town (known from early times) called Sâlim in the latter location and of modern ʿAinûn eight miles to the northeast favors the second site. Also, the latter location, being further south, seems to cohere better with the geographical markers of 3:22 and 4:3. In either case, if we assume the reconstruction of "Bethany near the Jordan" in 1:28 is correct (see comments), John has moved south.

Ceremonial washing (3:25). The issue of ritual purification, while of significant interest to first-century Jews (see also the Dead Sea Scrolls), is clearly peripheral to the ministries of Jesus and John the Baptist. Hence no further explanation is provided (see also 2:6; 11:55; 18:28; 19:31).

Rabbi (3:26). See comments on 1:38. This is the only place in John's Gospel where the Baptist is called "Rabbi." While the Baptist, who engaged predominantly in a prophetic-style ministry, may not fit the stereotype of a Jewish rabbi, the term was at that time still sufficiently wide to subsume the Baptist. Later, the term came to be used only for those who had undergone formal rabbinic training.

On the other side of the Jordan (3:26). Salim must be located on the west side of the Jordan (cf. 1:28: "Bethany on the other side of the Jordan," that is, east of the Jordan).

A man can receive only what is given him from heaven (3:27). In keeping with contemporary practice, John uses the word "heaven" to circumscribe the name of God (similarly, Jesus in 19:11: "from above"). John here tells his disciples that he must not exceed the calling he

TEL SALIM

received from God or compare himself with others (cf. 21:20–22).

Sent ahead of him (3:28). The phrase is used in the Old Testament for messengers sent ahead of a given person (e.g., Gen. 24:7; 32:3; 45:5; 46:28; cf. Ps. 105:17).

The bride belongs to the bridegroom. The friend who attends the bridegroom (3:29). John likens himself to the best man at a wedding who stands ready to do the bridegroom's bidding (e.g. *m. Sanh.* 3:5; *m. B. Bat.* 9:4).[90] He thus makes clear that the purpose of his ministry was to elevate Jesus, so that there was no rivalry between the two men. Jesus calls himself "the bridegroom" in Matthew 9:15 par.

Joy (3:29). Joy was the overriding theme at Jewish weddings.

Has certified (3:33). The word translated "has certified" (*sphragizō*) literally means "to seal" in the sense of confirming or authenticating something to be true.[91] The term is derived from the practice of signing important documents by pressing one's distinctive mark, which was engraved on one's signet ring, onto hot wax. Here the expression indicates that everyone who accepts Christ's testimony about himself agrees ("seals") that God is truthful. In 6:27, it is said that God has put his "seal of approval" upon the Son of Man.

For God gives the Spirit without limit (3:34). Literally, the text reads: "for he." Later Jewish rabbis were convinced that God gave his Spirit to the prophets in measured amounts: "Even the Holy Spirit resting on the prophets does so by weight [i.e., appointed measure], one prophet speaking one book of prophecy and another speaking two books. . . . Even the words of the Torah which were given from above were given by measure, namely Scripture, Mishnah, Talmud, *Halachah* [legal portions], and *Haggadah* [narrative portions]. One man becomes versed in Scripture, another in Mishnah, etc." (*Lev. Rab.* 15:2 on Lev. 13:2; attributed to R. Aḥa [c. A.D. 320]). Jesus, by contrast, is the One on whom the Spirit has come to rest in all his fullness, as the Baptist has previously testified (cf. John 1:32–33). In keeping with this notion, the Apocalypse portrays Jesus as the One who holds the seven spirits of God (Rev. 3:1) and as the Lamb who has seven horns and seven eyes, which are the seven spirits of God (5:6).

Has eternal life (3:36). The present tense "has" indicates that eternal life is not merely a future expectation but already a present experience. This exceeds Old Testament hopes and claims made by other world religions.

Will not see life (3:36). Similar to "see/enter the kingdom" and "do the truth," "see life" is a Jewish expression meaning "experiencing or enjoying life." The corresponding expression "see death" occurs in 8:51.[92]

Christ Witnesses to the Woman at the Well (4:1–26)

After an eventful stay in Jerusalem for the Passover and an extended baptizing ministry in the Judean countryside (2:13–3:36), Jesus journeys back north to Galilee. His trip leads him through Samaritan territory. But rather than rushing on in order to avoid religious defilement through an encounter with this despised race, Jesus takes the time to talk with a Samaritan woman at a well, which results in her entire village being evangelized. In the process, Jesus identifies himself as Messiah and is recognized by his converts as the Savior of the world.

The Pharisees heard that Jesus was gaining and baptizing more disciples than John (4:1). There were others baptizing in Judea during this period, but Jesus and John are distinctive in that they use baptism as an initiatory rite for Jews. The Pharisees have investigated John's credentials (1:19, 24); now they are looking into those of Jesus.

JUDEAN COIN

One of the first coins struck in the land of Israel. This one bears the inscription "Yehud" (Judea) and dates to 333 B.C.

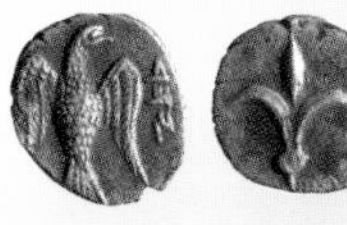

Had to go (4:4). "Had to" may indicate divine necessity: That is, Jesus' going through Samaria is according to the plan and will of God (cf. 9:4; 10:16; 12:34; 20:9).

Through Samaria (4:4). This was the usual trek taken by travellers from Judea to Galilee. As Josephus writes, "It was the custom of the Galileans at the time of a festival to pass through the Samaritan territory on their way to the Holy City" (*Ant.* 20.6.1 §118; cf. idem., *J.W.* 2.12.3 §232). Again, Josephus comments, "I further wrote to my friends in Samaria to provide for their safe convoy through that district; for Samaria was now under Roman rule and, for rapid travel, it was essential to take that route, by which Jerusalem may be reached in three days from Galilee" (*Life* 52 §269). Strict Jews, however, sought to bypass Samaria by opting for a longer, less direct route, which involved crossing the Jordan and traveling on the east side.

SAMARIA

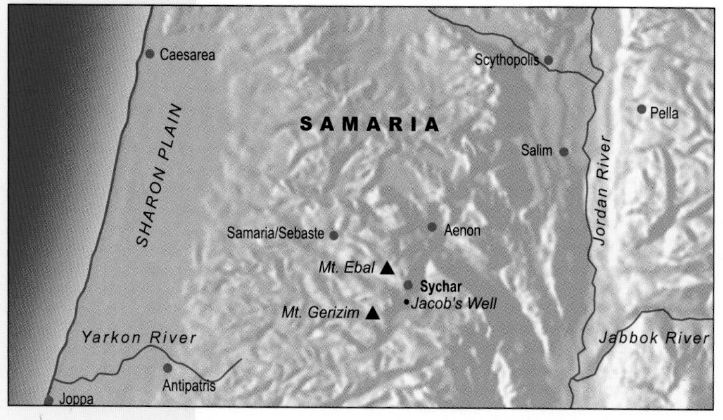

Sychar (4:5). The small village of Sychar was probably located at the site of modern ʿAskar about two miles east of Nablus, centrally situated just east of Mount Gerizim and Mount Ebal.[93] ʿAskar may also be the *ʿên Sokder* mentioned in the Mishnah (*m. Menaḥ.* 10:2).[94] An identification of Sychar with biblical Shechem (about a mile from ʿAskar) is unlikely, since Shechem was probably destroyed in 128 B.C. (or at least prior to 107 B.C.) by the Hasmonean high priest John Hyrcanus I (Josephus, *J.W.* 1.2.6 §63; *Ant.* 13.9.1 §§255–56). Subsequent to the conquest of Jerusalem by the Roman general Pompey (63 B.C.), Sychar apparently became the most important Samaritan city in place of Shechem. John is the first ancient author to mention Sychar/ ʿAskar.[95]

Near the plot of ground Jacob had given to his son Joseph (4:5). It was deduced from Genesis 48:21–22 and Joshua 24:32 that Jacob gave his son Joseph the land at Shechem which he had bought from the sons of Hamor (Gen. 33:18–19) and which later served as Joseph's burial place (Ex. 13:19; Josh. 24:32).[96]

Jacob's well was there (4:6). The reference to Jacob's well and the later mention of Mount Gerizim (4:20) places Jesus' encounter with the Samaritan woman within the framework of "holy geography," which Jesus is shown to transcend. Holy sites were—and still are—of great importance in Jewish and Samaritan life, as they are in all major world religions. Apparently, Jacob's well was a convenient stop for pilgrims travelling from Galilee to Jerusalem or vice versa.[97]

The site of Jacob's well is reasonably certain, although the Old Testament nowhere mentions Jacob digging a well here (or anywhere). The current well is about one hundred feet deep. Such a deep well is unusual in an area where there are many springs. ʿAskar is nearly a mile to the north and has its own well, but perhaps it did not two thousand years ago. Shechem, on the other hand, is only 250 feet from Jacob's well, which suggests to some that Shechem and not ʿAskar is the true Sychar (see comments on 4:5).

Tired as he was from the journey (4:6). Since it was about noon when Jesus sat down at the well (see below), he and his disciples would have been traveling for about six hours up to that point if they had started their journey at daybreak.

Sat down by the well (4:6). Wells were usually carved out from solid limestone rock, with a small curb remaining to guard against accident (cf. Ex. 21:33). This is probably where Jesus sat down to rest.[98]

About the sixth hour (4:6). This probably means around twelve noon (see comments on 1:39).

Samaritan woman came to draw water (4:7). Apparently, the woman is from the district, not the town, of Samaria (the town of Samaria is located several miles north of Sychar). If Sychar is ʿAskar, it is surprising that the woman does not go to the well there (Ain ʿAskar). Perhaps that well did not always flow or the woman lives closer to the well of Jacob. Women were more likely to come in groups to fetch water (Gen. 24:11; Ex. 2:16) and to do so either early in the morning or later in the day when the heat of the sun was not so fierce (Gen. 24:11: "toward evening"). By contrast, this Samaritan woman comes alone, and she comes in the heat of the midday sun. Both observations suggest that this woman is looked down upon in her community on account of her low reputation (see 4:16–18).

Will you give me a drink? (4:7). By asking a woman who has come to the well alone for a drink, Jesus, himself being alone (4:8), breaks all rules of Jewish piety (see comments on 4:9). His taking the initative is open to the charge of acting in a

THE SITE OF JACOB'S WELL

The structure is a Byzantine-era church rebuilt by the Crusaders and, later, the Orthodox church.

flirtatious manner. Also, the fact that Isaac and Jacob met their prospective wives at wells (Gen. 24:17; 29:10) creates the sort of precedent that would further have cautioned devout Jews.

His disciples had gone into the town to buy food (4:8). Apparently, Jesus and his disciples carry little or nothing to eat on their journeys (Matt. 12:1 par.; 16:6–7 par.; cf. 10:9–10 par.). Rather, they bring with them the necessary money to buy what they need on the way (cf. John 12:6; 13:29). Purchasing food, together with the preparation and cooking of food and waiting on tables, were common tasks of disciples.[99] That Jesus and his disciples are willing to purchase food from Samaritans indicates a certain freedom from the self-imposed regulations of the stricter Jews, who would have been unwilling to eat food handled by Samaritans. As Rabbi Eliezer (c. A.D. 90–130) used to say, "He that eats the bread of the Samaritans is like to one that eats the flesh of swine" (*m. Šeb.* 8:10). Moreover, with certain dry foods, there was no conveyance of defilement.

You are a Jew and I am a Samaritan woman. How can you ask me for a drink? (For Jews do not associate with Samaritans.) (4:9). Generally, Jews avoided contact with Samaritans, especially Samaritan women, although there would have been a certain spectrum depending on locale, class, education, and other factors.[100] Some Jews were willing to eat with Samaritans (*m. Ber.* 7:1; 8:8), but many were not because of ritual defilement. Samaritans were thought to convey uncleanness by what they lay, sat, or rode on, as well as by their saliva or urine. Samaritan women, like Gentiles, were considered to be in a continual state of ritual uncleanness: "The daughters of the Samaritans are [deemed unclean as] menstruants from their cradle" (*m. Nid.* 4:1).[101] Apart from these ethnic sensibilities, men would generally not want to discuss theological issues with women. Hence the woman's surprise: Did Jesus not know that even her water jar was considered unclean by his fellow-Jews?

The gift of God . . . living water (4:10). On a literal level, the expression "living water" refers to the much sought-after fresh spring water, as opposed to stagnant water (Gen. 26:19; Lev. 14:6; Jer. 2:13). Ultimately, God is known to be the source and giver of life. In Numbers 20:8–11, an incident to which Jesus may allude in the present passage, water gushes out of the rock, supplying the Israelites with much-needed refreshment. In Jeremiah 2:13, God laments that his people have forsaken him, "the spring of living water." In Isaiah 12:3, the prophet envisions the joy with which people "will draw water from the wells of salvation" in the last days.

For the ancient Jews, the greatest "gift of God" was the Torah (the law). Other "gifts of God," apart from the lights in the sky and rain, were considered to include peace, salvation, the land of Israel, and divine mercy (*Gen. Rab.* 6:5; attributed to Yoḥanan ben Zakkai [c. A.D. 70] and other rabbis). Rabbinic thought associated the provision of water with the coming of the Messiah: "As the former redeemer made a well to rise [cf. Num. 21:17–18], so will the latter Redeemer bring up water" (*Eccl. Rab.* 1:9; see comments on 6:31).

In John, Jesus is identified explicitly with God the Creator and Life-giver (John 5:26) and shown to dispense the gift of "living water," later unveiled as the Holy Spirit (7:37–39). This end-time blessing, bestowed after Jesus' exaltation, transcends John's water baptism (1:26, 33), Jewish ceremonial purification (2:6; 3:25), proselyte baptism (cf. 3:5), and the torch-lighting and water-pouring symbolism of the Feast of Tabernacles (chs. 7–8). It also supersedes nurturing or healing waters such as Jacob's well (ch. 4) or the pools of Bethesda and Siloam (chs. 5 and 9). In fulfillment of the Old Testament prophetic vision (Ezek. 47:9; Zech. 14:8), Jesus has inaugurated the age of God's abundance.

Sir (4:11). The word translated "sir" is *kyrios*, which can also mean "Lord." Here, however, it is merely a respectful address of Jesus without further Christological implications.[102]

Nothing to draw with and the well is deep (4:11). The well is still over one hundred feet deep and was probably deeper at that time. In fact, Jacob's well may have been the deepest well in all of Palestine.[103] John's use of a different

The Samaritans[A-15]

The Samaritans occupied a curious middle position between Jews and Gentiles. Their origins went back to the intermarriage of Israelites left behind during the Assyrian exile of the northern kingdom with Gentiles (2 Kings 17:24). The Samaritans themselves, however, claimed descent from Joseph by way of the tribes of Manasseh and Ephraim (Josephus, *Ant.* 9.14.3 §291; 11.8.6 §§341, 344). In contrast, at least some Jews preferred to trace the Samaritans' ancestry back to Shechem, the rapist of Dinah, the sister of Jacob's twelve sons (Gen. 34). Because they occupied territory that according to the Jews belonged to the two above-mentioned tribes (which had not yet returned from exile), they saw the Samaritans as an obstacle to the fulfillment of God's end-time promises to the Jews (cf. Sir. 50:26: "the foolish people that live in Shechem"; *T. Levi* 5–6).

In Jesus' day, relations between Jews and Samaritans were generally characterized by bitter hostility (e.g., *T. Levi* 7:2, which calls Shechem "City of the Senseless"). In an apparent attempt to ease the tension, Herod the Great married a Samaritan woman named Malthace, who bore him both Antipas and Archelaus (Josephus, *J.W.* 1.28.4 §562; *Ant.* 17.1.3 §20), but to little avail. On the whole, Samaritans were considered to be irremediably impure.

Despite their recognition of the five books of Moses, they were suspected of being an idolatrous cult on the basis of their veneration of Mount Gerizim as a holy mountain (cf. *m. Ḥul.* 2:8). The Jewish historian Josephus portrays the Shechemites as a refuge for Jewish religious apostates (*Ant.* 11.11.7 §§346–47). He also records an occasion (between A.D. 6–9) when some Samaritans tried to desecrate the Jerusalem temple on the eve of the Passover (*Ant.* 18.2.2 §§29–30) and another instance (in A.D. 52) when they attacked Jewish pilgrims on their way to Jerusalem (*Ant.* 20.6.1–3 §§118–36).

To call someone—especially a fellow-Jew—a "Samaritan" was a gross insult (cf. *b. Soṭah* 22a)[A-16] and may have been tantamount to accusing him of religious apostasy (cf. 8:48; Josephus, *Ant.* 11.8.6 §340). When Jesus sent out the Twelve, he explicitly instructed them not to enter any town of the Samaritans, thus upholding an ethnic (as well as salvation-historical) distinction between these people and the Jews (Matt. 10:5). At a later time, Jesus' disciples were indignant when they were not welcome in a Samaritan village because Jesus was headed for Jerusalem (Luke 9:51–56; cf. Josephus, *Ant.* 20.1.1 §6). Jesus himself broke with his Jewish contemporaries' hostility toward Samaritans (see Luke 10:33; 17:16). His coming had created a level playing field where ethnic distinctions gave way to spiritual considerations bound up with obedience to God and acceptance of Jesus as Messiah (cf. esp. John 4:23–24).

Greek word for "well" in the present passage (*phrear*; cf. 4:6: *pēgē*) may indicate that the cistern (*phrear*) is fed by an underground spring (*pēgē*). Travellers usually carried a skin bucket (*antlēma*) for drawing water, which they could let down the well with a rope. In the present instance, Jesus' disciples are probably carrying it with them, but they have gone to buy food, presumably taking it along (4:8); in any case Jesus could not get "living" water out of the well (see comments on 4:10).

Are you greater than our father Jacob (4:12). Jesus' significance surpasses that of all the major previous figures in the history of God's people, be it Abraham (8:53), Moses (1:17), Jonah, or Solomon (Matt. 12:41–42).

According to Josephus, the Samaritans claimed descent from Joseph through Ephraim and Manasseh (*Ant.* 11.8.6 §341). The Jews sharply disagreed (see "The Samaritans" at 4:9). Jesus himself seems to side with his fellow Jews when he refers to a Samaritan leper as a "foreigner" (Luke 17:18). Yet in the present passage, Jesus refuses to get sidetracked by this (for him) peripheral point (cf. John 4:19–20).

Who gave us the well and drank from it himself (4:12). This is sheer tradition. The book of Genesis does not record Jacob ever digging a well, much less drinking from it himself or giving it to any of his sons. Mention is merely made of Jacob's buying and giving Shechem to Joseph (Gen. 33:19; 48:22), in the vicinity of which Jacob's well is located (see comments on John 4:5–6).[104]

Will become in him a spring of water welling up to eternal life (4:14). Isaiah envisioned a time in the last days when people would joyfully "draw water from the wells of salvation" (Isa. 12:3).[105] In a dry, hot climate such as that of Palestine, people were particularly aware of their need for water and the blessing it represents. Similar terminology is found in the *Targum Neofiti* of Genesis 28:10: "When *our father Jacob* raised the stone from above the mouth of the well [at Haran], the well *overflowed* and came up to its mouth, and was *overflowing* for twenty years."[106] A Samaritan liturgy for the Day of Atonement says of the Taheb, the Samaritan Restorer, that "water will flow from his buckets" (cf. Num. 24:7).[107]

I have no husband (4:17). While technically truthful, the woman's statement is potentially misleading. On the face of it, it can be taken to imply that she is unattached and thus available (see comments on 4:7).[108] Jesus, with fine irony, quickly removes all doubt.

You have had five husbands, and the man you now have is not your husband (4:18). If the NIV rendering is correct, the woman is in conflict with Jewish law, since rabbis generally disapproved of more than three legal marriages in a lifetime, even in case of the death of previous husbands (*b. Yebam.* 64b; cf. *b. Nid.* 64a). However, it is perhaps more likely that this is another instance of a wordplay, here involving the word *anēr*, which can mean either "man" or "husband." Jesus may tell the woman that she had five "men" (with whom she lived in fornication) and that the one she is now living with is not her "man," that is, husband (though he may be that of another woman, note the emphatic position of "your" in the Greek). In other words, the woman is a serial fornicator.[109] Some argue that "five men or husbands" alludes to a tradition cited in Josephus, according to which the Samaritans had five gods (*Ant.* 9.14.3 §288; cf. 2 Kings 17:24, 30–31), just as "five colonnades" in 5:2 are taken to refer to the Jewish Pentateuch.[110]

You are a prophet (4:19). The woman acknowledges that Jesus knows her life circumstances without apparently having been told by anyone—hence he must be "a prophet" (cf. Luke 7:39).

Our fathers worshiped on this mountain (4:20). "Our fathers" refers back to Abraham (Gen. 12:7) and Jacob (33:20), who built altars in this region. Mount Gerizim was the site where the Israelites were blessed by Moses (Deut. 11:29; 27:12). The Samaritans held that many other significant events during the patriarchal period were associated with this mountain.[111] It is unclear precisely when the Samaritans built a temple at that location. Samaritan tradition places construction in the fifth century B.C., while Josephus claims that the temple was built in 332 B.C.[112] Since the names mentioned by Josephus coincide strikingly with those of Nehemiah 13:28, Samaritan tradition may be closer to the truth than Josephus.[113] In Hellenistic times, Antiochus IV Epiphanes converted the Samaritan sanctuary into a temple of Zeus Horkios ("the Guardian of Oaths"), while the Samaritans continued their worship at an altar erected on another peak of the mountain.[114] In 129 B.C., it was razed by John Hyrcanus and the Jews (*Ant.* 13.9.1 §§254–56).

The Jewish-Samaritan dispute regarding the proper place of worship had thus been raging for centuries when the Samaritan woman broached the subject with Jesus. Josephus tells of an argument between Egyptian Jews and Samaritans before Ptolemy Philometor in around 150 B.C. as to whether the sanctuary was to be on Mount Gerizim or Mount Zion (*Ant.* 13.3.4 §74; cf. 12.10).

That Samaritan beliefs regarding the sanctity of Mount Gerizim continued unabated is illustrated by an incident in A.D. 36 (recounted in *Ant.* 18.4.1 §§85–87) involving a Samaritan troublemaker put down by Pilate. "Although bereft of a sanctuary, the Samaritan high priest and priesthood continued to sacrifice on Mount Gerizim in the first century."[115] During Jesus' conversation with the Samaritan woman, Mount Gerizim would have been in full view. From Jacob's well, they may have even been able to see the temple's ruins, perhaps turning to look at them when the woman mentioned the place.

You Jews claim . . . Jerusalem (4:20). *Midr. Ps.* 91:7, commenting on Genesis 28:17, says that "when a man prays in Jerusalem, it is as though he prays before the throne of glory, for the gate of heaven is in Jerusalem, and a door is always open for the hearing of prayer." The Pentateuch, however, does not specifically identify

MT. GERIZIM

Jerusalem as the proper place of worship—though other portions of Scripture do (see 2 Chron. 6:6; 7:12; Ps. 78:68)—which led the Samaritans to establish their own sanctuary on Mount Gerizim. The Samaritans accepted only the Pentateuch as Scripture (see comments on 4:22).

A time is coming when you will worship the Father neither on this mountain nor in Jerusalem (4:21). The woman has just acknowledged Jesus as a prophet (4:19). Now he uses prophetic language: "a time is coming" (cf. 1 Sam. 2:31; 2 Kings 20:17; Jer. 31:31). Jesus' prophecy was literally fulfilled through the events of A.D. 66–70, when the Romans under Titus razed Jerusalem, including the temple (cf. Luke 21:20, 24). Spiritually speaking, the crucified and resurrected Christ would serve as a substitute for the Jerusalem temple as the new center of worship for God's people (John 2:19–22).

You Samaritans worship what you do not know (4:22). The Samaritans had greatly truncated their knowledge of God by restricting their canon to the Pentateuch. Jesus says "what" (neuter) rather than "whom" (masculine) you do not know, perhaps pointing to the less than personal character of Samaritan worship.

Salvation is from the Jews (4:22). See "The Jews" at 5:10. In Psalm 76:1, the psalmist exclaims, "In Judah God is known; his name is great in Israel." Jesus here acknowledges that the Jewish people are the instrument by which God's redemption is mediated to others. This contrasts with Samaritan religious ignorance (see previous comment). Nevertheless, while Jesus freely acknowledges Jewish salvation-historical preeminence, he does not allow it to become a barrier to keep others from benefiting from divine salvation blessings.[116] It was precisely the fact that the Jews wanted to keep God's gifts to themselves that drew God's judgment.

God is spirit . . . worship in spirit and in truth (4:24). "God is spirit" does not refer to the Holy Spirit but identifies God as a spiritual rather than material being. The spiritual nature of God is taught clearly in the Old Testament.[117] Because God is spirit, the Israelites were not to make idols "in the form of anything" as did the surrounding nations (Ex. 20:4).

Messiah (called Christ) is coming (4:25). See comments on 1:41. Although the Samaritan woman refers to a coming "Messiah," the Samaritans did not regularly use this expression until the sixteenth century,[118] preferring terms such as "Taheb" (meaning "the Restorer"). The figure of the Taheb apparently originated independently of Deuteronomy 18:15–18 and was only later identified with the "prophet like Moses."[119]

He will explain everything to us (4:25). Rather than looking for a royal Messiah from the house of David (as did the Jews), Samaritans apparently expected a "teaching" Messiah.[120]

The Disciples Rejoin Jesus (4:27–38)

Disciples . . . were surprised to find him talking with a woman (4:27). Some rabbis (such as Yose ben Yoḥanan, a very early rabbi) held that to talk too much to a woman, even one's own wife, was a waste of time, diverting one's attention from the study of the Torah. Potentially, this habit could grow to be a great evil leading even to hell (*m. ʾAbot* 1:5). Consequently, some rabbis taught that it was as inappropriate to provide one's daughter with a knowledge of the Torah as it was to sell them into prostitution (*m. Soṭah* 3:4; attributed to R. Eliezer [c. A.D. 90–130]).[121] As in other encounters with women, Jesus broke with this prejudice (cf. 7:53–8:11; 11:17–40; also Luke 7:36–50; 8:2–3; 10:38–42).

But no one asked, "What do you want?" or "Why are you talking with her?" (4:27). On other occasions, the disciples were not so bashful (e.g., Matt. 19:13 par.).[122] Perhaps the reason why they refrain from questioning Jesus here is that the woman is still there, so that an open challenge would have created an awkward situation. Generally, it was certainly considered appropriate in first-century Judaism for disciples to question their rabbi's actions, as long as this was done respectfully and appropriately.[123]

Leaving her water jar (4:28). The water jar was probably a large earthenware pitcher carried either on the shoulder or the hip.[124] The woman here abandons her original purpose for coming to the well (to draw water) in order to tell her townspeople about Jesus. "Leaving her water jar" may therefore have symbolic overtones.

Come, see a man who told me everything I ever did. Could this be the Christ? (4:29). Regarding the Samaritan Taheb as prophet-revealer, see comments on 4:25. "Who told me everything I ever did" is an obvious exaggeration, understandable in light of the woman's excitement. Rabbinic literature is somewhat ambivalent regarding the validity of a Samaritan's testimony. One relevant passage states, "No writ is valid which has a Samaritan as witness excepting a writ of divorce or a writ of emancipation" (*m. Giṭ.* 1:5). Yet the document proceeds, "They once brought a bill of divorce before Rabban Gamaliel . . . and its witnesses were Samaritans; and he pronounced it valid."

The witness of Samaritan *women*, especially those of low repute, may have been subject to further limitations. Regarding women witnesses in general, Josephus writes, "From women let no evidence be accepted, because of the levity [lightness, triviality] and temerity [overboldness, rashness] of their sex" (*Ant.* 4.8.15 §219). Yet the present instance represents not a formal courtroom scene, but an informal situation where a Samaritan woman goes back to her village and tells her fellow townspeople about a remarkable encounter she has had. Perhaps precisely *because* of the woman's reputation for immorality, her compatriots are curious to see for themselves what created such a remarkable change in the woman's disposition.

Rabbi, eat something (4:31). See comments on 1:38. Disciples regularly cared for the physical well-being of their master, a concern that extended from buying food to tending to him when he was sick and burying him after he had died.[125]

I have food to eat that you know nothing about. . . . My food . . . is to do the will of him who sent me (4:32–34). Jesus here asserts that fulfilling his mission is

◂ BREAD

more important to him than physical food (cf. Matt. 6:25; Mark 3:20–21). The present statement may echo Deut. 8:3: "Man does not live on bread alone but on every word that comes from the mouth of the LORD" (cf. Matt. 4:4; Luke 4:4). The Old Testament prophet Jeremiah testified, "When your words came, I ate them; they were my joy and my heart's delight" (Jer. 15:16).

To finish his work (4:34). In one sense, God was considered to have finished his work (Gen. 2:2). In another sense, it was recognized that God continues to sustain his creation (cf. John 5:17). In the present passage, Jesus affirms his commitment to complete the task God has given him to do, that is, his redemptive work on the cross (12:23–24; 17:4; 19:30).

Do you not say, "Four months more and then the harvest"? (4:35). Apparently, the saying quoted here by Jesus is a common proverb (cf. Matt. 16:2–3), though there is no independent evidence for its existence. Jesus' statement can be taken to imply that four months remain until the harvest. If so, the present event occurred some time in December or January, since the time of harvest extended from March until May (barley was harvested in March, wheat from mid-April until the end of May).

Alternatively, the proverb as commonly used may simply indicate the need for patience, similar to the saying, "Rome was not built in a day."[126] Jesus' point may be that while sowing and reaping are separated by (a minimum of) four months, his coming has ushered in the end-time harvest, so that sowing and harvest paradoxically coincide. Then again, the saying may have been a general proverb *and* have been uttered by Jesus about four months prior to harvest time, so that there is no need to choose between the above alternatives. See further the following comment.

Look at the fields! They are ripe for harvest (4:35). If the proverb quoted in the previous verse is to be taken literally, the fields are not actually ripe for harvest. Rather, Jesus' statement may be metaphorical rather than literal, pointing his disciples to the approaching mass of white-clothed Samaritans.[127] Elsewhere Jesus uses similar imagery (Matt. 9:37–38; Luke 10:2).

Even now the reaper draws his wages (4:36). Payment was usually made only for work completed. Thus, the disciples must not delay getting to work when others are already receiving wages.[128] R. Tarfon (c. A.D. 130) used to say, "The day is short and the task is great and the laborers are idle and the wage is abundant and the master of the house is urgent" (*m. ʾAbot* 2:15).

The sower and the reaper may be glad together (4:36). The joy of reaping a harvest is universally known. The Old Testament refers to it both literally (Deut.

WHEAT

16:13–14) and metaphorically (Ps. 126:5–6; Isa. 9:3). Sowing, on the other hand, was often laborious (Ps. 126:5). In the present instance, however, it is not just the reaper who is able to rejoice but also the sower. Jesus here conjures up images of a glorious, restored Edenic prosperity (cf. Amos 9:13: "The days are coming . . . when the reaper will be overtaken by the plowman"), a time when streams of blessing will flow from God's presence (cf. Ps. 36:8; 46:4; 87:7; Ezek. 47:1–12).

The saying "One sows and another reaps" is true (4:37). Usually, the saying points to the sad inequality of life: One sows without enjoying the benefits of the resulting crop, while another, who has not sown, reaps the fruit of that person's labor at a later time. In the case of the end-time spiritual harvest referred to by Jesus, however, the intervening time is collapsed, so that sower and reaper rejoice together (4:36). Nevertheless, as Jesus points out in the present verse, this does not mean that the distinction between sower and reaper is obliterated.[129]

REFLECTIONS

RATHER THAN BEING RUGGED Christian individualists—a contradiction of terms—we stand in a rich tradition of faith. We must seek to be ever more conscious of our place in salvation history and see ourselves as part of the historic Christian movement. North American Christians in particular at times operate as if they were the first Christians—but they are not. We can benefit from insights into Scripture gained by previous interpreters—patristic, medieval, or more recent. We can draw strength from the unswerving faith displayed by a succession of Christian martyrs in ages past. And we can be assured that when we get to heaven, we will be greeted by others in that "great cloud of witnesses" who have gone before us.

Many Samaritans Believe (4:39–42)

Many of the Samaritans . . . believed in him because of the woman's testimony (4:39). Apart from this instance, there is no precrucifixion evidence for a large contingent of Samaritan disciples; Acts 8:4–25 treats the evangelization of the Samaritans as a fresh venture. Historically, Jesus' Samaritan mission may have been preparatory for the early church's effort at evangelizing this group. Theologically, John may be seeking to show that the Samaritan mission of the early church was based on precedent in Jesus' own ministry (cf. Acts 1:8; 8:4–25). Jesus' pattern of ministry in John coincides with that of the mission of the early church (Acts 1:8): first Judea (Nicodemus, John 3), then Samaria (John 4), then the Gentiles (10:16; 11:52; 12:20–32).

That town (4:39). The village referred to is Sychar (cf. 4:5).

They urged him to stay with them, and he stayed two days (4:40). The Jews' concern regarding ritual purity, which caused them to refrain from association with Samaritans, was clearly not a major concern for Jesus (cf. 4:9).

Savior of the world (4:42). Interestingly, the Old Testament never calls the Messiah "Savior," and the expression was not a messianic title in first-century Judaism. The

Samaritans likewise did not view their Taheb as a redeemer. Philo calls God "Savior of the world" (*Spec. Laws* 2.198). The title "Savior" was also applied to many Greek gods and even Roman emperors, including Nero (A.D. 54–68).[130] By identifying Jesus as "Savior of the world," John thus challenges his surrounding culture (cf. Rev. 13:18; see also comments on John 20:28). In the present context, Jesus' large-scale harvest among the Samaritans is considered the first sign of the universal scope of his saving mission.

Return Trip to Galilee (4:43–45)

He left for Galilee (4:43). We are not told how long it takes Jesus to travel to Galilee or where in Galilee he goes prior to his return visit to Cana (4:46). But from Sychar to Cana is about forty miles, a trip that could be accomplished in two or three days.

A prophet has no honor in his own country (4:44). (Cf. 4:19.) This comment seeks to qualify the sense in which Jesus is "welcomed" at his return to Galilee. John may be assuming his readers' familiarity with Synoptic tradition, according to which Jesus is rejected in his native Galilee, including Nazareth.[131] The saying is also found in the *Gospel of Thomas* (Logion 31) and a papyrus document (P. Oxy. 1).

Jesus Heals the Royal Official's Son: His Second Sign in Cana (4:46–54)

A certain royal official (4:46). The term "royal official" (*basilikos*) usually refers to someone in the service of a king;[132] the official may also have been a centurion.[133] Perhaps he was "a wealthy aristocrat, probably much influenced by Greco-Roman culture and not very religious by general Palestinian Jewish standards."[134]

Whose son lay sick (4:46). The sickness of the royal official's son involves some kind of fever (4:52) and is apparently terminal (4:47, 49).

Capernaum (4:46). See comments on 2:12 and the following verse.

He went to him (4:47). To travel from Capernaum to Cana involves a day's journey of about fifteen miles. The trip is mostly uphill, since Cana lies in the Galilean hill country while Capernaum is several hundred feet below sea level. If the royal official leaves Capernaum at sunrise, he can reach Cana at noon, and at the seventh hour (i.e., 1 P.M.) hear Jesus' comforting words that his son will live (4:50). On the way back, however, he can complete only half of his journey on the same day, so that his servants meet him at the plain of Gennesaret on the following day (4:51–52).[135]

To come (4:47). Literally, "come down," for Capernaum is lower in elevation than Cana (see previous comment).

Miraculous signs and wonders (4:48). The expression probably harks back to the "signs and wonders" performed by Moses at the Exodus.[136]

Come down. . . . You may go. Your son will live (4:49–50). This is a rare instance of a long-distance miracle (on the unusual nature of Jesus' signs selected by John, see comments on 2:10). Another similar remarkable incident (that of the healing of the centurion's servant in Capernaum) is narrated in Matthew 8:5–13 (Luke 7:1–10 par.). See also the activities by the first-century Jewish miracle worker and faith healer Ḥanina ben Dosa. According to rabbinic tradition, when Rabban Gamaliel's son fell ill, he sent two disciples to this healer and asked him to pray for his son's healing. When Ḥanina ben Dosa had finished praying, he said to the messengers, "Go, the fever has left him." They wrote down the hour, and when they came back to R. Gamaliel, he said to them, "You have not been a moment too soon or too late, but so it happened: at that very moment the fever left him and he asked for water to drink" (*b. Ber.* 34b).[137]

Your son will live (4:50). This may be an allusion to Elijah and the woman of Zarephath in 1 Kings 17:23. If so, Jesus' messianic activity is here placed within the compass of the miraculous healing ministry of Elijah in the Old Testament (cf. Luke 4:23–27).

Seventh hour (4:52). The healing takes place around 1 P.M. (see "References to Time in John's Gospel" at 1:39).

Second miraculous sign . . . having come from Judea to Galilee (4:54). This is the second sign Jesus performs after having come from Judea to Galilee. In the interim, other signs have been performed in Jerusalem and the vicinity (2:23; 3:2; 4:45). Thus John closes the cycle of Jesus' first ministry circuit, starting and ending in Cana of Galilee.

REFLECTIONS

"THE MAN TOOK JESUS AT HIS word and departed." This is the essence of faith: taking Jesus at his word and acting on the basis that Jesus' word is true. Jesus was a man of his word. Am I? Can others take me at my word? Can my daughter count on me coming to her ballet recital when I have told her that I would be there? Can my wife count on me being home after work when I told her I would be? In the official's case, he was called to believe that Jesus could do something as difficult as healing at a long distance. His faith still challenges us today.

The Healing at the Pool of Bethesda (5:1–15)

A little while after completing his first "ministry circuit," Jesus travels to Jerusalem in order to attend an unspecified feast; this is the second of three trips by Jesus to the Jewish capital recorded in this Gospel (the time may be October, A.D. 31). Passing by the pool of Bethesda, Jesus takes pity on a lame man and heals him (the fourth sign in this Gospel). Healers were much sought after in the ancient world, both in Judaism and in Greco-Roman society. Rabbinic literature speaks of Ḥanina ben Dosa, who operated as a miracle worker and faith healer in first-century Galilee. In the Hellenistic world, shrines were dedicated to Asclepius and other gods of healing.[138] John must consider this event to be very important, since it is the only event he selects from Jesus' second year of ministry.

Some time later (5:1). This expression marks the passing of an indefinite period of time. Up to a year and a half may have passed since the last feast recorded, the Jewish Passover, at which Jesus had cleansed the temple and met with Nicodemus.

Went up to Jerusalem (5:1). It was customary for Jews at any place and any elevation in Palestine to use the expression going "up" to Jerusalem.

A feast of the Jews (5:1). This is the only unnamed festival in John. This feast was most likely one of the several festivals taking place in Jerusalem in September/October, perhaps the Feast of Tabernacles (which, if the year was A.D. 31, fell on October 21–28).[139] This is suggested by the fact that some manuscripts (such as Codex Sinaiticus) have "the" feast of the Jews, which was the conventional name for the Feast of Tabernacles.[140]

In Jerusalem near the Sheep Gate a pool (5:2).[141] A "Sheep Gate" is mentioned in the book of Nehemiah (3:1, 32; 12:39). In Jesus' day, this was apparently a small opening in the north wall of the temple. The sheep would have been washed in the pool before being taken to the sanctuary. This is also the place where invalids would lie in hopes of being healed. The upper class and those wishing to be ritually pure would avoid this area, but not Jesus.

Surrounded by five covered colonnades (5:2). The five colonnades may have been erected by Herod the Great.[142] Four covered colonnades enclose two separate pools (viewed as a unity)[143] in a rough trapezoid, with a fifth one separating them.[144] There the sick can lie and be partially protected from the weather. Some argue that "five" colonnades is also symbolic of the five books of Moses, the Pentateuch (see comments on 4:18).[145]

Which in Aramaic is called Bethesda (5:2). For John's translation of Aramaic or Hebrew terms, see the chart at 1:38. "Bethesda"[146] may mean "house of (divine) mercy"—which would be a fitting term, given the desperate state of the people lying there in hope of miraculous healing—or "house of the two springs," or the name may be derived from the root "pour out" or "slope."[147]

Here a great number of disabled people used to lie (5:3). Official Judaism almost certainly did not approve of the superstition associated with the alleged healing powers of the pool of Bethesda. After all, healing shrines were characteristic of pagan cults, such as the one surrounding the Greek god of healing, Asclepius. Apparently, however, the Jewish authorities looked the other way, tolerating this expression of popular religion. See comments on 5:7.

An invalid (5:5). Though the man's illness is not detailed, 5:7 suggests that he

POOL OF BETHESDA

(left) A model of the pool with the Sheep Gate in the upper left.

(right) Remains of the pool of Bethesda.

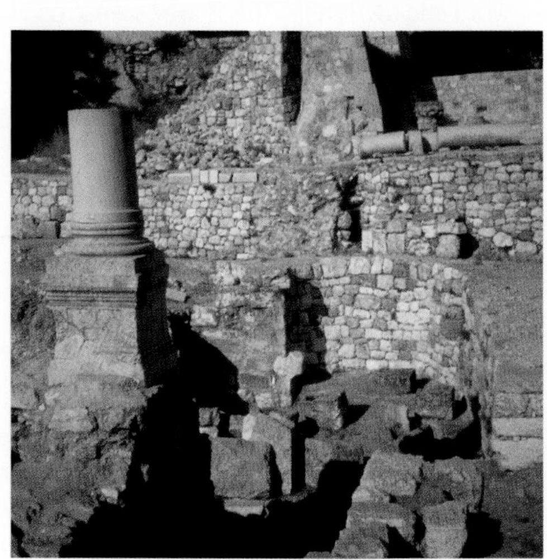

is paralyzed, lame, or extremely weak (the Gk. word used is the general expression for "disabled"). We do not know the invalid's age or exactly how long he has been lying there. A similar healing is recorded in Matthew 9:1–8 par.

For thirty-eight years (5:5). This man has been an invalid longer than many people in antiquity lived (average life expectancy for men barely exceeding forty years of age), roughly as long as Israel's wanderings in the desert (Deut. 2:14).[148] For all that time, nothing has cured him (cf. Mark 5:25–26; cf. Luke 8:43). The length of the man's plight is also in keeping with John's selection of "difficult" miracles performed by Jesus (see comments on John 2:10).

Jesus saw him . . . and learned that he had been in this condition for a long time (5:6). The Greek term rendered "learned" can just as well refer to supernatural knowledge rather than to knowledge gained through diligent inquiry (cf. 1:47–48; 4:17–18). Possibly Jesus' conversation with the invalid is occasioned by the man's request for alms (cf. Acts 3:1–5).

I have no one to help me (5:7). Contrast this with the paralytic in Mark 2:1–12, whose four friends carry him to Jesus by lowering his mat through a roof.

When the water is stirred (5:7). The stirring of the waters may have been created by intermittent springs or spring water. Superstition attributed the movement of the water to an angel of the Lord coming down from time to time and stirring up the waters. Some later manuscripts add: "from time to time an angel of the Lord would come down and stir up the waters."

Your mat (5:8). A mat (*krabattos*) was the poor man's bedding. The term is used in distinction from "bed" (*klinarion*; Acts 5:15). Normally made of straw, it was

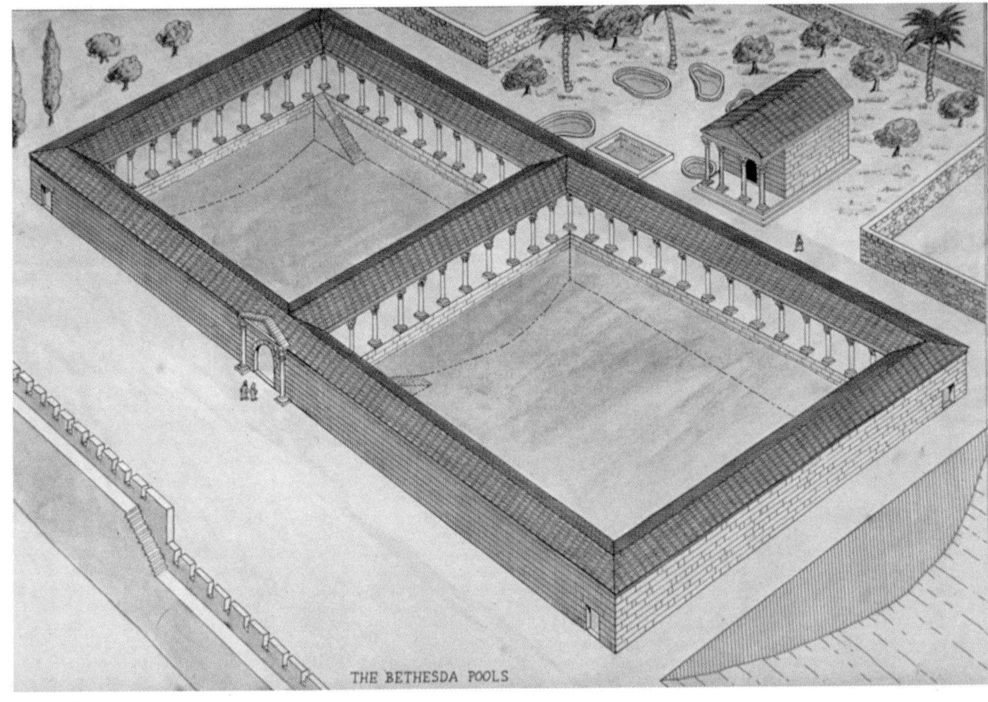

POOL OF BETHESDA

An artistic reconstruction.

Major Archaeological Finds Relating to John's Gospel

Site or Artifact	Location	Passage in John
Inscription barring Gentiles from entry into inner temple	Jerusalem	2:14–17
Herod's temple	Jerusalem	2:20
Jacob's well	Nablus	4:5–6
Pool of Bethesda	Jerusalem	5:2
Ancient fishing boat	Galilee	6:22–24; 21:8
Early synagogue	Capernaum	6:59
Pool of Siloam	Jerusalem	9:7
Siloam inscription	Jerusalem	9:7
Tomb of Lazarus	Bethany	11:38
Caiaphas tomb/inscription	Jerusalem	11:49; 18:13–14
Pilate inscription	Caesarea	18:29
Stone pavement	Jerusalem	19:13
Skeletal remains of crucified man	Jerusalem	19:18
Garden tomb[A-17]	Jerusalem	19:41–42

light and could be rolled up and carried about by any healthy person.

It is the Sabbath; the law forbids you to carry your mat (5:10). Although the Jews may have thought of Old Testament passages such as Exodus 31:12–17, Jeremiah 17:21–27, or Nehemiah 13:15, 19, the man is not actually breaking any biblical Sabbath regulations. According to Jewish tradition, however, the man is violating a code that forbids the carrying of an object "from one domain into another" (*m. Šabb.* 7:2; in the present instance, his mat). Apparently, it was permissible to carry a bed with a person lying on it, but not one that was empty (*m. Šabb.* 10:5). At this point, Jesus is accused, not of violating the law himself, but of enticing someone else to sin by issuing a command that will cause that person to break the law. "To forbid this man from carrying his bed was like forbidding a modern man to move a chair or a campstool. Either he must have left his bed at the pool, to be stolen, or he must have stayed there to watch it, or he must have been allowed to take it home with him."[149]

At the temple (5:14). The pool of Bethesda is located just north of the temple area. Jesus meets the man again just a short distance from where the original healing has taken place.

REFLECTIONS

IT IS NEVER TOO LATE TO TRUST JESUS. HERE IS A man who has been through an almost endless cycle of futility and frustration. For thirty-eight years he has been an invalid, and all his hopes for healing have been dashed time and time again. Then comes Jesus. Rather than rely on friends or superstition, the man must rely on Jesus. Jesus speaks the word, and the man gets well. The man born blind later has a similar experience. Many of us can gratefully testify that Jesus has redeemed us from a life of purposelessness and futility. Let's now live for him.

Stop sinning or something worse may happen to you (5:14). The comment seems to imply that at least sometimes—including in the case of the invalid?—sickness may be a result of sin (e.g., 1 Kings 13:4; 2 Kings 1:4; 2 Chron. 16:12). Jesus' Jewish contemporaries generally held that suffering was a direct result of sin (cf. John 9:2). Given expression already by the "miserable counselors" in the book of Job, rabbinic literature states the principle succinctly: "There is no death without sin, and there is no suffering without iniquity" (*b. Šabb.* 55a with reference to Ezek. 18:20; attributed to R. Ammi [c. A.D. 300]). However, the Old Testament features several instances where suffering is transparently not a result of sin (e.g., 2 Sam. 4:4; 1 Kings 14:4; 2 Kings 13:14). Jesus himself, likewise, rejects simple cause-and-effect explanations (cf. Luke 13:1–5; John 9:3). Nevertheless, Jesus acknowledges that sin may well lead to suffering. In the present instance, the "something worse" he threatens probably does not refer to a worse physical condition but rather to eternal judgment for sin (cf. 5:22–30).

Jesus' Defense (5:16–30)

The Jews charge Jesus not only with breaking the Sabbath but with blasphemy. In response, he declares that he has come, not to detract attention away from the Father, but to lead people to him. The Jews resist him out of personal ambition. Jesus himself claims to be the life-giver and judge, terms reserved in the Old Testament exclusively for God.

My Father (5:17). It would be highly unusual for a Jew of that day to address God simply as his "Father" without some qualifying phrase like "in heaven" in order to avoid undue familiarity.[150] The Jews' response in verse 18 confirms the perceived inappropriateness of Jesus' terminology.

Is always at his work to this very day (5:17). According to Genesis 2:2–3, God rested on the seventh day of creation. But if God observes the Sabbath, who sustains the universe? The consensus among Jewish rabbis at the end of the first century

"The Jews" in John's Gospel

In recent years, scholars have been troubled by the negative portrayal of "the Jews" in John's Gospel.[A-18] This has been taken by some as evidence that John is guilty of anti-Semitism. However, this charge is clearly unjustified. John's primary concern is not ethnic but salvation-historical. Acknowledging that "salvation is from the Jews" (4:22), John points to the fact that the Jewish nation, represented by its religious leadership, has rejected Jesus as Messiah. Note, of course, that all the members of Jesus' inner circle, the Twelve, are Jews, as are most of his first followers. Nevertheless, the Jews, *as a nation*, have joined the world in its sinful rebellion against God and his Sent One. Thus, Jesus must set up a new messianic community that will be able to carry on his work once he returns to God the Father. Jews are welcome in this community if they believe that Jesus is the Messiah. In fact, many believe that one of John's major purposes for writing is to reach out to unbelieving Jews.

A.D. was that God does indeed work constantly, but that this does not amount to his breaking the Sabbath. For the entire universe is his domain, so that he cannot be charged with transporting an object from one domain to another; and God lifts nothing to a greater height than himself (cf. *Gen. Rab.* 11:10; *Ex. Rab.* 30:9 citing Isa. 6:3; Jer. 23:24). The Letter of Aristeas (second century B.C.) says of God that he "is continually at work in everything" (210). Eusebius later wrote, "It is plainly said by our legislation that God rested on the seventh day. This does not mean, as some interpret, that God no longer does anything. It means that, after he had finished ordering all things, he so orders them for all time" (Frag. 5 in Eusebius, *Praep. Ev.* 13.12.11).[151]

And I, too, am working (5:17). Jesus could have objected to the—inaccurate—Jewish interpretation of the Old Testament Sabbath command that prohibited work normally done on the other six days of the week. These regulations (which refer to regular work) hardly apply to the man's picking up his mat after a miracle cure! But rather than taking this approach, Jesus places his own activity on the Sabbath plainly on the same level as that of God the Creator. If God is above Sabbath regulations, so is Jesus (cf. Matt. 12:1–14 par.).

Calling God his own Father (5:18). See 5:17. Just as Jesus is uniquely God's "own" Son (Rom. 8:32), God is uniquely "his own" Father (cf. John 10:29–30). The designation "my Father" for God was extremely rare in the Old Testament (but see Jer. 3:4; cf. Ps. 89:26).

Making himself equal with God (5:18). The Jews of the first century were committed monotheists, believing in only one God.[152] This became an important distinguishing characteristic of Jewish religion in a polytheistic environment. Thus the Roman historian Tacitus writes, "The Jews conceive of one God only" (*Hist.* 5.5).[153] Jesus' claim of a unique relationship with God seemed to compromise this belief by elevating him to the same level as the Creator, as if he were a second God.

The Son can do nothing by himself (5:19). Similarly, Moses affirms in the Old Testament, "This is how you will know that the LORD has sent me to do all these things and that it was not my idea" (Num. 16:28). Just like the Son, so believers can do nothing of eternal significance without Christ (John 15:5).

Just as the Father raises the dead and gives them life, even so the Son gives life to whom he is pleased to give it (5:21). Old Testament and intertestamental Jewish literature concur that raising the dead and giving life are the sole prerogatives of God.[154] Jesus' contemporaries therefore do not believe that the Messiah will be given authority to raise the dead. Rabbi Yoḥanan (c. A.D. 70), for instance, cites three prerogatives of God not delegated to others: the key of rain (cf. Deut. 28:12), the key of childbirth (cf. Gen. 30:22), and the key of raising the dead (cf. Ezek. 37:13; *b. Taʿan.* 2a).

The *Shemoneh ʿEsreh*, an ancient Jewish prayer dating to around A.D. 70–100,[155] likewise affirms:

> *You are mighty forever, O Lord;*
> *you restore life to the dead . . .*
> *who sustains the living out of grace,*
> *makes the dead alive out of great*
> *mercy. . . .*
> *Who is like you, O King,*
> *who makes dead and alive again. . . ?*

Sabbath and Sunday Observance

In the early church, a transition took place from the Jewish Sabbath to the Christian Sunday. This day was called "the Lord's Day" (Rev. 1:10), for on it Jesus had risen from the dead. It was considered to be "the first day of the week" (John 20:1 and Synoptic parallels) and was the day on which the early church met for worship (Acts 20:7; 1 Cor. 16:2). The first Christians did not think of Sunday as a mere substitute for the Sabbath. In fact, nowhere is the Old Testament command to "keep the Sabbath holy" repeated in the New Testament. Rightly understood, the fulfillment of the Sabbath is to be found in the salvation rest provided for believers by Jesus (Heb. 4:3, 9–11), ultimately pointing to heaven itself (6:20; 12:2).

In this life, Sunday (the name "Sunday" is not biblical but, like other names of days of the week, derives from Roman terminology) is to be a day celebrating Jesus' resurrection, a day not of legalistic preoccupation but of joyful liberty. That was already true for the intention underlying the Sabbath: "The Sabbath was made for man, not man for the Sabbath" (Mark 2:27). Communal worship, recreation, time spent with one's family and with God's people, and works of helpfulness, love, and necessity all have their place in using "the Lord's Day" in a way pleasing to the Lord.

And you are faithful to raise the dead.
Blessed are you, O Lord, who restores the dead.

This background renders Jesus' claim of being able to raise the dead and to give them life at will all the more startling. To be sure, Elijah was sometimes considered to constitute an exception because he was used by God to raise the dead. Yet Jesus' claim is much bolder than that of Elijah. For Jesus is not merely God's instrument in raising other people but he chooses to give life *to whom he is pleased to give it*.

The Father judges no one, but has entrusted all judgment to the Son (5:22). Genesis 18:25 states that God is "the Judge of all the earth" (cf. Judg. 11:27). In Psalm 2:2, "the LORD" is associated with "his Anointed One" in rule and judgment. The final judgment will take place after the resurrection on the last day (Rev. 20:11–15). According to the rabbis, God alone will judge the world. There is no passage in rabbinic literature that unambiguously places the judgment of the world in the hands of the Messiah. Apart from carrying out God's judgment on his enemies in keeping with Jewish nationalistic expectations (e.g., *Pss. Sol.* 17:21–27), the Messiah remains very much in the background as far as judgment is concerned, even in the Apocrypha. The singular exception is the Son of Man (or "Chosen One") in the Similitudes of Enoch.[156] See also the following comment.

He who does not honor the Son does not honor the Father, who sent him (5:23). In the Old Testament, Moses and the prophets were considered to be God's agents and mouthpieces who acted and spoke on God's behalf. The Jewish fundamental affirmation regarding a messenger (*šaliaḥ*) is that "a man's agent is like the man himself" (e.g., *m. Ber.* 5:5).[157] This is true of any messenger, particularly a trusted servant, and even more so of a man's son, especially his firstborn.[158] Thus, anyone who fails to acknowledge the authority of Jesus (the sent Son) in fact rejects his Sender, that is, the Father. Authorized representatives were not unique to Judaism. The Roman *legatus*, for instance, fulfilled a similar role. To this day, the failure to honor an ambassador is a failure to honor the government he or she represents.

The dead will hear the voice of the Son of God and those who hear will live (5:25). This statement is reminiscent of Ezekiel's vision of the valley of dry bones (Ezek. 37). There are no similar texts in intertestamental Jewish literature.

For as the Father has life in himself, so he has granted the Son to have life in himself (5:26). The Old Testament states repeatedly that God grants life to others.[159] But here Jesus claims that God has granted him life *in himself*, a divine attribute.

Because he is the Son of Man (5:27). Literally, the phrase reads, "he is Son of Man"—the only instance of this phrase without articles before both "Son" and "Man" in the entire New Testament. This may be accounted for in part by Colwell's rule (see comments on "The Word was God" at 1:1); it may also indicate an allusion to Dan. 7:13 (LXX), where the phrase "son of man" likewise does not feature any article (cf. Rev. 1:13; 14:14).[160]

All who are in their graves will hear his voice and come out—those who have done good will rise to live, and those who have done evil will rise to be condemned (5:28–29). In the first century, there was no consensus as to whether all would be raised or just the righteous (though see Dan. 12:2). Sheol was thought of as containing chambers where the dead are kept until the great day of judgment.[161]

By myself I can do nothing . . . I seek not to please myself but him who sent me (5:30). See comments on 5:19 and 23. The Mishnah cites a saying attributed to Rabban Gamaliel III, son of R. Yehudah the Patriarch (c. A.D. 200): "Do his will as if it was your will that he may do your will as if it was his will. Make your will of no effect before his will that he may make the will of others of no effect before your will" (*m. ʾAbot* 2:4).

Testimony Regarding Jesus (5:31–47)

If I testify about myself, my testimony is not valid (5:31). The interrogation of witnesses was central to Jewish legal procedure.[162] The need for multiple witnesses, already taught in the Hebrew Scriptures (Deut. 17:6; 19:15), is reiterated by Jewish tradition. According to the Mishnah, "None may be believed when he testifies of himself" (*m. Ketub.* 2:9), "for no individual can be deemed trustworthy in himself" (*m. Roš Haš.* 3:1). Josephus writes, "Put not trust in a single witness, but let there be three or at the least two, whose evidence shall be accredited by their past lives" (*Ant.* 4.9.4 §219).

There is another (5:32). The Jews may think of John the Baptist (cf. 5:33–35), but Jesus is referring to God the Father (5:37; see comments), in common Jewish fashion avoiding the name of God.

He has testified to the truth (5:33). Similarly, 18:37 (cf. 3 John 3, 12). The Qumran community considered itself as "founded on truth . . . true witnesses for the judgment" (1QS 8:5–6).

John was a lamp that burned and gave light (5:35). See 1:7–9. The verb "was" (past tense) may indicate that John is now dead or at least in prison (cf. 3:24). "A lamp" is more accurately rendered "the lamp" (note the Gk. article), pointing to a known person or phenomenon. Most likely, Psalm 132:17 is in view, where it is said that God will "set up a lamp" (*lychnos*) for his "anointed one." The book of Sirach portrays Elijah as having arisen "like fire [*pyr*], and his word burned like a torch [*lampas*]" (Sir. 48:1). While the Baptist earlier denies being Elijah (John 1:21), Jesus here identifies him as that "lamp" set up by God to cast its light on the coming Messiah. Inherent in the designation of the Baptist as a "lamp" is the recognition that his witness is small (though important) and of a temporary nature.

You chose . . . to enjoy his light (5:35). The word for "enjoy" also occurs in Psalm 132:16 (LXX; see previous comment), where it is said that the saints "will ever sing for joy." Josephus wrote that people "were aroused [*or* overjoyed] to the highest degree" by the Baptist's message (*Ant.* 18.5.2 §118).

◀ *left*

AN OIL LAMP

The Father . . . has himself testified concerning me (5:37). Jesus may here refer to the voice at his baptism (Matt. 3:17 par.), an event not explicitly mentioned in John, though the primary reference is probably to God's witness in Scripture.[163] In mishnaic teaching, God is also cast as a witness: "God . . . is the Judge, he is the Witness, he is the Complainant, and it is he that shall judge [i.e., render the ultimate judgment]" (*m.* ᵓ*Abot* 4:22).[164]

You have never heard his voice nor seen his form (5:37). Old Testament figures who heard the voice of God include Noah (Gen. 7:1–4), Abraham (12:1–3), Moses (Ex. 3:4–4:17; 19:3–6, 9–13; 33:11), Samuel (1 Sam. 3:4, 6, 8, 11–14), and Elijah (1 Kings 19:13, 15–18). Abraham (Gen. 18:1–2), Jacob (32:24–30), Moses (Ex. 33:11), and Isaiah (Isa. 6:1–5) all "saw" the Lord in one sense or another. While not seeing God directly, Israel received the Law at Mount Sinai and accepted it from God's servant Moses. Now the Jews are rejecting greater revelation from an even greater messenger (cf. John 1:17–18; 8:56–58; 12:41; Heb. 1:1–3; 2:1–3; 3:1–6).

Nor does his word dwell in you (5:38). The Old Testament depiction of a God-fearing individual is that of someone who has the Word of God living in his heart (Josh. 1:8–9; Ps. 119:11).

You diligently study the Scriptures (5:39). Jewish scribes "numbered the verses, words and letters of every book. They calculated the middle word and the middle letter of each. They enumerated verses which contained all the letters of the alphabet, or a certain number of them."[165] When copying the Scriptures, scribes were not to write more than one letter before looking at the original again (*b. Meg.* 18b).[166]

Because you think that by them you possess eternal life (5:39). The famous first-century Jewish rabbi Hillel used to say, "The more study of the Law the more life.... If a man ... has gained for himself words of the Law he has gained for himself life in the world to come" (*m. ʾAbot* 2:7). Similarly, the apocryphal work Baruch states: "She is the book of the commandments of God, the law that endures for ever. All who hold her fast will live, and those who forsake her will die" (4:1).

These are the Scriptures that testify about me (5:39). For John, it is not merely that individual sayings of Scripture are fulfilled in Jesus,[167] but Scripture in its entirety is oriented toward him.[168] See comments on 5:46–47.

I have come in my Father's name, and you do not accept me; but if someone else comes in his own name, you will accept him (5:43). Deuteronomy 18:19 says regarding the "prophet like Moses": "If anyone does not listen to my words that the prophet speaks in my name, I myself will call him to account." The false prophet Shemaiah is charged by the true prophet Jeremiah with speaking in his own name.[169] Jesus himself predicted the proliferation of false Christs as a sign of the end times (Matt. 24:5 par.), and Josephus reports a string of messianic pretenders in the years prior to A.D. 70.[170] The delegation sent to investigate John the Baptist (1:19–22) is no doubt aware of such stirrings.

You accept praise from one another (5:44). In the rabbinical schools, "Scripture study had become a world in which men sought fame by showing their intellectual prowess. One big authority was set over against another, and the result was barren logomachy [verbal disputes], where men sought *honour one of another*."[171]

Your accuser is Moses, on whom your hopes are set (5:45). See 9:28–29. With regard to Old Testament Israel, Moses frequently served as intercessor.[172] According to the first-century work *Assumption of Moses*, Moses, "in every hour both day and night, had his knees fixed to the earth, praying and looking steadfastly toward him who governs the whole earth with mercy and justice, reminding the Lord of the ancestral covenant" (11:17; cf. 12:6; *Jub.* 1:19–21). Yet both the "Song of Moses" and the Book of the Law are said to function as a witness against Israel (Deut. 31:19, 21, 26; cf. Rom. 3:19).

In Jesus' day, many Jews, in keeping with the Old Testament and intertestamental portrayal of Moses, saw the latter's role primarily as that of continuing mediator and advocate, who prayed for them in heaven as he had interceded for the Israelites on earth.[173] The Samaritans, too, increasingly regarded Moses as their intercessor in heaven.[174] Even many pagans knew Moses as Israel's lawgiver (e.g., Diodorus Siculus, *Bib. Hist.* 1.94.2.8; 34/35.1.3.9; first cent. B.C.). Jesus sharply rebukes this reliance on Moses' intercession; to him, Moses is not the Jews' advocate but their accuser.

Moses . . . wrote about me (5:46). See comments on 5:39. The reference may be to the first five books of the Old Testament, which are attributed to Moses, or to the prediction of a "prophet like [Moses]" in Deut. 18:15, or to both.

But since you do not believe what he wrote, how are you going to believe what I say? (5:47). This refers to the Jews' failure to grasp the true essence of Scripture, including its prophetic orientation toward Jesus (cf. Matt. 5:17). The argument is from the lesser to the greater, a customary rabbinic device used frequently by Jesus (3:12; 6:27; 7:23; 10:34–36), Paul (Rom. 5:15, 17; 2 Cor. 3:9, 11), and other New Testament writers (Heb. 9:14; 12:9, 25). Jesus' words in Luke 16:31 are similar: "If they do not listen to Moses and the Prophets, they will not be convinced even if someone rises from the dead." The same reasoning is found in an ancient Jewish commentary: "If . . . they believed in Moses, is it not implied by *Kal vaḥomer* [i.e., an argument from the lesser to the greater] that they believed in God?" (*Mek. Ex.* 14:31; 2d cent. A.D.).

Jesus Feeds the Five Thousand (6:1–15)

After defending himself against the charge of breaking the Sabbath, Jesus once again leaves Jerusalem. He returns to Galilee and is found on the east side of the Sea of Galilee, shortly before another Passover (April, A.D. 32). There Jesus performs another one of his startling messianic signs, feeding a large multitude. In keeping with Jewish expectation, Jesus reveals himself as the antitype to Moses, not only providing bread for his people (as Moses did the manna), but also revealing himself as the life-giving "bread" who will give his flesh for the world.

Some time after this (6:1). As much as half a year may have passed since the previous event recorded in John.

The far shore of the Sea of Galilee (that is, the Sea of Tiberias) (6:1). The "far shore" of the Sea of Galilee was normally considered to be the east side, since most Jewish activity occurred on the west side. In Old Testament times, the Sea of Galilee was referred to as Kinnereth because it was shaped like a lyre.[175] Around A.D. 17–18, Herod Antipas founded a city called Tiberias (cf. 5:23) on the west side of the lake in honor of his patron, the reigning Roman emperor Tiberius (A.D. 14–37; see Josephus, *Ant.* 18.2.3 §36). Tiberias is one of the few cities in the Holy Land that has kept its Roman name, probably because it was founded in Roman times and entirely supplanted the previously existing village of Rakkath (Josh. 19:35). Gradually, the name of the city was transferred to the lake. On a popular level, this transfer probably did not take place until late in the first century (around the time when John was writing his Gospel), hence his choice to provide both names (cf. 21:1). The name "Sea of Tiberias" is attested in first-century literature (*Sib. Or.* 12.104). It is also preserved in Jewish tradition (*Yamma shel Tiberya*; *t. Sukkah* 3:9) and by the Arabs, who call the lake *Bahr Tabariyeh*.[176]

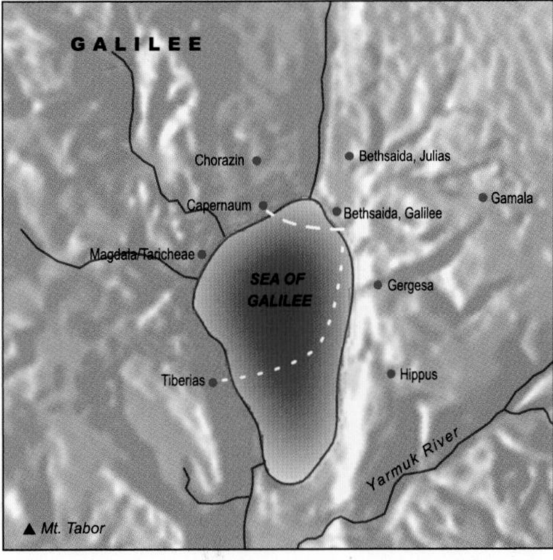

THE SEA OF GALILEE

Mountainside (6:3). "Mountainside" need not designate any specific mountain or hill but may refer simply to "the hill country" or "the high ground" east of the lake, known today as the Golan Heights.

Sat down (6:3). Like other rabbis, Jesus usually sat down to teach (Matt. 5:1; Mark 4:1; 9:35; Luke 4:20), although here teaching is not mentioned explicitly.

Jewish Passover feast was near (6:4). This is the second of three Passovers mentioned by John, and the only one Jesus spends in Galilee (in A.D. 32, Passover fell on April 13/14). In the life of the Jewish nation, Passover was a time of intense nationalistic zeal. The nearness of this feast provides the framework for the ensuing feeding of the multitude and Jesus' claim of being the "bread of life."

A great crowd coming toward him (6:5). People have apparently walked the several miles around the (shorter) north side of the lake and caught up with Jesus and the disciples.

Philip (6:5). Philip would be the natural choice, since, like Andrew (cf. 6:8) and Peter, he is a native of nearby Bethsaida (1:44).

Where shall we buy bread for these people to eat? (6:5). In the desert, Moses asked God a similar question: "Where can I get meat for all these people?" (Num. 11:13). There are several other parallels between John 6 and Numbers 11: the grumbling of the people (Num. 11:1; John 6:41, 43); the description of the manna (Num. 11:7–9; John 6:31); the reference to the eating of meat (Jesus' flesh) (Num. 11:13; John 6:51); and the striking disproportion between the existing need and the available resources (Num. 11:22; John 6:7–9).

Eight months' wages would not buy enough bread for each one to have a bite! (6:7). "Eight months' wages" ren-

SHORE OF THE SEA OF GALILEE

ders the phrase "two hundred denarii." One denarius was approximately one day's pay (Matt. 20:2; cf. John 12:5). Philip quickly estimates that it would take over half a year's income to feed the entire crowd (no pay on Sabbaths or other holy days).

◀ *left*

DENARIUS

A Tyrian silver denarius with the image of Alexander the Great.

A boy (6:9). This "boy" may be a teenager or even someone in his early twenties, though he may have been younger as well. The same word is used to refer to young Joseph in Genesis 37:30 (LXX); Daniel and his friends in Daniel 1 (LXX); and Tobit's son who is at a marriageable age in Tobit 6.

Five small barley loaves and two small fish (6:9). The common word for bread, *artos*, usually designates wheat bread; here it refers to bread made of barley. Barley was common food for the poor, its "lower gluten content, low extraction rate, less desirable taste, and indigestibility" rendering it "the staple of the poor in Roman times."[177] Philo writes that barley products are "suited for irrational animals and people in unhappy circumstances" (*Spec. Laws* 3.57). The more well-to-do preferred wheat bread (Philo, *Spec. Laws* 2.175), which was traded at twice or even three times the value of barley (2 Kings 7:1, 16, 18; Rev. 6:6; *m. Ketub.* 5:8). The fish were probably dried or preserved, perhaps pickled. The word used for "fish" here is the rare term *opsarion* (cf. 21:9–13), a diminutive form of *opson*, which originally meant cooked food and then came to refer to any relish taken with food.

Have the people sit down . . . the men sat down, about five thousand of them (6:10). In addition to the men, there were women and children (cf. Matt. 14:21). The total may have been as many as twenty thousand people.

There was plenty of grass in that place (6:10). Mark 6:39–40 mentions that the grass was green, which points to spring (near the Passover), before the summer heat would turn it brown.

Jesus . . . gave thanks (6:11). If Jesus used the common Jewish form of thanksgiving, he would have uttered a prayer such as the following: "Blessed are you, O Lord our God, King of the universe, who brings forth bread from the earth."[178]

Gather the pieces that are left over. Let nothing be wasted (6:12). Similarly, it is said of Ruth, "She ate all she wanted and had some left over" (2:14).[179] It was customary at Jewish meals to collect what was left over. Pieces of bread were not to be thrown around (*b. Ber.* 50b), and food the size of an olive or larger must be picked up (*b. Ber.* 52b).[180] The expression "that nothing may be lost" is also documented in rabbinic literature with reference to food: "Let the poor come and eat the food, so that it not go to waste" (*y. Sanh.* 6:6; *y. Ḥag.* 2:2). Jesus applies the same care to preserving all the Father has given him (John 10:28–29; 17:11–12, 15).

They gathered them and filled twelve baskets with the pieces of the five barley loaves left over (6:13). The baskets used to gather the leftovers were probably made of stiff material, perhaps wicker. "Twelve" baskets may allude to Jesus' restoration of Israel (the twelve tribes) by calling twelve disciples to form the core of his new messianic community.

LARGE WOVEN BASKET MADE FROM REEDS

Miraculous sign (6:14). See comments on 2:11.

The Prophet who is to come into the world (6:14). See 1:21; 6:31; 7:40. The underlying passage is doubtless Deuteronomy 18:15–18, which also featured significantly in the messianic expectations of the Qumran community (cf. 4QTest 5–8; 1QS 9:11). Jesus' multiplication of barley loaves is reminiscent of the miracle performed by Elijah's follower, Elisha (2 Kings 4:42–44). In 1 Kings 19, a parallel between Elijah and Moses is obvious (cf. Ex. 24:18; 34:28). The popular expectation expressed in John 6:14 may represent an amalgamation of the two figures.[181] In Jesus' day, the notion of the "Prophet" was apparently merged with that of "king" (John 6:15). Indeed, "the step from a prophet like Moses (6:14), the first Redeemer and worker of miracles, to a messianic deliverer was a short one for enthusiasts in contemporary Israel to make."[182] This figure also figured prominently in early Christian preaching (Acts 3:23; 7:57).

They intended to come and make him king by force (6:15). The present incident is reminiscent of the Zealots, a militant movement that found in Galilee fertile soil for its nationalistic brand of Judaism.

Withdrew again to a mountain by himself (6:15). Earlier Jesus had withdrawn to this mountainous area with his disciples (6:1–3). Now he goes by himself farther up what is known today as the Golan Heights (cf. Matt. 14:23; Mark 6:46).

Jesus Walks on the Water (6:16–24)

From the mountaintop of participating in the feeding of the multitudes, the disciples descend to the valley of experiencing a violent storm as they try to cross the

REFLECTIONS

PEOPLE IN JESUS' DAY STILL recounted Israel's wanderings in the desert and God's provision of manna, the heavenly bread, for his people through Moses. So caught up were they in their religious observances and remembrances that they were blind to the "new thing" God was doing in their midst that very day, even though God had plainly predicted it through the prophets. Jesus' "substitute presence," the Holy Spirit, is in our midst today, ready to do his work. Let us not get so caught up in the past that we miss God's will for us in the present.

Sea of Galilee. Many of them are fishermen and well acquainted with the lake. Nevertheless, they are gripped with fear and need to be rescued by Jesus. This is all the more remarkable since a similar incident has taken place earlier (Matt. 8:23–27 par.).

When evening came, his disciples went down to the lake, where they got into a boat and set off across the lake for Capernaum (6:16–17). Perhaps it is late afternoon, because only in the next verse has darkness set in. The disciples are on the east side of the lake and attempt to row the six or seven miles back to Capernaum on the northwest side.

By now it was dark. . . . A strong wind was blowing and the waters grew rough (6:17–18). "The Sea of Galilee lies about six hundred feet below sea level. Cool air from the south-eastern tablelands can rush in to displace the warm moist air over the lake, churning up the water in a violent squall."[183] Even today, power boats are to remain docked as the winds buffet the water. How much more could violent storms have wreaked havoc to the wooden boats used in Jesus' time.

Rowed three or three and a half miles (6:19). "Three or three and a half miles" translates "twenty-five or thirty stadia." A *stadion* was equivalent to 606.75 feet. The lake was about 61 stadia at its greatest width. If the multiplication of the loaves took place at the eastern shore of the Sea of Galilee, the shortest distance to Capernaum would be five to six miles. After rowing for about three and a half miles, the disciples were driven off course and found themselves halfway towards Magdala, where the lake was the widest.

The next day . . . in search of Jesus (6:22–24). Apparently, the crowd, which has been fed on "the far shore" (6:1), has remained there during the events of 6:16–24. Next, "some boats from Tiberias" end up where the crowd is (presumably east across the lake from Tiberias). Finally, the multitude and the people in the boats decide to head back to Capernaum across the northern quarter of the lake.

Boats from Tiberias (6:23). Tiberias is (even today) the chief city on the west side of the lake (see comments on 6:1). Whereas Capernaum is located on the northwest edge of the lake, Tiberias is several miles to the south, just about at the midpoint of the western shore.

Jesus the Bread of Life (6:25–59)

Jewish literature celebrated God's provision of manna for Israel in the desert. People expected the Messiah to perform a similar feat. The age of the Messiah would be an age of abundance, when God's blessings would be poured out on Israel. In the following discourse, Jesus presents himself as the fulfillment of these expectations. In contrast to popular belief, however, God's provision of life through his Messiah entails substitutionary suffering. Jesus will have to "give his flesh for the life of the world," and only those who "eat his flesh" and "drink his blood" will partake of God's salvation blessings.

On the other side of the lake (6:25). This refers to the area in or around Capernaum (see 6:24, 59).

Do not work for food that spoils, but for food that endures to eternal life (6:27).

As essential for human existence, bread and water are universal symbols of life. This symbolism may be applied to salvation, the law, the Scriptures, or wisdom. In Judaism, the Torah (law) was commonly called "bread." *Gen. Rab.* 54:1, for instance, interprets Proverbs 25:21 in terms of the "bread and water of the Torah" (see also *Gen. Rab.* 70:5; *Song Rab.* 1.2 §3). In Gnosticism, the imagery referred to knowledge (*gnōsis*), in the mystery religions to the sacramental meal.[184]

The Son of Man (6:27). See comments on 1:51.

God the Father has placed his seal of approval (6:27). See comments on 3:33.

To do the works God requires (6:28). Literally, "to work the works of God." "To work works" is a common Semitic expression.[185] The phrase "works of God," which may reflect Zealot parlance, refers in Jewish literature normally to works *done by God*, not those *required by him* (cf. 3:21; 9:3–4). Similar terminology is found in the Qumran scrolls: "I shall open your eyes so that you can see and understand the deeds of God" (CD 2:14).[186] The ensuing conversation is just the type that will have occurred in the synagogue (see comments on 6:59).

ANCIENT SEALS

Hebrew-inscribed clay bullae dating from the seventh century B.C.

The work of God is this: to believe in the one he has sent (6:29). In light of the Jewish emphasis on "works of the law,"[187] Jesus' answer is nothing less than stunning: God's requirement is summed up as believing in "the one he has sent," that is, the Messiah.

What miraculous sign then will you give that we may see it and believe you? (6:30). "Jews demand miraculous signs" (1 Cor. 1:22). In Judaism, a "sign from heaven" was considered to be the highest form of legitimation. In *Ex. Rab.* 9:1, the rainbow provided by God for Noah after the flood is called a wonder or sign.

Our forefathers ate the manna in the desert (6:31). The psalmist celebrated the memory of God's provision of manna in the desert: "He gave a command to the skies above and opened the doors of the heavens; he rained down manna for the people to eat, he gave them the grain of heaven. Men ate the bread of angels; he sent them all the food they could eat" (Ps. 78:23–25). The *Sibylline Oracles* state that "those who honor the true eternal God inherit life . . . feasting on sweet bread from starry heaven" (*Frag.* 3:49; 2d cent. B.C.?). A first-century Jewish work expresses the expectation of an end-time recurrence of God's provision of manna: "And it will happen at that time that the treasury of manna will come down again from on high, and they will eat of it in those years because these are they who will have arrived at the consummation of time" (*2 Bar.* 29:8; cf. Rev. 2:17).

The same expectation is also found in later rabbinic tradition. Thus R. Berechiah

(c. A.D. 340) said in the name of R. Isaac (c. A.D. 300): "As the first Redeemer was, so shall the latter Redeemer be. . . . As the former Redeemer [i.e., Moses] caused manna to descend [citing Ex. 16:4], so will the latter Redeemer cause manna to descend" (*Eccl. Rab.* 1:9). Similarly, "R. Eleazar Ḥisma [c. A.D. 120] says: You will not find it [the manna] in this world but you will find it in the world to come" (*Mek. Ex.* 16:25).

As it is written: "He gave them bread from heaven to eat" (6:31). The divine provision of manna for Israel in the desert (Ex. 16:4, 15) is celebrated in both Old Testament and intertestamental literature.[188] Philo interprets the manna as referring to the Word of God (the divine Logos) or wisdom.[189]

It is not Moses . . . but it is my Father who gives you the true bread from heaven . . . the bread of God (6:32–33). The Old Testament passages cited on 6:31 indicate that the Jews likewise regarded God as the giver of the manna, with Moses as his mediator. In Jewish thought, "bread [of God]" was taken to refer to the Torah or the bread of the Presence (*Gen. Rab.* 70:5), in keeping with Old Testament usage.[190]

Gives life to the world (6:33). In rabbinic teaching, the giving of the law at Sinai was described thus: "The earth trembled when he gave life to the world" (*Ex. Rab.* 29:9). In the present passage, the same function is fulfilled by Jesus (cf. 5:39).

He who comes to me will never go hungry, and he who believes in me will never be thirsty (6:35). Jesus plainly claims to fulfill Old Testament messianic expectations. One of the closest parallels is Isaiah 55:1: "Come, all you who are thirsty, come to the waters; and you who have no money, come, buy and eat!" (cf. Isa. 49:10, cited in Rev. 7:16).

The Jews began to grumble about him (6:41). There are obvious parallels between Jesus' Jewish opponents and Israel in the desert (cf. Ex. 16:2, 8–9; Num. 11:4–23). Just as the Israelites grumbled about the first giver of bread, Moses, they grumble about the second giver, Jesus.

Is this not Jesus, the son of Joseph, whose father and mother we know? (6:42). Even the Jews in Jesus' own part of Palestine are ignorant of his virgin conception. Note 4:44, where the evangelist refers to Jesus' saying that a prophet is not without honor except in his own country. The Jews here object, not to the notion that a man (like Jesus) can receive a divine calling, or even that someone like Elijah might appear on earth and live among human beings, but to Jesus' claim of descent from heaven in face of his obvious (or so it seemed) human origin.[191] See further 8:31–59 below, esp. v. 41.

SEAT OF MOSES

The "seat of Moses" from the synagogue at Chorazim in lower Galilee.

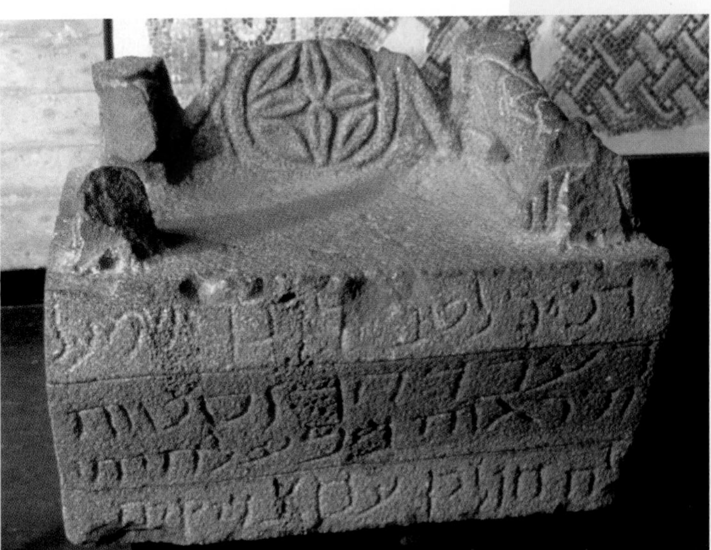

Capernaum and Its Synagogue

Jesus' headquarters, Capernaum ("village of Nahum"), located on the northwest shore of the Sea of Galilee, was a reasonably prosperous town apparently populated by both Jews and Gentiles in Jesus' day. It is probable that no more than a thousand people lived there in the first half of the first century A.D. After having been uninhabited for almost a thousand years, Capernaum, known as Tel-Hûm, was rediscovered by the American scholar Edward Robinson, who also recognized the remains of a synagogue. In 1866, Charles Wilson identified Tel-Hûm with Capernaum.

In subsequent years, several important structures have been found, including a fourth-century A.D. synagogue (with initial construction in the third century) and a fifth-century octagonal church built on top of a first-century house believed by some to have been the house of Simon Peter. According to Luke 7:5, the synagogue visited by Jesus in Capernaum was built by a Roman centurion. It is possible that the floor of basalt stones from the beginning of the first century A.D., discovered under the fourth-century synagogue, belonged to this building.[A-19]

No one can come to me unless the Father who sent me draws him (6:44). Rabbinic sources use the expression "to bring near to the Torah" with reference to conversion. Thus the first-century rabbi Hillel urged his followers to be those "loving peace and pursuing peace, loving mankind and bringing them near to the Law" (*m. ʾAbot* 1:12; see also Jer. 31:3; Hos. 11:4; comments on John 12:32).

It is written in the Prophets: "They will all be taught by God" (6:45). The expression "the Prophets" may refer to the general tenor of Old Testament prophetic teaching or to "the Prophets" as a division of the Old Testament. "They will all be taught by God" paraphrases Isaiah 54:13 (cf. Jer. 31:34). In Judaism, to learn the Torah was to be taught by God himself. The expression "disciples of God" (i.e., the ones taught by God) is also found in the Qumran writings (CD 20:4; 1QH 10:39; 15:10, 14). See also the messianic parallel in *Psalms of Solomon* 17:32: "And he will be a righteous king over them, taught by God . . . and their king shall be the Lord Messiah" (prior to A.D. 70).

He who believes has everlasting life (6:47). There is a certain affinity between John's teaching on predestination and the Qumran doctrine of the "two spirits" (1QS 3:14–4:6). The rabbinic view is summed up by the saying attributed to Rabbi Akiba (c. A.D. 135): "All is foreseen, but freedom of choice is given" (*m. ʾAbot* 3:16).

Unless you eat the flesh of the Son of Man and drink his blood, you have no life in you (6:53). For "Son of Man," see comments on 1:51. Old Testament teaching, in particular the Mosaic law, proscribed the drinking of blood as well as the eating of meat containing blood.[192] A midrash on Ecclesiates 2:24 reads, "All the references to eating and drinking in this book signify Torah and good deeds" (see a similar comment on Eccl. 8:15). The Hebrew idiom "flesh and blood" refers to the whole person. Later rabbinic theology speaks of "eating the Messiah" (*b. Sanh.* 99a).[193]

He said this while teaching in the synagogue in Capernaum (6:59). There is evidence that some synagogue services allowed the kind of exchange found in the present passage.[194] The discourse is particularly appropriate if the lectionary readings for that time of year were Exodus 16 and Isaiah 54.[195]

Many Disciples Desert Jesus (6:60–72)

Jesus' teaching on the "bread of life" is impossible to tolerate even for many of his disciples. The ensuing large-scale defection marks a watershed in John's Gospel. Chapter 6 thus ends on a note of failure (as ch. 12 does later). This does not mean that Jesus' ministry itself has failed. Rather, John shows how the scope of Jesus' followers is narrowed, so that in the end it is only a believing remnant (constituting the core group of the new messianic community) that is gathered to be instructed by the Messiah (chs. 13–16).

The Spirit gives life (6:63). The Old Testament depicts the Spirit as life-giving (Gen. 1:2; Ezek. 37:1–14; cf. *Midr. Mek. Ex.* 15:2b: "The words of the law which I have given you are life for you").[196] The rabbis said: "Great is the Law, for it gives life to those who practice it both in this world and in the world to come, as it is written (Prov. 4:22)" (*m. ʾAbot* 6:7).

The flesh counts for nothing (6:63). At Qumran, the dualism is between two spirits. Here and in 3:6, it is between flesh and spirit.

The words I have spoken to you are spirit and they are life (6:63). Life came into being through God's word (Gen. 1). Later, the Israelites were told, "Man does not live on bread alone but on every word that comes from the mouth of the LORD" (Deut. 8:3). The Old Testament viewed God's word as efficacious in and of itself (Isa. 55:11; Jer. 23:29), as did the New Testament writers (e.g., Heb. 4:12). The emphasis in the present passage lies on the fact that it is *Jesus'* words that are spirit and life (cf. John 5:40, 46–47). The Jews, however, believed that life was to

SYNAGOGUE REMAINS AT CAPERNAUM

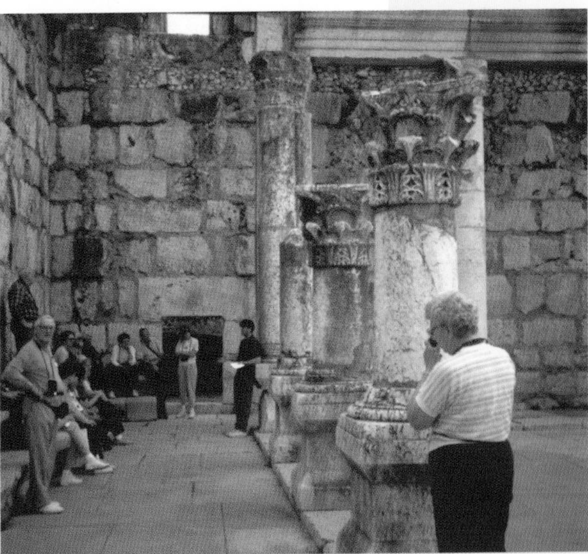

be found in the words of the law: "The words of the Torah which I have given you are life unto you" (*Mek. Ex.* 15:26, citing Prov. 4:22; cf. John 5:39).

Lord (6:68). Since the term *kyrios* here introduces a confession of Jesus as the "Holy One of God" (6:69), it does not merely (as in earlier passages, e.g., 6:34) address Jesus as "sir" but rather acknowledges him as Lord, which at least means "Master" and may allude to the name used for God in the LXX.

To whom shall we go? You have the words of eternal life (6:68). "To whom shall we go?" may refer to the possibility of transferring allegiance to a better Rabbi (cf. 1:35–37).

Holy One of God (6:69). See especially 1:34, "the Chosen One of God" (see comments). While there is no evidence that the expression "the Holy One of God" functioned as a messianic title in Judaism,[197] it clearly does so here. The term is also seldom used in the Old Testament, occasionally occurring with regard to people consecrated to God. The expression "the Holy One of Israel" is used with reference to God (Ps. 71:22; Isa. 43:3; 54:5), who is "the Holy One" par excellence.[198]

In John, the holy God is identified with Jesus (note the definite article "*the* Holy One"). The closest parallel in the present Gospel is probably 10:36, where Jesus refers to himself as "the one whom the Father set apart as his very own and sent into the world" (cf. John 17:17–19). This makes clear that holiness does not merely (or even primarily) refer to moral perfection but foremost of all to a setting apart for mission, in Jesus' case the revelation of God and the redemption of humanity.

Have I not chosen you, the Twelve? (6:70). In the Old Testament, the Israelites were God's "chosen people" (Deut. 10:15; 1 Sam. 12:22). In the New Testament, this designation is transferred to the community of believers in Jesus (e.g., Eph. 1:4, 11; 1 Peter 1:1–2; 2:9).

(He meant Judas, the son of Simon Iscariot) (6:71). At least six interpretations of "Iscariot" have been advanced, the most likely being "man of Kerioth."[199] It was common in that day for father and son to have the same last name, especially if "Kerioth" refers to their hometown. "Kerioth" may refer to the Kerioth Hezron in Judea (i.e., Hazor), mentioned in Joshua 15:25, or to the Kerioth in Moab referred to in Jeremiah 48:24. This means that Judas is the only non-Galilean among the Twelve.

Jesus Goes to the Feast of Tabernacles (7:1–13)

As much as an entire year may have passed since Jesus' last major clash with the Jerusalem authorities. In what may be the following year's Feast of Tabernacles (A.D. 32), Jesus braces himself once again for intense opposition. This is now the third (and, as it turns out, final) trip of Jesus to the Jewish capital, which finds Jesus spending two months in Jerusalem from Tabernacles to the Feast of Dedication (10:22). At this stage of Jesus' ministry, he is increasingly viewed within the matrix of messianic expectations. Was the Coming One to emerge from secret, mysterious beginnings or a known figure of Davidic descent? Did Jesus' miracles identify him as Messiah?

The Jews there were waiting to take his life (7:1). On "the Jews," see "'The Jews' in John's Gospel" at 5:10. Because

Galilee and Judea are under different jurisdictions (Herod Antipas and the Roman prefect, respectively), it affords a certain amount of protection for Jesus to stay away from Judea, where the Jews are "waiting" ("seeking" is more accurate) to take his life (but see Luke 13:31).

The Jewish Feast of Tabernacles was near (7:2). Almost half a year has passed since the Passover mentioned in 6:4.[200] The Feast of Tabernacles was celebrated from 15–21 Tishri, which fell in September or October (Lev. 23:34; in A.D. 32, it was celebrated September 10–17), after the grape harvest and exactly two months prior to the Feast of Dedication (see 10:22 below). Josephus calls it "the greatest and holiest feast of the Jews" (*Ant.* 8.4.1 §100). The mishnaic tractate called *Sukkah* ("The Feast of Tabernacles") provides some helpful information regarding the large crowds and festivities at this most popular of Jewish feasts (cf. esp. *m. Sukkah* 5:2–4). The Feast of Tabernacles is called the "Feast of Booths" in some translations, because the people lived in booths to commemorate God's faithfulness to the Israelites during their desert wanderings (Lev. 23:42–43; cf. Matt. 17:4 par.).

Jesus' brothers (7:3). The most natural understanding is that "brothers" refers to other naturally born sons of Mary—younger, of course, than Jesus.

The right time for me has not yet come; for you any time is right (7:6). "To the Jews it was a self-evident truth that every man had his time."[201] As the wise preacher had said, "There is a time for everything, and a season for every activity under heaven" (Eccl. 3:1; cf. *Eccl. Rab.* 3:1). Later rabbis concurred: "He [Simeon ben Azzai; c. A.D. 120–140] used to say: Despise no man and deem nothing impossible, for there is not a man that has not his hour and there is not a thing that has not its place" (*m. ʾAbot* 4:3). The Qumran community held similar views.[202] Jesus' statement that his brothers have no particular "time" but that their "time" is always present is therefore striking, even novel.

Not publicly, but in secret (7:10). Jesus does not make the journey to Jerusalem with the pilgrim caravan. Rather than traveling in public, Jesus goes later by himself. This he judges necessary in order not to hasten the time of his execution in light of mounting opposition. Moreover, the fact that he does not travel with his extended family (as was customary) points to Jesus' increasing isolation even among his flesh and blood relations. How large the company of travelers might be can be seen from the incident recounted in Luke 2:44, where Joseph and Mary traveled for an entire day thinking Jesus was in their company among their relatives and friends when in fact he was not.

No, he deceives the people (7:12). Matthew records a similar charge (27:63:

REFLECTIONS

AS JOHN REMINDED HIS READERS EARLIER, "JESUS himself had pointed out that a prophet has no honor in his own country" (4:44)—to which may now be added, "or even in his own family"! This underscores the extent to which Jesus' true identity remained a mystery even to those closest to him. Similarly, we may often find it most difficult to be God's witnesses in our natural families. But we must not relinquish this serious responsibility. In Jesus' case, both his mother and his brothers are found later among the circle of believers (Acts 1:12). With the necessary perseverance, and if this is God's sovereign will, we, too, may in due course reap a spiritual harvest in our own family.

"that deceiver"). Josephus names several first-century messianic pretenders or deceivers: Theudas, who in A.D. 45 or 46, claiming to be a prophet, promised to part the Jordan, and misled many (*Ant.* 20.5.1 §§97–98; cf. Acts 5:36); "the Egyptian," who also claimed to be a prophet and sought to reenact the conquest of Jericho, led the masses astray (*Ant.* 20.8.5 §§169–72; cf. *J.W.* 2.13, 5–6 §§261–65; Acts 21:38); an unnamed impostor (c. A.D. 61) who led his followers into the desert promised them salvation and deliverance (*Ant.* 20.8.10 §188); later (after A.D. 70) a certain Jonathan lured crowds into the desert and raised hopes of signs (*J.W.* 7.11.1 §§437–40).[203]

Jesus himself is called a deceiver in later Jewish literature. The Babylonian Talmud preserves a tradition to the effect that Jesus was executed on Passover Eve because he was a deceiver who practiced sorcery and led Israel astray (*b. Sanh.* 43a; cf. *b. Soṭah* 47a). According to Jewish law, the punishment for leading the people astray was stoning, further distinguishing between one who misleads an individual and one who leads an entire town astray (*m. Sanh.* 7:4, 10). Deuteronomy 13:1–11 stipulates that a false prophet must die "because he preached rebellion against the LORD your God . . . [and] has tried to turn you from the way the LORD your God commanded you to follow" (Deut. 7:5).

For fear of the Jews (7:13). "The Jews" here refers to the Jerusalem authorities, represented by the Sanhedrin.

Jesus Teaches at the Feast (7:14–24)

Halfway through the Feast (7:14). "Halfway" is a vague expression that may refer to the exact middle of the Feast (i.e., the fourth day) or merely to a time other than the first or the last day (7:37).

Go up to the temple courts and begin to teach (7:14). The main temple building (*naos*; cf. 2:19–21) was surrounded by several courts (*hieron*, here translated "temple courts"), including the Court of Women, the Court of (Israelite) Men, and the Court of the Gentiles. Jesus is probably teaching here in one of the outer porticoes.

The Jews (7:15). This probably refers to the Judean crowds as well as to the Jewish authorities.

How did this man get such learning without having studied? (7:15). A similar question is raised regarding Jesus' followers in Acts 4:13. It was common for Jewish males in Jesus' day to be able both to read and to have a basic understanding of the Scriptures. What is unusual, however, is Jesus' ability to carry on a sustained discourse in the manner of the rabbis, including frequent references to Scripture. Moreover, while the rabbis of Jesus' day teach by frequent appeal to other authorities, Jesus regularly prefaces his teachings by asserting unique authority: "You have heard that it was said . . . but I tell you" (cf. Matt. 5:21ff.); "I tell you the truth."[204]

Increasingly, however, it was not enough for a Jew to master the written Scriptures or even the oral law; formal rabbinic training became the norm, so that in the post-Jamnia period (after c. A.D. 90) the term "rabbi" came to refer exclusively to those who had undergone formal rabbinic training. According to one passage from the Babylonian Talmud, "If one has learnt Scripture and Mishnah but did not attend upon Rabbinical scholars, R. Eleazar (A.D. 80–120) says he is an *'am ha-ʾareṣ*; R. Samuel b. Naḥmani (c. A.D. 300) says he is a boor; R. Jannai (c. A.D. 240) says he is a Samaritan; R. Aḥab. Jacob (c. A.D. 300) says he is a magician [i.e., one who deceives the people]" (*b. Soṭah* 22a). See also 7:49 below.

My teaching is not my own (7:16). The age in which Jesus lived did not prize originality. If Jesus had acknowledged that he was self-taught or had originated his own message, he would have been immediately discredited for arrogance. In the Judaism of his day, there was only one way to teach and learn the word and will of God: through Scripture and its interpretation. There was no access to God other than through the Torah. In appealing to someone other than himself as the authority for his teaching, Jesus is not unlike other rabbis of his day. The rabbis referred back to the earlier rabbis; Jesus appeals to the Father, claiming direct knowledge from God (8:28).

He who speaks . . . there is nothing false about him (7:18). This verse is composed of maxims. The central contrast seems to be between a false prophet, who deserves to be executed (Deut. 18:9–22), and Jesus as the Son of God, who must be followed. The portrayal of Jesus concurs with the Palestinian Targum, where the dutiful son is one who is "concerned with the honor of his father" (*Tg. Ps.–J.* on Gen. 32:7 [8], 11 [12]).[205]

Has not Moses given you the law? (7:19). It was cause for great pride among the Jews that they were the recipients of the law (Rom. 2:17; 9:4). The Pharisees saw themselves as disciples of Moses (John 9:28).

Not one of you keeps the law (7:19). "Keeps the law" (lit., "does the law") is a rabbinic expression meaning to act in such a way that the law is done. Thus it is said of Abraham that he "kept [lit., did] the entire Torah even before it had come" (*t. Qidd.* 5:21).[206]

You are demon-possessed (7:20). Literally, "you have a demon" (cf. 8:48; 10:20; Matt. 12:24 par.). The same charge was levelled against John the Baptist (Matt. 11:18). Josephus (*Ant.* 6.13.7 §§300–309) recalls an incident at the Feast of Tabernacles several decades later (c. A.D. 62) where one Jesus, son of Ananias, prophesied Jerusalem's destruction under "some supernatural impulse" but was scourged severely and "pronounced a maniac" by Albinus the procurator.

Accusations Leveled Against Jesus by His Opponents in John's Gospel

Accusation	References
Galilean, Nazarene	1:46; 7:41, 52; 18:5, 7; 19:19
Breaking the Sabbath	5:16, 18; 9:16
Blaspheming	5:18; 8:59; 10:31, 33, 39; 19:7 (cf. Lev. 24:16)
Deceiving the people	7:12, 47
Demon-possessed	7:20; 8:48–52; 10:20–21
Illegitimate birth	8:41
Samaritan (apostate?)	8:48
A sinner	9:16, 24–25, 31
Madness	10:20
A criminal	18:30
Royal pretender, political threat	19:12; cf. 19:15, 21

I did one miracle (7:21). Here Jesus is probably referring to the healing of the invalid in 5:1–15.

Yet, because Moses gave you circumcision (though actually it did not come from Moses, but from the patriarchs) (7:22). As Jesus (John?) parenthetically points out, the Sabbath was actually instituted before Moses with Abraham (Gen. 17:9–14) in the time of the Patriarchs.

You circumcise a child on the Sabbath. Now if a child can be circumcised on the Sabbath so that the law of Moses may not be broken, why are you angry with me for healing the whole man on the Sabbath? (7:22–23). Jesus here uses the common rabbinic argument "from the lesser to the greater" (see comments on 5:47). The difficulty Jesus raises is that two commandments of God apparently conflict with one another. The Jews are to circumcise their males on the eighth day after birth (Lev. 12:3); yet no regular work is to be performed on the Sabbath. What should be done when the eighth day falls on a Sabbath? The Jews always concluded that it was permissible to go ahead and circumcise on the eighth day regardless of whether it fell on a Sabbath. Thus R. Yose b. Ḥalafta (c. A.D. 140–165) said, "Great is circumcision which overrides even the rigor of the Sabbath" (*m. Ned.* 3:11).[207]

So much for the "lesser" issue. What about the "greater" one of "healing the whole man"? Again, later rabbinic teaching generally concurs that, granted the lesser premise that circumcision (which "perfects" but one member of the human body) supersedes the Sabbath commandment, the saving of the entire body transcends it all the more. A saying attributed to R. Eliezer (c. A.D. 90) reads: "Now if on account of a single limb of a person, they override the prohibitions of the Sabbath, is it not logical that one should override the prohibitions of the Sabbath on account of [the saving of] the whole of him?" (*t. Šabb.* 15:16). R. Eleazar b. Azariah (c. A.D. 100) judged similarly: "If circumcision, which affects but one only of the two hundred and forty-eight members of the human body, suspends the Sabbath, how much more shall [the saving of] the whole body suspend the Sabbath!" (*b. Yoma* 85b; cf. *Mek. Ex.* 31:13).

Stop judging by mere appearances, and make a right judgment (7:24). This challenge has many formal Old Testament parallels.[208]

Is Jesus the Christ? (7:25–44)

Isn't this the man they are trying to kill? . . . they are not saying a word to him. Have the authorities really concluded that he is the Christ? (7:25–26). "They are not saying a word to him" is a rabbinic expression reflecting tacit approval (*t. Sukkah* 1:1). "The authorities" probably refers to the Sanhedrin (cf. 7:48; 12:42).

When the Christ comes, no one will know where he is from (7:27). According to rabbinic teaching, some believed the Messiah would be born of flesh and blood, yet be wholly unknown until he set out to procure Israel's redemption. Others in Judaism were sure about at least the geographic origin of the Messiah (Matt. 2:1–6); still, the Jewish leaders could tell Herod little else about the Messiah's family or circumstances. Some in the crowd were also convinced that the geographic origin of the Messiah was known (John 7:42). In a civilization without family names, the place of origin is equivalent to an identifying name, such as Joseph "of Arimathea" or Jesus "of Nazareth" (cf. Gen. 29:4; Judg. 13:6).

When the Christ comes, will he do more miraculous signs than this man? (7:31). While there is little direct evidence in the Old Testament that miracles were expected of the Messiah, this may be implied from the fact that Jews expected a prophet like Moses (Deut. 18:15, 18), and Moses performed miraculous signs at the Exodus (Ex. 7–11). Yet even if Jews in Jesus' day were not expecting a miracle-working Messiah, it would be natural for them to wonder, after witnessing Jesus' miracles, whether he might be the Messiah (see Mark 13:22; cf. Deut. 13:1–3).[209]

Then the chief priests and the Pharisees sent temple guards to arrest him (7:32). While there was technically only one "*chief* priest" at a given time (cf. 11:49, 51; 18:13), others who had formerly held this office apparently retained the title. The designation may also have extended to other members of the chief priestly families. Annas in particular, the patriarch of his family, skillfully controlled matters through his relations. Alternately, "chief priests" may not refer to present and past high priests but to principal priests, that is, higher temple officials including, besides the high priest himself, the captain of the temple, the temple overseer, and the treasurers.[210]

The *Pharisees* belonged to the Sanhedrin not as a party but as members of a group of men who knew the Scriptures. Josephus points to the Pharisees' influence among the people (*Ant.* 13.10.5 §288; 18.1.4 §17). Almost all the chief priests were Sadducees (cf. Acts 5:17; Josephus, *Ant.* 20.9.1 §199). The Sadducees and Pharisees made strange bedfellows. Faced with a common threat in the person of Jesus, they band together (John 7:32, 45; 11:47, 57; 18:3). Technically, only the chief priests have authority to arrest Jesus, but presumably the chief priests seek to arrest Jesus with Pharisaic support, perhaps even at Pharisaic urging.

The primary responsibility of the *temple guards*, who were drawn from the Levites, was maintaining order in the temple precincts as a kind of temple police force. Moreover, since the Romans granted the Jews a significant degree of autonomy in managing their own affairs, the Sanhedrin was able to deploy the temple guards also in matters removed from the actual sanctuary. If Jesus was still teaching in the vicinity of the temple, they would not have had to go far. The guards were commanded by "the captain of the temple," who was also drawn from one of the priestly families and whose authority in practical matters was second only to that of the high priest.

I am with you for only a short time (7:33). This is September/October (A.D. 32). Half a year later (March/April of A.D. 33) Jesus is crucified.

The Jews said to one another, "Where does this man intend to go that we cannot find him? Will he go where our people live scattered among the Greeks, and teach the Greeks?" (7:35). "The Jews" may refer to the authorities or the crowd in general. Old Testament parallels to the phrase "Where does this man intend to go that we cannot find him" may include Isaiah 55:6; Hosea 5:6; Amos 8:12. The expression "where our people live scattered" is a technical term referring to the Diaspora (Gk. "scattered"), that is, the large number of Jews living outside of Palestine in various parts of the empire and beyond.

The Greek word *diaspora* occurs about ten times in the LXX and regularly refers to the Jews' dispersion among the Gentiles.[211] A rabbinic source (*b. Sanh.* 11b) has Rabban Gamaliel (II, c. A.D. 90) address a letter "to our brethren the Exiles in Babylon and to those in Media, and to all the other exiled [sons] of Israel." Jews lived outside Palestine ever since the Babylonian exile. When they were allowed to return from exile, some went back but many did not. In later years, many cities boasted a considerable Jewish population, including Antioch, Alexandria, and Rome.

"Greeks" (cf. also 12:20) is regularly used in the New Testament in contrast with "Jews."[212] This suggests that the expression simply means "Gentile," whether literally Greek or of some other non-Jewish background. The phrase seems to have functioned as an umbrella term for Gentiles, owing to the dominance of Greek culture and language in the Greco-Roman world at large.[213] Interestingly, Jesus' Jewish interrogators do not think that Jesus will teach Diaspora Jews but Gentiles, presumably because it was assumed that only the latter need instruction in the Scriptures.

On the last and greatest day of the Feast (7:37). Every day during the Feast of Tabernacles, priests marched in solemn procession from the Pool of Siloam to the temple to pour out water at the base of the altar. The seventh day of the Feast of Tabernacles, the last day proper of the festival (Lev. 23:34, 41–42), was marked by a special water-pouring rite and lights ceremony (*m. Sukkah* 4:1, 9–10). This water rite, though not prescribed in the Old Testament, was firmly in place well before the first century A.D.[214] This rite was followed by a sacred assembly on the eighth day.[215] Hence, by the first century, many Jews had come to think of the Feast as an eight-day event.[216] The eighth day of the Feast of Tabernacles was set apart for sacrifices, the joyful dismantling of the booths, and repeated singing of the *Hallel* (Pss. 113–118).

Whether Jesus' words in John 7:37–38 and 8:12 are spoken on the climactic seventh day with its water-pouring and torch-lighting ceremonies or on the eighth day of joyful assembly and celebration, they would have a tremendous impact on the pilgrims who assemble for the Feast. Just when the events of the Feast and their attendant symbolism are beginning to sink into people's memories, Jesus' words promise a continuous supply of water and light, perhaps also alluding to the supply of water from the rock in the desert. If these words are spoken on the eighth day—when no water pourings were performed—Jesus' offer of spiritual water is particularly striking (cf. *m. Sukk.* 4:9; 5:1). The eighth day of this feast is also the last festival day in the Jewish year. Philo speaks of it as "a sort of complement (*plērōma*) and conclusion of all the feasts in the year" (*Spec. Laws* 2.213).

If anyone is thirsty, let him come to me and drink (7:37). The Feast of Tabernacles was associated with adequate rainfall (see Zech. 14:16–17, a passage read on the first day of the feast, according to the liturgy in *b. Meg.* 31a). Another Old Testament passage associated with this feast is Isaiah 12:3: "With joy you will draw water from the wells of salvation." The festival seems to speak of the joyful restoration of Israel and the ingathering of the nations. Here Jesus presents himself as God's agent to make these end-time events a reality.

As the Scripture has said, streams of living water will flow from within him (7:38). Possible scriptural allusions include those promising spiritual blessings,[217] including the blessing of the Spirit,[218] in line with the feast itself.[219] "From within him" probably refers to the one who believes in Jesus the Messiah. Jewish parallels abound. In a mishnaic passage, R. Eleazar b. Arak (c. A.D. 90–130) is called "an ever-flowing spring" (*m. ʾAbot* 2:8). A saying attributed to R. Meir (c. A.D. 140–165) affirms, "He that occupies himself in the study of the Law for its own sake merits many things . . . he is made like a never-failing spring and like

"STREAMS OF LIVING WATER WILL FLOW"

The Hazbani River in northern Galilee, one of the tributaries of the Jordan River.

a river that flows ever more mightily" (*m. ʾAbot* 6:1).

Also, according to certain traditions,[220] Jerusalem was situated in the *navel* of the earth, so that John may be using *koilia* (lit., "belly"; NIV simply translates as "him") as a synonym for Jerusalem.[221] "Said R. Joshua b. Levi [c. A.D. 250], 'Why is it [the court of women] called *place of drawing [water]*? For from there they draw the Holy Spirit, in line with the following verse of Scripture, 'With joy you will draw water from the wells of salvation' (Isa. 12:3)" (*y. Sukkah* 5:1).[222] In connection with the water from the rock, the Targum on Psalm 78:16 reads: "He made streams of water come from the rock and caused them to come down like rivers of flowing water." The idea of water flowing from the new Jerusalem (Ezek. 47:1–12) and from the rock are related in *t. Sukkah* 3:3–18.

By this he meant the Spirit (7:39). Occasionally in the Old Testament, water is used as a symbol for the Holy Spirit (cf. Isa. 44:3; Ezek. 36:25–27; Joel 2:28). Rabbinic parallels include *y. Sukkah* 5:1 (see previous comment); *Gen. Rab.* 70:8, where the "three flocks of sheep" in Genesis 29:1 are interpreted (among other things) as "the three festivals" (i.e., Passover, Pentecost, and Tabernacles) and "the well out of which they watered the flocks" as "the divine Spirit"; and *Ruth Rab.* 4:8: "'And drink of that which the young men have drawn' refers to the Festival of Water-Drawing. And why is it called 'Drawing'? For from there they drew the inspiration of the Holy Spirit, as it is said, 'Therefore with joy shall ye draw water out of the wells of salvation (Isa. 12:3).'" The most pertinent Qumran parallel is 1QS 4:20–21 (but there water is for cleansing rather than giving life).

Surely this man is the Prophet. . . . He is the Christ (7:40–41). "The Prophet" refers to "the prophet like Moses" (Deut. 18:15–18; see comments on John 6:14). In first-century thinking, the Prophet and the Christ were often viewed as two separate personages (cf. 1:21). The Qumran community looked forward to the coming of the Prophet and the Anointed Ones of Aaron and Israel (1QS 9:11), whereby the Prophet was held to be different from the priestly and royal Messiahs. Concerning the eschatological successor to Moses, we read in *Eccl. Rab.* 1:9, "As the former redeemer made a well to rise (Num. 21:17–18), so will the latter Redeemer bring up water (Joel 4:18)" (*Eccl. Rab.* 1:9).

How can the Christ come from Galilee? Does not the Scripture say that the Christ will come from David's family and from Bethlehem, the town where David lived? (7:41–42). There is ample scriptural support for people's contention that the Messiah would come from David's family and from Bethlehem, a village located south of Jerusalem in the heart of Judea.[223] Matthew 2:5–6 confirms that at least by the beginning of the first century A.D., Jewish scholars generally expected the Messiah to be born in Bethlehem (cf. Luke 2:1–2a).[224] No comparable evidence exists for a Galilean origin (cf. 7:52).

The Unbelief of the Jewish Leaders (7:45–52)

The temple guards . . . the chief priests and Pharisees (7:45). See comments on 7:32.

"No one ever spoke the way this man does," the guards declared (7:46). These guards were chosen from the Levites and were religiously trained. They were not, therefore, merely "brutal thugs." In the fulfillment of their duties, they would

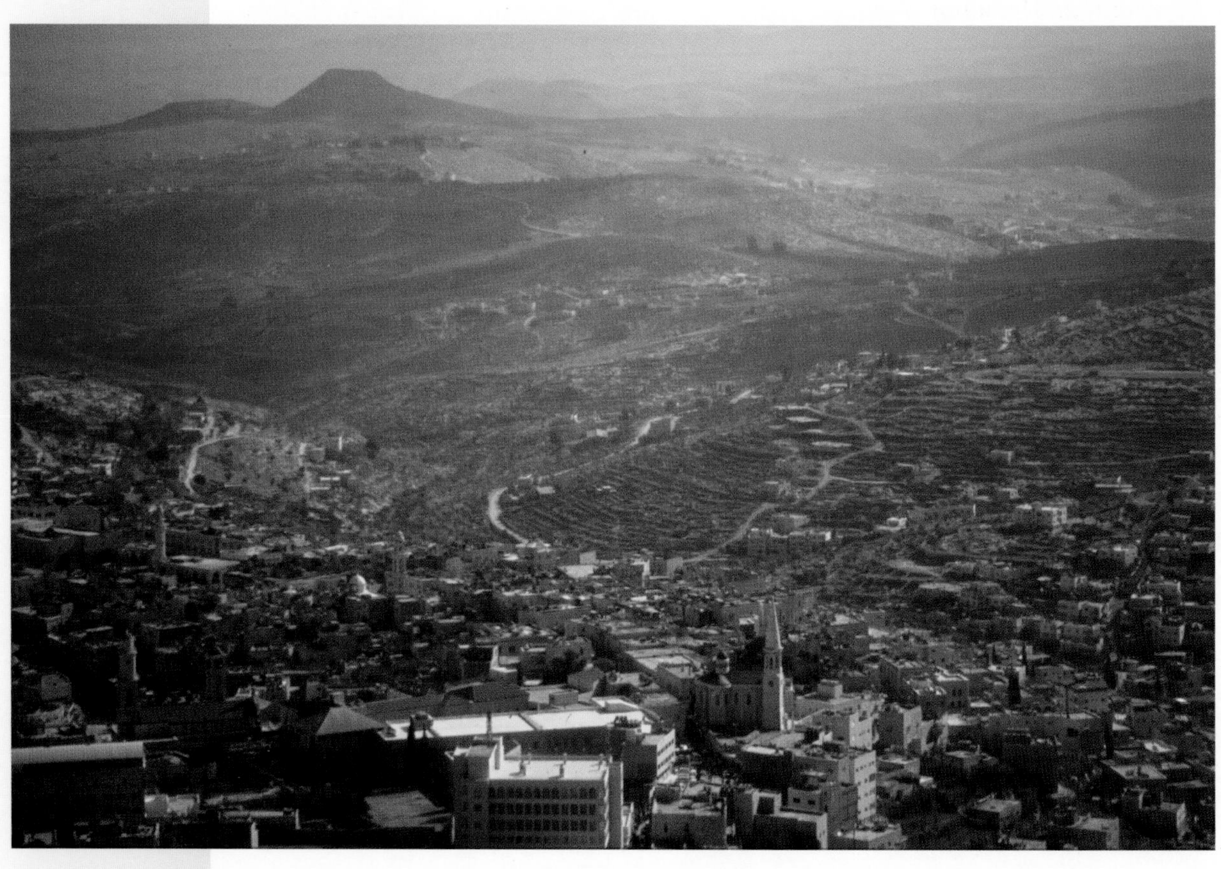

MODERN BETHLEHEM

The Church of the Nativity is in the lower left corner. The Herodium is visible in the background.

have heard many teach in the temple courts; even as biblical nonexperts, they recognize Jesus' teaching as unique.

This mob that knows nothing of the law—there is a curse on them (7:49). The disparaging designation "people of the land" (Heb. *ʿammê ha-ʾareṣ*; NIV: "this mob") is the way the unschooled masses were typically viewed by the rabbis. Originally, the whole nation was known by this expression (Ezek. 22:29); later, the term came to refer to the common folk as compared with the leaders (Jer. 1:18); finally, it came to represent the mixed population that settled in Samaria and Judea during the Exile, in distinction from the returning Jews (Ezra 10:2, 11).[225] Rabbi Hillel, living a generation before Jesus, said, "A brutish man dreads not sin, and an ignorant man (Heb. *ʿammê ha-ʾareṣ*) cannot be saintly" (*m. ʾAbot* 2:6). R. Dosa b. Harkinas (c. A.D. 90) commented, "Morning sleep and midday wine and children's talk and sitting in the meeting-houses of the ignorant people (Heb. *ʿammê ha-ʾareṣ*) put a man out of the world" (*m. ʾAbot* 3:11).

Nicodemus, who had gone to Jesus earlier and was one of their number (7:50). See 3:1–15.

Does our law condemn anyone without first hearing him to find out what he is doing? (7:51). See Acts 5:34–39, where, perhaps only two years later, Gamaliel, another rabbi, acts much like Nicodemus here. Old Testament law charges judges to investigate accusations against a person fairly (Deut. 1:16) and thoroughly (17:4; 19:18). In light of the fact that many of the Sanhedrin members have just expressed contempt toward the ignorant masses, John surely sees irony in Nicodemus's calling them to task on a point of simple Jewish—indeed, universal—legal procedure (cf. *m. Sanh.* 5:4). Consider the Roman Governor Festus's statement to King Agrippa: "It is not the Roman custom to hand over any man before he has faced his accusers and has had an opportunity to defend himself against their charges"[226] (Acts 25:16). Later rabbinic rulings concur: "Unless a mortal hears the pleas that a man can put forward, he is not able to give judgment."[227]

Are you from Galilee, too? Look into it, and you will find that a prophet does not come out of Galilee (7:52). The text may say "a prophet" or "the prophet" because of the manuscript tradition. Prophets had indeed come out of Galilee in the past, including Jonah (2 Kings 14:25) and possibly Elijah (1 Kings 17:1) and Nahum (Nah. 1:1). Rabbi Eliezer (c. A.D. 90), speaking in Upper Galilee, said, "There was not a tribe of Israel from which there did not come prophets" (*b. Sukkah* 27b). Similarly, *Seder ʿOlam Rabbah* 21: "You have no city in the land of Israel in which there has not been a prophet." Regarding contemporary attitudes of contempt for Galilee, see esp. *y. Šabb.* 16:8, where R. Ulla (c. A.D. 280) says of R. Yoḥanan ben Zakkai (d. c. A.D. 80) that he had lived for eighteen years in Galilee and had only been given two cases to decide. Hence he said, "O Galilee, Galilee, you have hated the Torah. You will end up working for tax farmers."

[Jesus and the Adulterous Woman (7:53–8:11)]

Both internal and external evidence indicate that the story of Jesus and the adulterous woman is not a part of the original Gospel but has been inserted at its present location by a later scribe. As far as external evidence is concerned, all the early papyri and the best major uncial manuscripts omit the account. Also, none of the early church fathers show awareness of this narrative, passing in their comments immediately from 7:52 to 8:12. The instability of the tradition is also apparent in that the text is inserted at various places in the Gospels, be it after 7:36, 7:44, or 21:25, or even in the Gospel of Luke after 21:38.

Internally, the insertion of John 7:53–8:11 clearly disrupts the unity and coherence of 7:1–52 and 8:12–59. Moreover, the account differs sharply in language and style from the rest of John. In fact, the pericope features a total of 14 unique words not elsewhere found in this Gospel, two and a half times as many as the next closest passage. For these reasons it is best not to treat the story as part of the Gospel and to consider it as a—possibly authentic—pericope that initially circulated separately in oral tradition and was eventually attached between 7:52 and 8:12.[228]

The Validity of Jesus' Testimony (8:12–30)

Still on the temple grounds, Jesus gets embroiled in renewed conflict with his Jewish opponents. After the Pharisees challenge the legitimacy of his witness, controversy centers in particular around the person of Abraham.

I am the light of the world (8:12). In the Old Testament, God himself (Ps. 27:1; 36:9) as well as his word (or "law"; Ps. 119:105; Prov. 6:23) are called a "light." Light imagery is also applied to the end-time servant of the Lord (Isa. 49:6; cf. 42:6) and to the Lord's own presence in the midst of his people in the last days.[229] Contemporary Judaism applied the phrase "light of the world" not only to God but also to Israel, Jerusalem, the patriarchs, the Messiah, famous rabbis (e.g., Yoḥanan ben Zakkai), the Torah, the temple, and even Adam.[230] The universality of "light" symbolism in religious language issues in numerous non-Jewish parallels.[231]

Here "light" terminology is applied to the symbolism of the Feast of Tabernacles. As part of the festivities, four golden lamps were put in place, and an abundance of oil was poured into large golden bowls. The lamps rose over the outside walls of the temple and were said to illumine the entire city of Jerusalem. In the ensuing joyous celebration, the pious danced with torches and spoke words of praise. Levites played their musical instruments, standing on the steps that led from the Court of the Israelites to the Court of Women. The dancing and singing lasted all night until dawn. Notably, the main candelabrum was left until the last night to remind the Israelites that they still awaited their full salvation in the future—but now, Jesus declares himself to be "the light of the world."[232] The celebration ended with two priests with trumpets slowly descending the steps, affirming people's loyalty to Yahweh (cf. *m. Sukkah* 5:2–4).

Whoever follows me will never walk in darkness (8:12). On the contrast between light and darkness in John, see comments on 1:5. Similar language is also found in the Dead Sea Scrolls[233] and Jewish intertestamental literature. In *Joseph and Asenath*, God is said to call people "from darkness to light, and from error to truth, and from death to life" (8:9).

Will have the light of life (8:12). The phrase "light of life" is found in the Old Testament as well as in other Jewish literature. Consider Psalm 36:9: "For with you is the fountain of life; in your light we see light." Psalm 56:13 reads, "that I may walk before God in the light of life" (cf. Job 33:30). Also, *Psalms of Solomon* 3:12: "Those who fear the Lord shall rise up to eternal life, and their life shall be in the Lord's light, and it shall never end" (cf. *4 Bar.* 9:3). In the Qumran scrolls it is said that man's "sins are atoned so that he can look at the light of life" (1QS 3:7). Similarly, apocalyptic literature: "The righteous ones shall be in the light of the sun and the elect ones in the light of eternal life" (*1 En.* 58:3; cf. 58:4–6; 92:4).

Here you are, appearing as your own witness; your testimony is not valid (8:13). Jesus himself earlier affirmed this: "If I testify about myself, my testimony is not valid" (5:31). Old Testament law required multiple witnesses in capital cases and other crimes (Num. 35:30; Deut. 17:6; 19:15). Later Jewish legislation adopted the principle and applied it to other legal situations: "None may be believed when he testifies of himself. . . . None may testify of himself" (*m. Ketub.* 2:9; cf. *m. Roš Haš.* 3:1).

Because I am not alone (8:16). Similarly, 16:32: "I am not alone, for my Father is with me." See also *m. ʾAbot* 4:8: "He [R. Ishmael, late second century A.D.] used to say: 'Judge not alone, for none may judge alone save One.'"

I stand with the Father, who sent me (8:16). Literally, "but I and he who sent me." According to later Jewish tradition (attributed to R. Yehudah, c. A.D. 150), when the priests marched in procession around the altar at the Feast of Tabernacles, singing the Hosanna of Psalm 118:25, they did not sing "O Lord" but rather "I and he" in order to avoid using the name of God (*m. Sukkah* 4:5; cf. *m. Yoma* 6:2), whereby "I and he" lent expression to the fellowship between Israel and Yahweh. Jesus' words "I and he who sent me" may correspondingly indicate that Christ had now taken the place of Israel in relation to God (cf. John 15:1).

In your own Law (8:17). By calling the Law "your own Law," Jesus distances himself from his Jewish opponents (cf. 10:34; see also 6:49: "your forefathers"; 7:56: "your father Abraham"; 15:25: "their Law").[234] Apparently, this is also how Gentiles referred to the Law when in dialogue with Jews.[235]

It is written that the testimony of two men is valid (8:17). See comments on 8:13. Apparently, "the Jews took this [the requirement of at least two witnesses] so seriously that they interpreted Scripture to mean 'two witnesses' wherever a witness is mentioned unless it is specifically laid down that only one is required."[236]

I am one who testifies for myself; my other witness is the Father, who sent me (8:18). Jesus here states plainly that he and his Father are the two witnesses that attest to his truthfulness.[237] There may be a hint of deity in Jesus' "I am" statement, recalling passages such as Isaiah 43:10. In Jewish tradition, the combined witness of father and son was not acceptable, at least for certain purposes (*m. Roš Haš.* 1:7). In the present instance, the Jews expect witnesses whose statements can be heard and compared with each other, so that it can be determined whether or not they agree. In John 5:31–39, Jesus had listed a whole series of witnesses, including the Father, John the Baptist, Jesus' own works, and the Scriptures.

Where is your father? (8:19). In the ancient Near East, "to question a man's paternity is a definite slur on his legitimacy."[238] See also 14:8: "Lord, show us the Father and that will be enough for us."

You do not know me or my Father. . . . If you knew me, you would know my Father also (8:19). "Like father, like son"—as well as the equivalent, "Like mother, like daughter" (Ezek. 16:44)—was a truism in the ancient Near East as much as it is in many parts of the world today. This family resemblance pertains both to external physical features and to character traits.

The temple area near the place where the offerings were put (8:20). The treasury stood in the Women's Court (cf. Mark 12:41–44 par.), not far from the hall where Sanhedrin meetings were held. The Court of Women also was the place where the celebration of lights took place during the Feast of Tabernacles (see comments on John 8:12). Each of the thirteen trumpet-shaped receptacles had inscriptions regarding the intended use of the respective offerings: "gold for the mercy seat," "frankincense," "bird offerings," "wood," "freewill offerings," etc. (cf. *m. Šeqal.* 6:5). There may actually have been several treasuries (cf. Josephus, *J.W.* 5.5.2 §200), the treasury so-called being the place where the alms boxes were set up. A number of chambers were also used to store valuable items, both temple and private property (cf. *J.W.* 6.5.2 §282; *Ant.* 19.6.1 §294).

I am going away . . . and you will die in your sin. Where I go, you cannot come (8:21). Dying in one's sins, with one's sins unrepented and unatoned for, renders one subject to the wrath and judgment of the holy God. How much better to repent, confess one's sins, believe, and live (Deut. 24:16; cf. Ezek. 3:16–21; 18).

Will he kill himself? (8:22). This misunderstanding reveals the contempt (or at least low moral esteem) in which the Jews held Jesus (for a list of accusations leveled against Jesus, see comments on 7:20). Exceptional cases—such as Samson (Judg. 16:30) or the holdouts against the Romans committing mass suicide at Masada (A.D. 73)—were viewed favorably, but generally Jewish people shuddered at the thought of someone's taking his or her own life (e.g. Judas: Matt. 27:3–10; Acts 1:18–19). The corpse of such a person was left unburied until sunset (Josephus, *J.W.* 3.8.5 §377), and there was no public mourning.

Moreover, it was believed that suicide excluded one from the future age. According to the rabbis, the person who committed suicide could not pay with his life for the shedding of his blood (cf. Gen. 9:5), so that he must spend the afterlife in a state of damnation. Josephus writes, "But as for those who have laid mad hands upon themselves, the darker regions of the nether world receive their souls, and God, their father, visits upon their posterity the outrageous acts of the parents" (*J.W.* 3.8.5 §375; cf. 7.8.6 §320–401). In contrast to this negative view, contemporary pagan philosophers frequently considered suicide as an "honorable death."[239]

You are from below; I am from above. You are of this world; I am not of this world (8:23). The contrast between an "upper" heavenly and a "lower" earthly realm was recognized in Judaism, yet these two spheres were considered to be related through the concept of creation. The realm of the dead was imagined as under the earth, and this underworld, the "darkness of the depths" (*Jub.* 7:29; cf. 5:14), was also regarded as the place of judgment (*Jub.* 22:22; prior to 100 B.C.). A mishnaic tractate affirms the mystery attached to the division between what is above and what is below: "Whosoever gives his mind to four things it were better for him if he had not come into the world—what is above? what is beneath? what was beforetime? and what will be hereafter?" (*m. Ḥag.* 2:1). For John, however, the "lower" realm entails a moral dimension.[240]

If you do not believe that I am [the one I claim to be] (8:24). The proper Old Testament background of this "I am" statement (also in 8:28 and 58) appears to be Exodus 3:13–14 as further developed in Isaiah 40–55.[241] Thus Isaiah 43:10 says, "'You are my witnesses,' declares the LORD, 'and my servant whom I have chosen, so that you may know and believe me and understand that I am he.'" In context, the phrase "I am he" in this passage means "I am (forever) the same," and perhaps even "I am Yahweh," alluding to Exodus 3:14. Anyone other than God who applied this designation to himself was guilty of blasphemy and subject to God's wrath (Isa. 47:8–9; Zeph. 2:15).

Lifted up the Son of Man (8:28). The phrase "lifted up" (*hypsoō*) probably harks back to the Suffering Servant of Isaiah, who "will be raised and lifted up and highly exalted" (Isa. 52:13).

I do nothing on my own but speak just what the Father has taught me (8:28). Jesus, as the sent Son, again affirms his dependence on the Father, in keeping with the Jewish maxim that "a man's agent (*shaliaḥ*) is like the man himself" (e.g., *m. Ber.* 5:5).

I always do what pleases him (8:29). David was "a man after God's own heart"[242]—yet he was guilty of adultery and murder. In Isaiah 38:3, Hezekiah prays, "I have walked before you faithfully and with wholehearted devotion and have done what is good in your eyes"; yet Hezekiah was hardly perfect. In all of human history, only Jesus can legitimately claim that he always does what pleases God.

The Jews' and Jesus' Relationship to Abraham (8:31–59)

Hold to my teaching (8:31). The measure of any disciple is whether or not one holds to the master's teaching (cf. 2 John 9). The perfect follower of a Jewish rabbi was one who had "fully absorbed his master's teaching" and "was drawing on it to spread it abroad" (*b. Yoma* 28a; see also *T. Jos.* 1:3: "I have not gone astray: I continued in the truth of the Lord"; *Gospel of Thomas* 19: "If you become my disciples and listen to my words . . .").

Then you will know the truth, and the truth will set you free (8:32). Judaism held that what made people free was the study of the law. "R. Nehunya b. Ha-Kanah [c. A.D. 70–130] said: 'He that takes upon himself the yoke of the Law, from him shall be taken away the yoke of the kingdom and the yoke of worldly care; but he that throws off the yoke of the Law, upon him shall be laid the yoke of the kingdom and the yoke of worldly care" (*m. ʾAbot* 3:5; cf. 6:2; 1QS 4:20–21).

In Greek philosophy, both freedom and truth constituted virtues along with self-restraint, justice, and courage.[243] Philo wrote an entire essay on the Stoic notion that only the wise man is free. The Stoics believed that freedom was acquired by living in accordance with

Reason. The Stoic philosopher Epictetus (c. A.D. 50–120), son of a slave woman and for many years a slave himself, devoted his entire life to a passionate quest for freedom and independence. He contended that "freedom by the truth" (to be understood in terms of intellectual emancipation against the background of Epictetus's own slave background) is found by following some great philosopher.[244] Jesus' words would surely have resonated in the minds of John's Greek-speaking audience: One greater than Plato and Aristotle was here.

REFLECTIONS

FREEDOM IS ONE OF HUMANITY'S most prized possessions. Yet freedom is more than being able to do whatever a person would like to do. Freedom must be founded on truth, including the truth of human sinfulness. Only the one who has faced his or her own sinfulness and acknowledged a need for a Savior—Jesus—can experience true freedom. Sin enslaves even those who deem themselves "free" merely because they enjoy a certain degree of personal or political independence. But those who have trusted in the "Lamb of God, who takes away the sin of the world" have been set free from their bondage to sin.

We are Abraham's descendants (8:33). Several Old Testament passages extol the blessings of descent from Abraham: "O descendants of Abraham his servant, O sons of Jacob, his chosen ones" (Ps. 105:6); "But you, O Israel, my servant, Jacob, whom I have chosen, you descendants of Abraham my friend" (Isa. 41:8). However, even then, physical descent from Abraham was considered insufficient by itself.[245] While both Ishmael and Esau were Abraham's offspring, they were not sons of promise.[246] Thus Paul concluded, "For not all who are descended from Israel are Israel. Nor because they are his descendants are they all Abraham's children" (Rom. 9:6–7).

Descent from Abraham was the Jews' pride and a major source of confidence regarding their salvation (cf. esp. Matt. 3:9 par., including John the Baptist's exhortation).[247] The Jews considered Abraham to be the founder of the worship of God; he recognized the Creator and served him faithfully.[248] Apart from descent from Abraham, it was God's deliverance of the Israelites from slavery in Egypt that was seen to ensure the Jews' freedom: "God brought Israel out of captivity . . . from darkness and the shadow of death . . . from a yoke of iron to the yoke of the Torah . . . from slavery to freedom . . . from servitude to redemption" (*Ex. Rab.* 15:11).

And have never been slaves of anyone (8:33). Freedom was considered the birthright of every Jew. God's law laid down that no Jew, however poor, must ever descend to the level of slave: "If one of your countrymen becomes poor among you and sells himself to you, do not make him work as a slave. . . . Because the Israelites are my servants, whom I brought out of Egypt, they must not be sold as slaves" (Lev. 25:39–42). According to the Talmud, R. Simeon b. Gamaliel, R. Simeon, R. Ishmael, and R. Akiba held that "all Israel are royal children" (*b. Šabb.* 128a; cf. Matt. 8:12: "subjects of the kingdom").

Everyone who sins is a slave to sin (8:34). Jewish ethics viewed human existence as conflict between the evil and good impulses (*yeṣer*; e.g., *m. Ber.* 9:5). The law served to restrain the evil impulse and to help the good impulse prevail.[249] The idea that serious offenses subject humankind to the power of sin is attested in both Jewish intertestamental and rabbinic literature. The second-century B.C. work *Testaments of the Twelve Patriarchs* features the following: "The prince of error blinded me, and I was ignorant—as a human being, as flesh, in my corrupt sins—until I learned of my own weakness after supposing myself to be invincible" (*T. Jud.* 19:4); "Flee from the evil tendency, destroying the devil by your good works. For those who are two-faced are not of God, but they are enslaved to their evil desires, so that they might be pleasing to Beliar and to persons like themselves" (*T. Ash.* 3:2).

Rabbinic Judaism concurred. "Happy is he who is [master] over his transgressions, but his transgressions are not [master] over him."[250] R. Akiba (d. c. A.D. 135) said, "At first it [the evil impulse] is like a spider's web, but eventually it becomes like a ship's rope" (*Gen. Rab.* 22:6). The reality of sin was also acknowledged by the Qumran community (CD 1:8–9: "And they realized their sin and knew that they were guilty men").[251] Greek philosophy, on the other hand, prized wisdom, self-control, and other virtues. According to the Stoics, only the wise are free; the fool is a slave. Socrates denied that an individual can be called free who is controlled by passions. In the present instance, Yom Kippur, the Day of Atonement, which had just passed, should have served as a reminder that the Jews, too, were sinners.[252]

A slave has no permanent place in the family, but a son belongs to it forever (8:35). Compare the reference to Genesis 21:10 in Galatians 4:30: "The slave woman's son will never share in the inheritance with the free woman's son." In both Palestine and the Hellenistic world, households included slaves as well as sons. For Jewish slaves, this dependent relationship lasted only six years; in the seventh year they must be set free. In the Greco-Roman world, too, slaves were occasionally granted freedom, though this was not formally mandated.

The notion of a "son" being set over God's house "forever" is found in an important messianic text: "I will be his father, and he will be my son. . . . I will set him over my house and my kingdom forever; his throne will be established forever" (1 Chron. 17:13–14). The special status of sons even with regard to taxation by earthly kings is affirmed by Jesus in Matthew 17:25–26. In Hebrews 3:5–6, Moses and Christ are contrasted in terms of the temporary status of servant and the permanent position of son.

If you were Abraham's children . . . then you would do the things Abraham did (8:39). In Genesis 18:1–8, Abraham welcomed divine messengers with eager hospitality. In 12:1–9; 15:1–6; 22:1–19, he displayed obedience to God (though the book of Genesis records less noble instances in Abraham's life as well). The rabbis frequently upheld Abraham as a moral example to be emulated by the Jews: "He in whom are these three things is of the disciples of Abraham our father. . . . A good eye and a humble spirit and a lowly soul—[they in whom are these] are of the disciples of Abraham our father" (*m. ʾAbot* 5:19); "Whoever is merciful to his fellow-men is certainly of the children of our father Abraham, and whosoever is not merciful to his fellow-men is certainly not of the children of our father Abraham" (*b. Beṣa* 32b).[253] In rabbinic literature, a distinction is made between people who act like Abraham and those who act like Balaam (*m. ʾAbot* 5:19). Generally, Abraham was believed to have fulfilled the whole Torah even before the law was given.

"You are doing the things your own father does." "We are not illegitimate children" (8:41). "Illegitimate children" translates the literal "have been born of sexual immorality" (*porneia*). The prophets had compared Yahweh's covenant with Israel to a marriage relationship: idolatry amounted to spiritual adultery.[254] The Jews' rebuttal may imply that they considered Jesus' birth illegitimate.[255] The earliest attestation of the Jewish belief that Jesus was born out of *porneia* may be *m. Yeb.* 4:13: "I found a family register in Jerusalem and in it was written, 'Such-a-one is a bastard through [a transgression of the law of] thy neighbour's wife (Lev. 18:20),' confirming the words of R. Joshua."[256]

The only Father we have is God himself (8:41). In 8:39, the Jews had said that Abraham is their father (cf. 8:33, 37). Now they say they have only one father, God. This is entirely in keeping with Old Testament teaching (though not necessarily Jewish practice): "This is what the LORD says: Israel is my firstborn son" (Ex. 4:22). "Is . . . the LORD . . . not your Father, your Creator, who made you and formed you?" (Deut. 32:6). "But you are our Father, though Abraham does not know us or Israel acknowledge us; you, O LORD, are our Father, our Redeemer from of old" (Isa. 63:16). "Yet, O LORD, you are our Father. We are the clay, you are the potter; we are all the work of your hand" (Isa. 64:8). "I am Israel's father, and Ephraim is my firstborn son" (Jer. 31:9). "Have we not all one Father? Did not one God create us?" (Mal. 2:10).

I came from God (8:42). In pagan religions, the term "come" (*hēkō*) was commonly used for the saving appearance of deity.[257] In Jesus' case, it refers to his divine origin. This is part of John's portrayal of Jesus as coming from God and returning to him (metaphorically depicted in terms of descent and ascent; cf. 16:28).[258]

You belong to your father, the devil. . . . He was a murderer from the beginning (8:44). The plot to kill Jesus (cf. 8:37, 40) is ultimately inspired by Satan himself (13:2, 27). The phrase "murderer from the beginning" primarily refers to the fall narrative in Genesis 3 rather than the first murder in Genesis 4. It was commonly recognized in Jewish intertestamental literature that death was the result of Satan's initiative: "God created us for incorruption, and made us in the image of his own eternity, but through the devil's envy death entered the world, and those who belong to his company experience it" (Wisd. Sol. 2:23–24; cf. Sir. 25:24; Rom. 5:12).

Still, a reference to Cain, the murderer of Abel, may be secondarily in view (cf. 1 John 3:15). If so, Jesus' comment may imply that the devil is the father of "the Jews" because they want to kill Jesus, their fellow-Jew, just as Cain killed his brother Abel.[259] Other Jewish intertestamental texts refer to those outside the community as "children of destruction" (*Jub.* 15:26), "sons of Beliar" (15:33), or "sons of darkness" (1QS 1:10; 1QM passim). Finally, Antiochus Epiphanes IV, who erected the "abomination of desolation" in the Jewish temple in 167 B.C. and who serves as a type of the Antichrist in biblical literature,[260] is called "murderer and blasphemer" in 2 Macc. 9:28 (see comments on John 10:38).

Not holding to the truth, for there is no truth in him (8:44). "Not holding to the truth" may refer to the fall of Satan (Isa. 14:12?), which preceded the fall narrative in Genesis 3. Parallels are found at Qumran: "The Community council shall be founded on truth . . . true witnesses for the judgment and chosen by the will (of God)" (1QS 8:5–6); "they look for you with a double heart, and are not firmly based in your truth" (1QH 12:14).

He is a liar and the father of lies (8:44). See Genesis 2:17; 3:4; and previous comment. In the Scrolls, the opponent of the Teacher of Righteousness is called the "Man of Lies" (1QpHab 2:1–2; 5:11; CD 20:15). The Teacher himself says of the people who want to divert him from his path, "They are sowers of deceit and seers of fraud, they have plotted evil against me . . . and are not firmly based in your truth" (1QH 12:9–10, 14).

Can any of you prove me guilty of sin? (8:46). In Isaiah 53:9, it is said regarding the Suffering Servant that there was no "deceit in his mouth." Alluding to this passage, *Testament of Judah* 24:1 speaks of the Star from Jacob, who will arise like the Sun of righteousness, "and in him will be found no sin" (this may be a Christian interpolation). Christ's sinlessness is affirmed by the unanimous testimony of the early church.[261] See also *Gospel of Thomas* 104: "What is the sin that I have committed, or wherein have I been defeated?"

You are a Samaritan and demon-possessed (8:48). The Jews' riposte challenges Jesus' *paternity* in return: If he says the Jews are of their "father the devil" (8:44), he will be charged with having been birthed by a Samaritan! The label *Samaritan* may also imply the charge of apostasy. Like the Samaritans, Jesus calls into question the legitimacy of the Jews' worship. Finally, "Samaritan" may intimate that Jesus' *miracles are due to demonic influence or magic*.[262] In the Babylonian Talmud, a person who learned Scripture and the Mishnah but did not study with a rabbi is described by one teacher as belonging to "the people of the land," by another as a Samaritan, and by a third as a magician.[263]

I honor my Father and you dishonor me (8:49). Christ's calm, non-retaliatory response evokes reminiscences of Isaiah's Suffering Servant (cf. 1 Peter 2:23 alluding to Isa. 53:7). According to Jewish law, rejection of someone's messenger was tantamount to rejection of the sender himself. In many non-Western societies, honor and shame are of utmost importance.[264] Dishonoring of a person is regarded as inexcusable.

Will never see death (8:51). The phrase is a common Jewish expression.[265] It serves as "a graphic expression of the hard and painful reality of dying," stressing the bitter fate awaiting all human beings.[266] However, exceptions such as Enoch or Elijah showed that the power of death was not absolute.

Abraham died and so did the prophets (8:52). The Old Testament Scriptures, Jewish tradition, and Greco-Roman beliefs agree that death is the common lot of humanity. "What man can live and not see death, or save himself from the power of the grave?" writes the psalmist (Ps. 89:48). "Where are your forefathers now? And the prophets, do they live forever?" declares the prophet (Zech. 1:5). Even people the Jews believed to have been exceptionally close to God were not exempt from death. A later rabbinic passage narrates God's response to Moses when the latter expresses reluctance to die: "Behold Abraham, who honored my name in the world and died" (*Tanḥ.* 6:11). Greco-Roman culture concurs. The great classical Greek poet Homer queries, "Now, friend, do you too die? Why do you lament thus?" (*Iliad* 21.107). Lucretius, a first-century B.C. writer, echoes these sentiments: "And the Master . . . Epicurus himself died. . . . And will *you* kick and protest against your sentence?" (*De Rer. Nat.* 3.1037–50).

You do not know him (8:55). The Jews do not "know" God, because they fail to "acknowledge" him. A similar charge was leveled against the Jews by some of the Old Testament prophets (e.g., Hos. 4:1; 6:6). Several later prophetic passages predict a time when people *would* know God (e.g., Isa. 11:9; Jer. 31:31–34; Hab. 2:14). But even the prophets could not claim to be free from sin or to know God the way Jesus claimed for himself.

Your father Abraham rejoiced at the thought of seeing my day; he saw it and was glad (8:56). "To say that Abraham saw the Messiah was neither new nor offensive to Jewish teachers; it was its application to Jesus that was unbelievable."[267] Appealing to Genesis 15:17–21, R. Akiba (d. c. A.D. 135) taught that God revealed to Abraham the mysteries of the coming age (*Gen. Rab.* 44:22; *4 Ezra* 3:14; *2 Bar.* 4:4; *Apoc. Abr.* 31). Abraham's "rejoicing" was taken by Jewish tradition to refer to his laughter at the prospect (or actual birth) of his son Isaac. This interpretation was based partly on Genesis 17:17 (interpreted as joy, not scorn, as in Philo, *Names* 154–69) and partly on Genesis 21:6 (cf. *Jub.* 15:17; 16:19–29; see also *Tg. Onq.*). It has been suggested that the reference here may be to Abraham's rejoicing when he announced to Isaac on the way to the sacrifice, "God himself will provide the lamb for the burnt offering, my son" (Gen. 22:8). In *Testament of Levi* 18:2, 6, Levi predicts the coming of a "new priest" for whom "the heavens will be opened, and from the temple of glory sanctification will come upon him, with a fatherly voice, as from Abraham to Isaac."

My day (8:56). The "day of the Lord" here has become *Jesus'* "day." While this expression usually refers to the final judgment, here it probably denotes his incarnation.

You are not yet fifty years old (8:57). According to Luke 3:23, Jesus was about thirty years old when he began his ministry. If this is the fall of A.D. 32, Jesus would be about thirty-five (perhaps almost thirty-six) years old. The age of fifty was commonly considered to mark the end of a man's working life and his attainment of full maturity (cf. Num. 4:3, 39; 8:24–25; *m. ʾAbot* 5:21: "at fifty for counsel").[268] Jesus, the Jews may be saying, has not even reached full maturity, and he makes claims such as having seen Abraham. Also, the book of *Jubilees* uses "fifty years" to measure the eras since the creation.[269] Note also the interesting reference in *Pesiq. Rab.* 21:12: "The letter *nun*, whose numerical value is fifty, signifies that Abraham was fifty years old when he recognized his Maker."

Before Abraham was born, I am (8:58). Jesus' language here echoes God's self-identification to Moses in Exodus 3:14 (cf. Isa. 43:10, 13). Thus Jesus does not merely claim preexistence—or he could have said, "before Abraham was born, I *was*"—but deity (see the people's reaction in 8:59). Note also *Gospel of Thomas* 19: "Jesus said, 'Blessed is he who came into being before he came into being.'"

At this, they picked up stones to stone him (8:59). Stoning was the prescribed punishment for blasphemy (Lev. 24:16; cf. Deut. 13:6–11; *m. Sanh.* 7:4). However, such punishment was to be the result of righteous judgment, not mob violence (Deut. 17:2–7).[270] Already in Old Testament times, people considered stoning righteous men such as Moses (Ex. 17:4), Joshua and Caleb (Num. 14:10), or David (1 Sam. 30:6). Stephen, the church's first martyr, was stoned on account of alleged blasphemy (Acts 7:57–60). Paul, too, was stoned repeatedly, although he escaped with his life (Acts 14:19; 2 Cor. 11:25), as were other Christian saints (Heb. 11:37). The availability of stones in the temple area points to the fact that the temple was still being renovated (cf. John 2:20; Josephus, *Ant.* 17.9.3 §216; *J.W.* 2.1.3 §§11–12).

Jesus Heals a Man Born Blind (9:1–12)

Healings of blind men by Jesus are also featured in the other canonical Gospels.[271] In John, this is the sixth sign and the third healing selected by the evangelist. Restoring sight to the blind is considered to be a messianic activity in the Old Testament (Isa. 29:18; 35:5; 42:7). The healing probably took place anywhere between October and mid-December (A.D. 32).

As he went along (9:1). The scene probably took place in the area south of the temple at one of the two southern gates, Jesus recently having left the temple grounds (8:59).[272]

A man blind from birth (9:1). The man's blindness from birth raises the ante for the ensuing miracle and makes it all the more striking (see comments on 2:10). In ancient Palestine, blind people were cast wholly on the mercy of others. They would frequently position themselves near sanctuaries on the assumption that passersby would be in a charitable mood. In the present instance, Jesus and his disciples would notice the begging man as they leave the temple grounds (8:59).

Rabbi (9:2). See comments on 1:38.

Who sinned, this man or his parents, that he was born blind? (9:2). Jewish rabbis generally believed in a direct cause-and-effect relationship between suffering and sin (cf. the book of Job). R. Ammi (c. A.D. 300) said, "There is no death without sin, and there is no suffering without iniquity" (*b. Šabb.* 55a). Jesus, however, while acknowledging the possibility that suffering may be the direct result of sin (cf. 5:14), denies that such is invariably the case (cf. Luke 13:2–3a). Underlying the disciples' statement is the concern not to charge God with perpetrating evil on innocent people (cf. Ex. 20:5; Num. 14:18; Deut. 5:9). Regarding the possibility that the man's blindness from birth may be the result of prenatal sin, one may note Jewish speculation surrounding the struggle of Jacob and Esau in their mother Rebecca's womb.[273]

There are also several parallels regarding the possibility that the man's blindness was the result of his parents' sin prior to his birth. Some texts refer to a mother worshiping in a pagan temple during her pregnancy, with the fetus's "participation" in the pagan rite (*Song Rab.* 1.6.3; *Ruth Rab.* 6:4). An Aramaic Targum tells of parents who brought a rebellious boy to the elders saying, "We have transgressed the decree of the Memra [word] of the Lord: because of this, this son of ours, born to us, is stubborn and rebellious; a glutton with meat and a drunkard with wine" (*Tg. Ps.-J.* on Deut. 21:20). Other sayings speak of children being born epileptic or leprous on account of the sins of their parents. However, several Old Testament and intertestamental passages strongly challenge the notion that children suffer for their parents' sin (e.g., Jer. 31:29–30; Ezek. 18; cf. Tobit 3:3).

This happened so that the work of God might be displayed in his life (9:3). (Cf. 11:4.) "Work of God" is literally "works of God."[274] The thought here is that even evil ultimately contributes to the greater glory of God. An instance of this is the pharaoh of the Exodus.[275]

As long as it is day, we must do the work of him who sent me (9:4). Compare the statement attributed to R. Tarfon (c. A.D. 130): "The day is short and the task is great and the laborers are idle and the wage is abundant and the master of the house is urgent" (*m. ᵓAbot* 2:15). Note also the statement attributed to R. Simeon ben Eleazar (c. A.D. 190): "Work so long as you can and it is possible for you and it is still within your power" (*b. Šabb.* 151b).

Night is coming, when no one can work (9:4). This statement has the ring of common sense, if not a proverbial saying (cf., e.g., Rom. 13:12: "The night is nearly over; the day is almost here. So let us put aside the deeds of darkness and put on the armor of light"). Another proverb that takes the night symbolism in a different direction is found in Menander: "The night refreshes, the day brings forth work."[276] Apart from rare exceptions (such as shepherds, night watchmen, or special messengers), no one works in the dark. Here, of course, "night" also connotes the world's spiritual darkness apart from Jesus (cf. John 9:5).

While I am in the world (9:5). Jesus' announcement to his disciples that his earthly role will be limited in time is contrary to the popular notion that the Messiah and the messianic age will last forever (cf. 12:34).

I am the light of the world (9:5). See comments on 8:12.

He spit on the ground, made some mud with the saliva, and put it on the man's eyes (9:6). Jesus' use of saliva is reminiscent of the healing of the deaf and mute man in the Decapolis (Mark 7:33) and of the blind man in Bethsaida (8:23). According to some Jewish rabbis, the saliva of a firstborn has healing properties.[277] In the surrounding pagan culture, however, saliva was frequently associated with magical practices—most frequently cited is the healing of the blind soldier, Valerius Aper, apparently by Asclepius, in which an eye-salve was used[278]—so that many rabbis seem to have condemned the use of saliva.[279] John may here wish to stress Jesus' superiority over pagan healers such as the well-known god Asclepius.

Similar to people in other cultures, Palestinian Jews apparently believed that human excreta (including saliva) were forms of dirt rendering a person ceremonially unclean. Under certain conditions, however, that very "dirt" could become an instrument of blessing in the hands of authorized individuals. Thus blood and saliva generally pollute, but in certain contexts blood cleanses and saliva cures. In the Old Testament, saliva may convey ceremonial uncleanness (Lev. 15:8). If the reversal of this taboo also applies, then by using saliva to cure a man, Jesus claims to possess unusual spiritual authority (cf. Matt. 8:1–4).[280]

Wash in the Pool of Siloam (this word means Sent) (9:7). A connection with the previous chapters is established by the fact that the water for the water-pouring rites of the Feast of Tabernacles was drawn from the pool of Siloam (cf. *m. Sukkah* 4:9–10). In the Old Testament, Elisha does not heal Naaman immediately but sends him to wash in the Jordan (2 Kings 5:10–13).

Regarding the Pool of Siloam itself, Isaiah speaks of "the gently flowing waters of Shiloah" (Isa. 8:6; cf. Neh. 3:15). The existence of a "basin of the latrines of Siloam" is attested by a reference in the Copper Scroll of Qumran (3Q15 10:16). Josephus frequently refers to the Pool of Siloam.[281] A part of the major water system built by King Hezekiah, this rock-cut pool was located southwest of the City of David (excavated in 1880).[282] Its water was "sent" (hence its name) via Hezekiah's tunnel from the Gihon spring in the Kidron valley (cf. 2 Chron. 32:30). There is some debate as to whether it is to be identified with the "Lower" or "Old Pool" (Isa. 22:9, 11), the "Upper Pool" (cf. 2 Kings 18:17; Isa. 7:3; 36:2), or some other pool.[283]

As in other places, John translates Semitic words: Siloam "means Sent" (see comments on 1:38). The underlying Old Testament reference may be Genesis 49:10, which was interpreted messianically by both Jewish and Christian interpreters: "The scepter will not depart from Judah until Shiloh comes."[284] Rabbinic sources mention the pool as a place of purification.

Isn't this the same man who used to sit and beg? (9:8). Begging as a way of life was a common feature in first-century Palestine.[285] It was about the only way a blind person could make a living in that day. Beggars were "the truly poor," whose "hand-to-mouth existence was considered hardly worth living" (on the poor, see *m. Pe᾿ah* 8).[286] In Judaism, the giving of alms was considered to be of greater significance than all the commandments (*b. B. Bat.* 9a,b), constituting, together

POOL OF SILOAM

(left) The remains of the pool in Jerusalem.

(right) An artistic reconstruction of the first-century appearance of the pool.

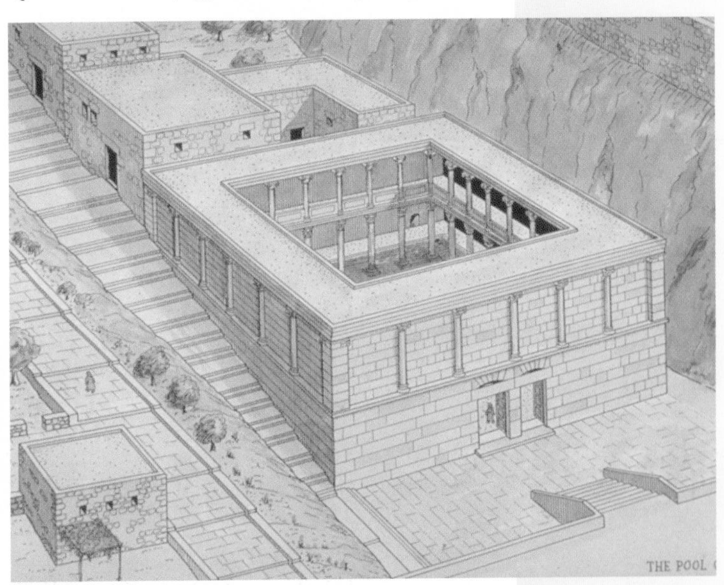

with the law and obedience, one of three pillars of the world (*m. ʾAbot* 1:2). Charitable deeds were viewed as a way to gain merit with God (*b. Šabb.* 151b; cf. Sir. 3:3–4; 35:1–2) and as protection against the devil (*Ex. Rab.* 31:1).

The Pharisees' First Interrogation of the Formerly Blind Man (9:13–17)

The day . . . was a Sabbath. . . . Some of the Pharisees said, "This man is not from God, for he does not keep the Sabbath" (9:14–16). According to the Pharisees, Jesus may have "broken" the Sabbath in the following ways: (1) Since he was not dealing with a life-or-death situation, Jesus should have waited until the next day to heal the man; (2) Jesus had kneaded the clay with his saliva to make mud, and kneading (dough, and by analogy clay) was included among the thirty-nine classes of work forbidden on the Sabbath (*m. Šabb.* 7:2; cf. 8:1; 24:3); (3) later Jewish tradition stipulated that it was not permitted to anoint eyes on the Sabbath, although opinion seems to have been divided. R. Yehudah (d. A.D. 299) said it was permissible to do so; R. Samuel declared it was not, but when his own eyes gave him trouble he asked the former if it was allowable, and Yehudah said it was so for others, but not for *him* (*b. ʿAbod. Zar.* 28b)!

Some of the Pharisees said, "This man is not from God, for he does not keep the Sabbath." But others asked, "How can a sinner do such miraculous signs?" So they were divided (9:16). The division apparent in this verse roughly follows the differing ways of reasoning followed by the schools of Shammai and Hillel. The former based its argument on foundational theological principles ("anyone who breaks the law is a sinner") while the latter argued from the established facts of the case ("Jesus has performed a good work").[287] Already in Old Testament times, the Israelites were warned against the appearance of a prophet or dreamer who would perform "a miraculous sign or wonder" to lead people astray (Deut. 13:1–5).

He is a prophet (9:17). The only notable miracle-working prophets were Elijah and Elisha (cf. 2 Kings 5:10–14). Another possible antecedent figure is Moses (Deut. 18:15, 18; 34:10–12).

The Pharisees' Interrogation of the Man's Parents (9:18–23)

The Jews . . . sent for the man's parents (9:18). On "the Jews," see "The 'Jews' in John's Gospel" at 5:10. The man's parents would be able to confirm whether or not he was actually born blind. It is possible that the man is staying under his parents' roof and spends his days begging in the temple courts.

Ask him. He is of age; he will speak for himself (9:21). "He is of age" probably means he is old enough to give legal testimony about himself, that is, at least thirteen. Beyond this, the man's age is not known. Alternatively, the phrase may indicate that the man is old enough to reason and answer the Pharisees' questions for himself.

His parents said this because they were afraid of the Jews, for already the Jews had decided that anyone who acknowledged that Jesus was the Christ would be put out of the synagogue (9:22). Confession of Jesus as Christ was the mark of the early Christians.[288] Expulsion from the assembly of the exiles is reported already in Ezra 10:8. Since the synagogue was the center not only of Jewish religious, but also of communal life, expulsion from it represented a severe form of social ostracism (as well as effectively barring a person from worshiping God in the company of his people).

The reference to expulsion from the synagogue is often considered to be anachronism, that is, a later practice (roughly sixty years later) being attributed back to this time. The discussion revolves around the liturgical Eighteen Benedictions, which were recited by all pious Jews three times a day.[289] The twelfth of these benedictions is believed to have been rewritten by Samuel the Lesser, a rabbi at the school at Jamnia (c. A.D. 85–90), in response to a request by R. Gamaliel II, leader of the school (cf. *b. Ber.* 28b). This revision, ironically called "the benediction of the heretics" (*birkat ha-minîm*), was supposedly prepared for the Sanhedrin that was reconstituted after the fall of Jerusalem in A.D. 70, in order to exclude Christian Jews from the synagogue by including in the liturgy a phrase no Christian could utter:

> *For the apostates let there be no hope,*
> *and let the arrogant government*
> *be speedily uprooted in our days.*
> *Let the Nazarenes [*noṣrim *= Christians?] and the Minim [heretics]*
> *be destroyed in a moment,*
> *and let them be blotted out of the book of life*
> *and not be inscribed together with the righteous.*

However, there are several questions regarding this reconstruction: (1) It is uncertain whether the twelfth benediction contained the term *noṣrim*.[290] (2) If it did, it is unclear whether this term meant "Christians." (3) Even if (1) and (2) are answered in the affirmative, this does not mean that a church-synagogue conflict around A.D. 90 was the exclusive or even primary factor behind John's references to synagogue expulsion. The historical background at the time of writing was considerably more complex, including the destruction of Jerusalem and the temple, rising Roman emperor worship, persecution of Christians, the threat of proto-Gnosticism, and other factors. (4) Even if John uses such terminology in order to reflect contemporary frictions, this does not mean that these references are anachronistic.[291]

The Pharisees' Second Interrogation of the Formerly Blind Man (9:24–34)

Give glory to God (9:24). This phrase constitutes a solemn exhortation to tell the truth and to make a confession, with the implication that the person so exhorted has done wrong.[292]

This man is a sinner (9:24). Especially the stricter rabbinic school of Shammai would infer that anyone who broke the Sabbath (and thus broke the law) was a sinner (see comments on 9:16).

"What did he do to you? How did he open your eyes?" . . . "I have told you already" (9:26–27). In Jewish jurisprudence, diligent cross-examination was considered vital in assessing the evidence: "The more a judge tests the evidence the more is he deserving of praise" (*m. Sanh.* 5:2).

Hurled insults (9:28). Pouring sarcasm was a common way of dealing with people of perceived lower status, which conveyed the notion that they were unworthy of receiving a direct answer.

We are disciples of Moses (9:28). There is some debate as to how common this self-designation was among the Jews of Jesus' day (cf., e.g., Matt. 23:2).[293] In *b. Yoma* 4a, it is applied to Pharisees as opposed to Sadducees. In *m. ʾAbot* 5:19, Jews are referred to as "the disciples of Abraham" while Christians are dismissed as "the disciples of Balaam the wicked" (i.e., Jesus!). The Pharisees indicate that they regard Moses, through whom God gave the law to Israel, as the paradigmatic teacher (often called "our teacher" by the rabbinate). "Those who call themselves his disciples consciously regard themselves as links in the chain which stretches back to Moses and at the beginning of which is the clear and unequivocal revelation to the will of God for the people through him."[294]

We know that God spoke to Moses (9:29). "The LORD would speak to Moses face to face, as a man speaks with his friend" (Ex. 33:11; cf. Num. 12:2–8). The Pharisees' comment harks back to the establishment of Israel as a nation through the giving of the Mosaic covenant at Sinai. However, according to the rabbis, this law consisted not merely of the written word (the Pentateuch) but also oral tradition passed on from generation to generation. Thus *m. ʾAbot* 1:1 states, "Moses received the [Oral] Law from Sinai and committed it to Joshua, and Joshua to the elders, and the elders to the Prophets; and the Prophets committed it to the men of the Great Synagogue."[295]

We know that God does not listen to sinners (9:31). Scripture clearly establishes a link between a person's righteousness and God's responsiveness to that person's prayer.[296] Later rabbis shuddered at the thought of God's listening to sinners. R. Akiba (c. A.D. 135) said, "God forbid that the Almighty should cause the sun to stand still at the behest of those who transgressed his will" (*b. Sanh.* 90a). Another rabbinic passage poses the rhetorical question, "Does the All-Merciful perform miracles for liars?" (*b. Ber.* 58a).[297]

He listens to the godly man who does his will (9:31). There is ample Old Testament substantiation for the cured man's contention. "The eyes of the LORD are on the righteous and his ears are attentive to their cry" (Ps. 34:15). "He fulfills the desires of those who fear him; he hears their cry and saves them" (Ps. 145:19). "The LORD is far from the wicked but he hears the prayer of the righteous" (Prov. 15:29). There are also rabbinic parallels: "If one is filled with the fear of God his words are listened to" (*b. Ber.* 6b; attributed to R. Ḥelbo [c. A.D. 300] in the name of R. Huna). "He who fulfills the will of God and prays with true earnestness is heard both in this world and also in that to come" (*Ex. Rab.* 21:3; cf. Isa. 65:24). The term *theosebēs* ("godly man"; only here in the New Testament) is occasionally used in Greek writings to mean "religious" or "pious."[298] It is also found in Josephus—with reference to David (*Ant.* 7.7.1 §130; 7.7.3 §153) and others (*Ant.* 12.6.3 §284; 14.12.3 §308; 20.9.11 §195; *Ag. Ap.* 2.14 §140)—and in Philo (*Names* 197), who likewise uses the expression in a broad sense to refer to a "God-fearing" person.

Nobody has ever heard of opening the eyes of a man born blind (9:32). Opening of the eyes of the blind is limited to unusual circumstances in the Old Testament (e.g., 2 Kings 6:8–23). Instances of blind persons being healed in Jewish tradition are extremely rare (Tobit 11:10–14; cf. 2:10). But the healing of *a man* *born blind* is without parallel. The phrase "nobody has ever heard" literally reads "not heard from of old" (i.e., from the world's beginning), a common Jewish expression in both the Old Testament and rabbinic literature (e.g., Isa. 64:4).[299]

You were steeped in sin at birth (9:34). The common rabbinic view of human nature implicitly denied universal human sinfulness by implying that people could act on their good impulses (*yeṣer*) and resist evil ones. Yet the reality of human sin is clearly taught in the Old Testament: "Surely I was sinful at birth, sinful from the time my mother conceived me" (Ps. 51:5). The apostle Paul establishes the same truth in his letter to the Romans (cf. Rom. 1–3, esp. 3:23; cf. 6:23). Thus the Pharisees are unduly self-righteous in linking the man's sinfulness from birth with his physical defect of blindness while failing to include themselves under the rubric "sinful from birth."

And they threw him out (9:34). This refers to the man's expulsion from the synagogue. The way in which this is carried out suggests an impulsive, impromptu decision rather than the culmination of a formal investigation issuing in a solemn act of excommunication. The Pharisees' prejudiced procedure of interrogating the blind man and his parents violates their own laws, which stipulate that witnesses are to be examined fairly and without prejudice (see comments on 5:31 and 9:26–27).

The Pharisees' Spiritual Blindness (9:35–41)

The blind will see and those who see will become blind (9:39). Both giving sight to the blind[300] and the blinding of those who see[301] are common Old Testament themes. Elsewhere, Jesus calls the Pharisees "blind guides" (Matt. 23:16; cf. 15:14; 23:26). The phrase "blind ones in heart" is found in an ancient papyrus (P. Oxy. 1.20–21). For the blinding effect of wickedness, see Wisdom of Solomon 2:21. In rabbinic Judaism this metaphorical usage is rare,[302] while Philo, under the influence of Greek philosophy, uses it frequently (e.g., *Agriculture* 81; *Heir* 48; *Spe. Laws* 4.189).

REFLECTIONS

FOR THE MAN BORN BLIND, THIS HEALING RESTORED his sight. "One thing I do know. I was blind but now I see!" But for John, the event also serves as a parable illustrating the condition of human blindness brought about by sin and spiritual pride. The Pharisees are quick to conclude that Jesus is a sinner because in their view he broke the Sabbath. But they are slow to find fault with themselves, haughtily claiming to be "disciples of Moses." "First take the plank out of your own eye," Jesus counseled, "and then you will see clearly to remove the speck from your brother's eye." If we fail to judge our own sin, we will see God do great things in the lives of those around us—but we ourselves will miss out.

The Shepherd and His Flock (10:1–21)

As winter (A.D. 32/33) approaches, the last winter prior to Jesus' crucifixion the following spring, Jesus talks about his relationship with his close followers. He portrays himself as the messianic shepherd and his disciples as "the sheep of his pasture" (Ps. 100:3; Ezek. 34:31). The Jewish leadership, on the other hand, proud claimants of Abrahamic heritage but spiritually blind, are not even among his "sheep."[303] Interestingly, a roughly contemporaneous passage, *2 Baruch* 77:11–16, portrays the law as a true shepherd (as well as light and water).

Thus, Jesus claims to fulfill the functions generally attributed to the law in his society.[304]

Enter the sheep pen by the gate (10:1). The sheep pen may have been a courtyard (cf. 18:15) near or bordering a house, surrounded by a stone wall and topped by briars, where one or several families kept their sheep. The gate, which probably could be locked, would have been guarded by a doorkeeper (cf. 10:3), who was hired to stand watch.[305]

Thief and a robber (10:1). The words "thief" and "robber" overlap in meaning and may reflect Semitic parallelism (cf. Obad. 5; Ep. Jer. 57), whereby "thief" may focus on the covert nature of entrance and "robber" on violence (cf. Luke 10:30, 36). Shepherds had to be on guard against either threat in order to avoid loss of sheep.

The man . . . is the shepherd of his sheep (10:2). The shepherd was the authorized caretaker of the flock. His task required dedication, courage, and vigilance. In Jesus' day, shepherds were regarded as vulgar and members of the lower class. This contrasts with the Old Testament designation of both God and his Messiah as shepherds.

The watchman opens the gate (10:3). On "the gate," see comments on 10:1. The watchman was an undershepherd who provided access to the flock. The existence of a watchman suggests that the pen in mind here is large enough to house several flocks and hence warrants the need of a doorkeeper.

The sheep listen to his voice (10:3). In the Old Testament, God communicated with his people preeminently through the Law (which spelled out God's moral expectations for his people) and the Prophets (who called people back to obedience to the law). People listened to God's voice by living in conformity with his revealed will. At the present time (from the perspective of the earthly Jesus), those who desire to follow God do so by listening to Jesus'

SHEPHERD AND HIS SHEEP

This was taken near Jericho.

words and by obeying his commandments (e.g., 15:10). In the future, God the Father (and Jesus) will speak to his own through the Spirit (16:13–15).

He calls his own sheep by name (10:3). Apparently, Palestinian shepherds used to give nicknames to some of their sheep.[306] Analogously, God in the Old Testament called some of his closest servants, as well as Israel as a whole, "by name" (e.g., Ex. 33:12, 17; Isa. 43:1). The shepherd's calling out of his own suggests the presence of more than one flock in the pen (see comments on John 10:3).

And leads them out. When he has brought out all his own (10:3–4). The wording is reminiscent of Old Testament passages such as Numbers 27:15–17 or Ezekiel 34:13. Jesus frequently uses sheep to illustrate people's helplessness and need for guidance. The leading out of sheep is a delicate task. It involves pushing the flock from the fold, where many of them are crowded, through the gate.

He goes on ahead of them (10:4). Western shepherds usually drive their sheep, often using a sheep dog. Their Near Eastern counterparts, on the other hand, both now and in Jesus' day, lead their flocks by beckoning them on with their voice. Often there is a helper watching the tail end of the flock.[307] Israel's exodus from Egypt is occasionally portrayed in terms of a flock being led by its shepherd.[308] Old Testament prophetic literature holds out similar visions of end-time deliverance for God's people (Mic. 2:12–13).

They will never follow a stranger; in fact, they will run away from him because they do not recognize a stranger's voice (10:5). In ancient times as well as today, sheep, while helpless and in need of guidance, are able to discern between their shepherd's voice and the call of strangers. This intimacy of a shepherd and his flock provides a beautiful illustration of the trust, familiarity, and bond existing between Jesus and his followers.

Jesus used this figure of speech, but they did not understand (10:6). The term "figure of speech" (*paroimia*) is roughly equivalent to the expression "parable" (*parabolē*). Both terms apparently render the broad Hebrew expression *mashal.* They occur side-by-side in several instances (e.g., Sir. 39:3; 47:17) and do not differ significantly in meaning.[309]

I am the gate for the sheep (10:7). The present verse begins to present an alternate scenario (continued through 10:18) to that portrayed in 10:1–5. "When the sheep were out on the hills in the warm season and did not return at night to the village at all, they were collected into sheep-folds on the hillside. These . . . were just open spaces enclosed by a wall. In them there was an opening by which the sheep came in and went out; but there was no door of any kind. What happened was that at night the shepherd himself lay down across the opening and no sheep could get out or in except over his body."[310] Jesus' words may hark back to messianic readings of passages such as Psalm 118:20, "This is the gate of the LORD through which the righteous may enter."

All who ever came before me were thieves and robbers (10:8). The Old Testament prophet Ezekiel refers to the "shepherds of Israel who only take care of themselves" but "do not take care of the flock" (Ezek. 34:2–4; see entire ch.). "All who ever came before me" hints at messianic pretenders who promise their followers freedom but instead lead them into armed conflict and doom. Jesus' statement also may have more overtly political overtones, evoking reminiscences of then-recent events in Jewish history, such as the Maccabean times when the high priests Jason and Menelaus betrayed their office and thus contributed to the desecration of the temple.

The spectrum of "thieves and robbers" may also encompass pseudoprophets, such as the ones mentioned by Luke and Josephus (cf. Acts 5:36–37; 21:38; see comments on John 7:12), the Zealots, and even the high-priestly circles that controlled Judaism in Jesus' day. Sadducees in particular were known to use temple religion for their own profit, and elsewhere both the Pharisees (Luke 16:14) and the teachers of the law (Mark 12:40) are denounced for their greed. Perhaps the closest connection in the present context is with the Pharisees, whose attitude toward the man born blind exemplifies a blatant usurpation of religious authority and a perversion of godly leadership (cf. John 9).

I am the gate; whoever enters through me will be saved (10:9). As attested in Greek literature since Homer, people in ancient times frequently thought of entering heaven by a gate. Jesus' claim to be "the door" resonates with this kind of thinking (cf. 1:51). The notion of a "gate to heaven" appears also in Jewish sources, both in the Old Testament and apocalyptic literature.[311] In the latter, the visionary receives a glimpse of the eternal truth of heaven, which is the source of final salvation (cf. Rev. 4:1). Apart from providing access to angels, the doors of heaven are the means by which knowledge and salvation are made known (e.g., *Odes Sol.* 17:6–11; 42:15–18; after A.D. 100). The Synoptics and Acts refer to "entering" God's kingdom as through a door or gate.[312]

SHEEPFOLD

A sheepfold and doorway in the area of Michmash pass in Benjamin.

He will come in and go out (10:9). Jesus' language (a Semitism) here echoes covenant terminology, especially Deuteronomic blessings for obedience (cf. Deut. 28:6; cf. Ps. 121:8). It is also reminiscent of Moses' description of Joshua (LXX: *Iēsous,* Jesus), who led Israel into the Promised Land: "May the LORD . . . appoint a man over this community to go out and come in before them, one who will lead them out and bring them in, so the LORD's people will not be like sheep without a shepherd" (Num. 27:16–17).

Find pasture (10:9). "Find pasture" is a common Old Testament expression (e.g., 1 Chron. 4:40). The psalmist basked in the assurance of God's provision (Ps. 23:2). The imagery is also found in Old Testament references to Israel's final restoration (Isa. 49:9–10) and deliverance from the nations (Ezek. 34:12–15).

Steal and kill and destroy (10:10). Threefold repetition of parallel expressions (positive or negative) is a device denoting emphasis in biblical literature (e.g., Matt. 7:7). The word for "kill" (*thyō*) is not the common term and may connote the abuse of the sacrificial system by the priestly authorities.

Have life, and have it to the full (10:10). On "life," see comments on 1:4. "Have life" means "to have eternal life," that is, "to be saved." But this does not merely entail participation in the age to come (as was the general view among Jews). According to John, Jesus gives a full life already in the here and now (which does not imply the absence of persecution, cf. 15:18–25). In the Old Testament, it is especially the prophet Ezekiel who envisions pasture and abundant life for God's people (cf. 34:12–15, 25–31).

I am the good shepherd (10:11). God is portrayed as the shepherd of his flock in numerous Old Testament passages.[313] The people of Israel, in turn, are described as "the sheep of his pasture."[314] God as the true shepherd is also contrasted with unfaithful shepherds, who are subject to divine judgment.[315] David (or the Davidic Messiah) is spoken of frequently as a (good) shepherd.[316] Moses, likewise, is portrayed as the "shepherd of his flock."[317] Philo speaks of a "good [*agathos*] shepherd" (*Agriculture* 44, 49) and applies shepherd terminology not only to kings and wise men but also to both God and his firstborn Son or Word (*Agriculture* 50–54; *Posterity* 67–68). In non-Jewish circles, too, gods and great men were described as shepherds.[318]

The good shepherd lays down his life for the sheep (10:11). Young David, first shepherd, then king, literally risked his life for his sheep (1 Sam. 17:34–37; cf. Sir. 47:3). Several Old Testament passages hint at the Messiah's self-sacrifice (Isa. 53:12; Zech. 12:10; 13:7–9).

The hired hand is not the shepherd . . . when he sees the wolf coming, he abandons the sheep and runs away. Then the wolf attacks the flock and scatters it. The man runs away because he is a hired hand and cares nothing for the sheep (10:12–13). Both Old Testament and later Jewish literature are replete with references to leaders who fail to perform their God-given responsibilities and as a result render their charge vulnerable to attack.[319] Shockingly, the shepherds themselves have turned into wolves (Ezek. 22:27). The "hired hands" of Israel (whose function is temporary) are contrasted with those who hold a permanent shepherding office: God and his Messiah, whose role is patterned after God's "good shepherd" par excellence, David (1 Sam. 17:34–36). The figure of the hired hand who abandons his sheep in times of adversity was well known in Jesus' day. As one intertestamental passage (c. A.D. 100) reads, "Do not forsake us, like a shepherd who leaves his flock in the power of savage wolves" (*4 Ezra* 5:18).

According to Old Testament legislation, the hired hand was not required to make restitution for an animal torn to pieces by a wild beast (Ex. 22:13). Later mishnaic law stipulated that if one wolf attacked the flock, the hireling must protect it. However, if two wolves threatened the sheep, no blame was attached to the hired man for any damage caused to the sheep (*m. B. Meṣiʿa* 7:8–9).[320] In Jesus' illustration, the "hired hand" is contrasted with "thieves and robbers" (John 10:1, 8, 10). While the latter are thoroughly wicked, the "hired hand" merely proves to be more committed to his own safety than to the sheep entrusted to his care. Under normal circumstances, he is willing to shepherd the flock for pay. In the face of danger, however, he puts self-interest first. Later in the Gospel, Jesus predicts that his disciples will be scattered (16:32). Elsewhere, Jesus sends his disciples out "as sheep among wolves" (Matt. 10:16; Luke 10:3). Paul likewise predicts that "savage wolves" will attack the Ephesian flock soon after his departure (Acts 20:29).

I know my sheep and my sheep know me . . . the Father knows me and I know the Father (10:14–15). Jesus' relationship with his followers ("know") is portrayed as an intimate, trusting relationship, in which Jesus, the good shepherd, cares deeply for those in his charge. This relationship is patterned after God's relationship with Old Testament Israel.[321] The saying "I know my sheep and my sheep know me" has a proverbial ring to it. Boring cites a Greek parallel, "I know Simon and Simon knows me."[322]

I have other sheep that are not of this sheep pen. I must bring them also (10:16). In light of Old Testament expectations of the incorporation of the Gentiles among God's people, the "other sheep that are not of this sheep pen" are probably Gentiles (see esp. Isa. 56:8).

REFLECTIONS

MANY, IF NOT MOST, HUMAN LEADERS LEAD OUT OF self-interest. They may project concern for those they lead, but when push comes to shove, it becomes clear that they only use others to accomplish their own ends. Tragically, this was the case with Israel's leaders for much of the nation's history. Even in Jesus' day, the Jewish religious leadership resembled "thieves and robbers" more than a "good shepherd." And what about church leaders today? Are our churches pastored by selfless, sacrificial servants or self-aggrandizing individuals who pursue their own agendas and ambitions under the guise of a religious office?

There shall be one flock and one shepherd (10:16). The notion of one flock being led by one shepherd as a metaphor for God's providential care for his united people is firmly rooted in Old Testament prophetic literature[323] and continued in later Jewish writings.[324] Yet while the Old Testament envisions primarily the gathering of the dispersed sheep of Israel, the present passage talks about the bringing together of Jews and Gentiles into one messianic community (cf. Eph. 2:11–22; 4:3–6).

In the Hellenistic world, likewise, leaders were prized who promoted unity. Thus Plutarch (A.D. 45–125) describes the primary principle underlying the philosophy of Zeno, founder of the Stoics, as follows: "that all the inhabitants of this world of ours should not live differentiated by their respective rules of justice into separate cities and communities, but that we should consider all men to be of one community and one polity, and that we should have a common life and an order common to us all, even as a herd that feeds together and shares the pasturage of a common field" (*De Alex.* 6).[325]

This command I received (10:18). Jesus here invokes covenantal language, relating his relationship with his disciples to the relationship between God and Israel in the Old Testament.[326]

Demon-possessed and raving mad (10:20). See 7:20; 8:48, 52. It appears that in ancient times insanity and demon-possession were frequently linked. See also a partial parallel in intertestamental literature, where the life of the righteous is considered madness (*mania*) by the unrighteous (Wisd. Sol. 5:4). The Sibyl likewise defends herself against the charge of madness: "Some will say that I am Sibylla born of Circe [a magic-working goddess] as mother and Gnostos as father, a crazy liar. But when everything comes to pass, then you will remember me and no longer will anyone say that I am crazy, I who am a prophetess of the great God" (*Sib. Or.* 3:814–18; c. 150 B.C.).

Can a demon open the eyes of the blind? (10:21). See John 9. The psalmist says that it is the Lord who gives sight to the blind (Ps. 146:8; cf. Ex. 4:11).

The Unbelief of the Jews (10:22–42)

Unlike Tabernacles and the other two major annual feasts celebrated in Jerusalem, the Feast of Dedication—with its festive lamps—was joyously commemorated in Jewish homes as well as in the temple. The feast fell near the time of the winter equinox (second half of December). A popular family celebration, it provided a stark contrast with the pagan Saturnalia, which were celebrated during the same period. Since there is no mention that Jesus went up to Jerusalem for the Feast of Dedication, it is possible that he spent the time from Tabernacles to Dedication (about two months) in Jerusalem. Alternatively, Jesus and his followers may have returned to Galilee subsequent to the Feast of Tabernacles only to embark on what turned out to be Jesus' final journey to Jerusalem (Matt. 19:1; Mark 10:1; Luke 9:51).[327]

The Feast of Dedication (10:22). This is the first reference to this feast by this name (*ta enkainia*) in Jewish literature.[328] The eight-day Feast of Dedication (also called *Ḥanukkah* or the Feast of Lights, *phōta*) celebrated the rededication of the temple in December, 164 B.C. The temple had been desecrated in 167 B.C. when the Seleucid ruler Antiochus IV Epiphanes offered a sacrifice to Zeus on a pagan altar (called "the abomination of desolation"[329]). A revolt started by the Jewish priest Mattathias issued in the miraculous defeat of Antiochus's troops through Mattathias's son Judas in 164 B.C. (1 Macc. 2:1–4:35), inaugurating a period of Jewish independence that lasted until 63 B.C., when the Roman general Pompey conquered Palestine. Judas immediately tore down "the abomination of desolation" and refurbished the temple (1 Macc. 4:36–51; cf. 2 Macc. 10:1–4). The temple was rededicated on the 25th of Chislev (Dec. 14), 164 B.C., three years after its desecration.[330]

There are similarities between the accounts of the Feast of Dedication, called "the festival of booths in the month of Chislev" (2 Macc. 1:9 [c. 124 B.C.]; cf. 10:6), and the Feast of Tabernacles (Lev. 23:42–43). Its association with the biblical Feast of Tabernacles lent Dedication a certain amount of scriptural legitimacy. Both festivals celebrated God's protection of Israel during her wanderings in the desert. Beyond this, the Feast of Dedication also commemorated God's intervention in the restoration of the temple, the apostasy among the Jews that had led to the temple's desecration, and the Jews' regaining of their religious (and national) freedom. As Josephus writes, "And from that time to the present we observe this festival, which we call the festival of Lights, giving this name to it, I think, from the fact that the right to worship appeared to us at a time when we hardly dared hope for it" (*Ant.* 12.7.7 §325; cf. 12.7.6–7 §§316–24).[331]

It was winter, and Jesus was in the temple area walking in Solomon's Colonnade (10:22–23). Probably owing to the cold winter weather (in A.D. 32, the Feast of Dedication fell on December 18), Jesus taught not in an open court but in the temple area called Solomon's Colonnade which, being about two hundred yards long,[332] offered protection from the raw east wind and was located on the east side of the temple (Josephus, *J.W.* 5.5.1 §§184–85; *Ant.* 15.11.3 §§396–401; 20.10.7 §§220–21). Solomon's Colonnade, which was commonly (but erroneously) thought to date back to Solomon's time and which in fact derived from the pre-Herodian Hasmonean period, formed part of a magnificent covered structure that surrounded the outermost court of the temple on all sides. It later became the gathering place for the early Jerusalem church (cf. Acts 3:11; 5:12).

If you are the Christ, tell us plainly (10:24). Owing to the political connotations of the term "Messiah" in first-century Palestine, Jesus avoided using the expression with reference to himself (cf. 6:14–15; 11:48). Similarly, Luke 22:67: "If you are the Christ, tell us."

No one can snatch them out of my hand (10:28). "Snatch" connotes the use of force (see comments on "robbers" in 10:1 and 8, above). The present assertion contrasts with the figure of the hireling, who abandons the flock in the face of danger (cf. 10:12–13). See also the references to the "hands" of the prophet and of God in Ezekiel 37:15–19, and the following note.

My Father . . . is greater than all; no one can snatch them out of my Father's hand (10:29). Jesus' reference to the Father's sovereign power recalls statements in both Old Testament and Jewish intertestamental literature that no one can deliver out of God's hand (Isa. 43:13) and that the souls of the righteous are in his hand (Wisd. Sol. 3:1).

I and the Father are one (10:30). This echoes the basic confession of Judaism: "Hear, O Israel: The LORD our God, the LORD is one" (Deut. 6:4). For Jesus to be one with the Father yet distinct from him amounts to a claim to deity (cf. John 1:1– 2). This challenged narrow Jewish

SOLOMON'S COLONNADE

A model of "Solomon's Colonnade"—a magnificent portico that surrounded the outermost court of the temple.

notions of monotheism, even though there are already hints in the Old Testament of a plurality within the Godhead.

The Jews picked up stones to stone him (10:31). See 5:18; 8:59. Stoning was to be carried out on the basis of a judicial sentence rather than as impulsive act of mob violence. But because the Roman authorities retained sole jurisdiction over capital punishment (cf. 18:31), and because large crowds could quickly turn volatile, especially in an oppressed nation replete with nationalistic fervor and religious fanaticism, lynching always remained a possible outcome (cf. Acts 7:54–60). In certain cases, Jewish law actually seems to have encouraged such a procedure (*m. Mak.* 3:2). In light of the relationship between the Feast of Dedication and the consecration of the temple and John's portrayal of Jesus as the temple's replacement (John 2:19–21), the Jews' attempt to stone Jesus for blasphemy is in fact presented by the evangelist as an effort on the Jews' part to blaspheme the "holy sanctuary of God," Jesus—and that at the Feast commemorating the rededication of the temple![333]

But for blasphemy, because you, a mere man, claim to be God (10:33). Later Jewish law limited blasphemy to pronouncing the name of God, the tetragrammaton ("Yahweh"): "'The blasphemer' is not culpable unless he pronounces the Name itself" (*m. Sanh.* 7:5; cf. 6:4); this Jesus is never recorded as doing. However, it is unlikely that the Sadducees—who controlled legal proceedings in the Sanhedrin, the highest Jewish court—ever adopted so narrow a definition of blasphemy in Jesus' day. Rather, a broader interpretation of blasphemy prevailed, based on passages such as Numbers 15:30–31 ("anyone who sins defiantly . . . blasphemes the LORD") or Deuteronomy 21:22 ("guilty of a capital offense"). See also Mark 14:61–64.[334]

Is it not written in your Law, "I have said you are gods"? If he called them "gods," to whom the word of God came . . . (10:34–35). The passage quoted is Psalm 82:6.[335] In the Old Testament, the phrase "to whom the word of God came" is often used with reference to those who speak or act in God's name. The phrase "the word of the LORD that came" is found at the opening of the prophetic books of Hosea, Joel, Micah, and Zephaniah (see also Luke 3:2). In the original context, the expression may have referred to: (1) Israel's corrupt judges, who were called "gods" because the administration of justice was a divine prerogative delegated to a few select individuals (Deut. 1:17; cf. Ps. 82:1–4); (2) angelic powers who abused the authority God had given to them over the nations (unlikely in light of the scarcity of references to angels in John); (3) Israel at the time of the giving of the law.[336] Arguing, in typical rabbinic fashion, from the lesser to the greater (see comments on John 5:47), Jesus' point here is that if Israel can in some sense be called "god" in the Scriptures, how much more is this designation appropriate for him who truly is the Son of God.[337]

The Scripture cannot be broken (10:35). Jesus' statement is evidence for his belief in the inviolability of God's written word (in the present instance, the Hebrew Scriptures). Elsewhere, Jesus contends that "until heaven and earth disappear, not the smallest letter, not the least stroke of a pen, will by any means disappear from the Law until everything is accomplished"

(Matt. 5:18). Paul and Peter concurred (2 Tim. 3:16; 2 Peter 1:20–21).

The one whom the Father set apart as his very own and sent into the world (10:36). In the Old Testament and intertestamental literature, the term "set apart" was used for those appointed to fulfill an important task or office, be it Moses the lawgiver (Sir. 45:4), Jeremiah the prophet (Jer. 1:5), or the Aaronic priests.[338] In the LXX, variants of the term *ta egkainia* ("Dedication," 10:22) refer to the dedication of the tabernacle altar (Num. 7:10–11), Solomon's temple (1 Kings 8:63), and the second temple (Ezra 6:16–17). Just as Jesus replaces the Sabbath (John 5, 9), the manna (ch. 6), and the light and water at the Feast of Tabernacles (chs. 7–9), so his reference to his own setting apart recalls the event behind the celebration of the Feast of Dedication: the consecration of the altar that replaced "the abomination of desolation" erected by Antiochus IV Epiphanes.

Believe the miracles (10:38). Old Testament figures recognized for performing unusual works were Elisha (who was given the key to the womb and enabled a barren woman to conceive), Elijah (who was given the key to the rain in answer to prayer), and both prophets together with Ezekiel (who were given the key to the graves and who raised the dead), all three works usually being reserved for God's direct intervention (*Midr. Ps.* 78 §5).[339]

The Father is in me, and I in the Father (10:38). Some have seen a parallel to Jesus' assertion of oneness with God in Antiochus Epiphanes's boast that he was "God Manifest" (the meaning of the Greek epithet "Epiphanes"). This claim made by Antiochus may also lie behind the Jews' charge that Jesus (like the Seleucid ruler, see 2 Macc. 9:28) was a blasphemer (cf. John 10:33, 36).[340]

Jesus went back across the Jordan to the place where John had been baptizing in the early days (10:40). See comments on 1:28. This probably refers to the region of Batanea in the tetrarchy of Philip in the northeast, a safe distance from the jurisdiction of the Jerusalem leaders. Notably, Jesus does not return to Galilee, his ministry there having come to a close (as far as the fourth evangelist is concerned) with the events of chapter 6.

John never performed a miraculous sign (10:41). Jewish sources do not praise putatively great men unless some miracle is attributed to them.[341] The Synoptic writers likewise never attribute miracles to John the Baptist, though Herod reportedly thought Jesus—who *did* perform miracles—was John the Baptist come back to life (Mark 6:14).

Jesus Learns of Lazarus's Death (11:1–16)

With the Feast of Dedication past (the year is now A.D. 33) and the threat to Jesus' life in Jerusalem and vicinity becoming increasingly severe, Jesus withdraws to the place where John had baptized in the early days of his ministry. (John had long been cast into prison and subsequently been killed.) One more great climactic miracle is about to follow, the seventh and final Johannine sign, which anticipates Jesus' own resurrection.

Now a man named Lazarus (11:1). "Now a [certain] man . . . was" recalls the similar introduction in 5:5 (cf. 1 Sam.

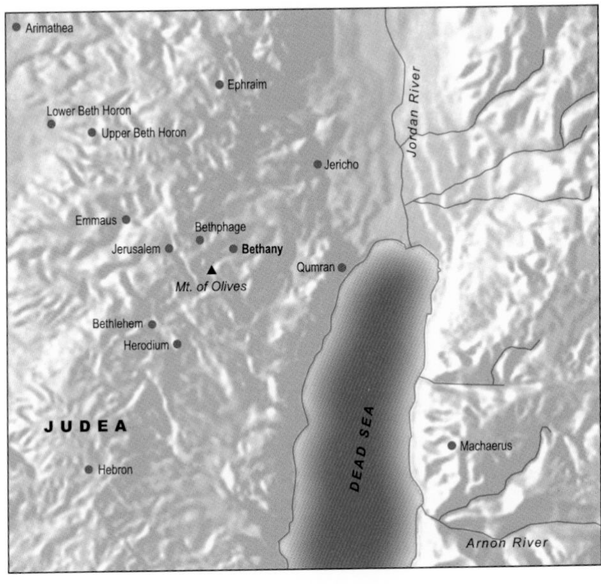

◀ left

JUDEA

Bethany was a village two miles east of Jerusalem.

1:1; Job 1:1). Lazarus is a shortened form of Eleazar (Heb. *El'azar*, "whom God helps," "whose help is God"). This was the name of the third son and successor of Aaron, whose descendants were the high priests of the house of Zadok. Ossuary inscriptions show that the name Eleazar was common in New Testament times.

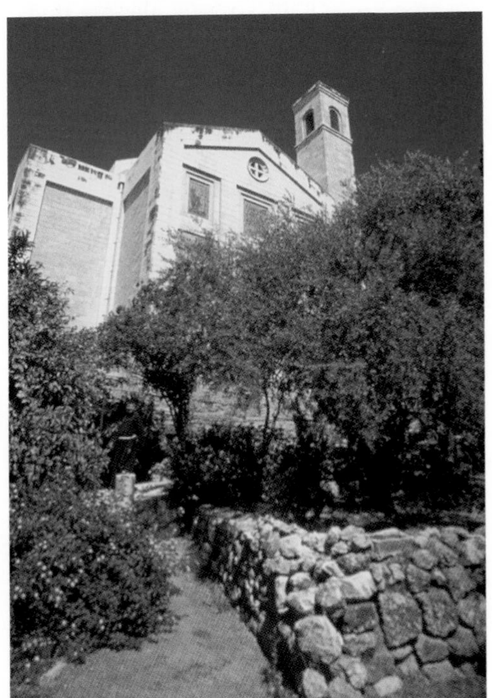

◀ left

BETHANY

The site of the village of ancient Bethany.

He was from Bethany, the village (11:1). The present Bethany (not previously mentioned in John's Gospel) must be distinguished from the Bethany featured in 1:28 and 10:40–42.[342] The village referred to here was situated east of the Mount of Olives, less than two miles from Jerusalem on the road to Jericho. This Bethany is mentioned elsewhere (together with Bethphage) as the place where Jesus stayed when visiting Jerusalem (Matt. 21:17; 26:6 par.). It is probably to be identified with the village of Ananyah mentioned in Nehemiah 11:32.[343] Today the town is called El-'Azariyeh in commemoration of Lazarus. The term "village" (*kōmē*) is elsewhere in John applied only to Bethlehem (John 7:42).

Mary and her sister Martha (11:1). Apparently, Martha was the older of the two sisters, since she acts as the hostess in the Lukan passage (cf. 12:2). Note also that she is named first in 11:5 below ("Martha and her sister"). The names Mary, Martha, and Lazarus were discovered in ossuary inscriptions in a tomb near Bethany in 1873.[344] Mary was a common name, the Greek form of the Hebrew Miriam. Martha was an Aramaic name, meaning "lady," feminine of *mar*, "Lord." The fact that of the three names in this family, one is Hebrew (Lazarus), one Aramaic (Martha), and one Greek (Mary), is typical of the end of the second temple period and attests to the way in which cultures interpenetrated each other. See comments on Luke 10:38–42.

He stayed where he was two more days (11:6). If the place where Jesus is staying when the news of Lazarus's illness reaches him is the region of Batanea, located approximately a hundred miles to the north-east of Jerusalem (see comments on 1:28; cf. 10:40–42), the following reconstruction of the events surrounding the raising of Lazarus best fits the evidence. Apparently, Lazarus is still alive when the initial news regarding his illness reaches Jesus (11:4). Two days later, Jesus, presumably by means of supernatural insight, announces to his followers that Lazarus has died, taking this as the divine signal to depart for Bethany.[345] If a person traveled an average of twenty to thirty miles a day on foot, it would take four days for Jesus to get to the scene (11:17).

Are there not twelve hours of daylight? (11:9). Similarly, *b. Sanh.* 38b: "R. Yoḥanan [Aḥa] b. Ḥanina (c. A.D. 300) said: 'The day consisted of twelve hours.'" Both Romans and Jews divided the day into twelve "hour" periods. Since the length of daylight extended, according to season, from ten to fourteen hours a day, the twelve "hours" of daylight varied accordingly. Most people did their work as long as there was daylight; once darkness came, it was time to stop working.

He has no light (11:10). The Greek adds the phrase "in him" (not represented in the NIV). This indicates a shift from the realm of nature (daylight) to symbolic language ("light" inside a person; cf. Matt. 6:23; par. Luke 11:35). In Semitic thought, the eye was regarded as light in a person's body. From there it is only a small step to the notion that a person is connected with the divine world of light. The shift in the image from *walking in* the light to light *being in a person* is also attested in the Qumran texts: "through your glory, my light becomes visible, for from darkness you make my light shine" (1QH 17:26–27). A similar statement appears in the *Gospel of Thomas*: "There is light within a man of light, and he lights up the whole world. If he does not shine, he is darkness" (*Gos. Thom.* 24). A possible Old Testament parallel is Jeremiah 13:16.

Lazarus has fallen asleep (11:11). The equivalent Old Testament phrase (esp. in the books of Kings and Chronicles) is he or she "slept with his [or her] fathers" (i.e., the person died), suggesting falling into an irrevocable sleep (cf. Job 14:11–12). Occasionally death is considered to be a sleep from which people will one day be awakened (Dan. 12:2; cf. *4 Ezra* 7:31–32).[346]

Thomas (called Didymus) (11:16). The name Thomas (both Heb. *tᵓōm* and Aram. *tᵓōmam* mean "twin") is not attested in literature prior to John's Gospel. However, the Greek term *didymos* (which also means "twin") is known also to have served as a proper name. It is therefore likely that Thomas was a genuine Greek name patterned after its Hebrew or Aramaic equivalents.[347]

Jesus Comforts Lazarus's Sisters (11:17–37)

By coming to console Martha and Mary after their brother's death, Jesus fulfills one of the most essential obligations in the Jewish culture of his day. The presence of a well-known teacher who has traveled a long distance would be particularly comforting to Lazarus's sisters. Yet, ultimately, Jesus has much greater things in mind (cf. 11:4, 15).

Lazarus had already been in the tomb for four days (11:17). Later Jewish sources attest the rabbinic belief that death was irrevocable three days after a person had died. "R. Abba b. R. Pappai and R. Joshua of Siknin said in the name of R. Levi (after A.D. 250): 'For three days [after death] the soul hovers over the body, intending to re-enter it, but as soon as it sees its appearance change, it departs' . . . Bar Kdappara said: 'The full force of mourning lasts for three days. Why? Because [for that length of time] the shape of the face is recognizable'" (*Lev. Rab.* 18:1 on Lev. 15:1; cf. *Eccl. Rab.* 12:6).

Burial usually followed shortly after death, as in the case of Ananias and Sapphira (Acts 5:6, 10). This is presupposed by the mishnaic stipulation that "evidence [of the identity of a corpse] may be given only during the first three days [after death]" (*m. Yebam.* 16:3) and the belief that one should visit a burial place of one newly buried for three days to ensure that the person was really dead. In the classic rabbinic text on death and mourning we read, "We go out to the cemetery and examine the dead within three days. . . . It once happened that [a man who was buried] was examined [and found to be living], and he lived for twenty-five years and then died. Another [so examined lived and] begat five children before he died" (*Sem.* 8 Rule 1).[348]

Bethany was less than two miles from Jerusalem, and many Jews had come . . . to comfort them (11:18–19). The original wording specifies that Bethany was fifteen *stadia* from Jerusalem. Since one *stadion* was approximately 200 yards, fifteen *stadia* equal about 3000 yards or just over 1.7 miles. It may be inferred that the "many Jews" who came to comfort Martha and Mary were from Jerusalem. If so, the family enjoyed considerable social standing, for although comforting the bereaved was generally regarded as a religious duty, not every villager would have been consoled by "many Jews" from a nearby city.[349]

Since burial in ancient Palestine took place on the day of death, mourning for the passing of a loved one followed burial. In Jesus' time, men and women walked separately in the funeral procession, and after the burial the women returned from the grave alone to begin a thirty-day mourning period. This included frequent expressions of loud wailing and other dramatic displays of grief.[350] The Talmud prescribes seven days of deep and thirty days of light

TOMB OF LAZARUS

mourning: "Three days for weeping and seven for lamenting and thirty [to refrain] from cutting the hair and [donning] pressed clothes" (*b. Mo'ed Qaṭ.* 27b).

Mary stayed at home (11:20). The Greek reads, "she was seated in the house." It was customary for those mourning the loss of a loved one to be seated when receiving the condolences of their friends (Job 2:8, 13; Ezek. 8:14; cf. *Ruth Rab.* 2:14). A sitting posture was also common for mourners in ancient Rome, being adopted, for example, by Cato when learning of the defeat at Pharsalus (Plutarch, *Cato Minor* 56.4). John's characterization of Mary and Martha agrees with Luke's Gospel, where Mary sits at Jesus' feet while Martha is busy with her household duties (cf. Luke 10:38–42).[351]

"Your brother will rise again." . . . "I know he will rise again in the resurrection at the last day" (11:23–24). Martha's affirmation of end-time resurrection is in keeping with Jesus' own teaching (cf. 6:39–44, 54), which in turn coheres with Pharisaic beliefs (cf. Acts 23:8; Josephus, *J.W.* 2.8.14 §163) and those of the majority of first-century Jews.[352] The Sadducees (as well as the Samaritans), flatly denied such a view.[353]

The resurrection of the dead was the subject of lively debate between the Pharisees and their opponents: "Sectarians [*minim*] asked Rabban Gamaliel [II; c. A.D. 90]: Whence do we know that the Holy One, blessed be He, will resurrect the dead? He answered them from the Torah, the Prophets, and the Hagiographa [i.e., the Writings], yet they did not accept it" (*b. Sanh.* 90b, referring to Deut. 31:16; Isa. 26:19; Song 7:9). Other mishnaic passages likewise denounce those who refuse to affirm the resurrection of the dead: "And these are they that have no share in the world to come: he that says there is no resurrection of the dead prescribed in the Law . . ." (*m. Sanh.* 10:1; cf. *m. Ber.* 9:5).

Belief in the resurrection is also evident from the second of the Eighteen Benedictions: "Lord, you are almighty forever, who makes the dead alive. . . . Blessed are you, Lord, who makes the dead alive" (cf. *m. Ber.* 5:2; *m. Soṭah* 9:15).[354] The old idea of Jewish corporate personality, where one continued to exist only in the lives of one's descendants, hardly provided satisfactory hope for many pious Jews in Jesus' day.[355]

The Christ, the Son of God, who was to come into the world (11:27). For "the Christ," see comments on 1:41. For "Son of God," see comments on 1:34 and 1:49. "[He] who was to come into the world" takes up the messianic expression derived from Psalm 118:26, which is applied to Jesus by others in the Gospels (see esp. Matt. 11:3 par.; John 12:13 par.).

The Teacher (11:28). "The teacher" was a natural way of referring to Jesus for any disciple in the pre-resurrection period. The fact that this term is here used by a woman (talking to another woman) is significant. While contemporary rabbis regularly refused to instruct women, Jesus took a radically different approach.

Supposing she was going to the tomb to mourn there (11:31). Literally, "to weep." In keeping with Jewish custom, Mary is expected to give way to her grief and weep at the tomb.[356]

The Jews who had come along with her also weeping (11:33). According to Jewish funeral custom, even a poor family was expected to hire at least two flute players and a professional wailing woman (*m. Ketub.* 4:4; attributed to R. Judah, c. A.D. 150), and Mary and Martha's family was anything but poor (cf. 12:1–3). The present heart-breaking scene would have been preceded by a formal funeral procession including burial, in which wailing women and flute-players as well as shouts of grief from the men in the procession punctuated laments sung in the house of death, on the way to the tomb, and during the burial itself (cf. Matt. 9:23 par.).[357]

Deeply moved in spirit and troubled (11:33). "Deeply moved" (NIV) hardly does justice to the underlying Greek word *embrimaomai*, which has the connotation of anger and snorting (in animals). The term occurs twice in the LXX (as verb or noun), both in the context of the venting of fierce anger (Dan. 11:30; Lam. 2:6). Thus, Jesus is shown here not merely to express empathy and grief but to be positively upset, even angry, in the face of the human suffering resulting from death (cf. John 12:27; 13:21). "Troubled" (*tarassō*) has connotations of being agitated and stirred up inside (cf. Est. 4:4: "in great distress"), like the waters of Bethesda (John 5:7) or the waves and breakers of a waterfall (Ps. 42:5–7). Being in anguish is an experience frequently described by David in his psalms.[358]

Jesus wept (11:35). The expression *dakryō* (only here in the New Testament) occurs occasionally in the LXX.[359] Owing to the force of the verb tense in the Greek original (an ingressive aorist), "Jesus burst into tears" would be a better translation. This is suggested by comparison with instances of *dakryō* in the same grammatical form in Greco-Roman and Hellenistic Jewish literature, where the term is regularly rendered this way.[360]

THE RAISING OF LAZARUS

A Roman catacomb fresco depicting the raising of Lazarus.

The Raising of Lazarus (11:38–44)

Old Testament instances of raisings of the dead include Elijah's raising of the widow's son (1 Kings 17:17–24), Elisha's raising of the son of the Shunammite woman (2 Kings 4:32–37), Elisha's "posthumous" raising of a dead man (2 Kings 13:21), and the witch of Endor's illicit bringing of Samuel out of the grave at King Saul's request (1 Sam. 28; see also Ezekiel's vision of the valley of dry bones in Ezek. 37:1–14). Raisings of the dead were generally viewed in light of the final resurrection and as an expression of God's power to bring it about.

The tomb. It was a cave with a stone laid across the entrance (11:38). "Archaeological surveys in the vicinity of Jerusalem have given us a clear idea of a well-to-do family tomb from the time of Jesus. Scores of such tombs have been found in the slopes of the valleys to the east and south of Jerusalem. . . . As the making of a tomb-cave required a vertical rock-face for the entrance, the sites chosen were often disused quarries. . . . The cave cut out of the rock usually consisted of a main hall, with a smaller vestibule. The bodies of the deceased were laid in a pit in the hall for the first year, till only the bones remained. Afterwards these were collected and placed in small stone boxes, the ossuaries. These miniature coffins were then placed in *loculi* (horizontal niches cut into the rock). The caves were closed by a stone door; for additional security a rolling stone was sometimes provided."[361]

Though the shaft of the cave could have been vertical or horizontal, from the way Lazarus came out as well as from archaeological evidence and mishnaic regulations, it would appear that the cave was horizontal. The burial place was outside the village in order for the living not to contract ritual impurity from contact with the corpse. There is ample Jewish evidence for the use of natural caves for burial, which were further prepared by artificial means (*m. B. Bat.* 6:8).[362] Jesus' own body would later be put in a similar tomb (Mark 15:46, par.).

There is a bad odor, for he has been in there four days (11:39). While the Jews used spices at burials (though not embalming as the Egyptians did), this did not prevent decomposition.[363]

Jesus looked up and said (11:41). An Old Testament antecedent to Jesus' prayer here is that of Elijah: "Answer me, O LORD, answer me, so these people will know that you, O LORD, are God" (1 Kings 18:37; cf. Ps. 118:21; 121:1; 123:1; cf. Matt. 11:25; John 6:11).[364] The gesture of looking up is rarely attested for the later period (cf. 1 Esd. 4:58; Josephus, *Ant.* 11.5.6 §162). The Jews generally believed that extraordinary things can be accomplished through the power of almighty God as a result of the prayer of his righteous servants (though magical practices made their way into Judaism as well).[365] Greco-Roman culture, by contrast, attributed superhuman powers to "divine men." Jesus' contemporaries frequently viewed him as a miracle-worker who was able to perform extraordinary feats by virtue of his supernatural power. Jesus' prayer counters this perception. It shows that he has no authority apart from the Father and that he is neither a magician nor a "divine man" by Greco-Roman standards.

Father (11:41). "Father" is the customary address for God used by Jesus in prayer, occasionally adorned by a divine attribute such as "Holy Father" (17:11) or "Righteous Father" (17:25).[366] At times, the address is "Our Father in heaven" (Matt. 6:9) or "Father, Lord of heaven and earth" (Matt. 11:25). The address "Father" is also found in Qumran scrolls (4Q372, frag. 1, 16).

Jesus called in a loud voice, "Lazarus, come out!" (11:43). "Wizards muttered their incantations and spells (cf. Isa. 8:19). Not so the Son of God."[367]

His hands and feet wrapped with strips of linen (11:44). "The corpse was customarily laid on a sheet of linen, wide enough to envelop the body completely and more than twice the length of the corpse. The body was so placed on the sheet that the feet were at one end, and then the sheet was drawn over the head and back down to the feet. The feet were bound at the ankles, and the arms were tied to the body with linen strips. . . . Jesus' body was apparently prepared for burial in the same way (cf. 19:40; 20:5, 7)."[368] The custom of wrapping the *hands and feet* of a dead person in linen cloths is not attested elsewhere in Jewish texts. Frequently, deceased loved ones were dressed in flowing and valuable garments, a practice later abolished by Rabbi Gamaliel II.[369] Yet contrary to pagan custom the Jews did not bind up their dead to prevent them from returning to life.

The word for "strips of linen" (*keiriai*) is used several times in fragments of medical papyri suggesting narrow strips tied around the body. "Fine linen" is frequently mentioned as an Egyptian export and is associated with the wealthy in the Old Testament.[370] In rabbinic times, it was thought that at the final resurrection the dead would rise in their clothes. "R. Ḥiyya b. Joseph [c. A.D. 260] further stated: The just in the time to come will rise [apparelled] in their own clothes" (*b. Ketub.* 111b). "R. Eliezer [c. A.D. 90] said: All the dead will arise at the resurrection of the dead, dressed in their shrouds . . . and the people who descend into the earth dressed (with their garments), will they not rise up dressed (with their garments)? . . . Learn from Samuel, the prophet, who came up clothed with his robe . . . (1 Sam. 28:14)" (*Pirqe R. El.* 33).

And a cloth around his face (11:44). The face was bound up with another cloth, called *soudarion* (a loan word from the Latin *sudarium*, "sweat-cloth"), which in life was often worn around the neck (cf. *b. Moʾed Qaṭ.* 27a).

REFLECTIONS

IN HEALING LAZARUS, WHO HAD been dead for four days, Jesus shows that he has power over death. The event also reveals Jesus'—and God's—heart in other ways. First, Jesus enters into close, loving friendship with other people. Mary and Martha send word to him that "the one you love" (Lazarus) was sick. Second, Jesus shows concern for those who mourn the loss of their loved one, whether he or she will be miraculously restored to life at present or not. He comes alongside Lazarus's sisters in their grief and mourns with them. What is more, third, he expresses deep inner outrage at the perversity of death. When brought to Lazarus's tomb, he "bursts into tears." May we, too, come to know God's love, friendship, and comfort in trying times and extend it to others.

The Plot to Kill Jesus (11:45–57)

Come to visit Mary (11:45). This may indicate that it is Mary rather than Martha who has an extensive circle of friends.

Chief priests and Pharisees (11:47). See comments on 7:32.

Called a meeting of the Sanhedrin (11:47). The term *synedrion* ("Sanhedrin") in the sense of "council meeting" is rare in the New Testament, yet frequent in secular Greek (e.g., Diodorus Siculus, *B.H.* 13.111.1), in the LXX (e.g., Prov. 31:23; 2 Macc. 14:5), and in Hellenistic Jewish literature.[371] Most large Jewish centers had a sanhedrin or local court, but the Supreme or Great Sanhedrin was located in Jerusalem. The Sanhedrin was the Jewish judicial, legislative, and executive body, which, under Roman overall jurisdiction, managed the nation's internal affairs. In Jesus' day, the Council's members were controlled by the chief priests, drawn from the extended family of the high priest who presided over the Sanhedrin. The vast majority of these priests were Sadducees, with Pharisees (most of whom were scribes or teachers of the law) constituting an influential minority.[372]

The calling of an official Sanhedrin meeting was legally the responsibility of the high priest. The wording of the NIV suggests an official meeting of the Sanhedrin, though a more informal gathering is equally plausible (in which case the word rendered "Sanhedrin" in the NIV may simply mean "gathering" or "assembly"). The latter alternative would explain why Caiaphas is called "one of them" (11:49), even though in a formal Sanhedrin meeting he would have presided over the proceedings of the Council. The casual way in which Caiaphas is introduced and the bluntness of his language also may indicate that this is not an official gathering of the Sanhedrin with the high priest presiding (contrast Matt. 26:57–66 par.).[373] From this point on, the Pharisees are only referred to infrequently in John's Gospel; control of proceedings against Jesus has now been seized by the chief priests.

If we let him go on like this, . . . the Romans will come and take away both our place and our nation (11:48). In Jewish literature, "the place" (Heb. *maqom*)

Jewish High Priests from 200 B.C. to the Time of Jesus (Selective List)[A-20]	
1. *Pre-Maccabean:*	
Simon the Righteous (after 200 B.C.)	Jason (175–172 B.C.)
Onias II (to 175 B.C.)	Menelaus (172–162 B.C.)
2. *Maccabean:*	
Jonathan (152–143/2 B.C.)	Aristobulus I (104–103 B.C.)
Simon (142/1–134 B.C.)	Alexander Jannaeus (103–76 B.C.)
John Hyrcanus I (134–104 B.C.)	Hyrcanus II (76–67 and 63–40 B.C.)
3. *Post-Maccabean:*	
Annas (A.D. 6–15)	Simon, son of Kamithos (A.D. 17–18)
Ishmael b. Phiabi I (c. A.D. 15–16)	Joseph Caiaphas (c. A.D. 18–36/7)
Eleazar, son of Annas (c. A.D. 16–17)	

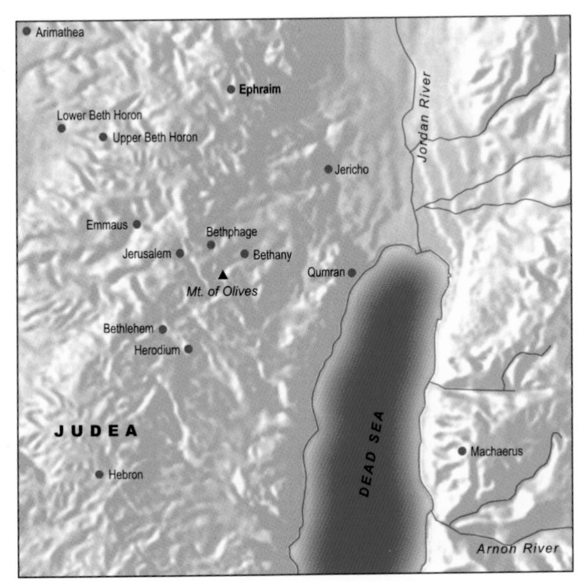

 *left*

JUDEA

Ephraim was located about 20 miles north of Jerusalem.

may refer metaphorically to the Lord (e.g. *Gen. Rab.* 68:9; *b. ʿAbod. Zar.* 40b), the Promised Land (2 Macc. 1:29), Jerusalem (*m. Bik.* 2:2), or the temple. Of these, the temple is the most concrete and climactic referent, since it is located in Jerusalem, the capital city of the Promised Land, and the place where God himself dwells. Importantly, the temple assumes a central role in God's judgment of Israel. Thus God announced the Babylonian exile through the prophet, "What I did to Shiloh I will now do to the house that bears my Name, the temple you trust in, *the place* I gave to you and your fathers. I will thrust you from my presence" (Jer. 7:14; cf. Neh. 4:7).

The next major instance of God's judgment on his people Israel involving the temple is the desecration of the temple by the Seleucid ruler Antiochus IV Epiphanes (see comments on John 10:22). In an important apocryphal passage, the fortunes of "the place" (i.e., the temple) and the Jewish "nation" are said to be closely linked. After recording the pillaging of the temple by Antiochus, the author writes, "But the Lord did not choose the nation for the sake of *the holy place*, but *the place* for the sake of *the nation*. Therefore *the place* itself shared in the misfortunes that befell *the nation* and afterward participated in its benefits; and what was forsaken in the wrath of the Almighty was restored again in all its glory when the great Lord became reconciled" (2 Macc. 5:19).

It appears, therefore, that the Jews' repeated, traumatic (albeit temporary) loss of land and temple elicited fear (at least on the part of its leaders) that God would once again visit the nation in judgment and allow them to be exiled and the temple to be destroyed if Israel was disobedient to God. This preoccupation, here expressed in relation to Jesus, surfaces again in a later Sanhedrin meeting, when false witnesses testify that Stephen "never stops speaking against *this holy place*," predicting that Jesus would "destroy *this place*" (Acts 6:13–14). Still later, Paul is likewise charged with teaching "all men everywhere against our people and our law and *this place*" as well as with defiling "*this holy place*" by bringing Greeks into the inner temple area (Acts 21:28).

"Take away our nation" (*ethnos*) refers to the feared removal of the Jews' semi-autonomous status by the Romans (cf. 2 Macc. 5:19; see comments on John 11:47). The Roman overlords were concerned to preserve public order. The Pharisees had strained to be free from domination, be it by Hasmoneans, Pompey, or Herodians, ever since their party had come into existence, in order to devote themselves fully to the practice of the law. Jewish sources indicate that the authorites had been nervous for some time prior to the Jewish War (A.D. 66–74). With this comports also the Pharisees' initial opposition to the armed revolt against Rome, which led to the destruction of the temple in A.D. 70 (cf. Josephus, *J.W.* 2.17.3–5 §§411–24). Josephus reports several portents of the end taking place in Jerusalem (*J.W.* 6.5.3–4 §§288–315; cf. *Ant.* 14.163–84).

Again, the irony would be all too apparent to John's readers (esp. after A.D. 70): What the Jewish leadership strenuously seeks to avoid, namely, for history to repeat itself and for God's judgment to fall on Israel's nation as typefied by the temple, is precisely what ensues in the wake of Jesus' crucifixion (cf. 2:13–22).[374]

Who was high priest that year (11:49). "That year" need not imply that the high priestly office rotated annually but may simply indicate that Caiaphas happened to be high priest in that fateful year when Jesus was tried and crucified. In fact, Caiaphas held on to his office for a remarkably long time (eighteen years; A.D. 18–36), longer than any other high priest in the first century. But John's remark may also convey the notion that the high priest's term generally lasted for a year and that considerable uncertainty attached to the high priestly office in that day. In fact, if a single one of his actions displeased the Roman governor, the high priest was subject to removal. Valerius Gratus, Pilate's predecessor, repeatedly deposed high priests after a short length of office. Thus the three high priests prior to Caiaphas (A.D. 15–18) as well as his immediate successor (A.D. 36) all held their office only approximately one year (cf. also the three high priests under Agrippa [A.D. 41–44] and the majority of high priests from A.D. 44–66).[375]

Joseph Caiaphas

Caiaphas's full name was Joseph Kayyafa, *Kaiaph* being the family name. He was made high priest by the Roman prefect Valerius Gratus (A.D. 15–26) in A.D. 18 (cf. Josephus, *Ant.* 18.2.2 §35) and held his position until A.D. 36, when he and Pontius Pilate were both removed from office by Vitellius, proconsul of Syria (cf. Josephus, *Ant.* 18.4.3 §95). The fates of Caiaphas and Pilate were closely linked, and it is possible that the former occupied his office through a financial arrangement with the latter. Throughout Caiaphas's tenure, his father-in-law Annas, who had been high priest for several years himself (A.D. 6–15), continued to exercise considerable influence (see 18:13 and comments on 11:47).

Caiaphas himself must have been a "genius of balance, diplomatically adept toward the prefect and the Herodian rulers, conscious of his powerful position yet not so hated by his Jewish contemporaries that he elicited prolonged protests."[A-21] Thus he managed to retain his office during the rule of two procurators, both of which must be judged difficult: Gratus, who in his first three years of office had changed high priests as many as four times, whereby Annas himself, Caiaphas's father-in-law had been his first victim (A.D. 15–18; cf. Josephus, *Ant.* 18.2.2 §§33–35), and Pilate (see comments on 18:29). Caiaphas is mentioned by name in connection with Jesus' death only in John and Matthew (26:57; but see Luke 3:2; Acts 4:6); he is named in Mark. Recent excavations in Jerusalem may have unearthed Caiaphas's tomb.[A-22]

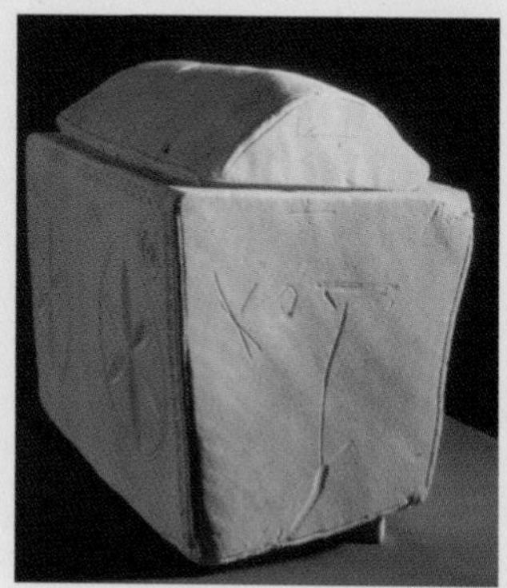

CAIAPHAS OSSUARY

Spoke up, "You know nothing at all!" (11:49). Caiaphas's opening words display a rudeness that was allegedly characteristic of Sadducees. Josephus (who, being a Pharisee, is hardly unbiased in this regard) states, "The Sadducees . . . are, even among themselves, rather boorish in their behavior, and in their intercourse with their peers are as rude as to aliens" (*J.W.* 2.8.14 §166).

It is better for you that one man die for the people than that the whole nation perish (11:50). Dying "for the people" invokes the memory of the Maccabean martyrs (2 Macc. 7:37–38). The question of whether Israelites should turn other Israelites over to the government was also discussed in rabbinic Judaism. Some argued that if there is good reason to turn over one person in particular, this was permissible. Others disagreed. One such passage takes its point of departure from 2 Samuel 20, where Sheba is slain while the city of Abel is spared. "It was taught: If a company of people are threatened by heathens, 'Surrender one of you and we will kill him, and if not we will kill all of you,' they should all be killed and not surrender one soul of Israel. But if they specified a particular person, as in the case of Sheba the son of Bichri [2 Sam. 20:1], they should surrender him and should not all be killed" (*Gen. Rab.* 94:9; cf. *t. Ter.* 7:20).

The same case is taken up in the Jerusalem Talmud, where Rabbi Yoḥanan (d. A.D. 279) appears to have prevailed over against R. Simeon b. Laqish with the view that even an innocent Israelite should be sacrificed for the rest: "[It applies] even if he is not subject to execution, as was Sheba the son of Bichri" (*y. Ter.* 8:10). Another incident involved Ulla the son of Kdosher who was wanted by the government. He fled to R. Joshua b. Levi, pursued by officers dispatched to arrest him. The rabbi's advice was for him to surrender: "Better that you should be executed rather than that the whole community should be punished on account of you" (*Gen. Rab.* 94:9). Yet another later rabbinic passage states categorically: "Better one life should be risked than all should be certain [to die]" (*Gen. Rab.* 91:10 on Gen. 48:10).[376] Caiaphas's ruling is thus firmly rooted within Jewish thought.

He did not say this on his own, but as high priest that year he prophesied (11:51). In the Old Testament, prophecy was occasionally associated with the high priest (Num. 27:21). Zadok the priest is called a "seer" (2 Sam. 15:27), and at one time the high priest sought to determine God's will by way of the Urim and Thummim (perhaps lots). Josephus recounts how Saul ordered the high priest to don his high priestly garments and to prophesy whether or not an attack on the Philistines would be successful. The high priest predicted victory, which did in fact ensue (*Ant.* 6.6.3 §§115–16; cf. 1 Sam. 14:15–23). As another instance where the high priest functioned as a prophet Josephus cites the high priest Jaddua's prediction that Alexander the Great would spare Jerusalem (*Ant.* 11.8.4 §327).[377]

The same Jewish historian also points to the prophetic gift of the Hasmonean ruler John Hyrcanus (135–104 B.C.), who is said to unite in himself the offices of king, priest, and prophet.[378] Apparently, in the vacuum of prophetic voices in the intertestamental period, the priestly class claimed the gift of prophecy for itself. Philo claims that "the true priest is necessarily a prophet" (*Spec. Laws* 4.192). The view that utterances could on occasion have a deeper prophetic meaning is found elsewhere in Judaism, though not with particular reference to the high priest, and prophecy was often considered to be unwitting (cf. Philo, *Moses* 1.274, 277, 283, 286). "R. Eleazar [c. A.D. 270] taught in the name of R. Jose ben Zimra [c. A.D. 220]: None of the Prophets, as they uttered their prophecies, knew that they were prophesying, except Moses and Isaiah who did know" (*Midr. Ps.* 90 §4).

The scattered children of God (11:52). Israel's end-time hopes were tied to the expectation that the "scattered children of God" (i.e., Jews in the dispersion) would be regathered in the Promised Land by the Messiah (or messiahs, cf. 1QS 9:11) to share in God's kingdom.[379] Yet at the same time, Old Testament prophetic literature frequently depicts the Gentiles as streaming toward the mountain of the Lord (Isa. 2:2–3; 56:6–8; 60:6; Zech. 14:16; cf. 1 Peter 1:1), and the Jerusalem temple is characterized as "a house of prayer for all nations" (Isa. 56:7; cited in Mark 11:17). In the present context ("for the Jewish nation, and not only for that nation . . ."), clearly "the scattered children of God" refers to the Gentiles (cf. esp. John 10:16; see also 12:20–21, 32). A similar thought appears in the *Odes of Solomon* 10:5–6: "And the Gentiles who had been scattered were gathered together . . . and they became my people for ever and ever" (after A.D. 100).[380]

He withdrew to a region near the desert, to a village called Ephraim (11:54). The reference is probably to Old Testament Ophrah (Josh. 18:23) or Ephron (2 Chron. 13:19), site of the modern village of Et-Taiyibeh, four miles northeast of Bethel (cf. Josephus, *J.W.* 4.9.9 §551) and less than twenty miles north of Jerusalem.[381]

The Jewish Passover, many went up from the country to Jerusalem (11:55). Passover is one of the three pilgrim feasts for which Jewish men were required to travel to Jerusalem. This is the third and final Passover mentioned by John. If the first Passover took place in A.D. 30 (see comments on 2:20), the year of Jesus' passion is A.D. 33.[382] Regarding the "many," recent scholarship estimates that the population of Jerusalem swelled from about 100,000 inhabitants to around a million during each of the three festivals.[383]

For their ceremonial cleansing before the Passover (11:55). Ceremonial uncleanness prevented a person from celebrating the Passover.[384] Need for purification arose particularly for those who lived in contact with Gentiles, since the latter frequently buried their dead near their houses, which would make their Jewish neighbors subject to the purification commanded by the law (Num. 19:11–12). Old Testament law stipulated the need for ceremonial cleansing before the Passover for anyone who had defiled himself, such as by touching a corpse (9:6–14). The appropriate purification rites might last as long as a week (19:12), so that many traveled to Jerusalem early, especially in light of the large numbers involved (Josephus, *J.W.* 1.11.6 §229; *m. Pesaḥ.* 9:1).

The chief priests and Pharisees had given orders that if anyone found out where Jesus was, he should report it so that they might arrest him (11:57). Both Old Testament and mishnaic legislation make provision for the kind of search ordered here by the chief priests and Pharisees. The Mosaic law obliged any Jew who heard a curse spoken aloud to report this to the authorities (Lev. 5:1).

The Mishnah stipulates a procedure for covertly capturing a person who leads people into idolatry (*m. Sanh.* 7:10).

Jesus Anointed at Bethany (12:1–11)

On the Friday evening before Passion week, Jesus arrives in Bethany, where a dinner is celebrated in his honor (it is now March, A.D. 33). The next day, "Palm Sunday," Jesus sets out for Jerusalem and is given a hero's welcome. The Pharisees are increasingly exasperated, while Jesus' appeal is shown to extend even to some Greeks who want to see Jesus.

Six days before the Passover (12:1). If John, as is likely, thinks of Passover as beginning Thursday evening (as do the Synoptics), "six days before the Passover" refers to the preceding Saturday, which began Friday evening.

A dinner was given in Jesus' honor (12:2). If Jesus arrives Friday evening, the festivity recounted here probably takes place on Saturday. "Dinner" (*deipnon*) refers to the main meal of the day. It was usually held toward evening but could commence as early as mid-afternoon, so that there is no perfect correspondence to our terms "lunch" and "dinner" today. Nevertheless, Jesus' words in Luke 14:12, "when you give a luncheon [*ariston*] or dinner [*deipnon*]," show that the midday and the evening meal were distinct. Moreover, "dinner" may refer to a regular meal or to a festive banquet (cf. Matt. 23:6 par.; Mark 6:21). Elsewhere in John's Gospel, the term is used of the Last Supper (13:2, 4; 21:20). In first-century Palestine, banquets usually started in the later hours of the afternoon and quite often went on until midnight. Banquets celebrating the Sabbath could begin as early as midday.

Martha served, while Lazarus was among those reclining at the table with him (12:2). Martha's serving at the table may indicate that by this time Sabbath has come to an end. Possibly, the meal is connected with the *Habdalah* service, which marked the end of a Sabbath (*m. Ber.* 8:5). It is probable that Lazarus, Mary, and Martha provide the meal, though a large dinner in this small village, celebrated in honor of a noted guest, may well have drawn in several other families to help with the work. "Reclining at the table" may indicate a banquet rather than a regular meal (see 13:2–5, 23).[385]

Jesus' Final Week (John 12–21; March 27–April 3, A.D. 33)

Time	Location/Event	Passage in John
Friday, March 27, 33	Jesus arrives at Bethany	11:55–12:1
Saturday, March 28, 33	Dinner with Lazarus and his sisters	12:2–11
Sunday, March 29, 33	"Triumphal entry" into Jerusalem	12:12–50
Monday-Wednesday, March 30–April 1, 33	Cursing of fig tree, temple cleansing, temple controversy, Olivet discourse	Synoptics
Thursday, April 2, 33	Third Passover in John; betrayal, arrest	13:1–18:11
Friday, April 3, 33	Jewish and Roman trials, crucifixion, burial	18:12–19:42

Then Mary took about a pint (12:3). A *litra* (a measurement of weight equivalent to the Latin *libra*) amounted to about eleven ounces or a little less than three-quarters of a pound (half a liter). Then, as today, this is a large amount of perfume.[386]

Pure nard, an expensive perfume (12:3). See Song 1:12; 4:13–16 (LXX). Nard, also known as spikenard, is a fragrant oil derived from the root and spike (hair stem) of the nard plant, which grows in the mountains of northern India.[387] This "Indian spike," used by the Romans for anointing the head, was "a rich rose red and very sweetly scented."[388] The Semitic expression is found in several papyri, including one from the early first century (P. Oxy. 8.1088.49). The rare term "pure" (*pistikēs*) may mean "genuine" (derived from *pistis*, "true, genuine") in contrast to diluted, since nard apparently was adulterated on occasion. "Perfume" (*myron*) is used here probably in the generic sense of "fragrant substance" (cf. Mark 14:3). The Synoptic parallels indicate that the perfume was kept in an "alabaster jar" (Matt. 26:7; Mark 14:3).[389] For "expensive," see comments on 12:5.

She poured it on Jesus' feet (12:3). "Poured" translates the Greek word *aleiphō*, which literally means "anoint." Anointing the head was common enough (Ps. 23:5; Luke 7:46), but anointing the feet was unusual (usually simply water was provided), even more so during a meal, which was definitely improper in Jewish eyes. Somewhat similar was the Babylonian custom for women to drip consecrated oil onto the heads of rabbis present at the wedding of a virgin, and for slave girls to bathe the hands and feet of a guest in oil.

The Greek poet Aristophanes cites an instance where a daughter is washing, anointing (*aleiphō*), and kissing her father's feet (*Vespae* 608). In the present instance, it is hard not to see royal overtones in Mary's anointing of Jesus, especially in light of the fact that the event is immediately followed by Jesus' triumphal entry into Jerusalem, where he is hailed as the king of Israel who comes in the name of the Lord (12:13, 15). Attending to the feet was servant's work (see comments on 1:27; 13:5), so Mary's action shows humility as well as devotion.

Wiped his feet with her hair (12:3). The use of hair rather than a towel for wiping Jesus' feet indicates unusual devotion. The act is all the more striking since Jewish women (esp. married ones) never unbound their hair in public, which would have been considered a sign of loose morals (cf. Num. 5:18; *b. Soṭah* 8a).[390] The fact that Mary (who was probably single, since no husband is mentioned) here acts in such a way toward Jesus, a well-known (yet unattached) rabbi, is sure to raise some eyebrows (see comments on 4:7). Also unusual is the wiping off of the oil.

Worth a year's wages (12:5). "A year's wages" translates "three hundred denarii." One denarius was the daily remuneration of a common laborer (cf. Matt. 20:2; see

ROMAN ERA GLASS CONTAINERS

comments on John 6:7). Three hundred denarii is therefore roughly equivalent to a year's wages, since no money was earned on Sabbaths and other holy days. This perfume is outrageously expensive owing to its being imported all the way from northern India. Its great value may indicate that Mary and her family are very wealthy. Alternatively, this may have been a family heirloom that has been passed down to Mary.

Money bag (12:6). The expression originally denoted any kind of box to hold the reeds of musical instruments. Later, the term was used for a coffer into which money is cast (2 Chron. 24:8, 10). In the present instance, what may be in mind is therefore not a "bag" (NIV) but a box made of wood or some other rigid material (cf. Plutarch, *Galba* 16.1; Josephus, *Ant.* 6.1.2 §11). The money kept in this container probably helps meet the needs of Jesus and his disciples as well as provide alms for the poor. The funds would be replenished by followers of Jesus such as the women mentioned in Luke 8:2–3, who supported his ministry.

REFLECTIONS

SHORTLY BEFORE JESUS' SACRIFICIAL death, Mary of Bethany lets her heart speak. She "wastes" a jar containing a large amount of expensive perfume on Jesus—at least that's what she is accused of doing by Judas, one of Jesus' twelve disciples. Wealth given freely to Jesus is better than overt concern for the poor that does not flow from genuine love for him in one's heart. "You will always have the poor among you, but you will not always have me."

It was intended that she should save this perfume for the day of my burial (12:7). While it was not uncommon for people in first-century Palestine to spend considerable amounts in funeral-related expenses, it is unusual that Mary here lavishly pours out perfume on Jesus while he is still alive. The word for burial (*entaphiasmos*) refers not so much to the event itself as to the laying out of the corpse in preparation for burial (cf. 19:40).

You will always have the poor among you, but you will not always have me (12:8). The allusion is probably to Deuteronomy 15:11: "There will always be poor people in the land." Jewish sources indicate that care of the dead was to take precedence over almsgiving. *b. Sukkah* 49b praises *gemilut ḥasadim* ("the practice of kindness") above charity, among other reasons because it can be done both to the living and the dead (by attending their funeral; cf. *t. Pe*ʾ*ah* 4:19).

The Triumphal Entry (12:12–19)[391]

The next day (12:12). This is probably Sunday of Passion week, called "Palm Sunday" in Christian tradition.

The great crowd (12:12). With Jerusalem's population at that time being about 100,000 and the amount of pilgrims amounting to several times the population of Jerusalem, the "great crowd" gathered at the Jewish capital at the occasion of the Passover may have numbered up to a million people. Many of these pilgrims were probably Galileans, who were well acquainted with Jesus' ministry.

The Feast (12:12). Passover (see 12:1 above and comments on 2:13).

Palm branches (12:13). Date palm trees did grow in the vicinity of Jerusalem, especially Jericho, the "City of Palms" (Deut. 34:3; 2 Chron. 28:15).[392] The palm tree served as a symbol of righteousness: "The righteous will flourish like a palm tree" (Ps. 92:12). In the Old Testament, palm branches are associated not with Passover but with the Feast of Tabernacles (Lev. 23:40). However, by the time of Jesus palm branches had already become a national (if not nationalistic) Jewish symbol (Josephus, *Ant.* 3.10.4 §245; 13.13.5 §372; cf. *Jub.* 16:31). Palm branches were a prominent feature at the rededication of the temple in Maccabean times (2 Macc. 10:7; 164 B.C.) and were also used to celebrate Simon's victory over the Syrians (cf. 1 Macc. 13:51; 141 B.C.). Later, palms appear on the coins minted by the insurrectionists during the Jewish wars against Rome (A.D. 66–70 and 132–135) and even on Roman coins themselves. Apocalyptic end-time visions likewise feature date palms (Rev. 7:9; *T. Naph.* 5:4).

In the present instance, people's waving of palm branches may signal nationalistic hopes that in Jesus a messianic liberator had arrived (cf. 6:14–15).[393] A later rabbinic source reads, "It is the one who takes the palm branch in his hand who we know to be the victor" (*Lev. Rab.* 30:2). The Greco-Roman world knew palm branches as symbols of victory (e.g., Suetonius, *Caligula* 32: "ran about with a palm branch, as victors do").

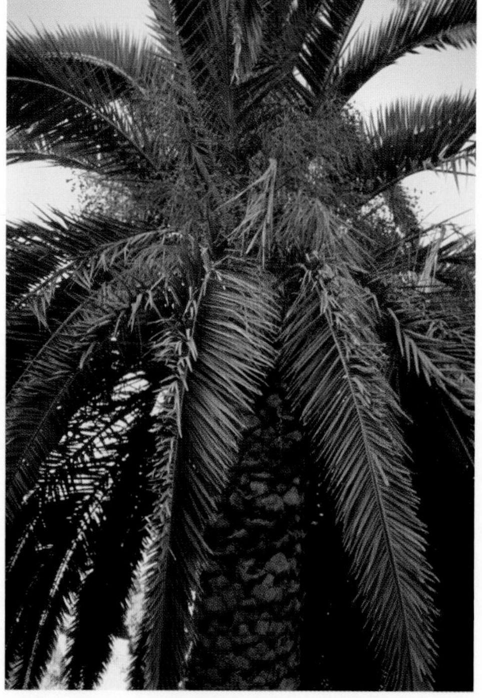

PALM BRANCHES

(right) A date palm in the Sinai region.

(bottom) A palm tree is depicted on a coin minted during the Bar Cochba revolt against Rome (c. A.D. 132).

Went out to meet him, shouting, "Hosanna!" (12:13). See Psalm 118:25. The phrase "went out to meet him" (rare in biblical literature) was regularly used in Greek culture, where such a joyful reception was customary when Hellenistic sovereigns entered a city. An instance of this is recorded by Josephus when Antioch came out to meet Titus (*J.W.* 7.5.2 §§100–101). The term "Hosanna," originally a transliteration of the identical Hebrew expression,[394] had become a general expression of acclamation or praise. Most familiar was the term's occurrence in the Hallel (Pss. 113–18; see esp. 118:25), a psalm sung each morning by the temple choir during various Jewish festivals (cf. *m. Pesaḥ.* 5:7; 9:3; 10:7). At such occasions, every man and boy would wave their *lulab* (a bouquet of willow, myrtle, and palm branches; *b. Sukkah* 37b; cf. Josephus, *Ant.* 3.10.4 §245) when the choir reached the "Hosanna!" in Psalm 118:25 (*m. Sukkah* 3:9).

Blessed is he who comes in the name of the Lord! (12:13). See Psalm 118:26. In its original context, Psalm 118 conferred a blessing on the pilgrim headed for Jerusalem, with possible reference to the

Davidic king. Later rabbinic commentary interpreted this psalm messianically (*Midr. Pss.* on Ps. 118:24). Note also the interesting connection between a donkey and the "ruler from Judah" in Genesis 49:11.

Blessed is the King of Israel! (12:13) For the title "King of Israel," see comments on 1:49.

Jesus found a young donkey and sat upon it (12:14). For a fuller description of how Jesus "found" the donkey, see Matthew 21:1–3 par. Two associations with the donkey were dominant in first-century Palestine: humility (see comments on 13:1–20) and peace (see comments on 14:27). In contrast to the war horse (cf. Zech. 9:10), the donkey was a lowly beast of burden: "Fodder and a stick and burdens for a donkey" (Sir. 33:25; cf. Prov. 26:3). Donkeys were also known as animals ridden on in pursuit of peace, be it by ordinary folk, priests, merchants, or persons of importance (Judg. 5:10; 2 Sam. 16:2). Jesus' choice of a donkey invokes prophetic imagery of a king coming in peace (Zech. 9:9; cf. 12:10: "He will proclaim peace to the nations"), which contrasts sharply with notions of a political warrior messiah (cf. 1 Kings 4:26; Isa. 31:1–3). The early Christians were often mocked as worshiping a donkey, a man in form of a donkey, or a donkey's head, such as in the famous graffito of a crucified slave with the head of a donkey and of another slave worshiping with the inscription "Alexamenos worships God" (early 3d cent. A.D.?).[395]

Do not be afraid, O Daughter of Zion; see, your king is coming, seated on a donkey's colt (12:15). See Zechariah 9:9. The phrase "Do not be afraid" does not occur in the Hebrew or other versions of Zechariah 9:9, replacing the expression "Rejoice greatly." It may be taken from Isaiah 40:9, where it is addressed to the one who brings good tidings to Zion (cf. Isa. 44:2; Zeph. 3:16).[396] "Daughter of Zion" is a common way of referring to Jerusalem and its inhabitants, especially in their lowly state as the oppressed people of God.

left

A YOUNG DONKEY IN MODERN JERUSALEM

right

A PALM SUNDAY PROCESSIONAL ON A JERUSALEM STREET

An early messianic prophecy speaks of a ruler from Judah who will command the obedience of the nations and who rides on a donkey (Gen. 49:10–11). Yet the rabbis had difficulty reconciling this notion of a humble Messiah with that of the Danielic Son of Man "coming on the clouds of heaven" (*b. Sanh.* 98a; c. A.D. 250). However, riding on a donkey does appear as one of the three signs of the Messiah in *Eccles. Rab.* 1:9 (c. A.D. 300), where the latter redeemer in Zechariah 9:9 is featured as the counterpart to Moses in Exodus 4:20. Note too 1 Kings 1:38, where Solomon (whose name means "peaceable") rode into Jerusalem for his coronation on King David's mule.

The whole world has gone after him! (12:19). "The whole world" constitutes a common Jewish hyperbolic phrase. So it is said that "all the world" followed the high priest (*b. Yoma* 71b); that Hezekiah taught the Torah to "the whole world" (*b. Sanh.* 101b); that "the people [lit., the world] were flocking to David" (*b. B. Meṣiᶜa* 85a; cf. 2 Sam. 15:13); and that "all the people [lit., world] came and gathered around" a certain rabbi (*b. ᶜAbod. Zar.* 19b). The early Christians were said to "have caused trouble all over the world" (Acts 17:6).

Jesus Predicts His Death (12:20–36)

There were some Greeks among those who went up to worship at the Feast (12:20). As elsewhere in the New Testament, the term "Greeks" refers not to people literally hailing from Greece, but to Gentiles from any part of the Greek-speaking world, including Greek cities in the Decapolis (see comments on 7:35). Most likely, these "Greeks" were God-fearers who had come up to Jerusalem to worship at the Feast (cf. Acts 17:4: "God-fearing Greeks"). Like the Roman Cornelius (Acts 10) or the centurion who had a synagogue built (Luke 7:5), such God-fearers were attracted to the Jewish way of life without formally converting to Judaism. They were admitted to the court of the Gentiles in the temple but forbidden entrance into the inner courts on the warning of death.

They came to Philip, who was from Bethsaida in Galilee (12:21). See 1:44. It is possible that the "Greeks" singled out Philip—and Andrew—because of their Greek names; although they were both Jews, they were the only two members of the Twelve with Greek names (with the possible exception of Thomas, see comments on 11:16). If these "Greeks" were from the Decapolis or from the territories north or east of the Sea of Galilee (such as Batanea, Gaulanitis, or Trachonitis), they may have known (or found out) who among Jesus' disciples it was who came from the nearest town—Philip, who hailed from Bethsaida (located in Gaulanitis). Galilee, in fact, was more Hellenized than much of the rest of Palestine and bordered on pagan areas (cf. Matt. 4:15). Moreover, Philip, because of his origin, would have been able to speak Greek.

Philip went to tell Andrew; Andrew and Philip in turn told Jesus (12:22). Philip is mentioned along with Andrew in 1:44 and 6:7–8 (cf. Mark 3:18).

For the Son of Man to be glorified (12:23). See comments on 1:51. The reference to the glorification of the Son of Man may well hark back to Isaiah 52:13, where it is said that the Servant of the Lord "will be raised and lifted up and highly exalted" (LXX: *doxasthēsetai*). In pre-Christian usage, the glory of the Son of Man and his function of uniting heaven and earth are conceived in primarily apocalyptic terms (Dan. 7:13; cf. *1 En.* 45–57, esp. 46 and 48; first century A.D.?).

Unless a kernel of wheat falls to the ground and dies, it remains only a single seed. But if it dies, it produces many seeds (12:24). The principle of life through death is here illustrated by an agricultural example. In rabbinic literature, the kernel of wheat is repeatedly used as a symbol of the eschatological resurrection of the dead. By an argument "from the lesser to the greater," "if the grain of wheat, which is buried naked, sprouts forth in many robes, how much more so the righteous, who are buried in their raiment" (*b. Sanh.* 90b).[397]

The man who loves his life will lose it, while the man who hates his life in this world will keep it for eternal life (12:25). The love/hate contrast reflects Semitic idiom, pointing to preference rather than actual hatred.[398] The present statement is couched in Hebrew parallelism, taking the form of a *mashal* with two antithetical lines. Such wisdom sayings use paradox or hyperbole to teach a given truth in as sharp terms as possible (cf. *b. Taᶜan.* 22a).

The paradox enunciated here has particular applicability if judged as Christ's verdict on Greco-Roman ideals of life. For the Greeks, the goal of human existence was bound up with self-fulfillment and the attainment of personal maturity. Following Christ, however, involves sacrifice of oneself and one's own interests, a truth seen supremely in Jesus' cross.

Whoever serves me must follow me; and where I am, my servant also will be (12:26). This teaching coheres closely with teacher-disciple relationships in first-century Palestine. "Being a disciple required personal attachment to the teacher, because the disciple learned not merely from his teacher's words but much more from his practical observance of the Law. Thus the phrase 'to come after someone' is tantamount to 'being someone's disciple.'"[399] What is more, the truth enunciated here extends beyond a disciple's earthly life to his eternal destiny (7:34, 36; 14:3; 17:24).

Father, glorify your name! (12:28). The glory of God as the ultimate goal of his salvific actions is a theme pervading the Old Testament.[400]

A voice came from heaven (12:28). This is one of only three instances during

left

HEADS OF WHEAT IN A FIELD

right

KERNELS OF WHEAT

Jesus' earthly ministry when a heavenly voice attests to his identity.[401] The rabbis called this voice *bat qol* (lit., "daughter of a voice"). Since it was commonly believed that the prophetic office had ceased and would not be renewed until the onset of the messianic age, the *bat qol* was the most that could be expected in the interim: "Since the death of the last prophets, Haggai, Zechariah and Malachi, the Holy Spirit [of prophetic inspiration] departed from Israel; yet they were still able to avail themselves of the *bat qol*" (*b. Sanh.* 11a; cf. *t. Soṭah* 13:3).[402]

A later rabbinic passage illustrates this belief: "One would hear not the sound which proceeded from heaven, but another sound proceeded from this sound; as when a man strikes a powerful blow and a second sound is heard, which proceeds from it in the distance. Such a sound would one hear; hence it was called 'Daughter of the voice'" (*Tosafot* on *b. Sanh.* 11a).[403] The all-important difference between the New Testament instances of the heavenly voice and the rabbinic notion of the *bat qol* is that while the rabbis thought of the divine voice as a mere echo, the heavenly voice attesting Jesus is the voice of God himself.

It had thundered (12:29). Thunder was considered to speak of the power and awesomeness of God (1 Sam. 12:18; 2 Sam. 22:14; Job 37:5). It was part of the theophany at Mount Sinai (Ex. 19:16, 19). God's intervention on behalf of his people is portrayed like a fierce thunderstorm sweeping down on his enemies (Ps. 18:7–15). In such instances, the power of the Creator is tied to that of Israel's Redeemer (Ex. 9:28; 1 Sam. 7:10; Ps. 29:3; cf. Sir. 46:16–17). The manifestations of God's power also highlight the contrast between his omnipotence and the idols' powerlessness (Jer. 10:13 = 51:16).

In New Testament times, light and sound accompanied the manifestation of the risen Christ to Saul (Acts 9:7; 22:9). In the Apocalypse, peals of thunder are shown to emanate from God's throne (Rev. 4:5; 8:5; 11:19; 16:18; cf. 2 Esd. 6:17). The *Sibylline Oracles* speak of a "heavenly crash of thunder, the voice of God" (*Sib. Or.* 5:344–45). The notion of heaven answering human speech in thunder is also found in the ancient Greek world. Thus in Homer's classic work, Odysseus's prayer is followed by divine thunder: "So he spoke in prayer, and Zeus the counselor heard him. Straightway he thundered from gleaming Olympus" (*Odyssey* 20.97–104).[404]

Others said an angel had spoken to him (12:29). In Old Testament times, angels (or the angel of the Lord) spoke to Hagar (Gen. 21:17), Abraham (22:11), Moses (cf. Acts 7:38), and Daniel (Dan. 10:4–11). In the New Testament, angels are said to minister to Jesus (Matt. 4:11; Luke 22:43; cf. Matt. 26:53), and at one point it was surmised that Paul, too, may have heard an angelic voice (Acts 23:9). Angelic voices are commonplace in the book of Revelation (Rev. 4:1; 5:2; 6:1; etc.).

Now the prince of this world will be driven out (12:31). "Prince" is literally "ruler" (*archōn*). Similar terminology is also found in Paul's writings (2 Cor. 4:4; 6:15; Eph. 2:2; 6:12). There are several Jewish (though no rabbinic) parallels to the phrase "prince of the world" with reference to Satan.[405] The title "prince of this world" occurs in relation to Beliar in the *Ascension of Isaiah* (1:3; 10:29; cf. 2:4). In *Jubilees*, "Mastema" is called "chief of the spirits" or simply "prince"

(10:8; 11:5, 11; etc.). More generally, the Qumran texts contain the notion that the "dominion of Belial" extends to his entire "lot."[406] However, unlike extensive intertestamental speculation regarding the demonic supernatural, John is much more restrained, limiting his treatment of Satan exclusively to his role in the plot against Jesus leading to the latter's crucifixion. See comments also on John 14:30; 16:11; also Luke 10:18.

Will draw all men to myself (12:32). "All men" is generic, "all people." This does not imply universalism (the ultimate salvation of all; see comments on 1:9). Rather, the approach of Gentiles prompts Jesus' statement that after his glorification he will draw "all kinds of people," even Gentiles, to himself (cf. 10:16; 11:52).

The Law (12:34). "The Law" may refer to the Hebrew Scriptures in their entirety rather than merely to the five books of Moses (cf. 10:34; 15:25).

The Christ will remain forever (12:34). Palestinian Judaism in Jesus' day generally thought of the Messiah as triumphant, and frequently also as eternal. Such expectations were rooted in the Son of David, of whom it was said that God would "establish the throne of his kingdom forever" (2 Sam. 7:13; cf. John 12:16). This prospect was nurtured both in the Psalms (e.g., Ps. 61:6–7; 89:3–4, 35–37) and prophetic literature (Isa. 9:7; Ezek. 37:25; cf. Dan. 7:13–14). It was also affirmed in intertestamental Jewish writings (*Pss. Sol.* 17:4; *Sib. Or.* 3:49–50; *1 En.* 62:14) and at the outset of Luke's Gospel (Luke 1:33).

Perhaps the closest parallel to the present passage is Psalm 89:37, where David's seed is said to "remain forever" (LXX: *menei eis ton aiōna*). Notably, this psalm is interpreted messianically both in the New Testament (Acts 13:22; Rev. 1:5) and rabbinic sources (*Gen. Rab.* 97, linking Gen. 49:10; 2 Sam. 7:16; Ps. 89:29). But probably Jesus refers not so much to any one passage but to the general thrust of Old Testament messianic teaching. Elsewhere in John, people express the expectation of a Davidic Messiah born at Bethlehem (John 7:42) and of a hidden Messiah to be revealed at the proper time (7:27; cf. 1:26).

The Christ . . . the Son of Man (12:34). It is unclear whether Palestinian Jews in Jesus' day, whose concept of Messiah was bound up largely with the expectation of the Davidic king, also linked the Coming One with the apocalyptic figure of the Son of Man (cf. Dan. 7:13–14).[407]

Walk while you have the light, before darkness overtakes you. The man who walks in the dark does not know where he is going. Put your trust in the light (12:35–36). The term "walk" (*peripateō*) frequently occurs in John's Gospel in a figurative sense in conjunction with light and darkness.[408] Similar terminology can be found in the Qumran literature: "the sons of justice . . . walk on paths of light,"

ROMAN CROSS

A model of a typical Roman cross with a nameplate on the top and two wooden beams for the arms and legs.

while "the sons of deceit . . . walk on paths of darkness" (1QS 3:20–21; cf. 4:11). The notion of "walking in the light" or "in darkness" in John resembles the thought in the Scrolls that there are two ways in which people may walk, light and darkness. Both John and the Scrolls hark back independently to Old Testament terminology, especially Isaiah: "Let him who walks in the dark, who has no light, trust in the name of the LORD" (Isa. 50:10); "the people walking in darkness have seen a great light" (9:2, quoted in Matt. 4:16). The important difference between John and the Scrolls is that the former calls people to "put their trust in the light," while the latter assume that the members of the community are already "sons of light."

Sons of light (12:36). "Son of . . ." reflects Hebrew idiom; the expression "sons of light," however, is not attested in rabbinic literature. A "son of light" displays the moral qualities of "light" and has become a follower of the "light" (cf. Luke 16:8; 1 Thess. 5:5; Eph. 5:8). The phrase is also common in the Dead Sea Scrolls, where it designates members of the Qumran community.[409] "Born of light" occurs in *1 Enoch* (108:11; cf. also *T. Naph.* 2:10: "so you are unable to perform the works of light while you are in darkness").

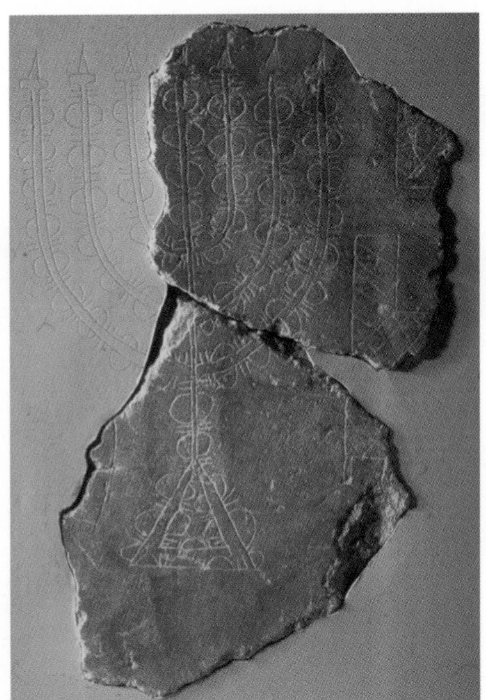

MENORAH

Fragments of plaster found in a Herodian-era house discovered in Jerusalem. This is the earliest depiction of the candelabrum, which stood in the temple.

The Jews Continue in their Unbelief (12:37–50)

Even after Jesus had done all these miraculous signs in their presence, they still would not believe in him (12:37). The Jews' failure to believe in Jesus' day is reminiscent of the unbelief of the desert generation, which had witnessed God's mighty acts of power (displayed through Moses) at the Exodus (Deut. 29:2–4). No greater sign than the raising of Lazarus—the seventh, climactic sign in John—could be given.

This was to fulfill the word of Isaiah the prophet (12:38). This leads off a whole series of fulfillment quotations in John's Gospel, stressing the fulfillment of Old Testament prophecy in the events of Jesus' life, especially the events surrounding his crucifixion.[410]

Lord, who has believed our message and to whom has the arm of the Lord been revealed? (12:38). The reference cited is Isaiah 53:1 (LXX; cf. Rom. 10:16). In the original context, Isaiah' message pertains to the Servant of the Lord, who was rejected by the people but exalted by God (cf. Isa.52:13–15). In John's Gospel, the passage is applied to Jesus the Messiah, who is that promised Servant, and to the rejection of his message and his miraculous signs ("arm of the Lord") by the Jewish people. Thus Jewish rejection of God's words is nothing new; as Isaiah's message had been rejected, so is Jesus'. The phrase "arm of the LORD" serves in the Old Testament frequently as a figurative expression for God's power.[411]

He has blinded their eyes and deadened their hearts, so they can neither see with their eyes, nor understand with their hearts, nor turn—and I would heal them (12:40). The reference cited is Isaiah 6:10 (here closer to the Hebrew than to the LXX). The Hebrew original moves from heart to ears to eyes and then back from sight to hearing to understanding. John does not refer to hearing but focuses instead on sight, probably owing to his mention of Jesus' miraculous signs in John 12:37. The Jews considered the heart to be the seat of mental as well as physical life (cf. Mark 8:17–21 par.).

Isaiah . . . saw Jesus' glory (12:41). In light of the preceding quotation of Isaiah 6:10, the background to the present statement is probably the call narrative in Isaiah 6. This is confirmed by the Targums (Aramaic paraphrases of the Old Testament). One Targum of Isaiah 6:1 changes "I saw the LORD" to "I saw *the glory* of the LORD," and changes "the King, the LORD Almighty" in Isaiah 6:5 to "*the glory of the shekinah of the eternal* King, the LORD of hosts" (*Tg. Ps.-J.,* 1st cent. B.C.–3d cent. A.D.). The notion of a preexistent Christ who was present and active in the history of Israel appears elsewhere in the New Testament (cf. 1 Cor. 10:4; see also Philo, *Dreams* 1.229–30). Later interpreters speculated that the prophet looked into the future and saw the life and glory of Jesus (*Ascen. Isa.* [2d cent. A.D.]).

But because of the Pharisees . . . for fear they would be put out of the synagogue (12:42). See comments on 9:22.

He does not believe in me only, but in the one who sent me (12:44). See comments on 5:23. The entire closing section (12:44–50) presupposes Jewish teaching on representation, according to which the emissary represents the one who sends him (cf. *m. Ber.* 5:5).[412]

That very word which I spoke will condemn him at the last day (12:48). Verses 48–50 echo the book of Deuteronomy (cf. 18:19; 31:19, 26).[413] There it is God who takes vengeance on the man who refuses to hear; in the Targums, it is God's *memra* or word. "And the man who does not listen to his words which he [the future prophet] will speak in the name *of my memra,* I *in my memra will be avenged of him*" (*Tg. Neof.* on Deut. 18:19); "*my memra* will take revenge on him" (*Tg. Ps.-J.* on Deut. 18:19).

Sometimes in intertestamental Jewish literature, the Law seems to take a more active part in the process of judging: "And concerning all of those [the sinners], their end will put them to shame, and your Law which they transgressed will repay them on your day" (*2 Bar.* 48:47); "and he will destroy them without effort by the law (which was symbolized by the fire)" (*4 Ezra* 13:38). In Wisdom of Solomon 9:3, wisdom is described as an assessor with God in judgment (cf. Philo, *Moses* 2.53).

I know that his command leads to eternal life (12:50). According to the book of Deuteronomy, God's commandments provide the framework within which Israel is to fulfill her calling as a people set apart for God (e.g., Deut. 8:3; 32:46–47). Jews commonly saw the law of Moses as the source of life (32:45–47; cf. John 5:39). The problem, however, is that no one keeps the law perfectly or is able to do so.

Jesus Washes His Disciples' Feet (13:1–17)

In the face of Jewish hardening, Jesus now turns his attention to the Twelve. After one final memorable demonstration of his love and after exposing the betrayer, Jesus prepares his followers for the difficult times ahead.

It was just before the Passover Feast (13:1). According to the Synoptics (Mark 14:12; Luke 22:15), Jesus and his disciples celebrated the Passover during the early hours of Nisan 15 (Thursday evening, with days beginning at sundown), with preparations having been made earlier that day, Nisan 14, the day on which the paschal lambs were slaughtered at the temple (usually between 3 and 5 P.M.). Some believe that John places the Last Supper on Nisan 14, Wednesday evening, with Jesus' crucifixion occurring on Thursday afternoon, when the lambs are slaughtered at the temple in preparation for Passover.[414] A closer look at the relevant passages, however, shows that none of these actually conflicts with the Synoptic accounts.[415]

His own (13:1). "His own" are now the Twelve, the representatives of the new messianic community, no longer the old covenant community, which had rejected Jesus as Messiah (cf. 1:11).

The evening meal was being served (13:2). On the Greek word for "evening meal" (*deipnon*), see comments on 12:2 (see also 1 Cor. 11:20).

Took off his outer clothing, and wrapped a towel around his waist (13:4). Jesus here adopts the stance of a menial (even

John's Gospel and Ancient Farewell Discourses[A-23]

Patterned after Moses' "farewell discourse" in Deuteronomy (31–33) and other similar Old Testament farewells,[A-24] the intertestamental period saw the production of an entire genre of such works.[A-25] Most of these testaments were written between the second century B.C. and the third century A.D. and include the following features:

1. Predictions of death and departure
2. Predictions of future challenges for the followers/sons of the dying man after his death
3. Arrangements regarding succession or continuation of family line
4. Exhortations to moral behavior
5. A final commission
6. An affirmation and renewal of God's covenant promises
7. A closing doxology

However, John's presentation of Jesus' "farewell discourse" (John 13:31–17:26) may not be consciously patterned after the intertestamental genre "testament" but merely build on the precedent of Moses' final words in Deuteronomy. In keeping with the genre's concern for proper succession, Jesus announces the coming of "another helping presence" (14:16; cf. 14:26; 15:26; 16:7), which would ensure continuation between his ministry and that of his disciples (see esp. 15:26–27; 16:8–11).

Yet important differences apply as well. Jesus' farewell is merely temporary—his followers will see him again "in a little while"—so that Jesus' final words focus on the future, while Jewish farewell discourses regularly consist of extended rehearsals of the past. Likewise, extensive detailed predictions regarding the future, common in intertestamental testaments, are almost entirely absent from Jesus' instructions to his followers. Also, the vine allegory in chapter 15 is without precedent in Jewish farewell discourses.

non-Jewish; cf. *Mek. Ex.* 21:2) slave, a position looked down on by both Jews and Gentiles. Other rabbis also stressed the virtue of humility, yet with certain limitations. R. Yehudah ha-Nasi (d. A.D. 217), for example, a highly respected Jewish teacher said to embody all the seven virtues listed by the sages for the righteous (*y. Sanh.* 11:3), "was said to be so humble that he would do anything for others except relinquish his superior position."[416] Jesus, for his part, knows no such boundaries.

The expression "wrap a towel around his waist" indicates that Jesus girds himself like a servant (Luke 12:37; 17:8). "Towel" (*lention*), which occurs in the New Testament only here and is not attested in earlier Greek literature, is a loanword from the Lat. *linteum* (similar to *soudarion*; see John 11:44).[417] It refers to a long towel fastened to the shoulder, which allowed Jesus to gird himself and still to use the end to dry the disciples' feet (cf. 1 Peter 5:5). Suetonius recalls an instance when the Roman emperor Caligula humiliated senators by having them wait on him in similar attire (*Caligula* 26.2).

He poured water into a basin and began to wash his disciples' feet (13:5). The Old Testament recounts several instances of footwashing as part of ancient hospitality.[418] Several intertestamental passages mention the washing of a guest's feet immediately prior to a meal.[419] The same custom was also common among the Greeks, as is illustrated by a reference to Odysseus having his feet washed after his return (*Odyssey* 19:386–88).[420] The disciples probably recline on mats around a low table, each leaning on his left arm, with the feet pointing outward (see comments on 13:23). In first-century Palestine, where people walked long distances in sandals and where roads were dusty, hospitality demanded that the host arrange for water to be available for the washing of feet (done upon arrival, not during the meal). Rather than washing the feet in the basin itself, water was poured over the feet from one vessel and caught in another (cf. 2 Kings 3:11).[421]

To perform acts of service for one's teacher was considered a common duty of a disciple.[422] In fact, it was maintained that "the service of the Torah is greater than the study thereof" (*b. Ber.* 7b).[423] The washing of feet, however, was considered too demeaning for disciples (or even a Jewish slave) and thus was assigned to non-Jewish slaves. "All manner of service that a slave must render to his master a student must render to his teacher, except that of taking off his shoe";[424] "the sages said: A Hebrew slave must not wash the feet of his master, nor put his shoes on him."[425] Jesus' adoption of the stance of (a non-Jewish) slave would thus be shocking to his disciples and cries out for an explanation. For while there are occasional exceptions featuring people other than non-Jewish slaves washing the feet of others,[426] the washing of the feet of an inferior person by a superior is not attested elsewhere in Jewish or Greco-Roman sources.[427]

No part with me (13:8). (Cf. 14:1–3; 17:24). The notion of "having a part [*meros*] in something" occurs elsewhere in the New Testament with regard to inheritance (Luke 15:12). In Old Testament times, each of the twelve tribes of Israel (except Levi) was to have its "share" in the Promised Land (Num. 18:20; Deut. 12:12; 14:27). Later, the expression is used with reference to people's being assigned a place in God's eternal kingdom, both in terms of fellowship with God (Rev. 20:6; 21:8; 22:19) or separation from him (Matt. 24:51; Luke 12:46). In Acts 8:21 Peter rebukes Simon Magus using similar language.

A person who has had a bath needs only to wash his feet; his whole body is clean (13:10). See 15:3. Two terms for washing are contrasted here: "have a bath" (*louō*) and "wash" (*niptō*).[428] "Have a bath" may refer to Jewish ceremonial cleansing in preparation for Passover (11:55). Alternatively, Jesus may allude to the custom (at least in some quarters) "for guests at a meal to take a bath before leaving home, and on arrival at their host's house to have their feet, but only their feet washed."[429] Thus according to Plutarch (first cent. A.D.), both Cato the Younger and Pompey had a bath (*louō*) before supper (*deipnon*).[430] In any case, Jesus' disclaimer would caution his followers (and John's readers) against interpreting his actions as a mandate for ritual washings common in Judaism (*katharismos*; cf. 2:6; 3:25).

You call me "Teacher" and "Lord" (13:13). John's Gospel regularly portrays Jesus as being addressed as "Teacher" and "Lord" by his disciples or others. The designation "Rabbi" was in keeping with Jewish teacher-disciple relationships. "Lord," however, was a word commonly applied to God in the LXX (though it could also simply mean "sir"; see 4:11, 15, 49; 5:7).

You also should wash one another's feet (13:14). As can be seen from 1 Timothy 5:10, the phrase "washing the feet of the saints," in extension of its literal application here, had already become an accepted figurative expression for Christian service by the time of the writing of John's Gospel.

An example (13:15). The Greek word *hypodeigma* can denote both an "example," be it good[431] or bad,[432] and a "pattern" (Heb. 8:5; 9:23; cf. Acts 7:44). In several Jewish intertestamental texts, *hypodeigma* is associated with exemplary death[433] or other virtues such as repentance (Sir. 44:16). Greco-Roman writers likewise use the term to denote examples of various virtues. Diodorus of Sicily says that the Roman senate left "models and patterns" (*typous kai hypodeigmata*) for all who strive for the empire (*Bib. Hist.* 30.8). Plutarch comments that the Romans, while skillful in warfare, left no examples of civil virtues such as gentleness and humanity (*Marc.* 20.1). Thus the major difference between Jesus and the Greco-Roman world is not so much the concept of leaving an example itself as the nature of this example: While Greeks and Romans prized virtues such as courage or military prowess, Jesus exemplifies humility, self-sacrifice, and love.

Now that you know these things, you will be blessed if you do them (13:17). Similar statements are attested in Greco-Roman sources. Several centuries before Christ, the Greek writer Hesiod remarked, "Blessed and fortunate is he who knowingly does all these things" (*Opera et dies* 826–27). The Roman Seneca, banished by Caligula and later tutor of the young Nero, stated, "He is not happy who only knows them [the things learned], but he who does them" (*Ep.* 75.7).

But this is to fulfill the scripture: "He who shares my bread has lifted up his heel against me" (13:18). On fulfillment quotations, see comments on 12:38. The text cited is Psalm 41:9. By Jesus' day, David had become a "type" or model of David's "greater Son," the coming Messiah on the basis of passages such as 2 Samuel 7:12–16 or Psalm 2. Several major themes of David's life are given a messianic application in the New Testament, especially those focusing on his suffering, weakness, and betrayal.[434] In rabbinic interpretation, Psalm 41:9 was taken to refer to Ahithophel's conspiracy with Absalom against David.[435] In ancient Semitic cultures, eating bread at the table of a superior amounted to a pledge of loyalty (2 Sam. 9:7–13; 1 Kings 18:19; 2 Kings 25:29), and "to betray one with whom bread had been eaten . . . was a gross breach of the traditions of hospitality."[436]

The expression "lifted up his heel against me" is capable of several interpretations. Carson (citing Bruce) sees it as "has given me a great fall" or "has taken cruel advantage of me" or "has walked out on me." Morris and others think the imagery may be that of a horse preparing to kick. Brown notes that "to show the bottom of one's foot to someone in the Near East is a mark of contempt . . . some [though not Brown himself] would see here a reminiscence of Genesis 3:15: 'You shall bruise his heel.'" Barrett suggests "the action of one who 'shakes off the dust of his feet against' another" (cf. Luke 9:5; 10:11).[437] From Jacob (in whose case the heel connotes trickery) to Achilles (whose heel, suggesting weakness, may be the most famous of all), it appears that the heel is patient of a wide variety of symbolic applications.

I am telling you now before it happens, so that when it does happen you will believe that I am He (13:19). The phrase chosen by Jesus echoes similar expressions referring to God in the Old Testament: "When this happens, you will know that I am the Sovereign LORD" (Ezek. 24:24); "'You are my witnesses,' declares the LORD, 'and my servant whom I have chosen, so that you may know and believe me and understand that I am he'" (Isa. 43:10; cf. 41:26; 48:3, 5–6).

Jesus was troubled in spirit (13:21). All three instances of Jesus' being troubled in spirit in this Gospel (cf. 11:33; 12:27) relate to the horror of human death (an effect of the work of Satan). This acknowledgment of inner turmoil on the part of Jesus contrasts sharply with the ideal of Greek philosophers to remain tranquil and unmoved in all circumstances, often on the basis of the view that one's fate had already been determined by the gods (cf. our expression "Stoic" today).[438]

The disciple whom Jesus loved (13:23). This expression probably refers to the historical figure of John the son of Zebedee as an oblique form of self-reference on part of the evangelist.[439] Since his recipients doubtless know him well, the author can dispense with his proper name.[440]

Reclining next to him (13:23). Reclining at meals was first introduced into Judaism from the Hellenistic world[441] and initially viewed as a sign of decadence (Amos 6:4–7). By New Testament times, however, reclining had become standard practice at banquets and feasts, including Passover celebrations. This leisurely way of observance—which symbolized freedom in contrast to Israel's bondage in Egypt[442]—stood in marked, self-conscious contrast with the haste that marked the first Passover on the night of the Exodus (Ex. 12:11).

> The usual arrangement at a formal meal was to have a series of couches arranged in a U around the table. The guests reclined with their heads toward the table and their feet stretched out obliquely away from it. They leaned on the left elbow, which meant that the right hand was free to secure food. The host, or the most important person, reclined in the center of the chief couch, a couch for three, placed at the junction of the two arms of the U. The place of honor was to the left of, and thus slightly behind, the principal person. The second place was to his right, and the guest there would have his head on the breast of the host.[443] The place of the beloved disciple, [sic] was clearly on the principal couch where he could lean back on Jesus' breast.[444]

While "the disciple whom Jesus loved" reclined at Jesus' right (rather than left), this was nonetheless the place of a trusted friend. In an interesting parallel, Pliny recounts an incident where Nerva, the Roman emperor, dined one evening with a few select friends, and one Veiento "was placed next to the Emperor, and actually reclined upon his bosom" (*in sinu recumbebat*; *Ep.* 4.22.4).

RECLINING AT THE TABLE

A model of a table, eating utensils, and terracotta pottery typical of the Roman period.

The one to whom I will give this piece of bread when I have dipped it in the dish (13:26). The host at a feast (here Jesus) may well dip a tasty bit into a common bowl and pass it on to someone as a sign of honor or friendship. "Piece of bread" (*psōmion*) refers to a morsel, usually bread, though sometimes meat. Perhaps the scene takes place "at an early point of the paschal meal when bitter herbs were dipped into a bowl of fruit puree, the haroset sauce of dates, raisins and sour wine."[445] The fact that Jesus can pass the morsel to Judas Iscariot so easily suggests that he is close by, possibly on Jesus' left.

Satan entered into him (13:27). Two interesting parallels are found in first-century Jewish documents: "I determined inwardly to destroy him [Joseph], because the Prince of Error blinded my mind" (*T. Sim.* 2:7); "if the mind is disposed toward evil . . . it accepts the evil and is overmastered by Beliar" (*T. Ash.* 1:8). The Qumran scrolls reveal the belief, also found in John (e.g., 8:44), that the relation between the devil and evil human beings is like that of father to child (see comments on 12:36; cf. Wisd. Sol. 2:24). In Judaism in general, however, a person's will was considered decisive in determining which of two impulses, that toward good or that toward evil, prevailed (see comments on 8:34). See comments on Luke 22:3.

Charge of the money (13:29). See comments on 12:6.

Some thought Jesus was telling him to buy what was needed for the Feast (13:29). This being the night of the Passover (Nisan

15), the disciples think Judas is being dispatched to buy what is needed for the Feast—not the Passover, but the Feast of Unleavened Bread (the *hagigah*). This festival started that very night and went on for seven days. Since the next day (Friday, still Nisan 15) was a high feast day, and the following day a Sabbath, Jesus may have considered it expedient to make necessary purchases (such as more unleavened bread) that night. While there is some debate on the subject (cf. *m. Pesaḥ.* 4:5), the making of such purchases was probably both possible and lawful (though not necessarily convenient). A similar piece of legislation is found in one rabbinic passage, which says, "In Jerusalem on the eve of Passover when it falls on a Sabbath, a man may leave his cloak and take his Passover-lamb and make his reckoning with the seller after the close of the Festival-day" (*m. Šabb.* 23:1).

Or to give something to the poor (13:29). Almsgiving was an important part of Jewish piety. As the famous rabbi Hillel said, "The more charity, the more peace" (*m. ʾAbot* 2:7). For pilgrims to Jerusalem, it was customary to give alms to the poor (Josephus, *Ant.* 4.8.19 §227). On Passover night, the temple gates were left open from midnight on, allowing beggars to congregate (*Ant.* 18.2.2 §§29–30).[446] Almsgiving was regarded as particularly meritorious when done in Jerusalem[447] (see comments on 9:8; 12:4–8).

A Talmudic maxim reflects a much older principle: "Even a poor man who himself lives from alms, should give alms" (*b. Giṭ.* 7b).[448] While Jesus himself is poor,[449] this does not keep him from showing concern for others who are poor. "Sell your possessions and give to the poor" is his advice both to the disciples and to the rich young ruler (Luke 12:33; 18:22). The early church remembered an otherwise unrecorded saying of Jesus, "It is more blessed to give than to receive" (Acts 20:35).

It was night (13:30). The main meal was usually eaten in the late afternoon, but the Passover celebration took place at night.[450] The present reference may also convey the notion of spiritual darkness entered by the betrayer (cf. Luke 22:53, "this is your hour—when darkness reigns"; cf. the statements in Matt. 26:20 [Mark 14:17], "when evening came"; 1 Cor. 11:23, "on the night he was betrayed").

NIGHT IN JERUSALEM

A group of people sitting at the second-century Roman cardo in Jesusalem. ▼

Jesus Predicts Peter's Denial (13:31–38)

God is glorified in him, God will glorify the Son in himself, and will glorify him at once (13:32). Once again, there are echoes of Isaiah (e.g., Isa. 49:3, where God says to the Servant of the Lord: "You are my servant, Israel, in whom I will display my splendor").

My children (13:33). Fulfilling the paschal role of head of the family, Jesus here addresses his followers as his "dear children." "The address is also very fitting if the Last Discourse is thought of as a farewell speech, for in this literary genre the scene is often that of a dying father instructing his children."[451]

A new command I give you: Love one another. As I have loved you, so you must love one another. By this all men will know that you are my disciples (13:34–35). The command to love one's neighbor as oneself was not new.[452] Love within the community was also highly regarded at Qumran (e.g., 1QS 1:10), and Josephus speaks similarly of the Essenes (*J.W.* 2.8.2 §119). Neighbor love is also emphasized by the famous first-century rabbi Hillel, who said, "Be of the disciples of Aaron, loving peace and pursuing peace, loving mankind and bringing them near to the Law" (*m. ʾAbot* 1:12). There are several parallels in other Jewish literature: "My children, beware of hatred . . . for hatred is not willing to hear the words of God's commandments concerning the love of one's neighbor" (*T. Gad* 4:1–2). "Now, my children, let each one of you love his brother . . . loving one another."[453] However, what is new is Jesus' commandment for his disciples to love one another *as he has loved them*—laying down one's life for others (cf. 13:1; 15:13). That the early Christians did love one another is attested in the famous statement by the church father Tertullian, "See how they love one another" (*Apol.* 39). Regarding the Jews, the Roman Tacitus wrote, "the Jews are extremely loyal toward one another, and always ready to show compassion, but toward every other people they feel only hate and enmity" (*Hist.* 5.5; cf. Josephus, *J.W.* 2.8.14 §166).

Before the rooster crows (13:38). Apparently, roosters in Palestine frequently crowed in the late night hours, so that the Romans assigned the label "cockcrow" to the watch between midnight and 3 A.M. (cf. Mark 13:35; see also comments on John 18:27).

Jesus Comforts His Disciples (14:1–4)

In the last few quiet moments before his arrest, Jesus prepares his followers for the time subsequent to his return to the Father. As far as they are concerned, nothing can be worse than the departure of their beloved teacher. But according to Jesus, this will actually work out to their benefit. For he will send another "Counselor" (14:16), who will take up Jesus'—and the disciples'—case. From his exalted position with the Father, Jesus will be able to grant his followers' requests and enable them to accomplish even greater works than he has done during his earthly ministry.

Do not let your hearts be troubled (14:1). In keeping with Semitic anthropology, the expression "heart" denotes the seat of a person's will and emotions. On

REFLECTIONS

"SEE HOW THEY LOVE ONE ANOTHER." CAN PEOPLE say that about Christians today? When doctors performing abortions are assassinated, when Christians are frequently belligerent, even hate-filled, how will the world know that we are Jesus' disciples? The answer is they will not. More important than being right or holding all the proper beliefs is that we are people of love. God so loved the world that he gave his Son. Will we who are saved be moved by his love and love fellow believers as well as those outside the faith? For this was—and still is—Jesus' burning desire: "that the world may know that you sent me."

"be troubled," see comments on 11:33; 12:27; 13:21. In the Old Testament, God's chosen servants as well as his people Israel were frequently told not to be afraid, whether the occasion was entering the Promised Land (Deut. 1:21, 29; 20:1, 3; Josh. 1:9) or threats from their enemies, such as the Babylonians (2 Kings 25:24) or the Assyrians (Isa. 10:24). Note too that in other farewell discourses, encouragement not to be afraid was common (*1 En.* 92:2; *T. Zeb.* 10:1–2; *Jub.* 22:23).

Trust in God; trust also in me (14:1). The Greek word *pisteuō*, elsewhere frequently translated "believe," denotes personal, relational trust in keeping with Old Testament usage (e.g., Isa. 28:16).

In my Father's house are many rooms (14:2). In Jesus' day, many dwelling units ("rooms")[454] were combined to form an extended household.[455] It was customary for sons to add to their father's house once married, so that the entire estate grew into a large compound (called *insula*) centered around a communal courtyard. The image used by Jesus may also have conjured up notions of luxurious Greco-Roman villas, replete with numerous terraces and buildings and situated among shady gardens with an abundance of trees and flowing water. Jesus' listeners may have been familiar with this kind of setting from the Herodian palaces in Jerusalem, Tiberias, and Jericho (cf. Josephus, *J.W.* 5.4.4 §§176–83).

Apocalyptic intertestamental literature provides extensive descriptions of heavenly dwelling places for the saints.[456] Philo regards heaven as a paternal house or city to which the soul returns after death: "So will you be able also to return to your father's house, and be quit of that long endless distress which besets you in a foreign land."[457] The rabbis believed that there were seven classes or departments, graded according to merit, in the heavenly Garden of Eden (*Midr. Ps.* 11 §6); the church fathers held similar views. John, however, is decidedly non-apocalyptic, and his treatment is much more restrained than Philo's existential allegorizing. The rabbinic notion of a compartmentalized heaven is likewise foreign to John.

Rather than elaborating on the characteristics of his Father's house, Jesus is content to stress that there is plenty of room and that the believers' future is bound up with a homecoming comparable to a son's return to his father's house (cf. Luke 15:11–32; note also Luke 2:49, where Jesus calls the temple "my Father's house"). In keeping with Jewish patriarchal culture, Jesus, the Son of the Father, establishes his followers "as members of the Father's household" and "makes his home accessible to them as a final place of residence."[458]

Prepare a place for you (14:2). Jesus' provision seems to be patterned after Deuteronomy, where God is said to have gone ahead and prepared a place for his people in the Promised Land (e.g., Deut. 1:29–33).[459] There may also be irony in the fact that the Jews fear that their "place" will be taken away from them by the Romans (11:48; a fear that materialized in A.D. 70), while Jesus' disciples can look forward to a "place" prepared for them by their master.[460]

I will come back and take you to be with me that you also may be where I am (14:3). This refers to the Second Coming (see 21:22–23; 1 Thess. 4:16–17).

Similar terminology is found in Song of Songs 8:2a, where the bride says she will bring her lover to her mother's house. Here Jesus, the messianic bridegroom (John 3:29), is said first to go to prepare a place for his own in his Father's house and then to come to take them home to be with him.

Jesus the Way to the Father (14:5–14)

As in the previous chapter, the farewell discourse is occasionally punctuated by questions from Jesus' disciples. The asking of clarification questions was an important aspect of the teacher-disciple relationship in first-century Judaism.[461]

I am the way and the truth and the life (14:6). In the Old Testament and intertestamental Jewish literature, "the way(s) of truth" is a life lived in conformity with God's law (e.g., Ps. 119:30; Tobit 1:3; Wisd. Sol. 5:6). In Psalm 86:11, "way" and "truth" occur in parallelism: "Teach me your way, O LORD, and I will walk in your truth." In 16:11, the notions of way, truth, and life are combined: "You have made known to me the path of life." A life devoted to walking in truth, in turn, will have eternal consequences: "The path of life leads upward for the wise to keep him from going down to the grave" (Prov. 15:24).

In the Dead Sea Scrolls, the ways of truth are contrasted with the ways of darkness and deceit.[462] The Qumran covenanters considered themselves to be "the Way" in absolute terms,[463] so that those who elected to join their ranks were said to have chosen "the Way" (1QS 9:17–18). At Qumran, "the Way" was understood to constitute strict legal observance as interpreted by the "Teacher of righteousness." The first Christians likewise considered themselves to be followers of "the Way."[464] Jesus' claim to be "the way," then, may reflect this whole chain of usage of "way" imagery, from the Old Testament to the early church. Because he in his very essence is truth and life, Jesus is the one and only way of salvation.

No one comes to the Father except through me (14:6). In keeping with Jesus' claim, the early Christians maintained, "Salvation is found in no one else, for there is no other name under heaven given to men by which we must be saved" (Acts 4:12). In the Old Testament, people expressed their faith in God by keeping the law; now that Jesus has come, he is the way. In the Jewish and Greco-Roman world of the first century as well as in today's pluralistic climate, Jesus' message is plain: He does not merely claim to be "a" way or "a" truth or "a" life, but "the way and the truth and the life," the only way to salvation.

If you really knew me, you would know my Father as well. From now on, you do know him and have seen him (14:7). The verb "to know," in the sense of "acknowledge," was part of Near Eastern covenantal language.[465] In the Old Testament, people are frequently exhorted to know God (e.g., Ps. 46:10; 100:3), with knowledge of God generally being anticipated as a future blessing rather than claimed as a present possession.[466]

Lord, show us the Father (14:8). In the Old Testament, Moses asked and was given a limited vision of God's glory: "Now show me your glory" (Ex. 33:18). The prophet Isaiah was granted a vision of "the Lord seated on a throne, high and exalted" (Isa. 6:1). Later, the same prophet predicted that in the day of the

Messiah the glory of the Lord would be revealed (40:5). In Jesus' day, many Jews longed for a first-hand experience of God.

The words I say to you are not just my own. Rather, it is the Father, living in me, who is doing his work (14:10). In Deuteronomy 18:18, God said regarding the prophet like Moses, "I will put my words in his mouth, and he will tell them everything I command him." In 34:10–12, Moses is said to have been sent by the Lord to do signs and works.

Anyone who has faith in me . . . will do even greater things than these (14:12). "Greater things" has a primarily qualitative dimension, marking Jesus' "signs" as preliminary and his disciples' ministry as "greater" in the sense that it is based on Jesus' completed work on the cross (12:24; 15:13; 19:30) and belongs to a more advanced stage in God's economy of salvation (cf. Matt. 11:11). Jesus' followers are benefiting from others' labors, reaping what they have not sown, and will bear fruit that remains (John 4:31–38; 15:8, 16).

Thus, in keeping with motifs current in both Jewish life in general and farewell discourses in particular, the disciples are designated as Jesus' successors, taking their place in a long string of precedessors that range from the Old Testament prophets to John the Baptist and climax in Jesus.[467] In this sense, Jesus' followers—not just his original disciples, but "anyone who has faith in me"—will do greater things even than Jesus, aided by answered prayer in Jesus' name (14:13) and in close, spiritual union with their exalted Lord (ch. 15).

REFLECTIONS

DO GREATER THINGS THAN JESUS did? This claim seems daring. The difficulty evaporates when one realizes that these "greater works" are still works of Jesus, now carried out from his exalted position with the Father through his commissioned, faithful followers. Because Jesus is now with the Father, we can expect to do greater works than even Jesus did: on the basis of his once-for-all death on the cross, and in answer to believing prayer for all that is necessary to accomplish the mission Jesus never relinquished.

Whatever you ask in my name (14:13). Praying in Jesus' name does not involve magical incantations but rather expresses alignment of one's desires and purposes with God (1 John 5:14–15). Jews frequently recalled the patriarchs in their prayers, hoping that God would be moved to hear them on account of these holy men.

Jesus Promises the Holy Spirit (14:15–31)

If you love me, you will obey what I command (14:15). Jesus' words echo the demands of the Deuteronomic covenant.[468]

Another Counselor (14:16). In secular Greek, "Counselor" (*paraklētos*) refers primarily to a "legal assistant" or "advocate" (though the word never became a technical term such as its Lat. equivalent *advocatus*). In John's Gospel, legal overtones are most pronounced in 16:7–11. In later rabbinic writings, the role of advocate (*sanêgôr*) is associated with the Holy Spirit (*Lev. Rab.* 6:1 on Lev. 5:1). R. Eliezer ben Jacob made the well-known statement, "He that performs one precept gets for himself one advocate (*p^e^raqlît*); but he that commits one transgression gets for himself one accuser (*qaṭêgôr*)" (*m. ʾAbot* 4:11). Also, both the noun *paraklēsis* and the verb *parakaleō* are used in the Old Testament with regard to the "consoling" expected to occur during the messianic era (e.g., Isa. 40:1; cf. *b. Makk.* 5b).

The Spirit of truth (14:17). The expression "spirit of truth" was current in Judaism. One first-century Jewish document says, "Two spirits await an opportunity with humanity: the spirit of truth and the spirit of error. . . . And the spirit of truth testifies to all things and brings all accusations" (*T. Jud.* 20:1–5). Similarly, the Qumran literature affirms that God placed within a human being "two spirits so that he would walk with them until the moment of his visitation; they are the spirits of truth and of deceit" (1QS 3:18; cf. 4:23–26). Yet the above parallels are merely those of language, not thought. For while these expressions are part of an ethical dualism in intertestamental literature (including Qumran), John's Gospel does not feature a "spirit of error" corresponding to the Spirit of truth (but see 1 John 4:6, where "the Spirit [or spirit] of truth and the spirit of falsehood" occur together). Rather, the Spirit of truth is the other "Counselor," who takes the place of Jesus' "helping presence" while on earth with his disciples.

I will not leave you (14:18). Compare Moses' parting words to Israel: "The LORD . . . will never leave you nor forsake you" (Deut. 31:6; cf. Josh. 1:5; Heb. 13:5).

Orphans (14:18). In Old Testament times, orphans needed someone to plead their case. Here, the term "orphan" is used in a metaphorical sense in connection with Jesus' departure and the resulting loss that his disciples will experience. In secular Greek, "orphans" can denote both children bereft of only one parent and disciples left without their master.[469] Plato wrote regarding the followers of Socrates that, in the face of their teacher's imminent death, "they felt that he was like a father to us and that when bereft of him we should pass the rest of our lives as orphans."[470]

On that day (14:20). The phrase frequently has end-time connotations and is commonly found in Old Testament prophetic literature (e.g., Isa. 2:11; 3:7, 18; 4:1–2).

Show myself (14:21). The Greek verb used here (*emphanizō*), along with its cognates, sometimes refers in the LXX to theophanies, that is, manifestations of God (e.g., Ex. 33:18).

Judas (not Judas Iscariot) (14:22). This Judas is probably the "Judas of James" mentioned in Luke 6:16 and Acts 1:13, not Jude, the half-brother of Jesus (Matt. 13:55; Mark 6:3).

If anyone loves me, he will obey my teaching (14:23). "Teaching" here is *logos*, often translated "word." The synonymous use of "word" and "command" (14:21) harks back to the Old Testament, where the Ten Commandments are called "words" of God (Ex. 20:1; cf. Deut. 5:5, 22). The expressions "commands" and "word[s]" are used interchangeably in Psalm 119 (e.g., 119:10, 25, 28).

We will come to him and make our home with him (14:23). This is the only place in the New Testament where the Father and the Son are both said to indwell believers. Elsewhere, it is Christ (Gal. 2:20; Eph. 3:17) or the Spirit (Rom. 8:9, 11; 1 Cor. 3:16). In Old Testament times, God dwelt among his people, first in the tabernacle (Ex. 25:8; 29:45; Lev. 26:11–12), then in the temple (Acts 7:46–47). In the New Testament era, believers themselves are the temple of the living God (1 Cor. 6:19; 2 Cor. 6:16; cf. 1 Peter 2:5).

Two interesting parallels to the phrase "make our home" are found in Josephus, where Jonathan is said to have "taken up residence" in Jerusalem (*Ant.* 13.2.1 §41) and Elijah is shown to "make his dwelling" in a cave (*Ant.* 8.13.7 §350). Philo frequently speaks of God or the Word (*logos*) as dwelling in people. People long for spiritual intimacy with their Creator; only the Lord Jesus Christ can fulfill this craving of the human heart (cf. John 14:6).

All this I have spoken (14:25). Literally, "all these things." This expression will recur a total of six times in the second part of the Farewell Discourse (15:11; 16:1, 4, 6, 25, 33). Reiterated phrases also occur in prophetic writings (e.g., "I the LORD have spoken" in Ezek. 5:13, 15, 17; 17:21, 24).

The Counselor (14:26). See comments on 14:16.

The Holy Spirit (14:26). The term "Holy Spirit" occurs only infrequently in the Old Testament (Ps. 51:11; Isa. 63:9–10). There are several references to the "Holy Spirit" in intertestamental literature (e.g., Wisd. Sol. 9:17; *Odes Sol.* 8).

Will teach (14:26). See the parallel in 16:13. Both passages together echo Psalm 25:5: "Guide me in your truth and teach me" (cf. 25:9). See also Nehemiah 9:20: "You gave your good Spirit to instruct them." Teaching in the sense of authentic exposition of Scripture was a vital part of Judaism. In Qumran, the primary teaching office was occupied by the "teacher of righteousness," who interpreted the Hebrew Scriptures prophetically with reference to the Dead Sea community. However, one important difference between the Holy Spirit and the "teacher of righteousness" is that the former will guide people into truth definitively while the latter will be followed by another "teaching righteousness" at the end of time (CD 6:11).

Will remind you of everything I have said to you (14:26). This promise has important implications for the life of the church and for the writing of the New Testament. "Remembering" was also an important part of the Jewish testament tradition.[471] There are several parallels in intertestamental literature between the consoling, teaching presence of the Paraclete and the period after the death of a revered leader in the testaments. In one such work the people tell Baruch, "Everything which we can remember of the good things which the Mighty One has done to us we shall remember, and that which we do not remember he knows in his grace" (*2 Bar.* 77:11). A literary parallel is found in the intertestamental book of *Jubilees*, where God reassures Jacob, "I will cause you to remember everything" (*Jub.* 32:25).

Peace I leave with you (14:27). In the Greek world, peace (*eirēnē*) was essentially a negative concept, denoting the absence of war.[472] Though this is also part of the term's range of meaning in Hebrew thought (e.g., Judg. 3:11, 30;

5:31; 8:28; etc.), the expression peace (*shālôm*) usually had much richer connotations, conveying the notion of positive blessing, especially that of a right relationship with God.[473] This is evident in the blessing given by Moses and Aaron: "The LORD bless you and keep you; the LORD make his face shine upon you and be gracious to you; the LORD turn his face toward you and give you peace" (Num. 6:24–26; cf. Ps. 29:11; Hag. 2:9).

The Old Testament prophetic writings in particular look forward to a period of peace inaugurated by the coming of the Messiah. The "Prince of Peace" (Isa. 9:6) will "command peace to the nations" (Zech. 9:10; cf. 14:9), and there will be good tidings of peace and salvation (Isa. 52:7; cf. 54:13; 57:19; Acts 10:36). Through the royal Messiah, God will make an everlasting "covenant of peace" with his people (Ezek. 37:26). This accords also with intertestamental notions that "the souls of the righteous are in the hand of God, and no torment will ever touch them . . . they are at peace" (Wisd. Sol. 3:1, 3).

The present phrase, "Peace I leave with you," reflects the customary Jewish greeting and word of farewell, whereby "leave" (*aphiēmi*) probably has the sense of "bequeath" (cf. Ps. 17:14; Eccl. 2:18). Here (as in John 16:33) the context of greeting is farewell; after the resurrection, it is welcome (20:19, 21, 26). By invoking "that day" anticipated by the prophets (14:20), Jesus places this period squarely within the context of Old Testament expectation. On the merits of his substitutionary death, the departing Lord bequeaths to his followers the permanent end-time blessing of a right relationship with God (cf. Rom. 1:7; 5:1; 14:17).

My peace I give you. I do not give to you as the world gives (14:27). On peace in general, see previous comment. Apart from his peace, the departing Jesus also bestows on his followers his love (15:9, 10) and joy (15:11). This triad is also

***ARA PACIS* IN ROME**

Caesar Augustus built the "altar of peace" in Rome to celebrate his inauguration of the age of peace.

found in Paul's teaching on the fruit of the Spirit (Gal. 5:22). The *pax Romana* ("Roman peace"), secured by the first Roman emperor, Augustus (30 B.C.–A.D. 14), had been obtained and was maintained by military might. The famous *Ara Pacis* ("altar of peace"), erected by Augustus to celebrate his inauguration of the age of peace, still stands in Rome as a testimony to the world's empty messianic pretensions.[474] The peace given by Jesus, by contrast, was not afflicted with the burden of having been achieved by violence (cf. John 18:11). Philo, the Hellenistic Jew, calls peace "the highest of blessings . . . a gift no human being can bestow" (*Moses* 1.304), holding up as the loftiest ideal "a soul, in which there is no warring, whose sight is keen, which has set before it as its aim to live in contemplation and peace" (*Dreams* 2.250).[475]

Do not be afraid (14:27). Moses' parting counsel in his farewell discourse is likewise, "Do not be afraid" (Deut. 31:6, 8).

The prince of this world (14:30). Lit., "the world's ruler." See comments on 12:31.

He has no hold on me (14:30). This phrase constitutes an idiomatic rendering of a Hebrew expression frequently found in legal contexts with the sense "he has no claim on me."[476] The present phrase does not mean "he has no *power* over me" (cf. 19:11: *kata*, not *en*; though this is of course true as well), but "he has no *legal claim* or hold on me." The reason for this is Christ's sinlessness (cf. 8:46).

Come now; let us leave (14:31). This may indicate that Jesus and his followers now leave the Upper Room and embark on a nightly walk, perhaps passing vineyards on the way, which would provide a fitting backdrop for Jesus' teaching on the vine and the branches (15:1–17). Some have suggested that Jesus' "vine" metaphor was occasioned by the golden vine overhanging the main entrance to the temple.[477] Alternatively, Jesus may have told his disciples it was time to go and then added some further instruction before finally getting underway (cf. 18:1).

The Vine and the Branches (15:1–17)

Vine imagery was common in the ancient world, as in the case of the cult of Dionysos, the Greek god of wine. The Old Testament frequently uses the vineyard or vine as a symbol for Israel, God's covenant people, especially in two "vineyard songs" found in Isaiah.[478] However, while the vine's purpose for existence is the bearing of fruit for its owner, references to Israel as God's vine regularly stress Israel's failure to produce good fruit, issuing in divine judgment.[479] In contrast to Israel's failure, Jesus claims to be the "*true* vine," bringing forth the fruit Israel has failed to produce. Thus Jesus, the Messiah and Son of God, fulfills Israel's destiny as the true vine of God (Ps. 80:14–17).[480] The intimate relationship between Jesus and his followers has already been depicted in terms of a shepherd and his flock (John 10). The

VINEYARD NEAR JERICHO

illustration of a vine and its branches, even more than that of a shepherd and his flock, focuses on the organic, vital connection between the branches and the vine.

I am the true vine (15:1). Joseph is called a "fruitful vine" in Genesis 49:22. The expression "true vine" is also found in Jeremiah 2:21 (LXX): "I had planted you like a choice *vine* of sound and *reliable* stock." Building on the Old Testament depiction of Israel as a vine, the vine in later years served as a symbol for wisdom (Sir. 24:17), the dominion of the Messiah (*2 Bar.* 39:7), and the Judaism of Jesus' day. The Jerusalem temple was adorned with a golden vine with large clusters of grapes (see comments on John 14:31). Coins of the first Jewish revolt (A.D. 66–70) feature a vine and branches as a symbol of Jerusalem, and the rabbinic school at Jamnia headed by R. Yoḥanan ben Zakkai after the destruction of the temple was known as a "vineyard" (*m. Ketub.* 4:6). Philo, characteristically, interprets the reference to Israel as a vine in Isaiah 5:7 in terms of "that most holy vineyard," the virtuous soul (*Dreams* 2.172–73).

THE GOLDEN VINE ON THE JERUSALEM TEMPLE

An artistic depiction of the golden vine on the entrance of the temple.

My Father is the gardener (15:1). The gardener (*geōrgos*) may merely be the one who tills the soil (the term is translated "farmer" in 2 Tim. 2:6 and James 5:7), which in Palestine was frequently all that was done for the vineyard. Yet the term can also refer more specifically to a vinedresser, as in the Synoptic parable of the tenants (Matt. 21:33–41 par.). Isaiah's first vineyard song, which constitutes the background of this parable, depicts God as spading, clearing, planting, and taking care of the vineyard, only to be rewarded with sour grapes (Isa. 5:1–7; cf. Ps. 80:8–9). The Roman writer Lucian portrays God as *geōrgos*, who acts without human collaboration (*Phal.* 2.8; second century A.D.).

He cuts . . . he prunes (15:2). The term "prune" (*kathairō*) is found frequently with reference to agricultural processes (though not necessarily pruning) in secular Greek (e.g., Xenophon, *Oecon.* 18.6; 20.11). The vinedresser does two things to ensure maximum fruit production. In the winter, he cuts off the dry and withered branches. This may involve pruning the vines to the extent that only the stalks remain. Later, when the vine has sprouted leaves, he removes the smaller shoots so that the main fruitbearing branches receive adequate nourishment.[481] Philo refers to "superfluous shoots . . . which are a great injury to the genuine shoots, and which the husbandmen cleanse and prune" (*Dreams* 2.9; cf. 2.64; *Agriculture* 10).

The pruning activity of the divine vinedresser resembles that of every earthly *geōrgos.*[482] Since the term underlying "cut" (*airō*) can mean either "cut off" (negative purpose) or "lift up" (restorative), some have argued that the present reference should be understood in the latter sense. But this is almost certainly erroneous. More likely, the antithetical parallelism of the first part of each statement ("every branch in me that bears no fruit"/"every branch in me that does bear fruit") is matched by corresponding divine action, be it judgment (negative; see 15:6) or discipline (positive).[483] In the case of Jesus' followers, Judas was an example of the former, Peter of the latter.

Branch (15:2). The term "branch" (*klēma*) occurs in the LXX regularly for the "shoot" of a vine (e.g., Num. 13:23; Ezek. 17:6) as distinct from the "branch" (*klados*) of other trees. The expression is used particularly of vine tendrils, though it occasionally refers to heavier branches as well.

Bears no fruit . . . does bear fruit . . . even more fruitful (15:2). The bearing of fruit is God's creative (Gen. 1:11–12, 22, 28) and redemptive purpose (cf. 15:8, 16). The Old Testament prophets envisioned a time when Israel would "bud and blossom and fill all the world with fruit" (Isa. 27:6; cf. Hos. 14:4–8).

Clean (15:3). See 13:10–11. The adjective "clean" (*katharos*) is occasionally used in Greek literature in connection with the growth of vines (Xenophon, *Oecon.* 20.20).

Remain in me, and I will remain in you (15:4). "In" language harks back to Old Testament covenant theology, including prophetic texts regarding a future new covenant.[484]

Like a branch that is thrown away and withers; such branches are picked up, thrown into the fire and burned (15:6). Verses 6 and 7 further develop the contrast of 15:2 (see comment). The present imagery may hark back to the parallel in Ezekiel, where a vine failing to produce fruit is said to be good for nothing but the fire (Ezek. 15:1–8; cf. 19:12). Fire is a common Jewish and biblical symbol for divine judgment.[485]

My joy may be in you and that your joy may be complete (15:11). See Psalm 19:8. In keeping with John's focus on believers' present experience of salvation blessings, he grounds their joy in Old Testament prophetic notions of end-time rejoicing.[486] John the Baptist epitomizes this salvation-historical fulfillment of joy (John 3:29; even already in his mother's womb: Luke 1:41, 44), as does Jesus' mother Mary (1:46–48). The early Christians likewise experienced this complete joy (Acts 13:52; Rom. 15:13; 2 Tim. 1:4).

As in the case of love, John's treatment of joy is remarkably restrained in comparison with other writings such as the *Odes of Solomon* (e.g., 15:1; 23:1; 31:3, 6; 40:4). In rabbinic thought, joy was imperfect in the present age, marred by the certain prospect of death and the worries of this life (*Gen. Rab.* 42:3; attributed to R. Samuel b. Naḥman, c. A.D. 260). Only the age to come, the messianic era, would see perfect joy.[487] Jesus' reference to "perfect joy" thus amounts to his claiming to be the Messiah.

Greater love has no one than this, that he lay down his life for his friends (15:13). Friendship was considered important in the Greco-Roman world. The supreme duty of friendship may involve self-sacrifice for one's friend even to the point of death. Aristotle wrote "that a virtuous man's conduct is often guided by the interests of his friends . . . and that he will if necessary lay down his life in their behalf" (*Eth. Nic.* IX.8.9).[488] Plato, writing on "love's peculiar power," commented, "Only such as are in love will consent to die for others" (*Symp.* 179B). Of the Epicurean Philonides it was said that "for the most beloved of his relatives or friends he was ready to offer his neck" (*Life Phil.* 22). The present statement would thus resonate particularly with John's Greco-Roman audience. Both the Old Testament and rabbinic literature recognize the sanctity of risking one's life for another, though this was not commanded but left up to the individual, and one's own life was often considered to take precedence over the life of another. Friendship was also the subject of extended reflection in intertestamental wisdom literature (esp. Sir. 6:5–17).[489]

You are my friends if you do what I command (15:14). In the Old Testament, only Abraham (2 Chron. 20:7; Isa. 41:8) and by implication Moses (Ex. 33:11) are called "friends of God." Other Jewish writings apply this designation, besides Abraham[490] and Moses,[491] to other Old Testament figures such as Isaac, Jacob, and Levi (*Jub.* 30:20; CD 3:3–4), or to the Israelites in general (e.g., *Jub.* 30:21), "holy souls" (Wisd. Sol. 7:27), and students of Torah (*m. ᵓAbot* 6:1). Because of Abraham's and Moses's unusual degree of access to God, later Jews speculated what revelations other than the ones recorded in Scripture they might have received, which sparked the development of a body of pseudepigraphal literature around these two figures. Here Jesus extends the same privilege of friendship to all believers, predicated on their obedience to his commands.

I no longer call you servants . . . I have called you friends (15:15). The disciples' role as servants is intimated in 13:16 and implied in 13:13.[492] Philo wrote, "It is folly to imagine that the servants of God take precedence over his friends in receiving their portion in the land of virtue" (*Migration* 45). The distinction between servants (*douloi*) and friends (*philoi*) is also found in Gnosticism and mystery religions. As Clement of Alexandria writes, "Wherefore also all men are His; some through knowledge, and others not yet so; and some as friends, some as faithful servants, some as servants merely" (*Strom.* 7.2). On friends, see comments on John 15:13–14.

You did not choose me, but I chose you (15:16). Election is hardly ever mentioned in the case of the Old Testament "friends of God" (Abraham and Moses). Only once is it said of Abraham (Neh. 9:7) and Moses (Ps. 106:23) that they were "chosen" by God. The Old Testament concept of election is primarily related to the king and people of Israel, God's "chosen people" (see comments on John 6:70).[493] In terms of teacher-pupil

REFLECTIONS

FRIENDSHIP IS A MUCH-TREASURED, THOUGH OFTEN elusive, prize. Hardly has there ever been a more unequal friendship than the one between Jesus and his followers: he the eternal, incarnate Word, they sinners in desperate need of redemption. Nevertheless, Jesus extended his friendship to believers. We can continue this cycle by befriending those who are unlike us or may seem unable to repay us for our friendship, especially those outside the faith.

relationships, Jesus here breaks with contemporary custom, for it was common in first-century Palestine for disciples to attach themselves to a particular rabbi, not vice versa, as is summed up by the well-known dictum of R. Joshua b. Perahyah (c. 100 B.C.): "Provide yourself with a teacher" (*m. ʾAbot* 1:6).

Appointed you (15:16). The same or a similar expression is used in the Old Testament for God's appointment of Abraham as father of many nations (Gen. 17:5; cf. Rom. 4:17), the ordination of Levites (Num. 8:10), and Moses' commissioning of Joshua (27:18). In the New Testament, the word used here (*tithēmi*) refers to being "set apart" for a particular ministry, such as Paul's apostolic work or a great number of other callings in the church; in Hebrews 1:2, the phrase even refers to Jesus' being made heir.

The World's Hatred of the Disciples (15:18–16:4)

If the world hates you (15:18). Jesus' disciples are to be known by their love; the world is characterized by hatred. The Qumran community stressed love within the brotherhood but hatred toward outsiders, preaching "everlasting hatred for the men of the pit" (1QS 9:21–22). Hatred in the world was experienced by Christians long before John wrote. The Roman historians Tacitus and Suetonius both called Christianity "a mischievous superstition" (*Annals* 15.44; *Nero* 16).

The following charges were regularly leveled against the early Christians: (1) insurrectionism (claiming Jesus is Lord); (2) cannibalism (eating Christ's body at the Lord's Supper); (3) immorality ("love feasts" [Jude 12], the kiss of love); (4) incendiaries (teaching that the elements will be dissolved and consuming fire will destroy the world [2 Peter 3:10]; thus Nero fastened the blame for the fire of Rome on the Christians); (5) disintegrating family relationships (divided families if the wife became a Christian but the husband did not).[494]

If they obeyed my teaching, they will obey yours also (15:20). As God assured Samuel, "It is not you they have rejected, but they have rejected me" (1 Sam. 8:7). Or as he told the prophet Ezekiel, "The house of Israel is not willing to listen to you because they are not willing to listen to me" (Ezek. 3:7).

Because of my name (15:21). The expression "because of my name" reflects Old Testament terminology pertaining to God and his great name.[495] The claim of Christians that Jesus—and he alone—is Lord (*kyrios*) pitted them against Roman imperial religion, which attributed this title to the Roman emperor. Domitian in particular, who probably reigned when John's Gospel was being written (A.D. 81–96), insisted on the designation *dominus et deus*, that is, Lord and God (cf. 20:28). However, John's Gospel is unequivocal that only those who know Jesus also know the Father.

They hated me without reason (15:25). The citation is from Psalm 35:19 or 69:4, the latter being more likely because Psalm 69 was widely regarded as messianic and frequently quoted elsewhere in the New Testament (see also 119:161, where the psalmist laments, "Rulers persecute me without cause"). In *b. Yoma* 9b, one of the causes for the destruction of the temple is given as "because therein prevailed hatred without cause," and "groundless hatred is considered as of even gravity with the three sins of idolatry, immorality, and bloodshed."

The Spirit of truth (15:26). In the present context, truth is required for the Spirit's role as a witness. At Qumran, the title "spirit of truth" was given to the leader of the forces of good against the forces of evil (e.g., 1QS 3:18). In 1QS 4:21, the expressions "spirit of holiness" (i.e., holy spirit) and "spirit of truth" occur in parallelism (see also the comments on 14:17).

You also must testify (15:27). In Old Testament prophetic literature (esp. Isaiah), God's end-time people are called God's "witnesses" to the nations (e.g., Isa. 43:10–12; 44:8). In the New Testament, believers are frequently promised the Spirit's help in times of persecution (Matt. 10:20; Mark 13:11; Luke 12:12). Particularly in Luke's writings, the Spirit is presented as vitally engaged in missionary outreach (Acts 1:8; cf. Luke 24:48; Acts 5:32; 6:10).

So that you will not go astray (16:1). Literally, "lest you be caused to stumble" (*skandalizō*). Encouraging words from a departing figure to stay true to the Lord God are a regular feature of Jewish farewell discourses. Note how decades after the composition of John's Gospel, Pliny the Younger, governor of Bithynia, wrote to the Roman emperor Trajan (A.D. 98–117):

> The method I have observed toward those who have been denounced to me as Christians is this: I interrogated them whether they were Christians; if they confessed it I repeated the question twice again, adding the threat of capital punishment; if they still persevered, I ordered them to be executed. . . . Others . . . at first confessed themselves Christians, and then denied it; true, they had been of that persuasion but they had quit it . . . many years . . . ago. They all worshipped your statue and the images of the gods, and cursed Christ (*Ep.* 10.96).[496]

Put . . . out of the synagogue (16:2). See comments on 9:22.

A time is coming (16:2). The expression is reminiscent of prophetic or apocalyptic expressions such as "the days are coming."[497]

Anyone who kills you will think he is offering a service to God (16:2). This probably refers to Jewish rather than Roman persecution.[498] In his pre-Christian days, Paul certainly reflected such misguided zeal for his ancestral traditions.[499] Some rabbinic authorities held that slaying heretics was an act of divine worship: "If a man sheds the blood of the wicked it is as though he had offered an offering" (*Num. Rab.* 21:3 with reference to Num. 25:13). However, such kinds of judgments rarely became public policy. For the most part, Jewish persecution of Christians was spontaneous, with seasoned voices counseling moderation.[500] According to Josephus, the Jewish authorities (i.e., the high priest Ananus II) were responsible for the stoning death of James the brother of Jesus in A.D. 62 (*Ant.* 20.9.1 §200). Regarding the preparations for the martyrdom of John's own disciple, the church father Polycarp, we read that "these things happened with so great speed, quicker than it takes to tell, and the crowd came together immediately, . . . and the Jews were extremely zealous, as is their custom, in assisting at this" (*Mart. Pol.* 13.1).

They will do such things because they have not known the Father or me (16:3). On the matter of passing judgment in want of all the facts, Epictetus writes, "When someone treats you ill or speaks ill of you, remember that he acts or speaks thus because he thinks that it is incumbent upon him. . . . If, therefore, you start from this point of view, you will be gentle with the man who reviles you. For you should say on each occasion, 'He thought that way about it'" (*Enchir.* 42).

The Work of the Holy Spirit (16:5–16)

The Counselor (16:7). See comments on 14:16.

I will send him (16:7). Old Testament prophetic literature is full of anticipation regarding the inauguration of the age of the kingdom of God by the pouring out of the Spirit.[501]

When he comes, he will convict (16:8). There are interesting parallels to this statement in Jewish documents. One first-century document says, "And the spirit of truth testifies to all things and brings all accusations. He who has sinned is consumed in his heart and cannot raise his head to face the judge [*kategoreō*]" (*T. Jud.* 20:5). *First Enoch* 1:9 (cited in Jude 15) deals with God's final judgment of the godless, where God will prove them guilty of all their godless works. Elsewhere Enoch functions as accuser of all the godless (cf. *Jub.* 4:23; 10:3–4, 17; *1 En.* 14:1). Another scribe (Michael?) has the task of writing down the transgressions of the seventy shepherds of the people and of reading aloud from this book at God's judgment (*1 En.* 89:62–63, 70; 90:17). The same terminology occurs in the Qumran scrolls where the term "rebuke" is used in a somewhat similar sense (e.g., 1 QS 9:16–17). Greek moralists (such as Philo) use the expression "to convict" (*elencheō*) primarily of the conscience. Occasionally, Philo speaks of the Word as an *elenchos* (e.g., *Worse* 146).

In regard to righteousness (16:10). Isaiah had confessed that all the "righteous acts" of people in his day were "like filthy rags" (Isa. 64:6). The world's (and Jewish) "righteousness" must thus be put in quotation marks; it is in fact the very opposite, *un*righteousness (cf., e.g., Rom. 2:12–24). This is what is here said to be prosecuted by the Spirit of truth in his legal function of *paraklētos*.

Prince of this world (16:11). See comments on 12:31.

Spirit of truth (16:13). See comments on 14:17; 15:26.

Guide . . . into all truth (16:13). Such divine guidance was already the psalmist's longing: "Show me your ways, O LORD, teach me your paths; guide me in your truth" (Ps. 25:4–5; cf. 43:3; 86:11); "may your good Spirit lead me" (143:10). Isaiah recounts how God led his people Israel in the desert by his Holy Spirit (Isa. 63:14) and predicts God's renewed guidance in the future (43:19). Wisdom literature applies guidance terminology to the figure of divine wisdom (Wisd. Sol. 9:11; 10:10, 17). The illuminating function of God's Spirit (or Wisdom) is also prominent in Philo, who writes, "For the mind could not have made so straight an aim if there was not also the divine spirit guiding it to the truth itself" (*Moses* 2.265). For Philo, Moses was the "teacher of divine things," who "has ever the divine spirit at his side, taking the lead in every journey of righteousness" (*Giants* 54–55). According to 1QS 4:2, "These are their [the spirits of light and darkness] paths in the world: to enlighten the heart of man, straighten out in front of him all the paths of justice and truth, establish in his heart respect for the precepts of God."

He will tell you what is yet to come (16:13). This same verb (*anangellō*, "declare, announce") occurs almost sixty times in Isaiah.[502] According to Isaiah, declaring things to come is the exclusive domain of Yahweh (Isa. 48:14). A close parallel to the present passage is Isaiah 44:7, where Yahweh challenges anyone to declare the things to come (cf. 42:9; 46:10). Another striking parallel is found in 41:21–29, where the idols of the nations are exhorted to interpret the meaning of past events and to "declare to us the things to come, tell us what the future holds, so we may know that you are gods" (41:22–23). In 45:19, Yahweh is said to declare truth—an expression combining two of the attributes of the Paraclete predicated on him in the present passage.

You will see me (16:16). The vision of God, denied as a possibility by John (apart from mediation through Jesus; 1:18; 5:37; 6:46) in keeping with Old Testament teaching (Ex. 33:20), is the aspiration of Hellenistic piety, and indeed most of the world's religions.

The Disciples' Grief Will Turn to Joy (16:17–33)

Weep and mourn (16:20). Both terms jointly refer to the loud wailing customary for mourning in the Near East. Similar terminology is already found in the Old Testament: "Do not weep for the dead king or mourn his loss" (Jer. 22:10).

Your grief will turn to joy (16:20). The Jewish feast of Purim celebrates "the time when the Jews got relief from their enemies, and . . . when their sorrow was turned into joy and their mourning into a day of celebration" (Est. 9:22). Old Testament Israel knew that it is God who is able to "turn their mourning into gladness" and to give them "comfort and joy instead of sorrow" (Jer. 31:13; cf. Isa. 61:2–3; 2 Esd. 2:27).

A woman giving birth to a child has pain because her time has come; but when her baby is born she forgets the anquish because of her joy that a child is born into the world (16:21). Everyone who has ever experienced or witnessed the birth of a child can relate to this illustration. In the prophetic portions of the Old Testament, the image of a woman in labor is common[503] and frequently applies to the coming of end-time salvation through the Messiah. The Day of the Lord is regularly portrayed as "a time of distress" (Dan. 12:1; Zeph. 1:14–15).

Intertestamental Judaism coined the phrase "the birth pains of the Messiah" to refer to the period of tribulation that precedes the final consummation.[504] This terminology is also used in Jesus' teaching on the end times, in which he speaks of "the beginning of birth pains" and times of "great distress" (Matt. 24:8, 21, 29 par.; cf. Rom. 2:9). The early church likewise saw present challenges in this larger perspective (Acts 14:22; 1 Cor. 7:26; 2 Cor. 4:17; Rev. 7:14).

You will rejoice (16:22). More literally, "your heart will rejoice." The same phrase occurs in Isaiah 66:14 in the context of the Lord's speaking words of comfort regarding Jerusalem (cf. 60:5). A general parallel is Psalm 33:21: "In him our hearts rejoice, for we trust in his holy name."

Figuratively . . . plainly (16:25). The term *paroimia* (translating Heb. *mašal* in the LXX) covers a wide range of parabolic and allegorical speech (e.g., Sir. 39:3; 47:17; see comments on John 10:6). However, the phrase *en paroimiais* does not necessarily mean "metaphorically" or "in a parable" but connotes the obscurity of Jesus' way of expression.

I came from the Father . . . going back to the Father (16:28). The present passage constitutes a Christological parallel to Isaiah's portrayal of the word of God in 55:11–12 (see comments on John 1:1).

You do not even need to have anyone ask you questions. This makes us believe that you came from God (16:30). Apparently, the disciples think that the promise of 16:23a has been fulfilled. In Jewish thought, the ability to anticipate questions and not needing to be asked is a mark of divinity. Thus Jonathan is said to swear to David by the God "who, before I have expressed my thought in words, already knows what it is" (Josephus, *Ant.* 6.11.8 §230). Elsewhere Jesus himself affirms, "Your Father knows what you need before you ask him" (Matt. 6:8).

You will be scattered (16:32). The present phrase alludes to Zechariah 13:7, a passage quoted in Matthew 26:31 par. Other Old Testament passages likewise refer to the scattering of God's flock.[505]

To his own home (16:32). The phrase also occurs in the LXX (Est. 5:10; 6:12), intertestamental literature (*3 Macc.* 6:27), and later in this Gospel (John 19:27). This probably refers to the disciples' temporary dwellings in Jerusalem rather than to their homes in Galilee.

You may have peace (16:33). See comments on 14:27.

I have overcome (16:33). The verb occurs only once in the LXX with God as the Conqueror (Ps. 51:4; cited in Rom. 3:4). It is also found in apocryphal and pseudepigraphical literature.[506]

Jesus Prays for Himself (17:1–5)

It was not uncommen for farewell discourses to conclude with a prayer (*Jub.* 22:28–30; Sir. 51:1–13; cf. *Jub.* 1:19–21; *4 Ezra* 8:19b–36). John 17 displays several thematic links with the Targums to Exodus 19–20.[507] More important still, Jesus' final prayer culminates John's portrayal of

GARDEN OF GETHSEMANE

A very old olive tree in the traditional site of the garden on the Mount of Olives.

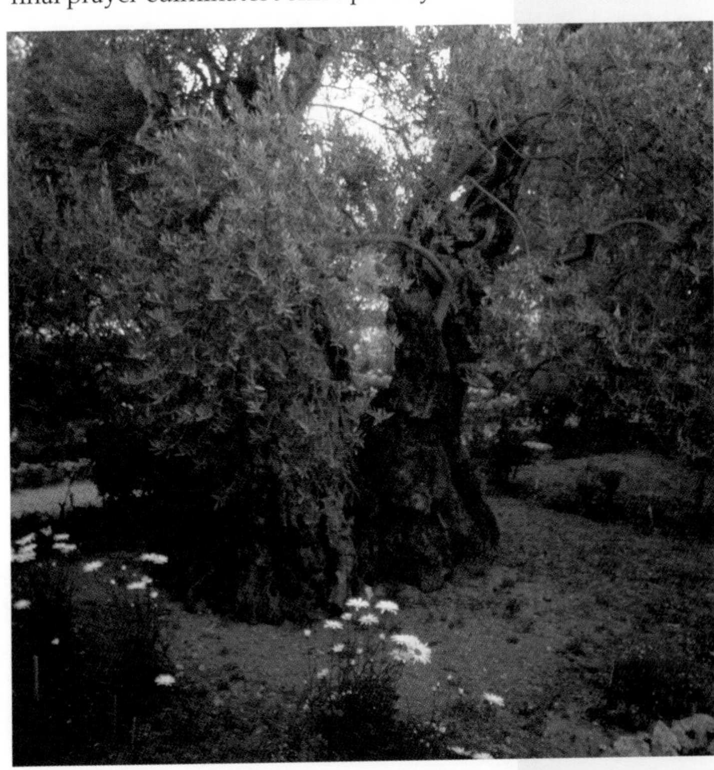

Jesus as the one sent from the Father who, after completing his mission, will soon return to the one who sent him (cf. Isa. 55:10–11).

He looked toward heaven and prayed (17:1). See comments on 11:41.

Father (17:1). See comments on 11:41.

Glorify your Son that your Son may glorify you (17:1). The Old Testament says that God will not give his glory to another (e.g., Isa. 42:8; 48:11). Jesus' sharing his Father's glory thus implies that he is God. In a religious papyrus, a miracle worker prays, "Isis . . . glorify me, as I have glorified the name of your son Horus" (P. Lond. 121.503–504).[508] However, while the terminology is strikingly similar, in the wonder-worker's case he prays to be glorified *because* he has glorified the name of Horus, while Jesus prays to be glorified *in order that* he many glorify the Father.[509]

You granted him authority (17:2). God's granting of authority to Jesus marks the inbreaking of a new era (cf. Isa. 9:6–7; Dan. 7:13–14).[510]

All people (17:2). Literally, "all flesh," a Semitism.

This is eternal life: that they may know you (17:3). The Old Testament relates life after death to the knowledge of God (e.g., Jer. 31:34). Hosea records the divine lament, "My people are destroyed from lack of knowledge" (Hos. 4:6), while both Isaiah and Habakkuk envision a future day when "the earth will be full of the knowledge of the LORD as the waters cover the sea" (Isa. 11:9; Hab. 2:14). God's people are to acknowledge him in all their ways (Prov. 3:6) and to live lives of wisdom (3:18; 11:9). The principle of wise living is also affirmed in later rabbinic teaching.[511]

"Knowing God" does not merely refer to head knowledge (the Greek conception). Rather, it means living in fellowship with God. Of course, God can also be known to a limited extent through creation (e.g., Wisd. Sol. 13:1–9; Rom. 1:18–25). But ultimately, knowledge of God is contingent on religious salvation, as was acknowledged even in Hellenistic Jewish literature: "For to know you is complete righteousness, and to know your power is the root of immortality" (Wisd. Sol. 15:3).

In the Qumran scrolls, "life" and "eternal knowledge" are set in close parallelism: "May he illuminate your heart with the discernment of life and grace you with eternal knowledge" (1QS 2:3; cf. 4:22; 11:3–4). The phrase "eternal life" is found in these writings as well (CD 3:20). In Hellenistic and oriental cults, it was the vision of God received by the initiate that was considered to be the source of life and salvation. Philo wrote, "holding that the knowledge of him is the consummation of happiness. It is also agelong life" (*Spec. Laws* 1.345; cf. *God* 143).

The only true God (17:3). This entire verse conforms closely to the pattern underlying 1 Corinthians 8:6: "there is but one God, the Father . . . and there is but one Lord, Jesus Christ." Similar expressions are also found in New Testament confessions of faith and liturgical formulas (e.g., 1 Thess. 1:9: "the living and true God"; 1 Tim. 1:17: "the only God"; 6:15–16: "God, the blessed and only Ruler . . . who alone is immortal"; 1 John 5:20: "the true God and eternal life"; Rev. 6:10: "Sovereign Lord, holy and true") as well as in Philo (*Alleg. Interp.* 2.68: "the only true God"; *Spec. Laws*

1.332: "the one true God . . . the Being who truly exists, even God"; *Embassy* 366: "the true God") and in other Jewish writings (*3 Macc.* 6:18: "most glorious, almighty, and true God"). See comments on John 5:44 ("the only God").

Jesus Christ (17:3). This phrase occurs elsewhere in this gospel only in 1:17; see also 1 John 4:2. It may strike the modern reader as curious that Jesus should call himself "Jesus Christ," but self-reference in the third person was common in antiquity (cf. John 21:24 and note).[512]

Before the world began (17:5). Preexistence is also ascribed to wisdom in intertestamental wisdom literature (e.g., Wisd. Sol. 7:25; 9:10–11) on the basis of its portrayal in the Old Testament book of Proverbs (esp. Prov. 8:23, 30); but see comments on John 1:1.

Jesus Prays for His Disciples (17:6–19)

You (17:6). Literally, "your name" (also in 17:26). God's "name" enshrines who God is (cf. Ex. 3:13–15). Because his name is glorious, God wants it to be made known.[513] In the Old Testament, knowledge of God's name implies a commitment of life (Ps. 9:10), and God's name is put on the central sanctuary (Deut. 12:5, 21). John takes over both aspects: Jesus' revelation of God's name to his followers must be met with obedience; and Jesus is shown to replace both tabernacle and temple, so that he has become the "place" where God has put his name (see also Isa. 55:13; 62:2; 65:15–16).

Speculation about the divine name was common in the Judaism of Jesus' day. In particular, people wondered about the angel of the Lord referred to in Exodus 23:20–21: "See, I am sending an angel ahead of you to guard you along the way and to bring you to the place I have prepared. . . . *My Name is upon him.*" In later Jewish literature, the name of God became enshrined in the sacred tetragrammaton (Yahweh), so that "the Name" served as a substitute for pronouncing this divine name.

The *Odes of Solomon* states that "the Messiah . . . was known before the foundations of the world, that he might give life to persons forever by the truth of his name" (41:15); moreover, God placed his name on the head of his people because they are free and they are his (42:20). In gnostic literature, "name" refers to the knowledge (*gnōsis*) mediated by the redeemer. This name is revealed only to certain individuals who thereby acquire a share in God's life, light, and joy.

I gave them the words you gave me (17:8). The portrayal of Jesus in the present passage is reminiscent of the description of the prophet like Moses in Deuteronomy 18:18.

Holy Father (17:11). The same phrase is found in *Odes of Solomon* 31:5. The concept goes back to Leviticus 11:44 (cf. Ps. 71:22; 111:9; Isa. 6:3). Similar addresses are found in Jewish literature: "O holy Lord of all holiness" (2 Macc. 14:36); "O Holy One among the holy" (*3 Macc.* 2:2); "You are holy and your Name is awesome" (*Shemoneh ʿEsreh* 3). Holiness is also ascribed to God in the book of Revelation (e.g., Rev. 4:8; 6:10). However, unlike in other Jewish contexts, Jesus' address of God as holy does not create a distance between him and God; for Jesus, God is his holy *Father.*

Protect them by the power of your name (17:11). The phrase "by the power of your name" is probably a Semitic expansion on "by [the instrumentality of] your name." Yet because God's name is powerful, it can be viewed as synonymous with power (see, e.g., Ps. 54:1, where "your name" and "your might" occur in parallelism). The psalmist knows that deliverance from his enemies and help in times of trouble are from the Lord: "Through your name we trample our foes" (44:5); "save me, O God, by your name, vindicate me by your might" (54:1); "our help is in the name of the LORD" (124:8).

The name you gave me (17:11). Exodus 23:21 says of the guardian angel of the people, "my Name is in him"; in Numbers 6:27, the "name" of Yahweh is "put on the Israelites" by the priestly blessing; according to Jeremiah 23:6, the "name" of the messianic King will be "The LORD Our Righteousness." As Paul sums it up, to Jesus God gave "the name that is above every name, that at the name of Jesus every knee should bow . . . and every tongue confess that Jesus Christ is Lord" (Phil. 2:9–10; cf. Rev. 19:12).

I protected them and kept them safe. . . . None has been lost (17:12). Jesus protected his disciples and kept them safe, just as Wisdom did Abraham: "Wisdom . . . preserved him blameless before God and kept him strong" (Wisd. Sol. 10:5). The juxtaposition of the verbs "protect" and "keep safe" reflects Semitic parallelism (see also Prov. 18:10)

The one doomed to destruction (17:12). Lit., "son of destruction." The expression can refer either to Judas's character[514] or his destiny.[515] The NIV rendering "doomed to destruction" suggests the latter, though of course both are true. The noun "destruction" (*apōleia*) commonly refers in the New Testament to final condemnation. The expression "son of perdition" also occurs in 2 Thessalonians 2:3, there with reference to "the man of lawlessness," that is, the antichrist. This suggests that "son of destruction" labels Judas Iscariot as part of a typology of evil personages across the sweep of salvation history seeking to thwart God's sovereign purposes. The phrase "son of" is a Semitism,[516] though it is also attested in classical Greek.[517] Similar expressions (in the plural) are also found in the Qumran writings.[518]

So that Scripture would be fulfilled (17:12). The antecedent passage is probably Psalm 41:10 (applied to Judas in John 13:18). Other Old Testament passages fulfilled through Judas are Psalm 69:25 and 109:8 (cited in Acts 1:20).

Not that you take them out of this world but that you protect them from the evil one (17:15). Parallel wording is attested in rabbinic literature both for "take out of this world"[519] and for "protect from the evil one."[520] Moses (Num. 11:15), Elijah (1 Kings 19:4), and Jonah (Jonah 4:3, 8) all asked to be taken out of this world, but none of their prayers was answered (though Elijah was taken up to heaven at a later time).

Sanctify (17:17). The address "Holy Father" in 17:11 would suggest to the Jewish mind that holiness was also expected of Jesus' followers, according to the principle enunciated in the book of Leviticus (11:44; 19:2; 20:26).

Your word is truth (17:17). The present phrase is similar to Psalm 119:142: "Your law is true" (cf. 119:151, 160). David likewise acknowledged, "Your words are trustworthy" (2 Sam. 7:28; cf. Ps. 19:7). In common Jewish prayer, it was acknowledged that God sanctifies people through his commandments.

As you sent me into the world, I have sent them into the world (17:18). A partial Old Testament parallel is the instruction to Moses, who had himself been consecrated by God (Sir. 45:4) in order to consecrate others so that they too may serve God as priests (Ex. 28:41).

For them I sanctify myself, that they too may be truly sanctified (17:19). Jesus' sanctification "for" (*hyper*) others is similar to atonement passages elsewhere in the New Testament (e.g., Mark 14:24; John 6:51; 1 Cor. 11:24). It is also reminiscent of the Old Testament notion of "setting apart" sacrificial animals (e.g., Deut. 15:19).

Jesus Prays for All Believers (17:20–26)

My prayer is not for them alone (17:20). See the parallel in Deuteronomy 29:14–15: "I am making this covenant . . . not only with you . . . but also with those who are not here today."

So that the world may believe that you have sent me (17:21). The coordination between unity and love is paralleled by exhortations to brotherly love and harmony in Jewish testamentary literature, which attributes this parting concern to Noah (*Jub*. 7:26), Rebecca (*Jub*. 35:20), Isaac (*Jub*. 36:4), Zebulon (*T. Zeb*. 8:5–9:4), Joseph (*T. Jos*. 17:2–3), and Daniel (*T. Dan*. 5:3).

Brought to complete unity (17:23). The Qumran covenanters also saw themselves as a *yaḥad* ("union") and displayed a keen consciousness of their election.[521]

To let the world know that you sent me (17:23). This phrase is reminiscent of Old Testament passages such as Zechariah 2:9: "Then you will know that the LORD Almighty has sent me."

Before the creation of the world (17:24). Literally, "before the foundation of the world." The phrase "from the beginning of the world" was frequently used in Judaism.[522] A suggestive parallel is found in *Odes of Solomon* 41:15, where the Messiah is said to have been "known before the foundations of the world, that he might give life to persons forever by the truth of his name."

Righteous Father (17:25). The Old Testament commonly teaches that God is righteous and just.[523] With Jesus' betrayal and innocent suffering imminent, he affirms the righteousness of God his Father.

REFLECTIONS

JESUS' PARTING PRAYER IS FOR believers' love and unity, so that unbelievers may come to know him through them. The church has miserably failed to live up to this longing of Jesus' heart. It has constantly been plagued by painful divisions, competitiveness, and an unforgiving spirit. How can we expect unbelievers to be attracted to Jesus if this is the state of the company of his followers? We must repent and make it our ambition to promote love and unity with other Christians so that those outside the faith will see Christ in us.

I myself may be in them (17:26). Subsequent to the giving of the law at Sinai, the glory of God displayed on the mountain (Ex. 24:16) came to dwell in the midst of Israel in the tabernacle (40:34). As the Israelites moved toward the Promised Land, God frequently assured them that he was in their midst (29:45–46; Deut. 7:21; 23:14). In John's prologue, Jesus is said to have come to dwell (lit., "tabernacle") among his people (John 1:14; see comments), and now Jesus' earthly presence is about to be transmuted into his spiritual presence in his followers in keeping with Old Testament notions of a new covenant.

Jesus' Arrest (18:1–11)

The Gospels narrate two trials of Jesus, one Jewish and one Roman.[524] The former started with an informal hearing before Annas (18:12–14, 19–24), while Sanhedrin members were probably summoned in order to stage a more formal trial. A meeting of the highest Jewish body (Matt. 26:57–68; Mark 14:53–65) then led to formal charges and the sending of a delegation to Pilate (Matt. 27:1–2; Luke 22:66–71). The Roman trial consisted of an initial interrogation by Pilate (Matt. 27:11–14; John 18:28–38a), followed by an appearance before Herod (Luke 23:6–12) and a final summons before Pilate (Matt. 27:15–31; John 18:38b–19:16).

Though Jewish law contained numerous stipulations regarding legal proceedings against those charged with serious offenses, many such stipulations could be breached if the matter was judged to be urgent (including the possibility of mob violence). Another factor in Jesus' case was that executions could proceed on feast days but not on a Sabbath. Thus if Jesus' arrest took place on Thursday evening, little time remained if he was to be tried and put to death before the onset of the Sabbath at sundown of the following day. Moreover, Roman officials such as Pilate worked only from dawn until late morning, so that the Jews' case against Jesus had to be prepared overnight.[525]

KIDRON VALLEY

The Kidron Valley (18:1). The Kidron Valley is frequently mentioned in the LXX and Jewish intertestamental literature.[526] Literally, the expression is "the brook [*cheimarros*] of Kidron," where "brook" refers to an intermittent stream that is dry most of the year but swells up during rainfalls, particularly in the winter (Josephus, *Ant.* 8.1.5 §17). The Kidron Valley, called "Wadi en-Nar," continues variously south or southeast until it reaches the Dead Sea (cf. Ezek. 47:1–12; Zech. 14:8).

An olive grove (18:1). To the east of the Kidron rises the Mount of Olives. The olive grove (*kēpos*, lit. "garden") on its slopes is called "Gethsemane" (meaning "oil press") in the Synoptics.[527] This garden may have been made available to Jesus and his followers by a wealthy person who supported Jesus' ministry. The phrase "there was" rather than "there is" may indicate that the garden had been destroyed by the time of the writing of John's Gospel.

Went into it (18:1). John's terminology ("went into it," later "went out") suggests a walled garden. According to Jewish custom (with reference to Deut. 16:7), Passover night was to be spent in Jerusalem, but in light of the large number of pilgrims, city limits were extended as far as Bethphage on the Mount of Olives (though Bethany lay beyond the legal boundary).[528]

A detachment of soldiers (18:3). A *speira* was a detachment consisting of a cohort of Roman soldiers.[529] A full cohort was led by a *chiliarchos* (lit., "leader of a thousand," rendered "tribune" or "commander") and consisted of one thousand men, though in practice it often numbered only six hundred.[530] The Romans could use surprisingly large numbers of soldiers even for a single person (like the 470 men protecting Paul in Acts 23:23), especially if they feared a riot. Roman troops were stationed in Caesarea, but during feast days gathered northwest of the temple by the fortress of Antonia. This enabled the Romans to keep a close eye on the large crowds during Jewish festivals and to quell any mob violence at the very outset.

Some officials from the chief priests and Pharisees (18:3). These "officials" (*hypēretai*) represented the temple police, the primary arresting officers. This unit was commanded by the captain of the temple guard (cf. Acts 4:1), who was charged with watching the temple at night (*m. Mid.* 1:1–2). Their arms and methods are recalled in a "street ballad":

> *Woe is me, for the house of Boethus:*
> *woe is me, for their clubs!*
> *Woe is me, for the house of Annas:*
> *woe is me, for their whisperings!*
> *Woe is me, for the house of Kdathros:*
> *woe is me, for their pen!*
> *Woe is me, for the house of Ishmael (ben Phabi): woe is me, for their fist!*
> *For they are the High Priests, and their sons the treasurers: their sons-in-law are Temple-officers, and their servants beat the people with their staves.*[531]

The chief priests (made up predominantly of Sadducees) and the Pharisees are regularly linked in this Gospel (cf. Josephus, *Life* 5 §21).

Chief priests (18:3). The rubric of "chief [or high] priests" included the incumbent high priest, former high priests still living (such as Annas), and members of aristocratic families from whom high priests were chosen.[532]

They were carrying torches, lanterns and weapons (18:3). Torches (*lampas*) consisted of resinous strips of wood fastened together.[533] Lanterns (*phanoi*) were "roughly cylindrical terracotta vessels with an opening on one side large enough for a household lamp to be inserted, its wick facing outward; a ceramic ring—or strap—handle on the top permitted easy carrying. Occasionally lanterns may have had built-in lamps."[534] Roman soldiers carried both kinds of lighting devices,[535] and the temple guard went on their rounds with "lighted torches" (*m. Mid.* 1:2). While this was the time close to the full paschal moon, lanterns might still be needed to track down a suspect who (it probably was suspected) was hiding from the authorities in the dark corners of this olive grove. "*They* were carrying" does not mean that all are carrying torches; it would have been sufficient for only some to do so. Regarding the carrying of weapons, it may be noted that sometimes the temple guards were unarmed,[536] but in the present instance both they and the Roman soldiers take no chances.

I am he (18:5). Literally, "I am." In light of people's response, the phrase probably has connotations of deity.

And fell to the ground (18:6). Falling to the ground is regularly a reaction to divine revelation.[537] Legend has it that Pharaoh fell to the ground speechless when Moses uttered the secret name of God.[538] Falling to the ground also speaks of the powerlessness of the enemies when confronted with the power of God. The phrase is reminiscent of certain passages in the Psalms.[539] Jewish literature recounts the story of the attempted arrest of Simeon: "On hearing his voice they fell on their faces and their teeth were broken" (*Gen. Rab.* 91:6). The reaction also highlights Jesus' messianic authority in keeping with passages such as Isaiah 11:4: "He will strike the earth with the rod of his mouth; with the breath of his lips he will slay the wicked" (cf. 2 Esd. 13:3–4).

Malchus (18:10). The name Malchus is not uncommon in the first century A.D. It occurs several times in Josephus, almost entirely of Natabean Arabs[540] as well as in the Palmyrene and Nabatean inscriptions.[541] The name probably derives from the common Semitic root *mlk* (*melek* means "king").

Sword (18:10). According to Luke 22:38, Jesus' disciples possessed a total of two swords. The term "sword" (*machaira*) may refer to a long knife or a short sword, with *rhomphaia* being the large sword. The fact that Peter's action is unforeseen suggests the short sword, which could be concealed under one's garments. It may have been illegal to carry such a weapon at Passover: "A man may not go out with a sword" (*m. Šabb.* 6:4; so the Sages with reference to Isa. 2:4, but not R. Eliezer [A.D. 90–130]: "They are his adornments").

right ▶

MODEL OF A ROMAN ERA SWORD

Right ear (18:10). Both Mark (14:47) and John use the term *ōtarion*, a double diminutive, equivalent to our "earlobe." It is possible that Peter deliberately chooses the right ear (which was considered to be the more valuable)[542] as a mark of defiance. While generally an injury to a slave would not have aroused much interest, Jesus shows concern even for this (by human standards) insignificant (Arab?) slave.

The cup (18:11). "Cup" serves here as a metaphor for death. In the Old Testament, the expression refers primarily to God's "cup of wrath," which evildoers will have to drink.[543] Similar terminology is found in later Jewish writings and the New Testament.[544] This imagery may have been transferred to the righteous, guiltless one taking on himself God's judgment by way of substitutionary suffering.[545]

Jesus Taken to Annas (18:12–14)

The detachment of soldiers . . . its commander . . . the Jewish officials (18:12). See comments on 18:3.

They bound him (18:12). "To be bound" is a customary expression in conjunction with arrest or imprisonment (e.g., Acts 9:2, 14, 21; already in Plato, *Leg.* 9.864E).

Annas (18:13). See "Annas the High Priest."

Caiaphas, the high priest that year. Caiaphas was the one who had advised the Jews that it would be good if one man died for the people (18:13–14). See comments on 11:49–52. Under Roman occupation, the high priests were the dominant political leaders of the Jewish nation.[546]

Peter's First Denial (18:15–18)

Another disciple . . . was known to the high priest (18:15). The "other disciple" is probably none other than "the disciple Jesus loved" (cf. 20:2).[547] While John was a fisherman, this does not mean that he stemmed from an inferior social background. John's father Zebedee is presented in Mark 1:20 as a man with hired servants, and either John and his brother James or their mother had prestigious ambitions (Matt. 20:20–28 par.). Moreover, it is not impossible that John himself came from a priestly family.[548] "Known" (*gnōstos*; used in John 18:15, 16) may suggest more than mere acquaintance. The term is used for a "close friend" in the LXX.[549]

The high priest's courtyard (18:15). The official high priest was Caiaphas, though Annas may have been referred to under

▸ Annas the High Priest

While Annas is also mentioned by Luke (Luke 3:2; Acts 4:6), John is the only evangelist to report that Jesus appeared before Annas. Annas ("Ananus the son of Seth[i]"; cf. Josephus, *Ant.* 18.2.1 §26) held the office of high priest from A.D. 6 until A.D. 15. He was appointed by Quirinius, the Roman prefect and governor of Syria, and removed from office by Pilate's predecessor, Valerius Gratus (A.D. 15–26; cf. Josephus, *Ant.* 18.2.2 §34). Even after his deposition, Annas continued to sway considerable influence, not only because his removal from office was thought by many Jews to reflect the arbitrary nature of priestly appointments of the day, but also because as many as five of his sons (Eleazar, Jonathan, Theophilus, Matthias, and Anan), as well as Joseph Caiaphas (his son-in-law) held the office at one point or another (*Ant.* 20.9.1 §§197–98; Annas's tomb is mentioned in *J.W.* 5.12.2 §506).

Thus, even though Caiaphas held the official position of high priest that year, many still considered Annas, the patriarch of this preeminent high priestly family, as the real high priest, especially since under Mosaic legislation the appointment was for life (Num. 35:25). As the Mishnah states, "And who is the anointed [High Priest]? He that is anointed with the oil of unction, but not he that is dedicated by the many garments."[A-26] Josephus indicates that it was customary for former high priests to continue to be called by that term (*J.W.* 5.151, 160). The family is mentioned several times in later Jewish writings; it was noted not only for its large size, wealth, and power,[A-27] but also for its greed (see the street ballad cited at 18:3). This family's wealth is reported later to have been destroyed by the Zealots.

this designation as well (see comments on 18:13). Presumably, he lived in the Hasmonean palace on the west hill of the city, which overlooked the Tyropoeon Valley and faced the temple. It is possible that Caiaphas and Annas lived in the same palace, occupying different wings bound together by a common courtyard.

The high priest (18:15–16). The sequence of references to "the high priest" in this chapter (esp. 18:13–14, 19, 24) shows that Annas is in view and that the courtyard (*aulē*) is the atrium connected with his house. The mention of a "girl on duty" confirms that the scene takes place outside the temple area, for there only men held such assignments (see also comments on 18:18). Caiaphas's quarters may have shared the same courtyard, so that even the second stage of the investigation would have been relatively private (though with at least some Sanhedrin members present). The formal action taken by the Sanhedrin (at about dawn) is not recorded in John's Gospel (cf. Matt. 27:1–2 par.).

The girl on duty . . . the girl at the door (18:16–17). On women gatekeepers, see 2 Samuel 4:6 (LXX) and Acts 12:13 ("servant girl named Rhoda").[550] The same word (*paidiskē*) is rendered "bondwoman" (in distinction from "free woman") in Galatians 4:22–31. Apparently, the female doorkeeper was a domestic female slave, probably of mature age, since her responsibility required judgment and life experience.[551]

It was cold (18:18). Nights in Jerusalem, which is only half a mile above sea level, can be cold in the spring.

The servants and officials (18:18). The soldiers have returned to their barracks, entrusting the role of guarding Jesus to the temple guards.

A fire (18:18). The presence of a fire confirms that these preliminary proceedings against Jesus take place at night, when the cold would incite people to make a fire to stay warm. Even at night, fires were not normally lit,[552] and night proceedings were generally regarded as illegal. Moreover, the fact that a fire was kept burning in the Chamber of Immersion so that the priests on night duty could warm themselves there and that lamps were burning even along the passage that led below the temple building (*m. Tamid* 1:1) suggest that the courtyard referred to in the present passage is private.

Jesus Before the High Priest (18:19–24)

The high priest (18:19). Again, Annas is referred to as "the high priest." The appropriateness of such a designation even after he was removed from office is confirmed both by the Mishnah (where the high priest is said to retain his obligations even when no longer in office; *m. Hor.* 3:1–2, 4) and Josephus (where Jonathan is called high priest fifteen years after his deposition; *J.W.* 2.12.6 §243; cf. 4.3.7–9 §§151–60). There may even be an element of defiance in the Jewish practice of continuing to call previous high priests by that name, challenging the Roman right to depose officials whose tenure was to be for life according to Mosaic legislation (Num. 35:25). Apparently, the seasoned, aged Annas still wielded considerable high priestly power while his relatives held the title.

Questioned Jesus (18:19). The fact that Jesus is questioned—a procedure considered improper in formal Jewish trials where a case had to rest on the weight of witness testimony (e.g. *m. Sanh.* 6:2)—suggests that the present hearing is informal (see comments on 18:21). On the Sadducees' reputation for judging in general, Josephus writes that "the school of the Sadducees . . . are indeed more heartless than any of the other Jews . . . when they sit in judgment" (*Ant.* 20.9.1 §199).

His disciples and his teaching (18:19). The question here addressed to Jesus indicates that the authorities' primary concern is theological, though a political rationale is later given to Pilate (cf. 19:7, 12). The Jewish leadership seems to view Jesus as a false prophet (see later *b. Sanh.* 43a), who secretly entices people to fall away from the God of Israel, an offense punishable by death (Deut. 13:1–11).[553] Apparently, Annas hopes Jesus might incriminate himself on those counts.

I have spoken openly to the world. . . . I always taught in synagogues or at the temple, where all the Jews come together. I said nothing in secret (18:20). Some see in the present statement an echo of the motif of Wisdom speaking to the people in public (Prov. 8:2–3; 9:3; Wisd. Sol. 6:14, 16; Bar. 3:37). More likely, Jesus is simply pointing to the public nature of his instruction, which has made it possible for the Jewish authorities to gather ample eyewitness testimony from those who have heard him teach. See further comment on "I said nothing in secret" below.

At the temple (18:20). This refers to the temple precints, variously translated "temple courts" or "temple area" in the NIV.

I said nothing in secret (18:20). Note the earlier acknowledgment by the people of Jerusalem that Jesus was "speaking publicly" (7:26). Jesus' words here echo Yahweh's in Isaiah 45:19; 48:16: "I have not spoken in secret." Socrates answered his judges similarly: "But if anyone says that he ever learned or heard anything privately from me, which all the others did not, be assured that he is not telling the truth" (Plato, *Apol.* 33B). The Qumran community, by contrast, preferred secret teaching, as did the mystery religions.

Why question me? Ask those who heard me. Surely they know what I said (18:21). Jesus' challenge is understandable especially if the questioning of prisoners was considered improper in his day (see comments on 18:19). This is further confirmed by the recognized legal principle that a person's own testimony regarding himself was deemed invalid (see 5:31). While an accused could raise an objection (which had to be heard: see 7:50–51; see also the apocryphal story of Susanna), a case was to be established by way of testimony, whereby witnesses *for* the defendant were to be questioned first (*m. Sanh.* 4:1; cf. Matt. 26:59–63 par.). If the testimony of witnesses agreed on essential points, the fate of the accused was sealed. This violation of formal procedure strongly suggests that Jesus' hearing before Annas is unofficial.

Ask those who heard me (18:21). Jesus is asking for a proper trial where evidence is established by interrogation of witnesses; the present informal hearing does not meet such qualifications. Such display of self-confidence before authority is in all likelihood startling. As Josephus tells us, those charged normally maintained an attitude of humility before their judges, assuming "the manner of one who is fearful and seeks mercy" (*Ant.* 14.9.4 §172).

One of the officials (18:22). The official (*hypēretēs*) in question is one of the temple guard who took part in Jesus' arrest (cf. 18:3, 12).

Struck him in the face (18:22). This is not the only ill-treatment Jesus has to endure during his Jewish trial before the Sanhedrin. According to Matthew, "they spit in his face and struck him with their fists. Others slapped him" (26:67). The word used here (*rhapisma*) denotes a sharp blow with the flat of one's hand (cf. Isa. 50:6 LXX). Striking a prisoner was against Jewish law.[554] Compare the similar incident involving Paul in Acts 23:1–5, where the high priest Ananias ordered those standing near Paul to strike him on the mouth.

Is this the way you answer the high priest? (18:22). A proper attitude toward authority was legislated by Exodus 22:28: "Do not blaspheme God or curse the ruler of your people" (quoted by Paul in Acts 23:5). See also Josephus, *Ag. Ap.* 2.24 §§194–95: "Anyone who disobeys him [the high priest] will pay the penalty as for impiety towards God himself."

If I said something wrong (18:23). Literally, "spoke in an evil manner," that is, "if I said something that dishonored the high priest." Jesus implicitly refers to the law of Exodus 22:28 (see previous comment) and denies having violated it. The LXX uses the expression "speak evil" for cursing the deaf and blind (Lev. 19:14), one's parents (20:9), the king and God (Isa. 8:21), and the sanctuary (1 Macc. 7:42).

Then Annas sent him, still bound, to Caiaphas the high priest (18:24). Before Jesus can be brought to Pilate, charges must be confirmed by the *official* high priest, Caiaphas, in his function as chairman of the Sanhedrin.[555] Just where the Sanhedrin met at that time is subject to debate.[556] A mishnaic source specifies the Chamber of Hewn Stone on the south side of the temple court (*m. Mid.* 5:4), while the Babylonian Talmud indicates that the Sanhedrin ceased meeting in this location "forty years" (not necessarily a literal time marker; e.g., *b. Yoma* 39a) prior to the destruction of the temple, moving to the marketplace.[557] Then again, "sent" need not imply movement to another building at all but may merely refer to changing courtrooms in the temple.

Peter's Second and Third Denials (18:25–27)

A relative of the man whose ear Peter had cut off (18:26). Being one of Jesus' disciples was not a legal offence, though it could have been surmised that open confession might lead to trouble, especially if Jesus is found guilty and executed (cf. 20:19). Of more immediate concern for Peter may have been the earlier incident in which he drew a weapon (perhaps carried illegally) and assaulted one of the high priest's servants (Malchus). Peter's denial of association with Jesus may therefore stem from a basic instinct of self-preservation and a self-serving desire on his part not to incriminate himself.

A rooster began to crow (18:27). While mishnaic legislation forbids the raising of fowl in Jerusalem (*m. B. Qam.* 7:7: "They may not rear fowls in Jerusalem"), it is unlikely this prohibition is strictly obeyed in Jesus' day.[558] Exactly when cocks crowed in first-century Jerusalem is subject to debate; estimates range from between 12:30 to 2:30 A.M. to between 3:00 and 5:00 A.M. Some have argued that reference is made here not to the actual crowing of a rooster but to the trumpet signal given at the close of the third watch, named "cockcrow" (midnight to 3:00 A.M.).[559] If so, Jesus' interrogation by Annas and Peter's denials would have concluded at 3:00 A.M. See comments on 13:38.

Jesus Before Pilate (18:28–40)

The palace of the Roman governor (18:28). Jesus is led to the Praetorium, the headquarters of the Roman governor. While based in Caesarea in a palace built by Herod the Great (cf. Acts 23:33–35), Pilate, like his predecessors, made it a practice to go up to Jerusalem for high feast days in order to be at hand for any disturbance that might arise. It is unclear whether Pilate's Jerusalem headquarters is to be identified with the Herodian palace on the western wall (suggested by the NIV's "palace") or the Fortress of Antonia (named after Mark Antony; Josephus, *J.W.* 1.21.1 §401) northwest of the temple grounds.[560]

Herod the Great had both palaces built, the former in 35 B.C. (on the site of an older castle erected by John Hyrcanus, see Josephus, *Ant.* 18.4.3 §91) and the latter in 23 B.C., whereby especially Philo identifies the (former) Herodian palace as the usual Jerusalem headquarters of Roman governors.[561] Yet the discovery of massive stone slabs in the Fortress of Antonia in 1870 has convinced some that it is this building that is in view (see further comments on 19:13).[562] On balance, the Herodian palace is more likely, especially in light of the above cited evidence from Philo and Josephus.[563]

Early morning (18:28). The expression "early morning" (*prōi*) is ambiguous. The last two watches of the night (from midnight to 6:00 A.M.) were called "cockcrow" (*alektorophōnia*) and "early morning" (*prōi*) by the Romans. If this is how the term is used here, Jesus is brought to Pilate before 6:00 A.M. This coheres with the practice, followed by many Roman officials, of starting the day very early and finishing the workday by late morning: "The emperor Vespasian was at his official duties even before the hour of dawn, and the elder Pliny, most industrious of Roman officials, had completed his working day, when Prefect of the Fleet, by the end of the fourth or fifth hour [i.e., 10:00 or 11:00 A.M.]. In Martial's account of daily life at the capital, where two hours are assigned to the protracted duty of *salutatio*, the period of *labores* ends when the sixth hour begins [noon]. Even a country gentleman at leisure begins his day at the second hour [7:00 A.M.]."[564] In light of Jewish scruples to try capital cases at night (see comments on 18:18), it is more likely that "early morning" means shortly after sunrise, when the Sanhedrin meets in formal session and pronounces its verdict on Jesus (Matt. 27:1–2 par.).

To avoid ceremonial uncleanness the Jews did not enter the palace; they wanted to be able to eat the Passover (18:28). Jews who entered Gentile

FORTRESS OF ANTONIA

A model of the fortress, which stood in the northwest corner of the temple grounds.

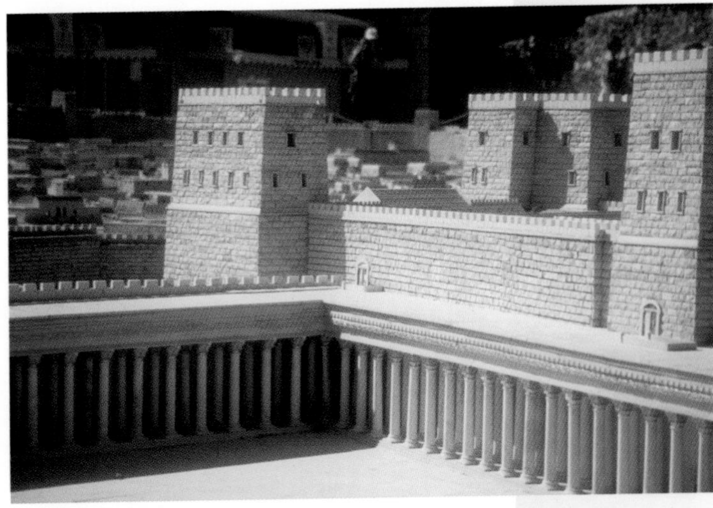

homes were considered unclean,[565] which would prevent them from celebrating the Passover. The present reference may not merely be to the Passover itself but to the Feast of Unleavened Bread, which lasted for seven days,[566] in particular to the offering (*hagigah*) brought on the morning of the first day of the festival (cf. Num. 28:18–19). "Eat the Passover" probably simply means "celebrate the feast" (cf. 2 Chron. 30:21).[567]

Pilate (18:29). See "Pontius Pilate."

Take him yourselves and judge him by your own law (18:31). Like Gallio after him (Acts 18:14–15), Pilate is not interested in being a judge of internal Jewish disputes.

But we have no right to execute anyone (18:31). Despite instances where the Jewish authorities are involved in executions, such as the stonings of Stephen (Acts 7) and of James the half-brother of Jesus in A.D. 62 (Josephus, *Ant.* 20.9.1 §200) and the burning of a priest's daughter accused of committing adultery (*m. Sanh.* 7:2)—all of which involved lynch law or breaches of authority—the Sanhedrin did not have the power of capital punishment.[568] As Josephus reports, "The territory of Archelaus was now [A.D. 6] reduced to a province, and Coponius, a Roman of the equestrian order, was sent out as procurator, entrusted by Augustus with full powers, including the infliction of capital punishment" (*J.W.* 2.3.4 §117).

The same writer tells of a case where the high priest had sentenced some people to death by stoning, a sentence that was protested by some apparently for the reason that the Sanhedrin did not have the authority to impose the death penalty during the period of Roman rule in Judea. Sure enough, the high priest was deposed for his presumption (*Ant.* 20.9.1 §§197–203). This comports with the acknowledgment in Talmudic literature that the Jews had lost this power "forty years" before the destruction of Jerusalem.[569] Not only was this consistent with general Roman practice in provincial administration, capital punishment was the most jealously guarded of all governmental powers.[570]

Moreover, an equestrian procurator such as Pilate in an insignificant province like Judea had no assistants of high rank who could help him carry out his administrative and judicial duties. Thus, he must rely on local officials in minor matters while retaining the right to intervene in major cases, including "crimes for which the penalty was hard labor in mines, exile, or death."[571] Also, in handling criminal trials, the prefect or procurator was not bound by Roman law,

PASSOVER SCENE

A model of the court of priests in the Jerusalem temple showing the altar of sacrifice.

which applied only to Roman citizens and cities. For this reason it is difficult to determine with certainty Pilate's motives in offering to give the case back to the Jewish authorities.

Kind of death he was going to die (18:32). Crucifixion was looked upon by the Jews with horror, as when Alexander Jannaeus had eight hundred of his captives crucified in the center of Jerusalem.[572] Execution on a cross was considered to be the same as hanging (Acts 5:30; 10:39), for which Mosaic law enunciated the principle, "Anyone who is hung on a tree is under God's curse" (Deut. 21:23; cf. Gal. 3:13). If Jesus had been put to death by the Sanhedrin, stoning would have been the likely mode of execution, since that is the penalty specified in the Old Testament for blasphemy,[573] the most common charge against Jesus in John. Other forms of capital punishment sanctioned by mishnaic teaching are burning, beheading, and strangling (*m. Sanh.* 7:1).

Pilate . . . asked him (18:33). In contrast to Jewish practice (see comments on 18:9 and 21), Roman law made provisions for

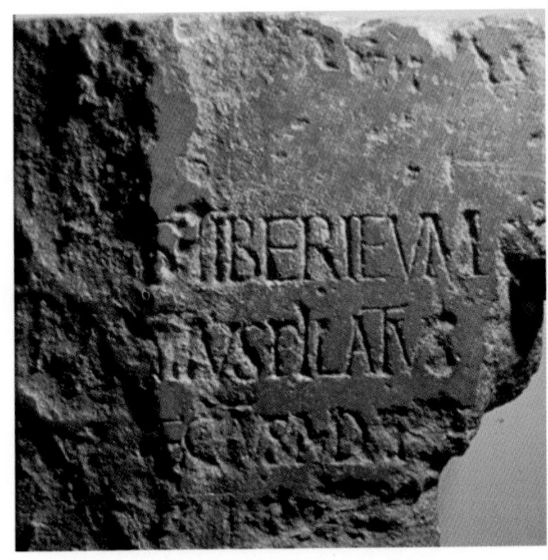

PONTIUS PILATE INSCRIPTION

Pontius Pilate

Pontius Pilate, governor of Judea, was appointed to his post by the emperor Tiberius in A.D. 26 and held this position for about ten years until A.D. 36/37.[A-28] According to Philo, Pilate owed his appointment to Sejanus, the commander of the Praetorian Guard in Rome (*Embassy* 159). If the chronology I presented in John 1 is correct, Pilate would have been governor for about seven years (the year of Jesus' trial being A.D. 33). The Synoptists use the generic title "governor" (*hēgemōn*) with regard to Pilate (e.g., Matt. 27:2, 11; Luke 20:20). Tacitus, the Roman historian, calls him *procurator* (*Ann.* 15.44); Josephus uses the equivalent expression *epitropos* (*J.W.* 2.9.2 §169). The famous Latin "Pilate inscription," found in Caesarea in 1961, identifies him as "prefect" (*praefectus*) of Judea: [PON]TIUS PILATUS [PRAEF]ECTUS IUDA[EA]E.[A-29]

Apparently, Pilate could act from a position of strength until the death of his mentor Sejanus (Oct. 18, A.D. 31), after which he had to tread much more lightly.[A-30] Since the Gospels portray Pilate's conduct at Jesus' trial as accommodating the Jews and as vulnerable personally, it is likely that his trial took place after A.D. 31 (i.e., in A.D. 33). Pilate was of equestrian rank, of lower nobility than senator, since Judea was considered to be a lesser imperial province.

Jesus' trial and crucifixion under Pilate is also attested by non-Christian sources, such as the Roman historian Tacitus, who writes, "Christ had been executed in Tiberius' reign by the procurator of Judea, Pontius Pilate" (*Ann.* 15.44). Pilate's tenure came to an end in A.D. 36/37, when he was deposed and sent to Rome by Vitellius, legate of Syria, on account of his brutal action in a Samaritan uprising (Josephus, *Ant.* 18.4.2 §§88–89).[A-31] He arrived in Rome after Tiberius's death (March 16, A.D. 37).

detailed questioning of persons charged with crimes, whether they were Roman citizens (*accusatio*) or not (*cognitio*).[574] These hearings were public and awarded the accused person with sufficient opportunity to defend himself against the charges, as seems to be presupposed in Jesus' case by the Synoptics.

The palace (18:33). See comments on 18:28.

Are you the king of the Jews? (18:33). "King of the Jews" may have been used by the Hasmoneans who ruled Judea prior to the Roman subjugation of Palestine. Josephus recounts that a golden vine or garden with the inscription "From Alexander, the king of the Jews" was given to the Roman general Pompey by Alexander, son of Alexander Jannaeus, and later transported to Rome and put in the temple of Jupiter Capitolinus (*Ant.* 14.3.1 §36). The title "king of the Jews" is also applied to Herod the Great (*Ant.* 16.10.2 §311).

Thus the designation "king of the Jews" has clearly political overtones, and Pilate's question is designed to determine whether Jesus constitutes a political threat to Roman imperial power.[575] Pilate's gubernatorial tenure was punctuated by outbursts of ethnic nationalism, which rendered him ever more alert to potential sources of trouble, especially since Judea was "infested with brigands" (*Ant.* 20.10.5 §215) and "anyone might make himself king as the head of a band of rebels" (*Ant.* 17.10.8 §285).[576]

My kingdom is not of this world. . . .But now my kingdom is from another place (18:36). Earlier, Jesus refused people's efforts to make him king (6:15). The answer given by the grandchildren of Jude, Jesus' half-brother, at a trial before Domitian echoes Jesus' words: "And when they were asked concerning Christ and his kingdom, of what sort it was and where and when it was to appear, they answered that it was not a temporal nor an earthly kingdom, but a heavenly and angelic one, which would appear at the end of the world" (Eusebius, *Eccl. Hist.* 3.20.6). Jesus' description of the nature of his kingdom echoes similar passages in Daniel (e.g., Dan. 2:44; 7:14, 27).

My servants (18:36). The term rendered "servant" (*hypēretēs*) has previously been used for the temple police. In the LXX, the expression refers to the minister or officer of a king (Prov. 14:35; Isa. 32:5; Dan. 3:46) or even kings themselves (Wisd. Sol. 6:4: "servants of his kingdom").

What is truth? (18:38). With this flippant remark, Pilate dismisses Jesus' claim that he has come to testify to the truth and that everyone on the side of truth lis-

REFLECTIONS

THE JEWISH LEADERS OF JESUS' day may well have known that Pilate, in the wake of his mentor Sejanus's demise, was in danger of losing his "friend of Caesar" status with the emperor in Rome, and they took full advantage of it: "If you let this man go, you are no friend of Caesar." Jesus did not play politics this way. In the face of accusations, he remained silent. When asked about his kingdom, he claimed that it was not of this world. Wherever you and I are empire-building, let us make sure the empire we are building is the kingdom of God.

tens to him. Rather than being philosophical in nature, Pilate's comment may reflect disillusionment (if not bitterness) from a political, pragmatic point of view. In his seven years as governor of Judea, he frequently clashed with the Jewish population. More recently, his position with the Roman emperor has become increasingly tenuous (see comments on 18:29).

He went out again to the Jews (18:38). Pilate returns to the outer colonnade (cf. 18:28–29).

I find no basis for a charge against him (18:38). (Cf. Luke 23:4.) Pilate's thrice-repeated exoneration of Jesus (cf. 19:4, 6) stands in blatant contrast with the actual death sentence pronounced in deference to the Jewish authorities.

It is your custom for me to release to you one prisoner at the time of the Passover (18:39). Literally, "at Passover."[577] There is little extrabiblical evidence for the custom of releasing one prisoner at Passover. The practice may go back to Hasmonean times and may have been continued by the Romans after taking over Palestine.[578] The release probably served as a gesture of goodwill designed to lessen political antagonism and to assure people that "no one coming to Jerusalem would be caught in the midst of political strife."[579] One mishnaic passage, which stipulates that the Passover lamb may be slaughtered for a variety of people whose actual condition is uncertain, including "one whom they have promised to bring out of prison" (*m. Pesaḥ.* 8:6), suggests that such releases were common enough to warrant legislation. Roman law provided for two kinds of amnesty: pardoning a condemned criminal (*indulgentia*) and acquitting someone prior to the verdict (*abolitio*); in Jesus' case, the latter would have been in view.[580]

No, not him! Give us Barabbas! (18:40). Generally, Zealot-style political extremism was condemned. Yet here the Jews, at the instigation of the high priests, ask for the release of Barabbas, a terrorist, while calling for the death of Jesus of Nazareth, who has renounced all political aspirations. Apart from the irony of making such a one out as a political threat, this demonstrates both the influence the Sanhedrin had over the Jewish people at large as well as the Jewish authorities' determination to have Jesus executed in order to preserve their own privileged position (11:49–52).

Barabbas (18:40). Nothing is known of this man apart from the Gospel evidence. "Barabbas" is not a personal name but a patronymic (like Simon *Barjonah*, i.e.,"son of Jonah") that occurs also in the Talmud.[581] Very possibly John saw in this designation a play on words: Bar-abbas literally means "son of the father," and John has presented Jesus as the Son of the Father throughout the Gospel.

Taken part in a rebellion (18:40). Barabbas was a *lēstēs* (lit., "one who seizes plunder"). This probably refers not merely to a robber but to an insurrectionist, one who destabilized the political system by terrorist activity (cf. Mark 15:7). Luke indicates that Barabbas "had been thrown into prison for an insurrection in the city, and for murder" (Luke 23:19). Josephus frequently uses the term for those engaged in revolutionary guerilla warfare, who, harboring mixed motives of plunder and nationalism, roamed the Jewish countryside in those volatile days. The term applies particularly to the Zealots, who had made armed resistance against Rome the consuming passion of their lives and who were committed to attain to national liberty by all means, including risk of their own lives.[582] In Matthew 27:16, Barabbas is characterized as "notorious" (*episēmos*), a word used by Josephus to describe Zealot leadership (John, son of Levi; *J.W.* 2.21.1 §585).

Jesus Sentenced to Be Crucified (19:1–16a)

After the Jewish phase of the trial and Jesus' interrogation by Pilate, we now enter the sentencing stage. The day is April 3, A.D. 33,[583] and Jesus' execution is imminent. Despite the Roman governor's thrice-repeated "I find no basis for a charge against him," Pilate yields to Jewish demands for Jesus' crucifixion. The preferred Roman capital punishment for non-Roman citizens, crucifixion is one of the most cruel and tortuous form of death invented and inflicted in human history. The mob's raucous relentlessness in asking for Jesus' execution contrasts with Jesus' quiet dignity in submitting to his fate in keeping with the will of the Father. As John points out, the events surrounding Jesus' crucifixion both confirm Jesus' kingship and fulfill Scripture.

Pilate (19:1). See "Pontius Pilate" at 18:29.

Had him flogged (19:1). From least to most severe, there were three forms of flogging administered by the Romans: (1) the *fustigatio*, a beating given for smaller offences such as hooliganism, often accompanied by a severe warning; (2) the *flagellatio*, a more brutal flogging to which criminals were subjected whose offenses were more serious; and (3) the *verberatio*, the most terrible form of this kind of punishment, regularly associated with other reprisals such as crucifixion.[584]

In the present instance, the flogging probably in view is the least severe form, the *fustigatio*, which is intended in part to appease the Jews and in part to teach Jesus a lesson.[585] After the sentence of crucifixion, Jesus is scourged again, this time in the most severe form, the *verber-*

Illegalities in Jesus' Trial Surfacing in John

1a. Jewish trial before Annas

1. Jesus is questioned about his disciples and his teaching (18:19); but first witnesses must be produced to establish an accused person's guilt.
2. Jesus is struck in the face (18:22); he challenges his accusers to furnish testimony of actual wrongdoing (18:23).

1b. Jewish trial before Caiaphas

1. No details are provided by John (cf. 18:24, 28), so no illegalities can be determined from his account alone.

2. Roman trial before Pilate

1. No charges are brought against Jesus (18:29); the Jews merely call him a criminal they want to have executed (18:30–31). Pilate reiterates three times that he finds no basis for a charge against Jesus (18:37; 19:4, 6; similarly, Luke 23:4, 14, 22).
2. No witnesses are ever produced.
3. Jesus never actually stands trial.
4. The verdict is clearly based on political expediency, not evidence.

◀ *left*

CROWN OF THORNS

The branches of this tree contains the kind of thorns that may have been used in the construction of the degrading crown.

atio. This explains why Jesus is too weak to carry his own cross very far (see comments on 19:17). Also, the nearness of the special Sabbath means that the agony of crucifixion must be kept short in order not to interfere with religious festivities (19:31–33).[586]

A crown of thorns (19:2). Apparently, some branches are twisted together from the long spikes of the date palm or from the common thornbush (Isa. 34:13; Nah. 1:10),[587] shaped into a mock "crown," the radiant *stephanos* (Lat. *corona*) that adorns rulers' heads on many coins of Jesus' time.[588] The crown is also reminiscent of depictions of oriental kings worshiped as gods.[589] These thorns, up to several inches long, would sink into the victim's skull, which caused blood to gush out and distort a person's face, resulting in considerable pain.

A purple robe (19:2). Probably a military cloak is used as a mock royal robe.[590] The Matthean parallel (27:28) refers to a "scarlet robe," a red chlamys or outer cloak worn by the emperor, minor officials, and soldiers alike. John uses the term *himation*, which denotes a person's "outer clothing" or "robe." As in Mark 15:17, John gives the robe's color as purple, the imperial color (1 Macc. 8:14); yet in the book of Revelation, "purple and scarlet" are mentioned side by side (Rev. 17:4; 18:16). Because purple dye (taken from shellfish) was expensive, a genuine purple cloak was not as easily obtained as a red one.

Hail (19:3). The soldiers' greeting mimics the "Ave Caesar" extended to the Roman emperor. Their mocking of Jesus as king seems to copy scenes frequently featured on stage and in Roman circuses.[591] The game of "mock king," scratchings of which are preserved on the stone pavement of the fortress of Antonia (see comments on 19:13), was played by soldiers during the Roman Saturnalia.

Philo tells of people's mocking a certain madman named Carabas in the gymnasium of Alexandria in A.D. 38, who, dressed in a rug for a royal robe with a sheet of byblus as a diadem on his head and a papyrus "scepter" in his hand, received "homage" and was saluted as king and hailed as "lord," apparently in imitation of familiar pantomimes (*Flaccus* 36–42; c. A.D. 50).

Dio Chrysostom (A.D. 40–120) refers to a Persian custom in which "they take one of their prisoners, who has been condemned to death, set him upon the king's throne, give him the royal apparel, and permit him to give orders. . . . But after that they strip and scourge him and then hang him," for the purpose of showing "that foolish and wicked men frequently acquire this royal power and title and then after a season of wanton insolence come to a most shameful and wretched end" (*Regn.* 4.67–68).

Here is the man (19:5). "Man" may hark back to Old Testament messianic passages such as Zechariah 6:12: "Here is the man whose name is the Branch."[592] In classical literature, the expression occasionally means "the poor fellow," "the poor creature."[593] To be sure, in his mock regal garments, Jesus must have been a heart-rending sight. In John's context, Pilate's statement may also accentuate Jesus' humanity.

You take him and crucify him (19:6). Pilate here uses sarcasm; he knows full well that the Jews do not have the authority to impose the death penalty; if they did, they would stone rather than crucify Jesus (see comments on 18:31).

We have a law, and according to that law he must die, because he claimed to be the Son of God (19:7). A Roman prefect was responsible both for keeping peace and for maintaining local law. "We have a law" may refer to Leviticus 24:16: "Anyone who blasphemes the name of the LORD must be put to death." Jesus has frequently been accused of blasphemy (John 5:18; 8:59; 10:31, 33); yet in both the Old Testament and other Jewish literature the claim of being God's Son need not be blasphemous and may refer to the anointed king of Israel (2 Sam. 7:14; Ps. 2:7; 89:26–27) or to the Messiah (4QFlor; see comments on 1:49).[594] Even Israel could be called God's son (Ex. 4:22; Hos. 11:1). In Greco-Roman circles, "son of god" frequently occurs in inscriptions as a title for the emperor, especially Augustus.[595]

ECCE HOMO ARCH

An arch built by the emperor Hadrian in A.D. 135. It is located on the Via Dolorosa and is identified by tradition as the site where Pilate presented Christ to the crowd saying, "Behold the man!"

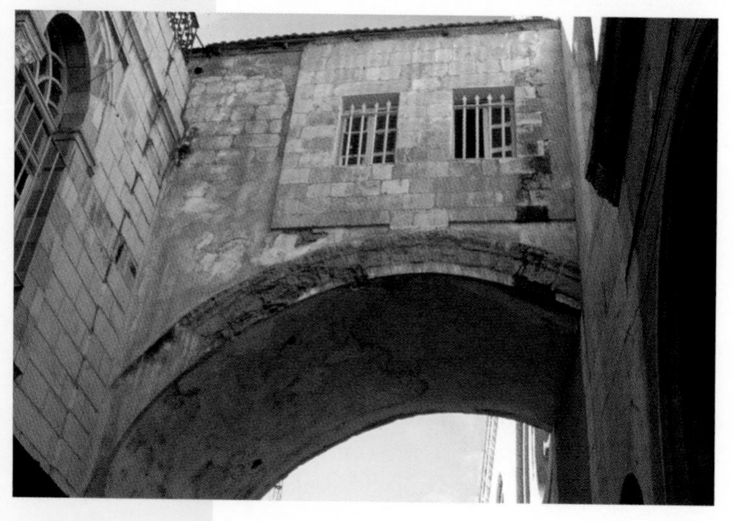

When Pilate heard this, he was even more afraid (19:8). Alternatively, "very afraid." While Roman officials may have been cynical, they were also often deeply superstitious. In pagan ears, the designation "son of god" conjured up notions of "divine men," persons believed to enjoy certain divine powers. Two instances of such fear by a judge of one accused whom he came to recognize as a higher being are relayed by Philostratus (b. A.D. 172).[596] Ancient pagans concluded commonly enough that "the gods have come down to us in human form" (Acts 14:11). If Jesus was a "son of a god," Pilate may have reasoned, he might incur the wrath of the gods for having Jesus flogged (cf. Matt. 27:19).

Alternatively, the root of Pilate's apprehension may have been political. He may have feared that the Jewish leaders would report to Rome that he failed to respect local religious customs, which was an accepted principle of provincial administration (see the later incident recounted in Philo, *Embassy* 299–305 and the parallel in Josephus, *J.W.* 2.9.2–3 §§169–74).[597] This depiction of Pilate hardly fits with Josephus's portrayal of the early years of the Roman governor's tenure, where he ruthlessly broke up riots and stubbornly resisted Jewish demands. Yet John's account fits perfectly with Pilate's tenuous position subsequent to the execution of his mentor Aelius Sejanus in A.D. 31.[598] Another pertinent issue is the designation "friend of Caesar" (see comments on 19:12).

The palace (19:9). See comments on 18:28.

Where do you come from? (19:9). In a parallel recorded by Josephus, the Roman procurator Albinus summons the prophet Jesus, son of Ananias, who had proclaimed the destruction of Jerusalem and the temple, inquiring who he was and where he came from (*J.W.* 6.5.5 §305). During the course of his ministry, Jesus' origins have frequently been at issue in his dealings with his opponents (e.g., 7:27–28; 8:14; 9:29–30). On a literal level, Jesus' Galilean provenance places him under Herod Antipas's jurisdiction (cf. Luke 23:6–7). In the Johannine context, however, there are clearly spiritual overtones as well (18:36–37).

Jesus gave him no answer (19:9). Jesus' silence brings to mind the Suffering Servant of Isaiah: "As a sheep before her shearers is silent, so he did not open his mouth" (Isa. 53:7; cf. 1 Peter 2:22–23). If Nicodemus and the Jewish authorities could not understand where Jesus has come from, how can this Roman governor be expected to grasp Jesus' true origin? The Greco-Roman pantheon was replete with gods having sexual union with women resulting in human offspring; a mind saturated with such myths would have grave difficulty comprehending Jesus' relationship with his Father.

There was also a Greco-Roman tradition, harking back to Socrates, holding that silence constituted a virtue when faced by accusers. Thus Philostratus writes, "For my own part I am sure that silence constitutes a fourth excellence much required in a law-court" (*Life of Apollonius* 8.2; early third cent. A.D.). However, Philostratus also acknowledged that remaining silent did not prove advantageous to Socrates. In the same passage, Philostratus records one person's objection, "And what good did it do him, seeing that he died just because he would say nothing?" (see comments on John 18:38).

I have power (19:10). According to Josephus, Coponius, the first Roman governor of Judea (A.D. 6–9), "was sent out as

▸ Friend of Caesar

Pilate had reason to fear the threat of the Jewish leaders—who had conveyed their displeasure with Pilate to the emperor on earlier occasions—for Tiberius was known to act decisively when suspicions were cast on the conduct or loyalty of his subordinates.[A-32] By the time of Vespasian (A.D. 69–71), "friend of Caesar" had become virtually an official title; even in Jesus' day, the term may have had semi-technical force.[A-33]

It is possible that Pilate acquired "friend of Caesar" status through his mentor Sejanus,[A-34] especially in light of Tacitus's statement that "the closer a man's intimacy with Sejanus, the stronger his claim to the emperor's friendship" (*Ann.* 6.8). But since Sejanus has recently fallen from grace (executed October 18, A.D. 31), Pilate has ample reason to be concerned that his favored status with the emperor will likewise be removed.

In Hellenistic times, "friends of the king" was a special group honored by the ruler for their loyalty and entrusted by him with responsible tasks.[A-35] In the early empire, the "friends of Augustus" were a well-known group. Later, the inscription PHILOKAISAR, "friend of Caesar," frequently occurs on coins of Herod Agrippa I (A.D. 37–44; cf. Philo, *Flacc.* 40).

procurator, entrusted by Augustus with full powers, including the infliction of capital punishment" (*J.W.* 2.8.1 §117).

From above (19:11). In good Jewish manner, Jesus here uses "from above" as an expression for God.

From then on, Pilate tried to set Jesus free (19:12). Apparently Pilate remains unconvinced of Jesus' guilt. Perhaps also owing to his superstitious nature and because he is impressed by Jesus' courage in the face of death (considered virtuous in the Greco-Roman world), he is reluctant to have Jesus crucified. Yet, as in other instances, Pilate would eventually yield to Jewish demands (Philo, *Embassy*, 38.301–2).

Friend of Caesar (19:12). See "Friend of Caesar."

Caesar (19:12). Originally the cognomen of Gaius Julius Caesar, the name was taken over by Augustus, Caesar's great-nephew, and his successors. The shift from proper name to title (equivalent to "emperor") had certainly occurred by the time of Vespasian and the Flavian rulers, who had no blood relations to the Julian dynasty. But an earlier date (supported also by the present reference) is likely. While Tiberius and Caligula could claim the name Caesar by virtue of adoption, Claudius could not. Moreover, already under Augustus, Judean coinage bore the name KAISAROS and a date, supporting the notion that "Caesar" functioned as an imperial title in Jesus' day.

The judge's seat (19:13). The Greek term *bēma* (originally "platform") denotes a judge's bench. This *bēma* or *sella curilis* normally stood in the forecourt of the governor's residence. It was elevated so that the judge could look over the spectators. Matthew depicts the entire trial with Pilate seated on the judge's seat and Jesus standing before him. Similar accounts are given of trials before the governors Festus (Acts 25:6, 17) and Florus (Josephus, *J.W.* 2.14.8 §301).

The Stone Pavement (19:13). The Greek term *lithostrōtos* may refer to different kinds of stone pavement, ranging from

PAVEMENT FROM THE FORTRESS OF ANTONIA

The "Lithostratos"—a Roman era pavement stone found near the location of the fortress where Jesus carried his cross.

simple ones consisting of identical pieces to elaborate ones of fine mosaic. In light of the pavement's location in front of the governor's residence, where traffic would have been heavy, a simple pavement of large stones may be the most likely. A paved court measuring about 2,300 square yards has been excavated on the lower level of the fortress of Antonia, one of the two possible sites of the governor's residence (the other is Herod's Palace in the northwest part of the Upper City; see comments on 18:28).[599] The blocks making up this pavement are more than a yard square and a foot thick. This kind of structure may well have been famous as "the stone pavement." However, it is unclear whether the excavated pavement was part of the fortress of Antonia in Jesus' time.

Which in Aramaic is Gabbatha (19:13). The meaning of "Gabath" (cf. Gibeah, birthplace of Saul; 1 Sam. 11:4) is given as "hill" by the Jewish historian Josephus (*J.W.* 5.2.1 §51).

Day of Preparation of Passover Week (19:14). Some argue that "day of Preparation" refers to the day preceding *Passover*, that is, the day on which preparations for Passover are made (in the present case, Thursday morning). If so, John indicates that Jesus is sent to be executed at the time Passover lambs are slaughtered in the temple. The Synoptists, however, clearly portray Jesus and his disciples as celebrating the Passover the night prior to the crucifixion. Moreover, Matthew, Mark, Luke, and Josephus alike use "Preparation Day" to refer to the day preceding the Sabbath (Matt. 27:62; Mark 15:42; Luke 23:54; *Ant.* 16.6.2 §§163–64). The term used here should therefore be taken to refer to the day of preparation *for the Sabbath* (i.e., Friday; cf. *Did.* 8:1; *Mart. Pol.* 7:1).[600]

If this is accurate, *tou pascha* means not "of the Passover" but "of Passover Week" (cf. NIV). Indeed, "Passover" may refer to the day of the actual Passover meal or, as in the present case, the entire Passover week (both Passover day and Feast of Unleavened Bread).[601] "Day of Preparation of Passover Week" is thus best taken to refer to the day of preparation for the Sabbath (i.e., Friday) of Passover week (see comments on 19:31). Thus all four Gospels concur that Jesus' Last Supper was a Passover meal eaten on Thursday evening (by Jewish reckoning, the onset of Friday).

About the sixth hour (19:14). Reckoning time from dawn to dark, "sixth hour" is about noon. Mark 15:25 indicates that Jesus' crucifixion takes place at the "third hour," that is, about 9:00 A.M. But since people related the estimated time to the closest three-hour mark, any time between 9:00 A.M. and noon may have led one person to say an event occurred at the third (9:00 A.M.) or the sixth hour (noon).[602]

We have no king but Caesar (19:15). The Old Testament frequently reiterates that Yahweh alone is the true king of Israel (e.g., Judg. 8:23; 1 Sam. 8:7). None of the foreign overlords qualified, be it Persian, Greek, or Roman. As Isaiah affirms, "O LORD, our God, other lords

CAESAR

A silver denarius with the image of the emperor Tiberius (A.D. 14–37).

besides you have ruled over us, but your name alone do we honor" (Isa. 26:13). The very feast of Passover, which the Jews are in the process of celebrating, is built on God's unique and supreme role in the life of the nation. The eleventh of the ancient Eighteen Benedictions prays, "Reign over us, you alone." Yet here, by professing to acknowledge Caesar alone as their king, the Jewish leaders betray their entire national heritage as well as deny their own messianic expectations based on the promises of Scripture. See also comments on John 19:12.

Handed him over to them to be crucified (19:16). The usual form of death sentence was *Ibis in crucem*, "On the cross you shall go" (Petronius, *Satyr.* 137). Latin literature usually uses the indirect expression *duci iussit*, "He ordered him to be led off" (e.g., Pliny, *Ep.* 10.96: "ordered . . . to be executed").[603] Upon pronouncement of the sentence, the criminal was first scourged, then executed (Josephus, *J.W.* 2.14.8 §308: "scourge before his tribunal [*bēma*] and nail to the cross"). The present statement is echoed by Tertullian, who says that the Jews extorted from Pilate a sentence giving Jesus up "*to them* to be crucified" (*Apol.* 21.18).

The Crucifixion (19:16b–27)

The soldiers took charge of Jesus (19:16). It was at this point that Jesus receives his second flogging, the brutal *verberatio*. In this form of punishment, the victim was stripped naked, tied to a post, and beaten by several soldiers with a whip "whose leather thongs were fitted with pieces of bone or lead or other metal." The scourgings were so severe that persons subjected to this torture sometimes died; others were left with their bones and entrails exposed.[604] Josephus reports that a certain Jesus, son of Ananias, was brought before Albinus and "flayed to the bone with scourges" (*J.W.* 6.5.3 §304). Eusebius writes that certain martyrs at the time of Polycarp were "lacerated by scourges even to the innermost veins and arteries, so that the hidden inward parts of the body, both their bowels and their members, were exposed to view" (*Eccl. Hist.* 4.15.4).

Carrying his own cross (19:17). As Plutarch attests, "Each criminal who goes to execution must carry his own cross on his back" (*Sera Num. Vind.* 554 A/B). Artemidorus (2d cent. A.D.) likewise affirms that "the man who is to be nailed to it [the cross] carries it beforehand" (*Onir.* 2.56), as does Chariton (c. 25 B.C.–A.D. 50), who tells of the crucifixion of sixteen men, who "were duly brought out, chained together at foot and neck, each carrying his own cross. The executioners added this grim public spectacle to the requisite penalty as a deterrent to

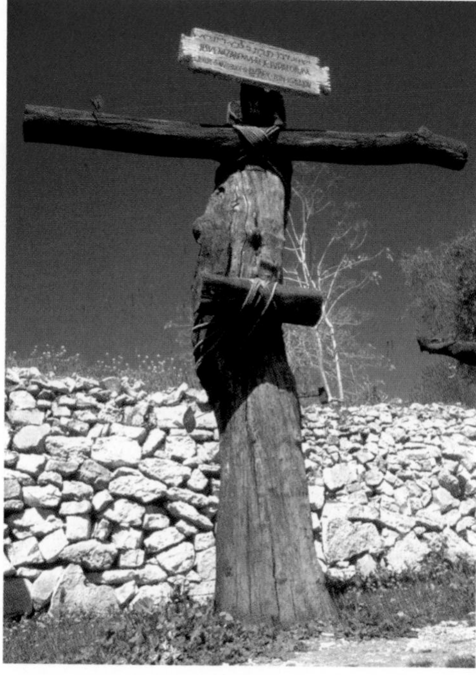

right ▶

ROMAN CROSS

A model of a typical Roman cross with a nameplate on the top and two wooden beams for the arms and legs.

others so minded" (*Chaereas and Callirhoe* 4.2.7).

The person would carry his cross to the site of crucifixion, where the upright beam (*stipes*, which was about nine feet high) had already been staked into the ground. There the criminal would be made to lie with his back on the ground, his arms stretched out, and his hands, wrists, or forearms tied or nailed to the crossbar.[605] After this, the crossbar was stood up and affixed to the upright beam. To this beam, the person's feet were tied or nailed, often not very high off the ground, whereby the legs were bent and twisted so that a single nail was driven through both heels. An optional piece of wood (*sedecula*) served further to increase the victim's agony. Later Jewish literature draws parallels between the crucifixion and Isaac's carrying the wood "like one carries his stake [=cross] on his shoulder" (*Gen. Rab.* 56:3 on Gen. 22:6).

He went out (19:17). Jewish custom prescribed that stonings were to take place outside the camp or city.[606] By extension, the same principle applied to crucifixions (cf. Heb. 13:12).

The place of the Skull (which in Aramaic is called Golgotha) (19:17). Greek "Golgotha" transliterates the Aramaic expression for skull. The Latin equivalent (found in the Vulgate of all four Gospels) is "Calvary." The location may have derived its name from its skull-like appearance. A site just outside Gennath Gate, not far from the Church of the Holy Sepulchre, is the most likely option.[607] See comments on 19:13.

They crucified him (19:18). In ancient times, crucifixion was synonymous with horror and shame, a death inflicted on slaves (Cicero, *In Verrem* 2.5.65.168), bandits (Josephus, *J.W.* 2.13.2 §253), prisoners of war (*J.W.* 5.11.1 §451), and revolutionaries (*Ant.* 17.10.10 §295).[608] Josephus terms it "the most pitiable of deaths" (*J.W.* 7.6.4 §203; cf. 1.97), Cicero calls it "that cruel and disgusting penalty" (*In Verrem* 2.5.64.165). Those crucified were made a public spectacle, often being

GOLGOTHA

The center of this picture of a model of ancient Jerusalem focuses on Golgotha, where the Church of the Holy Sepulcher is today.

affixed to crosses in bizarre positions, and their bodies left to be devoured by vultures.[609] No Roman citizen could be subjected to this terrible punishment without sanction by the emperor.

For hours (if not days), the person would hang in the heat of the sun, stripped naked and struggling to breathe. In order to avoid asphyxiation, he must push himself up with his legs and pull with his arms, triggering muscle spasms causing unimaginable pain. The end would come through heart failure, brain damage caused by reduced oxygen supply, suffocation, or shock.[610] Atrocious physical agony, length of torment, and public shame combined to make crucifixion a most terrible form of death. The remains of a crucified man aged 24–28 years dating roughly to Jesus' day were found in north Jerusalem in 1968.[611] The crucifixion of Jesus is corroborated by extrabiblical writers. For example, according to the Roman historian Tacitus, Jesus was "executed in the reign of Tiberius by the procurator Pontius Pilate" (*Ann.* 44.3). The Jewish historian Josephus likewise reports that "Pilate . . . condemned [Jesus] to the cross" (*Ant.* 18.63–64).

With him two others—one on each side and Jesus in the middle (19:18). See Isaiah 53:12: "numbered with the transgressors." Matthew and Mark identify these two others as bandits (*lēstai*; Matt. 27:38 par.), possibly insurrectionists like Barabbas (Mark 15:7). While later Jewish legislation forbade condemning two persons on the same day (*m. Sanh.* 6:4: "two ought not to be judged in one day"), it is unlikely that this law was already in effect in Jesus' day, and if so, whether it would have been honored by the Romans. Earlier, the Jewish high priest Alexander Jannaeus (88 B.C.) had crucified eight hundred persons at the same time (Josephus, *J.W.* 1.10.2 §97). The evangelists may find Jesus' crucifixion between two criminals reminiscent of Psalm 22:16: "a band of evil men has encircled me." According to Jewish convention, "when three persons were present, custom prescribed that the most honored take his place in the middle."[612]

Pilate had a notice prepared (19:19). Literally, "Pilate wrote a notice." The NIV rendering makes clear that Pilate probably did not write this notice himself but used the services of a literate slave.[613]

A notice prepared and fastened to the cross (19:19). This "notice" (the Latin word is *titulus*) was written on a board whitened with gypsum (*sanis, leukoma*). According to the Roman historian Suetonius, its purpose was the public exposition of the person's specific crime, presumably in order to deter others from committing similar acts. Thus the emperor Domitian had an unfortunate spectator dragged from his seat and thrown into the arena to dogs, with this placard (*titulus*): "A favorer of the Thracians who spoke impiously" (*Domitian* 10.1). However, while instances are known in which a person carried the notice around his neck or had it carried in front of him—such as "Attalus the Christian" during Marcus Aurelius's reign in the amphitheater in Lyons (Eusebius, *Eccl. Hist.* 6.44)—there is little or no evidence for the custom of affixing it to a cross.

Many of the Jews read this sign (19:20). The literacy level among first-century Palestinian Jews was high. "A pious Jew [in Jesus' day] . . . could read and write."[614]

The place where Jesus was crucified was near the city (19:20). See comments on 19:17.

The sign was written in Aramaic, Latin and Greek (19:20). If the order given reflects the order in which the inscriptions were written, Aramaic, the language most widely understood by the Jewish population of Palestine, would have taken pride of place. Of the three languages, Aramaic (see comments on 5:2) was the language commonly in use in Judea (cf. Acts 21:40); Latin was the official language of the Roman occupying force; and Greek was the "international language" of the empire, understood by most Diaspora Jews as well as by Gentiles.[615] By writing the sign in those three languages, the Romans ensured widest possible circulation of its contents, as a deterrent to every segment of the population.[616]

Aramaic: ישוע הנצרי מלך היהודים
Latin: IESUS NAZARENUS REX IUDAEORUM
Greek: ΙΗΣΟΥΣ Ο ΝΑΖΩΡΑΙΟΣ Ο ΒΑΣΙΛΕΥΣ ΤΩΝ ΙΟΥΔΑΙΩΝ

What I have written, I have written (19:22). "No longer faced with the possibility of mob unrest or a complaint to Tiberius, Pilate returns to his characteristic lack of cooperation."[617] Similar words are recorded of the Seleucid ruler Demetrius: "And the things we have guaranteed to you have been guaranteed" (1 Macc. 13:38). This grammatical construction is also found in the Old Testament (Gen. 43:14: "if I am bereaved, I am bereaved"; Est. 4:16: "if I perish, I perish") and Jewish literature (*b. Menaḥ.* 3a: "what he has offered, he has offered"; *b. Ketub.* 96a: "what she seized, she seized"; *b. Yebam.* 106b: "what he did is done"). Similar phrases are also found in a Roman context.[618] The request of the Jewish authorities clashes with the Roman respect for written documents, a legal decision that could not be reversed. For John, Pilate's firmness may again relate to his speaking better than he knew, for Jesus is the King of kings and Lord of lords, and there is no other.

A BILINGUAL INSCRIPTION

This inscription is part of the mosaic floor of the fifth-century A.D. Jewish synagogue at Tiberias. The Greek (top) and Hebrew *(bottom)* text honor the major donor for the construction of the synagogue.

◀ *left*

They took his clothes (19:23). In a collection of Roman law from the first century B.C. through the third century A.D. compiled in A.D. 530, we read that "on [a man's] condemnation to lose life . . . [his] property is confiscated." However, "neither may torturers claim these things of their own accord for themselves, nor their assistants ask for them, from those being stripped at the moment of execution; and governors . . . may . . . reward soldiers if they have performed bravely" (Justinian, *Digesta* 48.20).[619] Thus it appears that the soldiers were to take Jesus' clothes into custody but not necessarily arrogate them for themselves.

Romans normally stripped crucified persons naked. It is possible, however, that in deference to the Jewish dislike for public nudity Jesus was left with his underclothing (a dispute regarding whether a man about to be stoned should be completely stripped or not, involving R. Yehudah [c. A.D. 150], is recorded in *m. Sanh.* 6:3). This is suggested by the word *himatia*, which generally refers to the outer garment in distinction from the undergarment (called *chitōn*). People of that day wore a loin cloth, undergarments, the outer garment, a belt, a head covering, and sandals.[620]

Dividing them into four shares, one for each of them (19:23). It is unclear whether the soldiers overstepped legal bounds when dividing up Jesus' robe among themselves (see previous comment). "Four shares" indicates that the execution squad consisted of four soldiers, half the amount of the basic unit of the Roman army (i.e., eight soldiers sharing a tent [*contubernium*]), which was sometimes assigned to particular tasks (in Acts 12:4 Peter is "guarded by four squads of four soldiers each").[621] According to the Synoptics, a centurion was present as well. It is possible that additional soldiers were involved in preparing the other two men for crucifixion.

This garment was seamless, woven in one piece from top to bottom (19:23). Using a seamless piece of cloth precluded the possibility that two materials had been joined together, something forbidden in the Old Testament law. Such a garment could be woven without exceptional skill and was not necessarily a luxury item. Josephus notes that the high priestly robe (*chitōn*) was "not composed of two pieces . . . [but] one long woven cloth" (*Ant.* 3.7.4 §161; cf. Ex. 28:31; Rev. 1:13), while Philo uses a robe as symbolic of the Logos, which binds all things together in unity (*Flight* 110–12). In the Old Testament, it was Joseph who was stripped of his robe (Gen. 37:3, 23), which in later Jewish thought was interpreted in salvific terms (*Gen. Rab.* 84:8).

LOTS
Dice made of bone found in Jerusalem and dating to the early Roman period.

That the scripture might be fulfilled (19:24). The passage referred to is Psalm 22:18.[622] On the "fulfillment quotations" in the latter half of John's Gospel, crescendoing in the passion narrative, see comments on John 12:38.

Near the cross of Jesus (19:25). Crucified persons may have been surrounded by family, friends, and relatives. According to one Talmudic passage, a rabbi stood under the gallows of a hanged disciple and wept (*b. B. Meṣiʿa* 83b).[623]

His mother, his mother's sister, Mary the wife of Clopas, and Mary Magdalene (19:25). The Greek wording allows for the reference to be taken to two, three, or four. The wording adopted by the NIV (which represents the most likely alternative) interprets there to be four women: (1) Mary, Jesus' mother (here, as elsewhere, not named in this Gospel; see comments on 2:1–5); (2) his mother's sister (perhaps Salome, the mother of the sons of Zebedee mentioned in Matthew and Mark); (3) Mary the wife of Clopas (cf. Luke 24:18?); and (4) Mary Magdalene (John 20:1–18; cf. Luke 8:2–3).

"Dear woman, here is your son." . . . "Here is your mother" (19:26–27). Jesus' mother, who is almost certainly widowed and probably in her early fifties with little or no personal income, was dependent on Jesus, her oldest son. In keeping with the biblical injunction to honor one's parents (Ex. 20:12; Deut. 5:16), Jesus makes provision for his mother subsequent to his death.

In the LXX, the adoption formula is generally "you are" rather than "here is," as in the present passage.[624] In antiquity, a dying person would ordinarily entrust his mother to another with a direct charge, such as the following: "I leave to you my mother to be taken care of."[625] Thus the second-century writer Lucian writes, "The bequest of Eudamidas was, 'I leave to Aretaeus my mother to support and cherish in her old age" (*Toxaris* 22).

Dear woman (19:26). See comments on 2:4.

The Death of Jesus (19:28–37)

So that the Scripture would be fulfilled, Jesus said, "I am thirsty" (19:28). The allusion may be to Psalm 69:21: "They . . . gave me vinegar for my thirst." Another relevant psalm is 22:15: "My tongue sticks to the roof of my mouth." Psalm 69:21 is also cited in the Qumran hymn 1QH 12:11: "In their thirst they have given them vinegar to drink."

Wine vinegar (19:29). This cheap, sour wine was used by soldiers to quench their thirst (Mark 15:36; cf. Ps. 69:21). It differs from the "wine mixed with myrrh" Jesus was offered (and refused) on the way to the cross (Mark 15:23). While the latter was a sedative, "wine vinegar" prolonged life and therefore pain.

Put the sponge on a stalk of the hyssop plant (19:29). Hyssop is "a small bushy plant that can grow out of cracks in walls, a plant that 1 Kings 4:33 classifies as the humblest of shrubs."[626] It was used for the sprinkling of blood on the doorpost at the original Passover (Ex. 12:22). In the present instance, the branches at the end of the stalk would have formed a little "nest" into which the soggy sponge is placed. Since crucified people were not raised very high, the soldiers have to lift the stalk barely above their own heads.

Gave up (19:30). The same verb is used in Isaiah 53:12 to describe the death of the Suffering Servant: "His soul was *handed over* to death . . . and he was *handed over* because of their sins."

Day of Preparation (19:31). See comments on 19:14.

Special Sabbath (19:31). The Sabbath was special because it was the Sabbath of Passover week. An important sheaf offering was made on this day as well (Lev. 23:11).[627]

Because the Jews did not want the bodies left on the crosses during the Sabbath (19:31). The Romans left crucified persons on their crosses until death ensued (which could take days) and their bodies were devoured by vultures. Nevertheless, Roman law does seem to have allowed burial of crucified people, as a passage attributed to the first-century A.D. rhetorician Quintilian indicates: "But bodies are cut down from crosses, executioners do not prevent executed criminals from being buried" (*Decl.* 6.9; 2d cent. A.D.?). There is also evidence that at times, especially during feast days, bodies were taken down and given to relatives (Philo, *Flaccus* 83). The Jews' attitude was based on Deuteronomy 21:22–23 (cf. Josh. 8:29), according to which bodies of hanged criminals were not to defile the land by remaining on a tree overnight. According to Josephus, application of this passage was later extended to cover the crucified (*J.W.* 4.5.2 §317: "Even malefactors who have been sentenced to crucifixion are taken down and buried before sunset"; cf. Gal. 3:13).

They asked Pilate to have the legs broken and the bodies taken down (19:31). In order to hasten death, the crucifieds' legs (and sometimes other bones) would be smashed with an iron mallet, a practice called *crurifragium* ("breaking of bones"). This prevented the person from prolonging his life by pushing himself up with his legs to be able to breathe. Arm strength soon failed, and asphyxiation ensued. In the case of the body of a man crucified in the first century found north of Jerusalem (see comments on 19:18 above), one leg was fractured, the other broken to pieces.[628]

Pierced Jesus' side . . . bringing a sudden flow of blood and water (19:34).[629] The spear may have pierced Jesus' heart, resulting, either directly or via chest and lung, in the flow of blood and water.[630] The flow of blood and water underscores that Jesus died as a full human being.[631] The parallel 1 John 5:6–8 refers to "the Spirit, the water and the blood"; Jesus gave up his spirit when he died (John 19:30), leaving behind blood and water.

John also may be alluding to Exodus 17 and especially 19:6: "Strike the rock, and water will come out of it for the people to drink" (cf. Num. 20:11). Later Jewish thought held that Moses struck the rock twice, and that it yielded first blood, then water (*Ex. Rab.* 3:13 on Ex. 4:9). An allusion to the Passover may also be in view,[632] consisting of (1) the hyssop (John 19:29); (2) the unbroken bones (19:33, 36); and (3) the mingled blood (19:34).[633] Moreover, Jewish sacrificial law required that the victim's blood not be congealed but flow freely at the moment of death so it could be sprinkled (*m. Pesaḥ.* 5:3, 5). Jewish law also insisted that the priest "slit the [lamb's] heart and let out its blood" (*m. Tamid* 4:2).

With a spear (19:34). Roman soldiers used primarily two kinds of weapons: a short sword for close combat, and a lance or javelin for attacks from a distance. The lance (*pilum*) was about three and a half feet long and was made up of an iron point or spearhead (*lonchē*) joined to a shaft of light wood.[634] Later the term *lonchē* (the word used in the present passage) came to be used for a spear or lance itself.

The scripture would be fulfilled: "Not one of his bones will be broken" (19:36). Remarkably, Jesus did not only escape the breaking of his legs (unlike those crucified with him), his body was also pierced by a spear, yet again without sus-

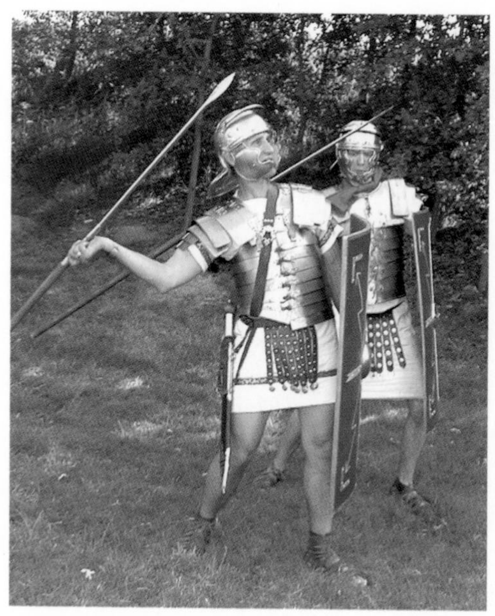

right ▶

ROMAN SPEAR

A reenactment group demonstrates the size and appearance of a Roman spear.

taining bone damage. Two sets of Scripture converge: (1) Psalm 34:20, depicting God's care for the righteous man: "He protects all his bones, not one of them will be broken"; and (2) Exodus 12:46 and Numbers 9:12, specifying that no bone of the Passover lamb may be broken (applied to Jesus in 1 Cor. 5:7; 1 Peter 1:19). Moreover, "in Jewish thought disfiguration was an obstacle to resurrection," which may further explain why John takes pains to stress that no bone was broken.[635]

As another scripture says, "They will look on the one they have pierced" (19:37). The passage in view is plainly Zechariah 12:10 (cf. Rev. 1:7). While the Hebrew of this passage appears to refer to the piercing of Yahweh himself (fig., with sorrow), later messianic interpretation developed this notion into the belief that the Messiah the son of Joseph would be pierced and people would look to Yahweh (*b. Sukkah* 52a). John, for his part, saw the fulfillment of Zechariah 12:10 at the crucifixion as confirmation that the Messiah was Jesus (cf. John 20:31). A related Old Testament figure that may have been in John's mind is that of the Suffering Servant of Isaiah 53:5, 10, who was "pierced for our transgressions" and "crushed" and "caused to suffer."

The Burial of Jesus (19:38–42)

Joseph of Arimathea (19:38). A member of the Sanhedrin (Mark 15:43; Luke 23:50), Joseph is wealthy (Matt. 27:57; cf. Isa. 53:9) yet "waiting for the kingdom of God" (Mark 15:43; Luke 23:51). Joseph's intervention fulfills another Scripture, "He was assigned a grave with the wicked, and with the rich in his death" (Isa. 53:9).[636] Of the several suggestions for the location of Arimathea, none is in Galilee, which would make Joseph one of Jesus' Judean disciples.[637]

Asked Pilate for the body of Jesus (19:38). The Romans usually handed over executed criminals to the closest relative. In the case of crucifixion, however, the rotting bodies were left to the vultures, both as a stern public warning and as the epitome of shame. The Jews, by contrast, buried even such people; yet rather than allowing their corpses to desecrate previously buried ones (the result if placed in a family tomb), a separate burial site was provided just outside the city.[638] Doubtless the Jewish authorities' request that the bodies be taken down (19:31) presupposes this arrangement. Joseph of Arimathea, however, uses his position as member of the Sanhedrin to gain access to Pilate and to secure a more dignified burial for his master. Joseph's act takes some courage, since Jesus has been accused of subversive activities both against the Jews and the Romans.

Nicodemus (19:39). Like Joseph of Arimathea, Nicodemus is a member of the Sanhedrin, a "ruler" (see comments on 3:1; 7:50–52).

A mixture of myrrh and aloes, about seventy-five pounds (19:39). Literally, one hundred *litrai* (see comments on 12:3) or about sixty-five pounds (rather than

MYRRH

Lumps of the aromatic gum from the Myrrh plant, which was used as an ingredient in perfumes and incense.

seventy-five pounds as in the NIV). Myrrh, a fragrant resin used by Egyptians in embalming (Herodotus, *Hist.* 2.86; the Romans often cremated their dead), was turned by the Jews into a powder and mixed with aloes, itself a powder of aromatic sandalwood, with whom it is regularly associated in the Old Testament (cf. Ps. 45:8; Prov. 7:17; Song 4:14). In the Jewish context, the mixture was to overcome the smell of putrification. Judging from the narrative, Joseph takes care of legal matters while Nicodemus brings the spices. Very possibly, servants are used to carry the aromatic mixture, take Jesus' body down from the cross, transport it to the burial place, and prepare it for burial. During the times of Israel's monarchy, King Asa died and was laid on "a bier covered with spices and various blended perfumes" (2 Chron 16:14). Later, "five hundred servants carrying spices" participated in the funeral procession of Herod the Great (Josephus, *Ant.* 17.8.3 §199).

The two of them wrapped it, with the spices, in strips of linen. This was in accordance with Jewish burial customs (19:40). "The two of them wrapped it" need not necessarily imply that Joseph and Nicodemus perform this task themselves. More likely, they use slaves in order not to contract ritual impurity (Num. 19:11: "unclean for seven days"), which would prevent them from celebrating the Passover (cf. John 18:28). Apparently, spices were spread along the linen wrappings (*othonia*; see comments on 11:44)[639] as well as underneath and perhaps around Jesus' body. Then the strips were wound around the corpse. Further spices may have been spread near the entrance of the tomb. In Jesus' day, burial clothes still tended to be luxurious; in around A.D. 90, R. Gamaliel II simplified procedures by having the dead buried in simple linen robes (*sadin*). Remarkably, the washing of Jesus' body, the most important service rendered to a dead person, is not mentioned by any of the evangelists.

At the place where Jesus was crucified (19:41). See comments on 19:17, 20.

GARDEN TOMB

An alternative (although unlikely) site of Jesus' tomb. The tomb is associated with the site that General Charles Gordon suggested as the location of Golgotha in 1883.

There was a garden (19:41). The term for "garden" (*kēpos*) points to a more elaborate structure, such as an orchard or a plantation (cf. 18:1: "olive grove"; note the later mention of a gardener in 20:15). Later Jewish legislation discouraged the planting of fruit trees near burial sites. In Old Testament times, Manasseh king of Judah was buried in the family tomb in his "palace garden" (2 Kings 21:18), as was his son and successor Amon (2 Kings 21:26: "buried in his grave in the garden of Uzza [=Uzziah?]"). According to Nehemiah 3:16 (LXX; cf. Acts 2:29), the popular tomb of David was situated in a garden as well.

A new tomb, in which no one had ever been laid (19:41). Burying a crucified person in a fresh tomb was doubtless less offensive to the Jewish authorities than using a grave that had previously been used (cf. 19:38). The location of the tomb is probably on the site of the Church of the Holy Sepulchre (built by Constantine) rather than the popular "garden tomb."[640] The vestiges of a nearby garden were still visible in Cyril of Jerusalem's day (c. A.D. 350): "It was a garden where he was crucified. For though it has now been most highly adorned with royal gifts, yet formerly it was a garden, and the signs and the remnants of this remain" (*Catechesis* 14.5). The tomb's proximity to Golgotha and its location in a garden concur with speculation that the site of the crucifixion is just outside the second north wall of the city (comments on 19:17, "he went out"). In fact, one of the four openings in the north wall was the Garden Gate ("Gennath"; cf. Josephus, *J.W.* 5.4.2 §147). This (prestigious) area also housed the tombs of the Hasmonean high priests John Hyrcanus and Alexander Jannaeus (*J.W.* 5.6.2 §259; 5.7.3 §304). For information on tombs in first-century Palestine, see comments on 11:38.

Jewish day of Preparation (19:42). See comments on 19:14.

Since the tomb was nearby, they laid Jesus there (19:42). Sabbath was rapidly approaching, when all work must cease, including that of carrying spices or transporting a corpse.[641] While it was allowed for a dead body to remain without burial overnight if time was needed to obtain "a coffin and burial clothes" (*m. Sanh.* 6:5), the nearby tomb was a welcome instance of divine providence.

The Empty Tomb (20:1–9)

It is now Sunday morning, "the first day of the week." Mary Magdalene and several other women decide to attend to some unfinished business; carrying spices, they head for the tomb to anoint Jesus' body.

Mary Magdalene (20:1). Earlier, Mary was found near the cross as part of a group of women (19:25). Her surname suggests that she is from Magdala on the northwest shore of the Sea of Galilee, approximately seven miles southwest of Capernaum. Mary's witness was not used as significantly in the preaching of the early church as that of Peter, doubtless because evidence provided by a woman was held in lesser esteem (e.g., *m. Roš Haš.* 1:8).

Went to the tomb (20:1). Regarding mourning at a gravesite, see comments on 11:31. A seven-day mourning period was customary—though people would often visit tombs within three days after the burial—so that Mary may have remained at home had she not sought to complete

Gospel Accounts of the Resurrection

Four angelic announcement shown in one scale drawing

Matthew 28: 1–7 Mark 16:1–7 Luke 24:1–8 John 20:1–16

In the Gospel of Matthew account, Mary Magdalene and "the other Mary" set out for the tomb, but Mary Magdalene apparently entered the tomb later, by herself.

Verses 2, 3, and 4 refer to an earthquake, rolling back of the stone and the guards, even which took place before the women arrived, possibly during the night. this gospel does not describe the actual entry of "the other Mary", but goes directly to the announcement of one angel, as in Mark and Luke, "He is not here; he has risen, just as he said. Come and see the place where he lay."
Matthew 28:1–7

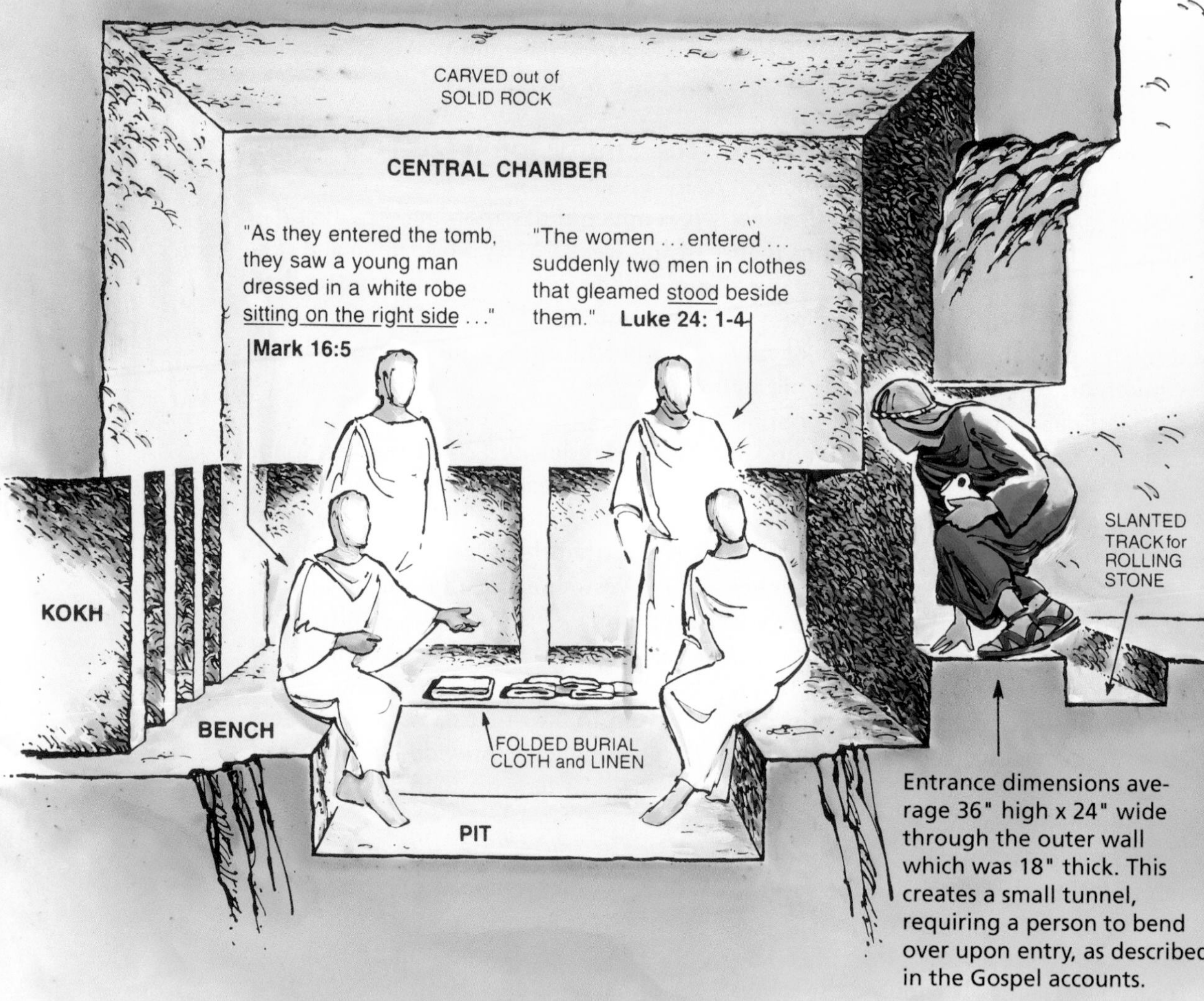

Entrance dimensions average 36" high x 24" wide through the outer wall which was 18" thick. This creates a small tunnel, requiring a person to bend over upon entry, as described in the Gospel accounts.

Reconstruction of the tomb of Joseph of Arimathea based upon average measurements of 62 Kokhim/Rolling-Stone tombs in Israel and Jordan by E. L. Nitowski, Ph.D.

Two angelic beings are shown here seated on the BENCH to illustrate the **John 20: 11, 12** account. These same two angels are also drawn in a standing position as they were seen by several women in **Luke 23:4**. The **Mark 16:5** gospel noes only the angel who spoke without specifically accounting for the other.

work left undone owing to the Sabbath (cf. 19:42). Rabbinic commentary, in the context of a dispute regarding whether intense mourning may be cut to two days in certain cases, cites the view of R. Bar Qappara (c. A.D. 200) that "on the third day . . . mourning is . . . at its height" (*Gen. Rab.* 100:7 on Gen. 50:10). According to a minor tractate in the Babylonian Talmud, one may "go out to the cemetery and examine the dead within three days and not fear [being suspected of] superstitious practices" (*b. Sem.* 8:1).

The stone had been removed from the entrance (20:1). One entered the cave tomb—which is probably horizontal rather than vertical (see comments on 11:38)—on ground level through a small doorway. This opening was usually no higher than a yard, so that people had to "bend down" to crawl in (20:5). Tombs could be sealed simply by a large stone rolled against the entrance, though more elaborate gravesites had a wheel-shaped "rolling slab" put in front, similar in effect to a sliding door (e.g., *b. Mo'ed Qaṭ.* 27a). The former is suggested in Jesus' case by the Synoptics (cf. Matt. 28:2). On the inside, larger tombs had a hallway leading to several burial chambers further back. Arrangements included (1) tunnels (*kōkīm*), into which the body was inserted head first; (2) semicircular niches (*arcosolia*), cut so as to leave a flat shelf or trough on or into which a body could be laid; (3) tombs where the body was placed on a bench that ran around three sides of the burial chamber. The second is most likely in Jesus' case (20:12).[642]

ENTRANCE TO A TOMB

The first-century tomb of Queen Helena. The large stone has been rolled to the side. ▼

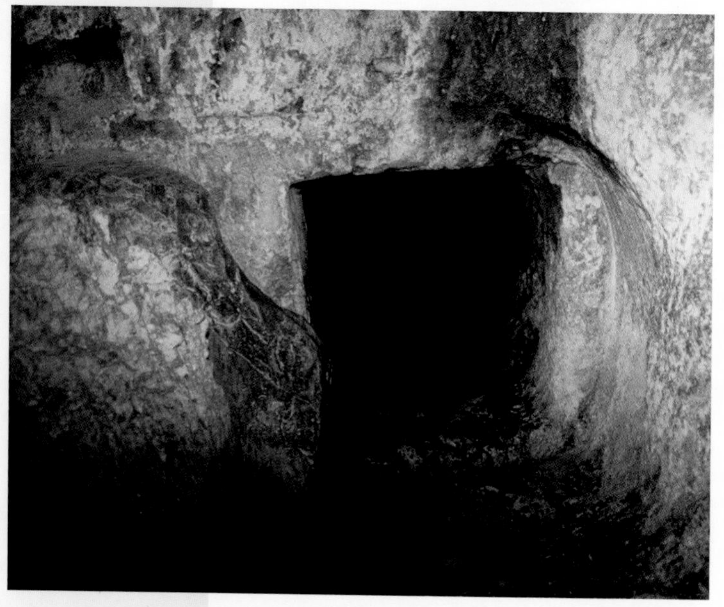

They have taken the Lord out of the tomb (20:2). Mary has no thought of resurrection. The charge of the Jewish leaders that Jesus' disciples stole his body (Matt. 27:62–66; 28:11–15) suggests that grave robbery was not uncommon. An inscription discovered in the neighborhood of Nazareth indicates that the emperor Claudius (A.D. 41–54) subsequently ordered capital punishment for those convicted of this crime.[643]

We don't know where they have put him (20:2). The plural "we" may indicate that Mary comes in the company of other women. This is further suggested by the fact that she goes to the tomb while it is still dark; for women would unlikely not venture outside the city by themselves at this time of day, especially during religious festivals when Jerusalem was crowded with visitors of uncertain character.[644]

He bent over and looked in at the strips of linen lying there (20:5). Apparently, by now there is enough daylight to see inside the burial chamber through the small, low opening in the cave tomb. The word "bend over" (*parakyptō*) is in the LXX regularly used for peering through a door or

◀ **MAGDALA**

Also known as Migdal, this was the site of the small town on the western shore of the sea of Galilee.

window.[645] For the "disciple Jesus loved," the linen strips (*ta othonia*; see comments on 19:40) are sufficient evidence that the body has not simply been moved. Moreover, grave robbers certainly would not leave behind expensive linen wrappings or spices. "There" probably refers to the place where the body has been, on the *arcosolium* (see comments on 20:1).

The burial cloth that had been around Jesus' head (20:7). In contrast to Lazarus, who came out of the tomb still wearing his graveclothes (11:44), Jesus' resurrection body has apparently passed through the linen wrappings very much in the same way as he later is able to appear to his disciples in a locked room (20:19, 26). The grave clothes may have passed under the chin and been tied on top of the head to keep the corpse's mouth from falling open. According to talmudic tradition, "Formerly they were wont to uncover the face of the rich and cover the face of the poor . . . and the poor felt shamed; they therefore instituted that everybody's face should be covered, out of deference for the poor" (*b. Mo*ʾ*ed Qaṭ*. 27a).

The cloth was folded up by itself, separate from the linen (20:7). John draws attention to the care that has been taken in the way the tomb is left. The phrase "folded up" (NIV) may actually mean "rolled up" (*entylissō*), which either points to neatness or indicates that the cloth is still in the exact same position as when Jesus' body was wrapped in it. This rules out grave robbers, who would have acted in haste (and probably taken these items with them). Also, it renders the Jewish story of the disciples' stealing Jesus' body implausible, because they likewise would hardly have left the face cloth and linen wrappings behind.

Finally the other disciple . . . saw and believed (20:8). The fact that two men see the items mentioned in 20:5–7 renders the evidence admissible under the Jewish legal system (Deut. 17:6; 19:15).

(They still did not understand from Scripture that Jesus had to rise from the dead) (20:9). The singular "Scripture" (*graphē*) may indicate that a specific Old Testament text is in view—suggestions range from Psalm 16:10 to Isaiah 53:10–12 to Hosea 6:2—though it cannot be ruled out that the reference is to Scripture in its entirety (cf. Luke 24:25–27, 32, 44–47).

Jesus Appears to Mary Magdalene (20:10–18)

To their homes (20:10). Literally, "to them" (*pros autous*), that is, the things belonging to them, which means their homes (cf. Josephus, *Ant.* 8.4.6 §124). Elsewhere, John uses the equivalent expression *eis ta idia* (1:11; 16:32; 19:27; cf. Num. 24:25). In all probability, the "disciple Jesus loved" brought the good news of Jesus' resurrection to Jesus' mother whom he had taken "into his home" (19:27).

Crying (20:11). The term "to cry" (*klaiō*) denotes the loud wailing typical of people in the ancient Near East (see comments on 11:31). Mary weeps, not because Jesus has died, but because his body has vanished; abuse of the dead was considered an abhorrent offense. An Old Testament example is the Philistines' exposure of the bodies of Saul and his sons and the bodies' recovery and proper burial by the brave men of Jabesh-Gilead (1 Sam. 31:9–13).

Two angels in white (20:12–13). In that day and culture, angelic appearances were no less real than what in modern parlance is called "evidence." Angels or celestial visitors are often depicted as clad in white.[646] The appearance of angels in pairs is likewise not uncommon in descriptions of heavenly visitations.[647]

One at the head and the other at the foot (20:12). This probably refers to an angel sitting at either end of the burial shelf (see comments on 20:1).

The gardener (20:15). Apart from grave robbers or other mourners—neither of whom would have been likely visitors at this early morning hour—gardeners attending to the grounds where a tomb was located (cf. 19:41) would have been the only people around. Mary's guess indicates that at first blush the resurrected Jesus is indistinguishable from an ordinary person.

Carried him away (20:15). The expression "carry away" (*bastazō*) is found elsewhere in the context of disposing of a corpse (Josephus, *Ant.* 3.8.7 §210; 7.11.7 §287).

In Aramaic, "Rabboni!" (which means Teacher) (20:16). See comments on 1:38.

Go instead . . . and tell them (20:17). In light of the limitations placed on women's witness in first-century Judaism (*m. Roš Haš.* 1:8), Jesus' entrusting Mary with this important message is surely significant.[648]

Jesus Appears to His Disciples (20:19–23)

Were together (20:19). The location is probably a house in Jerusalem, presumably the same place where the disciples were when Mary Magdalene came to them with the news that she has seen the Lord (20:18; cf. Luke 24:33: "Jerusalem").

The disciples are probably still there to mourn. Also, the Feast of Unleavened Bread is still in progress.

With the doors locked for fear of the Jews (20:19). Concerning the plural "doors" (cf. 20:26), the reference may be to a door at the house entrance and one into the room. "Proper residences were equipped with bolts and locks. Bolted doors would prevent anyone from entering (a heavy bolt could be slid through rings attached to the door and its frame)."[649]

Peace be with you! (20:19). This common Jewish greeting (e.g., 1 Sam. 25:6), representing Hebrew *šâlōm ʿalêkem* (repeated twice more in vv. 2, 26 below), is still used today. On "peace," see comments on 14:27. The expression "peace" may also function as a "formula of revelation." Thus when Gideon is gripped by fear at the sight of the angel of the Lord, the Lord says to him, "Peace! Do not be afraid. You are not going to die" (Judg. 6:23). Similarly, an angel reassures the frightened Daniel, "Peace! Be strong now; be strong" (Dan. 10:19). Jesus' greeting reassures any fears on the part of his followers related to their desertion of him prior to the crucifixion (John 16:32).

As the Father has sent me, I am sending you (20:21). This commissioning statement (cf. Matt. 28:18–20; Luke 24:46–49) climaxes the characterization of Jesus as the sent Son. Succession is important both in the Old Testament and in intertestamental literature. The most well-known Old Testament narratives involving succession are those featuring Joshua (following Moses) and Elisha (succeeding Elijah).

He breathed on them and said, "Receive the Holy Spirit" (20:22). The present reference represents a symbolic promise of the soon-to-be-given gift of the Spirit, not the actual giving of it (which happened fifty days later at Pentecost, see Acts 2). The Greek verb *emphysaō* means "breathe *on*" rather than "breathe *into*." The theological antecedent is Genesis 2:7, where the same verb and actual form is used.[650] There God breathes his Spirit into Adam at creation, which constitutes him as a "living being." Here, at the occasion of the commissioning of his disciples, Jesus constitutes them as the new messianic community, in anticipation of the outpouring of the Spirit subsequent to his ascension.

If you forgive anyone his sins, they are forgiven; if you do not forgive them, they are not forgiven (20:23). The second part of the present saying reads literally, "if you retain [anyone his sins], they are retained." In Matthew, this power is attributed to Peter in a universal, salvation-historical sense (Matt. 16:19; cf. Acts 1–12) and to the disciples in an inner-church context (Matt. 18:18).[651] Both evangelists may echo the reference to the one who is given "the key to the house of David" in Isaiah 22:22 (cf. Rev. 3:7).[652] If so, what is at stake is the authority to grant or deny access to God's kingdom.

In a Jewish context, the phrase "binding and loosing" originally described the activity of a judge who declared persons brought before him innocent or guilty, thus "binding" or "loosing" them from the charges made against them.[653] The rabbis used "binding" and "loosing" to declare what was forbidden or permitted by the law.[654] The same terminology was applied to the imposing or relieving of a ban or to a person's expulsion from or restitution to the synagogue.

If this meaning resonates in the present passage as well, Jesus would be declaring his new messianic community—not the Jewish leadership represented by the Sanhedrin and the Pharisees—as authorized to accept or deny acceptance into the believing (new) covenant community (cf. 9:22, 34, 35; 12:42; 16:2). On a secondary level, if Jewish nonmessianic synagogues in John's day have begun to expel Christians on a larger, more formal and organized scale, the present passage would serve as a reminder that Christians, not nonmessianic Jewish synagogues, now hold the key to membership in the messianic community.

Jesus Appears to Thomas (20:24–31)

Thomas (called Didymus) (20:24). See comments on 11:16.

The nail marks in his hands and put my finger where the nails were, and put my hand into his side (20:25). Apparently, Thomas thinks the disciples may have seen a ghost. Note that the Gnostics later taught Jesus only *appeared* to be human (the heresy of Docetism, from *dokeō*, "to seem"). Just as in the case of the incarnation (1:14), John takes pains to affirm that Jesus "came in the flesh" (a major concern in John's letters; cf. 1 John 4:2–3; 2 John 7), which entails also that his resurrection body is not merely that of a phantom or spirit apparition but a "fleshy" (albeit glorified) body.

ROMAN NAILS

These iron nails were discovered in Judea and date to the Roman period.

A week later (20:26). Literally, "after eight days." This refers to Sunday, one week after Easter.

His disciples were in the house again (20:26). Now that the Feast of Unleavened Bread is over, the disciples would soon be returning home to Galilee (barring instructions to the contrary). See comments on 20:19.

My Lord and my God (20:28). "Lord" and "God" are frequently juxtaposed in the Old Testament with reference to Yahweh (e.g., Ps. 35:23–24). The expression seems to have made its way into Roman emperor worship via Mediterranean cults; an inscription dated 24 B.C. dedicates a building "to the god and lord Socnopaeus."[655] The most pertinent parallel is that of the Roman emperor Domitian (A.D. 81–96), who wished to be addressed as "dominus et deus noster" ("our lord and god"; Suetonius, *Domitian* 13.2). Only decades later, Pliny attests that Christians worshiped Christ as God (*Ep.* 10.96; before A.D. 115).

Because you have seen me, you have believed; blessed are those who have not seen and yet have believed (20:29). A saying attributed to R. Simeon b. Laqish

(c. A.D. 250) contrasts Israel (who saw) and the Gentile proselytes (who still had not fully believed) thus: "The proselyte is dearer to God than all the Israelites who stood by Mount Sinai. For if all the Israelites had not seen the thunder and the flames and the lightnings and the quaking mountain and the sound of the trumpet they would not have accepted the law and taken upon themselves the kingdom of God. Yet this man has seen none of all these things yet comes and gives himself to God and takes on himself the yoke of the kingdom of God. Is there any who is dearer than this man?" (*Tanḥ*. 6 [32a]).[656] However, this ethnic distinction is not found in John. Rather, the saying accentuates the different mode of existence between the followers of the earthly Jesus and those whose faith depends on their witness. See also 2 Esdras 1:37: "I call to witness the gratitude of the people that is to come, whose children rejoice with gladness; though they do not see me with bodily eyes, yet with the spirit they will believe the things I have said."

Jesus did many other miraculous signs in the presence of his disciples, which are not recorded in this book. But these are written that you may believe (20:30–31). On Jesus' signs in John's Gospel, see "Jesus' Signs in John's Gospel" at 2:1. Parallels to this type of concluding statement can be documented from both secular and intertestamental Jewish literature.[657] After describing God's creative work and the marvels of nature, one intertestamental book concludes a section with the words, "We could say more but could never say enough; let the final word be: 'He is the all'" (Sir. 43:27). Even closer in wording is 1 Maccabees 9:22: "Now the rest of the acts of Judas . . . and the brave deeds that he did . . . have not been recorded, but they were very many."

Jesus is the Christ, the Son of God (20:31). See comments on 1:41, 49; 11:27.

By believing you may have life in his name (20:31). Regarding "life," see comments on 1:4. On "believing in his name," see comments on 1:12.

Jesus and the Miraculous Catch of Fish (21:1–14)

The present chapter, an epilogue mirroring in function the opening prologue, focuses primarily on two final issues: the special commissioning of Peter and the laying to rest of a rumor that the "disciple Jesus loved" would not die prior to Jesus' second coming.

Afterward (21:1). With the week-long Feast of Unleavened Bread now past, the disciples have left Jerusalem and returned to Galilee (cf. Luke 2:43).[658]

Sea of Tiberias (21:1). See comments on 6:1.

SEA OF GALILEE

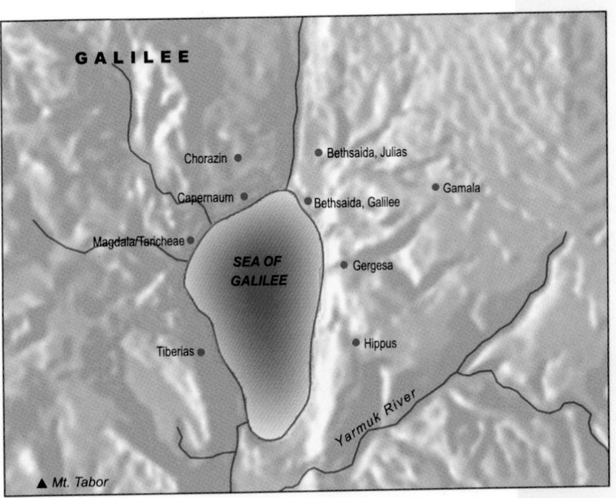

The sons of Zebedee (21:2). Their names are given in the Synoptics as James and John (e.g., Matt. 4:21 par.). Luke mentions that they were "Simon's partners" in fishing prior to being called by Jesus (5:10).

That night they caught nothing (21:3). Nighttime was the preferred time of day for fishing in ancient times, including first-century Galilee (e.g., Luke 5:5: "all night"). That way any fish caught before daybreak could be sold fresh in the morning.

Haven't you any fish? (21:5). The rare term translated "fish" (*prosphagion*) is not found elsewhere in biblical literature. The reference is most likely to a "bite to eat," which in first-century Galilee would often have been a piece of fish.

Throw your net (21:6). Three different kinds of net were used: one cast by hand; a trawlnet spread out from a boat and dragged through the water with cables on poles; and one stretched out in deep water. In the present instance, the trawlnet is most likely.[659]

Simon Peter . . . wrapped his outer garment around him (for he had taken it off) and jumped into the water (21:7–8). The "outer garment" in the present case is probably a fisherman's coat (*ependytēs*) that Peter wears in the morning chill. "For he had taken it off" is literally translated "for he was naked," but this may merely mean that Peter is wearing only his undergarment (so rightly the NIV), probably the short tunic of the Greek workman.[660] He tucks in his outer garment in order to be able to swim (rather than wade; the shoreline drops off rather rapidly at most parts of the lake) ashore more easily and to be properly dressed for greeting Jesus.[661]

Towing the net full of fish (21:8). The word for "towing" or "dragging" (*syrō*; used elsewhere in the New Testament only figuratively) occurs in connection with a trawlnet in Plutarch (*Soll. Anim.* 977.F).

About a hundred yards (21:8). Literally, "about two hundred cubits"; one cubit is about half a yard.

SUNRISE ON THE SEA OF GALILEE

A fire of burning coals (21:9). See comments on 18:18.

With fish on it (21:9). The singular "fish" (*opsarion*) here may suggest there is just one large fish being cooked. But then Jesus encourages the disciples to bring some of the fish they just caught (21:10).

Full of large fish, 153 (21:11). Various attempts have been made to interpret the number 153 symbolically, but more likely it simply represents the number of fish counted. Large numbers elsewhere in John are meant literally as well (e.g., 2:6; 12:3). An abundant catch of fish was considered evidence of God's favor.[662]

Come and have breakfast (21:12). First-century Jews normally ate two meals a day (cf. Luke 14:12), with "breakfast" (*ariston*) being the first of these. It was generally eaten before starting a day's work (though it could be an early lunch as well; cf. Luke 11:37–38).

Jesus came, took the bread and gave it to them, and did the same with the fish (21:13). Jesus here performs the act of the Jewish host, pronouncing the blessing at a meal (cf. 6:11, 23).

Jesus Reinstates Peter (21:15–25)

Simon son of John (21:15). See comments on 1:42.

Feed my lambs. . . . Take care of my sheep. . . . Feed my sheep (21:15–17). Shepherd imagery abounds in the Old Testament, which is pervaded by a yearning for shepherds who are devoted to God, care for his sheep, and carry out his will (Isa. 44:28; Jer. 3:15; Ezek. 34; see comments on John 10). At Qumran, the metaphor is applied to the authoritative overseer (*mebaqqer*): "He . . . will heal all the strays like a shepherd his flock" (CD 13:9).

The term "feed" (*boskō*) regularly occurs in the LXX for feeding sheep (e.g., Gen. 29:7; 37:12); the metaphorical sense is found in Ezekiel 34:2. The two verbs "feed" and "take care of" are contrasted in Philo: "For those who feed (*boskō*) us supply nourishment . . . whereas those who tend (*poimainō*) have the power of rulers and governors" (*Worse* 8.25). Jointly, they span the fullness of the task given to Peter (cf. 1 Peter 5:1–3).

◀ left

FISH FROM THE SEA OF GALILEE

A SHEPHERD FEEDING HIS SHEEP NEAR JORDAN

Jesus' Resurrection Appearances		
Location	**Time**	**Reference**
Empty tomb (Mary Magd. et al.)	Early Sunday morning	Matt. 28:1–10 par.; John 20:1–18
Road to Emmaus (two disciples)	Sunday noon	Luke 24:13–32
Jerusalem (Peter)	Sunday	Luke 24:34; 1 Cor. 15:5
Upper room (ten disciples)	Sunday evening	Luke 24:36–43; John 20:19–25
Upper room (eleven disciples)	Following Sunday	John 20:26–31; 1 Cor. 15:5
Sea of Galilee (seven disciples)	Later	John 21:1–23
Mountain in Galilee (eleven disciples)	Some time later	Matt. 28:16–20
Unknown (more than 500; James)	Some time later	1 Cor. 15:6–7
Mount of Olives (eleven disciples)	40 days after resurrection	Luke 24:44–49; Acts 1:3–8

Jesus' threefold repetition of his question may reflect the Near Eastern custom of reiterating a matter three times before witnesses in order to convey a solemn obligation, especially with regard to contracts conferring rights or legal dispositions. By analogy, Jesus' threefold question lends solemnity to the occasion of his commissioning Peter to his special shepherding task.

Stretch out your hands (21:18). In the ancient world, this expression (*ekteinō tas cheiras*) was widely taken to refer to crucifixion.[663] This is illustrated by the following passages: Epictetus, *Disc.* 3.26.22: "stretched yourself out like men who have been crucified"; Seneca, *Consol. ad Marciam* 20.3: "others stretch out their arms on a *patibulum*"; Dionysius of Halicarnassus, *Ant.* 7.69: "stretched out both his arms and fastened them to a piece of wood"; Tertullian, *De Pudic.* 22: "on the cross, with body already outstretched." The "stretching" occurred when a condemned criminal was tied to the horizontal crossbar called *patibulum* (see comments on 19:17) and compelled to carry his cross to the place of execution. Patristic interpreters interpreted Isaiah 65:2 ("All day long I have held out my hands to an obstinate people") with reference to the crucifixion.[664]

To indicate the kind of death by which Peter would glorify God (21:19). By the time John wrote his Gospel, Jesus' prediction had been fulfilled. According to Clement of Rome (c. A.D. 96), Peter suffered martyrdom under Nero (A.D. 54–68; *1 Clem.* 5.4), probably during the final years of Nero's reign (c. A.D. 64–66).[665] Later, Tertullian (c. A.D. 212) asserts that Peter was crucified.[666]

"Lord, what about him?" . . . "If I want him to remain alive until I return, what is that to you?" . . . Because of this, the rumor

spread among the brothers that this disciple would not die. But Jesus did not say that he would not die (21:21–23). Interestingly, the final chapter of Matthew is likewise given to dispelling a rumor—in Matthew's case that the disciples stole Jesus' body (Matt. 28:11–15; cf. 27:62–66). It is not impossible that these final verses were penned by John's disciples subsequent to his death in order to counter the charge that Jesus' prediction had been proven erroneous by John's death. More likely is the suggestion that John himself, while still alive, seeks to lay to rest the rumor that Christ has promised to return during his lifetime.[667]

This is the disciple who testifies to these things and who wrote them down. We know that his testimony is true (21:24). This verse, in its formal, solemn posture, represents the signature and statement of autography also common in epistolary postscripts.[668] It comes on the heels of two retrospective references to "the disciple Jesus loved" in 21:7 and 20 and a third resumptive passage in 21:14. The function of the entire chapter is to confirm the Beloved Disciple as author of this Gospel and to substantiate the authority of his eyewitness account.

The present verse identifies the fourth evangelist, the author of John's Gospel, with the literary character of "the disciple Jesus loved." This figure, in turn, relates historically to John the apostle, the son of Zebedee. The present verse is cast in the third person in order to affirm the credibility of the author's own witness.[669] In the second part of the verse, the author shifts to the first person plural,[670] and in verse 25 to the first person singular (*oimai*, "I suppose"). Here the author strikes a more informal, familiar tone to underscore his personal involvement and not to appear unduly detached from the events recorded earlier (see also comments on 19:35; 1 John 1:1–4).

Jesus did many other things as well. If every one of them were written down, I suppose that even the whole world would not have room for the books that would be written (21:25). Hyperbolic statements such as these were well-established literary convention at the time in both Greco-Roman and Jewish literature. The Old Testament book of Ecclesiastes ends with the acknowledgment that the wise Teacher had searched out many proverbs but "of making many books there is no end" (12:9–12). The following saying is attributed to R. Yoḥanan ben Zakkai (c. A.D. 80): "If all the heavens were sheets, all the trees quills and all the seas ink, they would not suffice for recording my wisdom which I acquired from my masters" (*b. Sop.* 16:8).

Philo frequently resorts to the kind of hyperbole found in the present passage. In one of his works he writes, "Were he [God] to choose to display his own riches, even the entire earth with the sea turned into dry land would not contain (*chōrēsai*) them" (*Posterity* 43.144). At another place he says, "their gifts are so boundless in number that no one, not even . . . the world, can contain them" (*Drunkenness* 9.32). Once again, the Jewish philosopher comments, "He who should wish to describe . . . the universe, would find life too short, even if his years were prolonged beyond those of all other men" (*Moses* 1.38.213).[671] Thus, John reinforces the selection principle already mentioned in 20:30–31 and further draws attention to the multitude of remarkable works performed by Jesus the Messiah (see comments on 20:30–31).

ANNOTATED BIBLIOGRAPHY

Commentaries

Barrett, C. K. *The Gospel According to St. John.* 2d ed. Philadelphia: Westminster, 1978.

Still one of the best commentaries on John, especially with regard to Greco-Roman backgrounds.

Brown, Raymond E. *The Gospel According to John.* 2 vols. AB 29A–B. New York: Doubleday, 1966, 1970.

Critical, yet extensive, including helpful excurses on major Johannine themes.

Carson, D. A. *The Gospel According to John.* Grand Rapids: Eerdmans, 1991.

One of the best evangelical commentaries on John now available, especially on difficult exegetical issues.

Moloney, Francis J. *The Gospel of John.* Sacra Pagina 4. Collegeville, Minn.: Liturgical, 1998.

The most recent thorough exegetical commentary, including helpful up-to-date bibliographies.

Morris, Leon. *The Gospel According to John.* NICNT. Rev. ed. Grand Rapids: Eerdmans, 1995.

The fruit of a lifetime of research on John's Gospel, this work is a model of judiciousness and even-handedness.

Ridderbos, Herman. *The Gospel of John: A Theological Commentary.* Trans. John Vriend. Grand Rapids: Eerdmans, 1997.

The new standard on theological synthesis. Less detailed than Carson, but more overtly theological in orientation.

Schnackenburg, Rudolf. *The Gospel According to St. John.* HTCNT. 3 vols. Trans. Kevin Smyth et al. New York: Crossroad, 1990 (1965, 1971, 1975).

Very thorough, moderately critical, always worth consulting. One caveat: Jewish background material is not always reliable and frequently seems to have been derived second-hand.

Special Studies

Bauckham, Richard. *The Gospels for All Christians: Rethinking the Gospel Audiences.* Grand Rapids: Eerdmans, 1997.

A seminal work on the universal orientation of the Gospels. Powerful refutation of the "Johannine community hypothesis."

Carson, D. A. "John and the Johannine Epistles." In *It Is Written: Scripture Citing Scripture,* eds. D. A. Carson and H. G. M. Williamson. Cambridge: Cambridge Univ. Press, 1988, 246–64.

A good starting point for the study of the Old Testament background to John's Gospel.

Charlesworth, James H., ed. *John and the Dead Sea Scrolls.* New York: Crossroad, 1991.

A helpful introduction to the relevance of Dead Sea Scrolls research for Johannine studies.

Culpepper, R. Alan, and C. Clifton Black, eds. *Exploring the Gospel of John. In Honor of D. Moody Smith.* Louisville, Ky.: Westminster John Knox, 1996.

A recent collection of essays that replaces more dated anthologies in relevance.

Köstenberger, Andreas. *The Missions of Jesus and the Disciples According to the Fourth Gospel.* Grand Rapids: Eerdmans, 1998.

An exegetical and theological study that endeavors to articulate a biblical theology of missions in the Fourth Gospel.

_____. *Encountering John. The Gospel in Historical, Literary, and Theological Perspective.* Grand Rapids: Baker, 1999.

A detailed introduction and survey of John's Gospel.

Pryor, John W. *John: Evangelist of the Covenant People: The Narrative and Themes of the Fourth Gospel.* Downers Grove, Ill.: InterVarsity, 1992.

Pryor shows convincingly that the substructure of John's narrative is salvation-historical, linking Jesus' new covenant community systematically with Old Testament antecedents.

Main Text Notes

1. For a general survey, see D. H. Johnson, "Logos," *DJG*, 481–84.
2. M. J. Harris, *Jesus As God* (Grand Rapids: Baker, 1992), 67.
3. For thorough discussion see Richard Bauckham, *God Crucified: Monotheism and Christology in the New Testament* (Grand Rapids: Eerdmans, 1998); Larry W. Hurtado, *One God, One Lord: Early Christian Devotion and Ancient Jewish Monotheism* (Philadelphia: Fortress, 1988).
4. Cf. E. C. Colwell, "A Definite Rule for the Use of the Article in the Greek New Testament," *JBL* 52 (1933): 12–21; Lane C. McGaughy, *Toward a Description Analysis of EINAI as Linking Verb in New Testament Greek* (SBLDS 6; Missoula, Mont.: Society of Biblical Literature, 1972).
5. See C. T. R. Wayward, "The Holy Name of the God of Moses and the Prologue of St. John's Gospel," *NTS* 25 (1978): 16–32.
6. See Thomas H. Tobin, "Logos," *ABD*, 4:348–56.
7. See D. H. Johnson, "Life," *DJG*, 469–71; G. F. Shirbroun, "Light," *DJG*, 472–73.
8. See also Isa. 42:6–7 and 49:6. Cf. John 12:46 with Matt. 4:16; Luke 2:32; 2 Cor. 4:6; Eph. 5:8; 1 John 1:5–7.
9. See Richard Bauckham, "Qumran and the Fourth Gospel: Is There a Connection?" in Stanley E. Porter and Craig A. Evans, eds., *The Scrolls and the Scriptures: Qumran Fifty Years After* (Sheffield: Sheffield Academic Press, 1997), 267–79.
10. Note that the Gk. word "understood" in v. 5 may actually mean "overcome" (see NIV footnote; cf. 12:35; 16:33).
11. See R. Kysar, "John, Gospel of," *ABD*, 3:886.
12. See Rom. 4:3, 20–24; Gal. 3:6; Heb. 11:8–12; James 2:23.
13. See esp. W. Horbury, *Jewish Messianism and the Cult of Christ* (London: SCM, 1998), 92–93, 99–100, who also discusses rabbinic interpretations.
14. See Charles H. Talbert, *Reading John* (New York: Crossroad, 1992), 74; cf. Elaine Pagels, "Exegesis of Genesis 1 in the Gospels of Thomas and John," *JBL* 118 (1999): 477–96.
15. For further discussion and relevant passages, see Köstenberger, "What Does It Mean to Be Filled with the Spirit?" *JETS* 40 (1997): 230.
16. See Ps. 5:7; 51:1; 69:16; 106:45; Lam. 3:22–23; see also 1QS 4:4.
17. See 3:16; Rom. 8:32; Gal. 4:4; see also Heb. 1:1–2; 2:2–3; 3:1–6.
18. See Hoehner, *Chronological Aspects*, 31–37; Finegan, *Handbook*, 340; B. Messner, "'In the Fifteenth Year' Reconsidered: A Study of Luke 3:1," *SCJ* 1 (1998): 201–11, with reference to the Roman historians Tacitus, *Ann.* 4.1, and Suetonius, *Tib.* 73, both of whom date the beginning of Tiberius's reign at A.D. 14 (the precise date is August 19, the day of Emperor Augustus's death); see comments on 2:20.
19. See R. A. Horsley, "Messianic Movements in Judaism," *ABD*, 4:791–97.
20. Matt. 16:14 par.; 17:3–4, 10 par.; 27:47, 49 par.; Sir. 48:10; *m. Šeqal.* 2:5; *m. Soṭah* 9:15; *m. B. Meṣiʿa* 1:8; *m. ʿEd.* 8:7; probably also 1QS 9:11. Quotations from the Mishnah are taken from H. Danby, *The Mishnah* (Oxford: Oxford Univ. Press, 1933).
21. See also Mark's conflation of Mal. 3:1 ("I will send my messenger") and Isa. 40:3 (also found in John 1:23 and Synoptic parallels) in Mark 1:2–3.
22. See Acts 3:22; 7:37; see also 1 Macc. 4:46; 14:41; *T. Benj.* 9:2.
23. Cf. J. Macdonald, *The Theology of the Samaritans* (Philadelphia: Westminster, 1964), 197–98, 362–71, 443.
24. C. S. Keener, *BBC* (IVPNTC; Downers Grove, Ill.: InterVarsity, 1993), 266.
25. E. W. Burrows, "Did John the Baptist Call Jesus 'The Lamb of God'?" *ExpTim* 85 (1974): 245–49.
26. Cf. D. Daube, *The New Testament and Rabbinic Judaism* (London: Athlone, 1956), 266–67.
27. This would seem to invalidate the recent claims, made by Mohammed Waheeb, an archaeologist heading the Jordanian excavations in the Jordan area, to have discovered the "Bethany beyond the Jordan" at a site about five miles north of the Dead Sea ("Site of Jesus' Baptism Found—Again," *BAR* 25/3 [1999]: 14–15). Cf. R. Riesner, "Bethany Beyond the Jordan (John 1:28): Topography, Theology and History in the Fourth Gospel," *TynBul* 38 (1987): 47; now succinctly presented in R. Riesner, "Archeology and Geography," *DJG*, 35–36; I am indebted to Riesner also for some of the following material.
28. For a general survey, see I. H. Marshall, "Lamb of God," *DJG*, 432–34.
29. Alternatively, the Baptist may have proclaimed Jesus as the apocalyptic warrior lamb who would bring judgment (cf. *1 En.* 90:9–12; *T. Jos.* 19:8; *T. Benj.* 3:8); cf. D. A.

Carson, *The Gospel According to John* (Grand Rapids: Eerdmans, 1991), 150. For the Baptist's message of judgment, see esp. Matt. 3:7–12; Luke 3:7–17.

30. See Num. 11:25; Judg. 3:10; 6:34; 11:29; 14:19; 1 Sam. 11:6; 16:13; 2 Chron. 15:1; 20:14.
31. Cf. Köstenberger, "What Does It Mean?" 229–30.
32. See Isa. 32:15; 44:3; Ezek. 36:25–27; Joel 2:28–32; cf. *Jub.* 1:23; 2 Esd. 6:26; *T. Jud.* 24:3; 1QS 4:20–21.
33. Cf. M. G. Abegg and C. A. Evans, "Messianic Passages in the Dead Sea Scrolls," in *Qumran Messianism*, ed. J. H. Charlesworth et al. (Tübingen: Mohr-Siebeck, 1998), 202.
34. Hoehner, *Chronological Aspects*, 37–38; idem., "Chronology," *DJG*, 119; C. J. Humphreys and W. G. Waddington, "The Jewish Calendar, a Lunar Eclipse and the Date of Christ's Crucifixion," *TynBul* 43 (1992): 351. For a dissenting voice, see Finegan, *Handbook*, 344–45, who places Jesus' birth in 3/2 B.C. (see pp. 278, 291), in which case Jesus would quite literally have been "about thirty years old." However, Finegan's date makes it hard to reckon with Herod's successors (according to a personal corespondence from H. Hoehner, dated Jan. 11, 2001).
35. For further rabbinic parallels, see Köstenberger, "Jesus As Rabbi in the Fourth Gospel," *BBR* 8 (1998): 119.
36. Cited in J. Lightfoot, *A Commentary on the New Testament from the Talmud and Hebraica* (Peabody, Mass.: Hendrickson, 1989 [1859]), 3:245.
37. J. Jeremias, *The Eucharistic Words of Jesus* (London: SCM, 1966), 45, n. 1.
38. For a general survey of this title, see L. W. Hurtado, "Christ," *DJG*, 106–17.
39. On messianism in the Old Testament, see Horbury, *Jewish Messianism and the Cult of Christ*, ch. 1.
40. See CD 2:12; 12:23–13:1; 14:19; 19:10–11; 20:1; 1QSa 2:14, 20; 4Q521 line 1; 11QMelch 2:18.
41. See *Pss. Sol.* 17:32; *1 En.* 48:10; 52:4; *4 Ezra* 7:28–29; 12:32; *2 Bar.* 29:3; 30:1; 40:1; 70:9; 72:2. Cf. J. C. O'Neill, *Who Did Jesus Think He Was?* (Leiden: Brill, 1995), 25–26; Abegg and Evans, "Messianic Passages," 191–94; Horbury, *Jewish Messianism*, ch. 2.
42. See O. Cullmann, "Πέτρος, Κηφᾶς," *TDNT*, 6:100–101.
43. For general (including archaeological) information on Bethsaida, see esp. F. Strickert, *Bethsaida: Home of the Apostles* (Collegeville, Minn.: Liturgical, 1998); H.-W. Kuhn and R. Arav, "The Bethsaida Excavations: Historical and Archaeological Approaches," in *The Future of Early Christianity. Fs. H. Koester*, ed. B. A. Pearson (Minneapolis: Fortress, 1991), 77–106; "Searching for the New Testament Site of Bethsaida," *BAR* 48/4 (Dec. 1985): 207–16.
44. Cf. L. P. Trudinger, "An Israelite in Whom There Is No Guile: An Interpretive Note on John 1:45–51," *EvQ* 54 (1982): 117–20.
45. See 4Q246 2:1; cf. 1QSa 2:11–12; *4 Ezra* 7:28–29.
46. See G. F. Hawthorne, "Amen," *DJG*, 7–8.
47. See the discussion in Carson, *John*, 163.
48. Cf. M. Hengel, "The Dionysiac Messiah," in *Studies in Early Christology* (Edinburgh: T. & T. Clark, 1995), 293–331.
49. Cf. Riesner, "Bethany Beyond the Jordan," 46.
50. So R. H. Mounce, "Cana," *ISBE*, 1.585.
51. Cf. R. M. Mackowski, "'Scholar's Qanah.' A Re-examination of the Evidence in Favor of Khirbet-Qanah," *BZ* 23 (1979): 278–84; G. H. Dalman, *Sacred Sites and Ways* (London: SPCK, 1935), 101–6; R. Riesner, "Archeology and Geography," *DJG*, 36–37.
52. M. Avi-Yonah, *The World of the Bible: The New Testament* (Yonkers, N.Y.: Educational Heritage, 1964), 138.
53. See Riesner, "Bethany Beyond the Jordan," 47, referring to Mackowski, "Scholar's Qanah," 278–79. Cf. Dalman, *Sacred Sites and Ways*, 101.
54. See the helpful discussion of vv. 1–11 in Derrett, *Law in the New Testament*, 229–44.
55. See Jer. 31:12; Hos. 14:7; Amos 9:13–14; Matt. 22:1–14 par.; 25:1–13; *2 Bar.* 29:5; *1 En.* 10:19.
56. So Keener, *BBC*, 268.
57. Compare 19:26; the NIV softens Jesus' address by translating the phrase as "dear woman," but there is no equivalent for "dear" in the original.
58. See 4:21; 20:13, 15; cf. Matt. 15:28; Luke 13:12; 22:57.
59. Cf. R. E. Brown et al., eds., *Mary in the New Testament* (Philadelphia: Fortress, 1978), 188.
60. See Judg. 11:12; 2 Sam. 16:10; 1 Kings 17:18; 2 Kings 3:13; 2 Chron. 35:21.
61. Cf. Derrett, *Law in the New Testament*, 240–41.
62. Cf. 1 Esd. 8:20 and Bel 3 (Theod.); BAGD, 514 further lists several inscriptions and papyri.
63. L. Abbott, *Illustrated Commentary on the Gospel According to St. John* (New York/Chicago: A. S. Barnes & Co., 1879), 30.
64. See Roger Aus, *Water into Wine and the Beheading of John the Baptist* (Atlanta: Scholars, 1988), 15–17.

65. For general information, see J. C. H. Laughlin, "Capernaum: From Jesus' Time and After," *BAR* (Sept./Oct. 1993): 54–61, 90; A. Schlatter, *The History of the Christ* (Grand Rapids: Baker, 1997), 111–12.
66. On the relationship between this temple cleansing and that recorded by the Synoptics, see Köstenberger, *Encountering John* (Grand Rapids: Baker, 1999), ch. 5.
67. While this was not always possible for those living at a distance, Galileans were not so remote as to be prevented from attending regularly. See Ferguson, *Backgrounds*, 521.
68. Hoehner, *Chronological Aspects*, 60.
69. Cf. E. Stern et al., eds., *The New Encyclopedia of Archaeological Excavations in the Holy Land* (New York: Simon & Schuster, 1992), 2:744; A. Millard, *Discoveries from Bible Times* (Oxford: Lion, 1997), 243. See also *m. Kelim* 1:8 and Josephus, *Ant.* 15.11.5 §417; *J.W.* 5.5.2 §193; 6.2.4 §125.
70. On the temple tax, see Ex. 30:13–14; 2 Chron. 24:9; Neh. 10:32; Matt. 17:24–27 (cf. Josephus, *Ant.* 3.8.2 §§193–96).
71. Cf. *m. Šeqal.* 1:3: "On the 25th thereof [the month of Adar] they [the tables of the money-changers] were set up in the Temple." On Tyrian shekels, see P. Richardson, "Why Turn the Tables? Jesus' Protest in the Temple Precincts," in *SBL 1992 Seminar Papers*, ed. E. H. Loving Jr. (Atlanta: Scholars, 1992), 514–18. On the half-shekel offering, see J. Liver, "The Half-Shekel Offering in Biblical and Post-biblical Literature," *HTR* 56 (1963): 173–98.
72. Cf. C. K. Barrett, "The House of Prayer and the Den of Thieves," in *Jesus und Paulus*, ed. E. E. Ellis and E. Grässer (Göttingen: Vandenhoeck & Ruprecht, 1975), 13–20; C. A. Evans, "From 'House of Prayer' to 'Cave of Robbers': Jesus' Prophetic Criticism of the Temple Establishment," in *The Quest for Context and Meaning*, ed. C. A. Evans and S. Talmon (Leiden: Brill, 1997), 417–42. On Gentile worship at the Jerusalem temple, see "Appendix: Gentile Participation in Worship at Jerusalem," in E. Schürer, *The History of the Jewish People in the Age of Jesus Christ*, rev. and ed. G. Vermes et al. (Edinburgh: T. & T. Clark, 1979), 2:309–13 (henceforth Schürer, *HJP*[2]).
73. Moreover, the use of Tyrian shekels involved religious compromise, since these coins bore the image of the Tyrian god Melkart. P. M. Casey, "Culture and Historicity: The Cleansing of the Temple," *CBQ* 59 (1997): 306–32, esp. 313–15.
74. See W. J. Heard, "Revolutionary Movements," *DJG*, 688–98; M. Hengel, *The Zealots* (Edinburgh: T. & T. Clark, 1988).
75. See "Appendix B: The Fourth Philosophy: *Sicarii* and Zealots," in Schürer, *HJP*[2], 2:598–606.
76. This reading of John 2:20 and a date of A.D. 30 for Jesus' first Passover and the temple cleansing are advocated by Hoehner, *Chronological Aspects*, 38–43; idem., "Chronology," *DJG*, 119; Humphreys and Waddington, "The Jewish Calendar, a Lunar Eclipse and the Date of Christ's Crucifixion," 351; Finegan, *Handbook*, 346–49.
77. Schürer, *HJP*[2], 1:308–9.
78. See 1 Sam. 16:7; 1 Chron. 28:9; Ps. 139:1–18, 23–24; Jer. 17:10; Rom. 8:27; Heb. 4:12–13; Wisd. Sol. 1:6; *Pss. Sol.* 14:8; 17:25.
79. See also 1:48; 2:4, 19; 3:14; 4:17–18; 6:51, 70; 7:6; 8:28; 9:3; 10:15–18; 11:4, 14; 12:24, 32; 13:10–11, 38; 15:13; 21:18–19.
80. See Richard Bauckham, "Nicodemus and the Gurion Family, *JTS* 47 (1966): 1–37.
81. See A. J. Saldarini, "Sanhedrin," *ABD*, 5:975–80; G. H. Twelftree, "Sanhedrin," *DJG*, 728–32.
82. See Köstenberger, "Seventh Johannine Sign," 87–103.
83. For an extended discussion, see Carson, *John*, 191–96, esp. 194–95. See also W. L. Kynes, "New Birth," *DJG*, 574–76, esp. 575.
84. Cf. E. F. F. Bishop, "The Authorised Teacher of the Israel of God," *BT* 7 (1956): 81–83.
85. See e.g., Ps. 14:2; 33:14; 103:19. See C. R. Schoonhoven, "Heaven," *ISBE*, 2:654–65; J. D. Tabor, "Heaven, Ascent To," *ABD*, 3:90–91.
86. See Tabor, "Heaven, Ascent To," 3:91–94.
87. See R. A. Muller, "World," *ISBE*, 4:1115; J. Guhrt, "Earth, Land, World," *NIDNTT*, 1:525–26.
88. Ferguson, *Backgrounds*, 313–14.
89. The first is mentioned as early as Eusebius's *Onomasticon* (4th cent. A.D.). The second is defended by the eminent archaeologist W. F. Albright in *HTR* 17 (1924): 193–94, followed by B. W. Bacon, *JBL* 48 (1929): 50–55; see also J. Finegan, *The Archeology of the New Testament*, rev. ed. (Princeton, N.J.: Princeton Univ. Press, 1992), 70. R. Riesner ("Archeology and Geography," *DJG*, 35) suggests Ain Farah, eight miles northwest of Shechem.
90. For the role of the bridegroom's friend, see R. Gower, *The New Manners and Customs of Bible Times* (Chicago: Moody, 1987), 64–66.
91. R. Schippers, "Seal," *NIDNTT*, 3:497–501.
92. For Old Testament parallels, see Job 10:22 LXX; Isa. 26:14; Eccl. 9:9 LXX (cf. Ps. 33:13 cited in 1 Peter 3:10).
93. R. Riesner, "Archeology and Geography," *DJG*, 40.
94. Avi-Yonah, *World of the Bible*, 140.

95. "A city in Samaria" in Acts 8:5 may refer to Sychar as well; see Hengel, "Das Johannesevangelium als Quelle des antiken Judentums," in *Judaica, Hellenistica et Christiana* (WUNT 109; Tübingen: Mohr-Siebeck, 1999), 301.
96. Cf. J. Neyrey, "Jacob Traditions and the Interpretation of John 4:10–26," *CBQ* 41 (1979): 419–37; Dalman, *Sacred Sites and Ways*, 212–16.
97. Hengel, "Johannesevangelium als Quelle," 302, referring to Dalman.
98. Abbott, *Illustrated Commentary*, 52.
99. See *y. Šeb.* 9:9; *Lam. Rab.* 3:17; *y. Ber.* 8:5; *t. Ber.* 6:4–5. Cf. Köstenberger, "Jesus As Rabbi," 122.
100. See R. G. Maccini, *Her Testimony Is True* (JSNTSup 125; Sheffield: Academic Press, 1996), 131–44.
101. See D. Daube, "Jesus and the Samaritan Woman: The Meaning of *synchraomai* (Jn 4:7ff)," *JBL* 69 (1950): 137–47; idem, *NT and Rabbinic Judaism*, 373–82; J. D. M. Derrett, "The Samaritan Woman's Purity (John 4.4–52)," *EvQ* 60 (1988): 291–98.
102. See 4:15, 19, 49; 5:7; 6:34; 9:36; 12:21.
103. This is suggested by R. D. Potter, "Topography and Archaeology in the Fourth Gospel," in *Studia Evangelica I*, ed. K. Aland et al. (Berlin: Akademie, 1959), 331.
104. See esp. Neyrey, "Jacob Traditions," 421–22.
105. Cf. also Isa. 44:3; 49:10; 55:1; see also John 6:63; 7:38; Sir. 24:21; *1 En.* 48:1.
106. Cf. J. R. Díaz, "Palestinian Targum and the New Testament," *NovT* 6 (1963): 76–77.
107. Cited in Carson, *John*, 220.
108. Keener, *BBC*, 273.
109. Cf. C. H. Giblin, "What Was Everything He Told Her She Did?" *NTS* 45 (1999): 148–52.
110. So Hengel, "Johannesevangelium als Quelle," 307, 315.
111. For Samaritan views about Mount Gerizim, see J. Macdonald, *The Theology of the Samaritans* (London: SCM, 1964), 327–33.
112. See *Ant.* 11.8.4 §§321–24; cf. 13.9.1 §256. Josephus further attests to the temple's existence in 323 B.C., the year of Alexander the Great's death (*Ant.* 11.8.7 §346; cf. 11.8.3 §310). See Jeremias, *Jerusalem*, 352, n. 2. On archaeological excavations related to Mount Gerizim, see esp. Crown, *Samaritans*, 165–74.
113. R. Schnackenburg, *The Gospel According to St. John* (New York: Crossroad, 1990), 1:434, n. 44.
114. Avi-Yonah, *World of the Bible*, 141.
115. Bond, *Pontius Pilate*, 90.
116. Contra Keener, *BBC*, 273, who reads the present passage in terms of "racial reconciliation." But this does not square with the emphasis of the present passage on the Jews being *the source of salvation*.
117. For a helpful discussion contrasting biblical with Hellenistic concepts of God see Schnackenburg, *John*, 1:440.
118. Cf. Kippenberg, *Garizim und Synagoge*, 303, n. 216.
119. M. E. Boring, ed., *Hellenistic Commentary to the New Testament* (Nashville: Abingdon, 1995), 264–65.
120. Cf. J. Bowman, "Samaritan Studies," 298–308; repr. in *Samaritan Studies* (Manchester: Manchester Univ. Press, 1958).
121. See L. Morris, *The Gospel According to John*, rev. ed. (Grand Rapids: Eerdmans, 1995), 242–43, n. 67, for other primary quotes.
122. The spirit of open interchange between Jesus and his disciples—or even those of John the Baptist—is illustrated by passages such as 9:2; 11:8, 12, 16; 13:6–10, 36–38; 14:5, 8, 22; 21:21; also Matt. 9:14; 11:3; 13:10, 36; 15:12, 15; 17:10, 19; 18:21; 24:3 and the parallels in Mark and Luke.
123. See the discussion and references in Köstenberger, "Jesus As Rabbi," 120–22. Contra Keener, *BBC*, 274, who refers to "the general principle that one ought not to challenge one's teacher."
124. Gower, *New Manners and Customs*, 44.
125. See Köstenberger, "Jesus As Rabbi," 122–23.
126. H. Ridderbos, *The Gospel of John* (Grand Rapids: Eerdmans, 1997), 168, n. 194.
127. G. R. Beasley-Murray, *John* (WBC 36; Waco, Tex.: Word, 1987), 63.
128. Morris, *John*, 247.
129. Note Old Testament allusions in Josh. 24:13; Eccl. 2:18–21; Mic. 6:15 (cf. Matt. 25:24).
130. A. Deissmann, *Light from the Ancient East*, rev. ed. (London: Hodder & Stoughton, 1927), 364–65. Cf. Boring, *Hellenistic Commentary*, 268; Craig R. Koester " 'The Savior of the World' (John 4:41)," *JBL* 109 (1990): 665–80, esp. 666–67.
131. Alternatively, "own country" may here refer to both Jewish Galilee *and* Judea in contrast to Samaria (see discussion in Carson, *John*, 234–38). See also W. D. Davies, *The Gospel and the Land* (Berkeley: Univ. of California, 1974), 321–31.
132. In the present instance, the "king" was probably Herod Antipas (cf. Mark 6:14), though Antipas did not technically hold that title but was tetrarch of Galilee (4 B.C.–A.D. 39). See H. W. Hoehner, *Herod Antipas* (SNTSMS 17; Cambridge: Cambridge Univ. Press, 1972).
133. See A. H. Mead, "The βασιλικός in John 4.46–53," *JSNT* (1985): 69–72.
134. Keener, *BBC*, 275. It has been speculated that the royal official is to be identified with Cuza, the manager of Herod's household mentioned in Luke 8:3.
135. See Dalman, *Sacred Sites and Ways*, 105.

136. See Köstenberger, *Missions of Jesus and the Disciples* (Grand Rapids: Eerdmans, 1998), 58–59, esp. n. 43.
137. On Ḥanina ben Dosa, see B. M. Bokser, "Wonder-Working and the Rabbinic Tradition: The Case of Ḥanina ben Dosa," *JSJ* 16 (1985): 42–92; G. Vermes, "Ḥanina ben Dosa: A Controversial Galilean Saint from the First Century of the Christian Era," *JJS* 23 (1972): 28–50; 24 (1973): 51–64.
138. R. M. Mackowski, *Jerusalem, City of Jesus* (Grand Rapids: Eerdmans, 1980), 81–83, even believes that behind the account of John 5:2–9 is the story of a pagan sanctuary that he argues was an Asclepieion; but this is categorically ruled out by Hengel, "Johannesevangelium als Quelle," 313. Nevertheless, Hengel does point to the significance of the Asclepios cult for John's Asia Minor audience (315). See also the ancient and bibliographic references cited in Boring, *Hellenistic Commentary*, 266–67.
139. So, e.g., Hengel, "Johannesevangelium als Quelle," 308, 321.
140. See 1 Kings 8:2, 65; 12:32; 2 Chron. 5:3; 7:8; Neh. 8:14, 18; Ps. 81:3; Ezek. 45:25; see also John 7:2, 10, 14, 37.
141. Helpful treatments include Avi-Yonah, *World of the Bible*, 142; J. Jeremias, *The Rediscovery of Bethesda* (Louisville, Ky.: Southern Baptist Seminary, 1966); Mackowski, *Jerusalem, City of Jesus*, 79–83; E. J. Vardaman, "The Pool of Bethesda," *BT* 14 (1963): 27–29; D. J. Wieand, "John V.2 and the Pool of Bethesda," *NTS* 12 (1966): 392–404. R. Riesner, "Archeology and Geography," *DJG*, 41, prefers the translation "There is in Jerusalem by the Sheep Pool the [site] with five porticoes called in Hebrew [i.e., Aramaic] Bethesda."
142. See Hengel, "Johannesevangelium als Quelle," 310–12.
143. The existence of these pools, if not the name "Bethesda," may be attested by the copper scroll from Qumran (3Q15), which dates from between A.D. 35 and 65. See Hengel, "Johannesevangelium als Quelle," 309–10.
144. The northern, smaller pool may go back to monarchial times; the southern pool may be that established in the second century B.C. by Simon the high priest (Sir. 50:3). For ancient sources, see Hengel, "Johannesevangelium als Quelle," 310. The site favored by most scholars is located under the Monastery of St. Anne in the northeast quarter of the Old City. Cf. Jeremias, *Rediscovery of Bethesda*; Vardaman, "Pool of Bethesda," 28. Regarding the archaeological identification of Bethesda, see esp. Wieand, "John V.2 and the Pool of Bethesda," 396–400.
145. See Hengel, "Johannesevangelium als Quelle," 315.
146. Some manuscripts read "Bethzatha" (preferred by Nestle/Aland) or "Bethsaida" (cf. 1:44; 12:21), but "Bethesda" is attested much more widely and is clearly the superior reading. Cf. Hengel, "Johannesevangelium als Quelle," 309: "One should by all means read 'Bethesda.'"
147. Barrett, *John*, 252–53; Hengel, "Johannesevangelium als Quelle," 313 (with further references in n. 74).
148. Hengel, "Johannesevangelium als Quelle," 316, with references to Jewish commentaries and targumim.
149. Abbott, *Illustrated Commentary*, 65–66.
150. See L. Morris, *The Lord from Heaven* (Downers Grove, Ill.: InterVarsity, 1974), 31–35; J. Jeremias, *New Testament Theology* (London: SCM, 1971), 61–67.
151. Cited in Boring, *Hellenistic Commentary*, 267.
152. See Num. 15:37–41; Deut. 6:4; 11:13–21. On the Jewish confession of God as "one God," called the *Shema* (from Heb. "to hear"), see Schürer, *HJP*², 2:454–55. See also L. W. Hurtado, "First-Century Jewish Monotheism," *JSNT* 71 (1998): 3–26.
153. Cf. S. S. Cohon, "The Unity of God: A Study in Hellenistic and Rabbinic Theology," *HUCA* 26 (1955): 425–79, who also cites affirmations of God's uniqueness in *Sib. Or.* 3:11–12, 545–61; *Let. Aris.* 132–38; Wis. 13–15; Philo (*Moses* 1.75; *Decalogue* 52–81; QG 4.8); and Josephus (*Ant.* 2.5.4 §§75–76).
154. See Deut. 32:39; 1 Sam. 2:6; 2 Kings 5:7; Tobit 13:2; Wis. 16:13.
155. Schürer, *HJP*², 2:455–63.
156. *1 En.* 37–71; esp. 49:4; 61:9; 62:2–6; 63:11.
157. See K. Rengstorf, "ἀπόστολος," *TDNT*, 1:414–20.
158. See Köstenberger, *Missions of Jesus and the Disciples*, 115–21.
159. See Gen. 2:7; Job 10:12; 33:4; Ps. 36:9.
160. See Carson, *John*, 259.
161. See *1 En.* 22:13; 51; *4 Ezra* 7:32; *2 Bar.* 30:1–2; 42:7–8; 50:2.
162. On the trial motif in John's Gospel, see Andrew T. Lincoln, *Truth on Trial: the Lawsuit Motif in the Fourth Gospel* (Peabody, Mass.: Hendrickson, 2000).
163. See John 5:45–47; also Luke 24:27, 44; Acts 13:27; 1 John 5:9.
164. The passage is attributed to R. Eliezer ha-Qappar (after A.D. 160). See also *Ex. Rab.* 1:20 (where God is said to bear witness to Moses) and Wisd. Sol. 1:6.
165. F. Kenyon, *Our Bible and the Ancient Manuscripts* (London: Eyre & Spottiswoode, 1939), 38, cited in Morris, *John*, 292.

166. The saying is attributed to Rabbah b. Bar Ḥanah in the name of R. Yoḥanan (c. A.D. 70).
167. See 12:38; 13:18; 15:25; 17:12; 19:24, 36–37.
168. See 1:45; 2:22; 3:10; 5:45–47; 12:41; 20:9; cf. Luke 24:27, 44–45 and Matthew's "fulfillment quotations." Cf. F. F. Bruce, *The Time Is Fulfilled* (Exeter: Paternoster, 1978), 35–53.
169. Jer. 29:25, 31; cf. Deut. 18:20; Jer. 14:14–15; 23:25; 29:9.
170. *Ant.* 20.5.1 §§97–99; 20.9.6 §§171–72; *J.W.* 2.13.4–6 §§258–65. Cf. P. W. Barnett, "The Jewish Signs Prophets—A.D. 40–70: Their Intentions and Origin," *NTS* 27 (1980–81): 679–97; O. A. Piper, "Messiah," *ISBE*, 3:332–33; A. S. van der Woude and M. de Jonge, "χρίω, Χριστός," *TDNT*, 9:509–27.
171. Morris, *John*, 294, n. 125, citing R. H. Strachan, *The Fourth Gospel* (London: SCM, 1955).
172. See Ex. 32:11–14, 30–32; Num. 12:13; 14:19–20; 21:7; Deut. 9:18–20, 25–29.
173. See *Ex. Rab.* 18:3 on 12:29, where Moses is called "a good intercessor."
174. Schnackenburg, *John*, 1:470, n. 139.
175. Another explanation for the name is the proximity of the nearby town Tell el-'Oreimeth, which was lyre-like in shape. See W. S. Lasor, "Galilee, Sea of," *ISBE*, 2:391–92. For general information, see also R. Riesner, "Archaeology and Geography," *DJG*, 37.
176. Avi-Yonah, *World of the Bible*, 143.
177. B. Malina and R. L. Rohrbaugh, *Social-Science Commentary on the Gospel of John* (Minneapolis: Fortress, 1998), 127.
178. Carson, *John*, 270.
179. Cf. D. Daube, *The New Testament and Rabbinic Judaism*, 46–51.
180. This reflects the view of both Hillel and R. Yoḥanan (cf. *b. Ḥul.* 105b, attributed to Abaye, c. A.D. 280–339).
181. R. E. Brown, *The Gospel According to John* (AB 29; Garden City, N.Y.: Doubleday, 1966), 1:234–35.
182. Beasley-Murray, *John*, 88; R. A. Horsley, "Popular Messianic Movements Around the Time of Jesus," *CBQ* 46 (1984): 471–95.
183. Carson, *John*, 275.
184. R. Bultmann, *The Gospel of John* (Oxford: Blackwell, 1971), 223–24.
185. See Matt. 26:10 par.; John 9:4; Acts 13:41 (quoting Hab. 1:5); 1 Cor. 16:10.
186. Cf. 1QS 4:4; 1QH 13:36; CD 1:1–2; 13:7–8.
187. Cf. Rom. 3:20, 27–28; Gal. 2:16; 3:2, 5, 10; cf. Phil. 3:6, 9.
188. See Ps. 78:24; 105:40; Neh. 9:15; Wisd. Sol. 16:20. Cf. Maarten J. J. Menken, "The Provenance and Meaning of the Old Testament Quotations in John 6:31," *NovT* 30 (1988): 39–56.
189. Logos: *Alleg. Interp.* 3.169–76; *Worse* 118; *Heir* 79; wisdom: *Names* 259–60; *Heir* 191.
190. NIV: "food of God"; see Lev. 21:6, 8, 17, 21, 22; 22:25.
191. Cf. H. Odeberg, *The Fourth Gospel* (Amsterdam: B. R. Grüner, 1968), 264–65, n. 3.
192. See Gen. 9:4; Lev. 17:10–14; Deut. 12:16. Cf. C. Koester, *Symbolism in the Fourth Gospel* (Minneapolis: Fortress, 1995), 98–100.
193. Talbert, *Reading John*, 138.
194. I. Abrahams, *Studies in Pharisaism and the Gospels* (Cambridge: Cambridge Univ. Press, 1917), 1:1–17, esp. 4.
195. Note the absence of the article before synagogue: Jesus taught "in synagogue" (similar to our "in church").
196. See Raymond E. Brown, *The Gospel According to John* (AB; Garden City, N.Y.: Doubleday, 1966, 1970), 1:297.
197. But cf. Ps. 16:10, applied to Jesus in Acts 2:27 and 13:35.
198. E.g., Ex. 15:11; Lev. 11:44–45; 19:2; 20:7; 1 Sam. 2:2; 6:20; Isa. 6:3; 8:13; 10:17; frequently in the Psalms.
199. D. A. Carson, *Matthew* (*EBC* 8; Grand Rapids: Zondervan, 1984), 239–40.
200. For helpful information on the particulars of the Feast, see Avi-Yonah, *World of the Bible*, 144. Old Testament references include Lev. 23:33–43; Num. 29:12–39; Neh. 8:13–18; Hos. 12:9; Zech. 14:16–19.
201. Odeberg, *The Fourth Gospel*, 279, cited in Morris, *John*, 353.
202. E.g., 1QS 8:4; 9:12–21; 10:1–5; 1QM 1:5, 11–12; 14:13: "the times indicated by your eternal edicts"; 15:5; 1QH 5:19–20; 9:16–20; 20:4–9.
203. For a general survey, see W. J. Heard, "Revolutionary Movements," 688–98.
204. Cf. esp. R. Riesner, *Jesus als Lehrer* (WUNT 2/7; Tübingen: Mohr-Siebeck, 1981), 97–245.
205. M. McNamara, *Targum and Testament* (Shannon: Irish Univ. Press, 1972), 142.
206. See also Rom. 2:13; Gal. 2:14; 3:10 (quoting Deut. 27:26), 12 (citing Lev. 18:5).
207. Cf. *m. Šabb.* 18:3; 19:1–3; *Tanḥ.* 19b.
208. E.g., Deut. 16:18–19; Isa. 11:3–4; Zech. 7:9.
209. Cf. W. A. Meeks, *The Prophet-King* (NovTSup 14; Leiden: Brill, 1967), 162–64.
210. Schürer, *HJP*², 2:275–308; Jeremias, *Jerusalem*, 160–81.
211. See Deut. 28:25; 30:4; Neh. 1:9; Ps. 146 [147]:2; Isa. 49:6; Jer. 15:7; 41 [34]:17; Dan. 12:2; Judith 5:19; 2 Macc. 1:27; cf. *Pss. Sol.* 8:28; 9:2.

212. See Acts 14:1; 16:1; 18:4; 19:10, 17; 20:21; Rom. 1:16; 2:9, 10; 3:9; 10:12; 1 Cor. 1:22, 24; 10:32; 12:13; Gal. 3:28; Col. 3:11.
213. Note that there is a separate term for "Greek-speaking (or Grecian) Jews," the word *Hellēnistēs*, which occurs in Acts 6:1 and 9:29.
214. Some rabbinic sources which may or may not reach back to the first century are *Pesiq. Rab.* 52:3–6; *t. Sukkah* 3:3–12. Cf. B. H. Grigsby, "'If Any Man Thirsts . . .': Observations on the Rabbinic Background of John 7, 37–39," *Bib* 67 (1986): 101–8.
215. See Lev. 23:36; Num. 29:35; Neh. 8:18.
216. See Josephus, *Ant.* 13.8.3 §245; *b. Sukkah* 48b; *m. Sukkah* 5:6; 2 Macc. 10:6.
217. Isa. 58:11; cf. Prov. 4:23; 5:15; Zech. 14:8.
218. Isa. 12:3; 44:3; 49:10; Ezek. 36:25–27; 47:1; Joel 3:18; Amos 9:11–15; Zech. 13:1.
219. See Neh. 9:15, 19–20; other relevant passages include Ex. 17:6; Ps. 105:41; Prov. 18:4; Isa. 43:19–20; 55:1; Jer. 2:13; 17:13; see also 1QH 16:4–40. Cf. M. J. J. Menken, "The Origin of the Old Testament Quotation in John 7:38," *NovT* 38 (1996): 160–75.
220. See *b. Sanh.* 37a; Ezek. 5:5; 38:12; *Jub.* 8:19.
221. Cf. I. Abrahams, *Studies in Pharisaism and the Gospels* (Cambridge: Cambridge Univ. Press, 1917), 1:11, referring also to Zech. 14:8.
222. Cf. J. Marcus, "Rivers of Living Water from Jesus' Belly (John 7:38)," *JBL* 117 (1998): 328–30.
223. See 2 Sam. 7:12–16; Ps. 89:3–4; Isa. 9:7; 11:1; 55:3; esp. Mic. 5:2.
224. Targumic parallels (probably of a later date) confirm that there were at least some rabbinic connections between Mic. 5:2 and Messiah's origin (see Beasley-Murray, *John*, 118, who also refers to *Pirqe R. El.* 3[2b]; *y. Ber.* 5a; and *Midr. Rab.* 51 on Lam. 1:16); see also R. E. Brown, *The Birth of the Messiah*, updated ed. (New York: Doubleday, 1993), 513, n. 2.
225. See Appendix E by G. F. Moore in F. Jackson and K. Lake, *The Beginnings of Christianity*, 5 vols. (1920–1933, repr. Grand Rapids: Baker, 1979), 1:439–45.
226. Cf. Josephus, *Ant.* 14.9.3 §167; *J.W.* 1.10.6 §209. Cf. S. Pancaro, "The Metamorphosis of a Legal Principle in the Fourth Gospel: A Closer Look at Jn 7, 51," *Bib* 23 (1972): 340–51.
227. *Ex. Rab.* 21:3, a rabbinic commentary on Ex. 14:15 attributed to R. Eleazar b. Pedat (d. A.D. 279).
228. For helpful discussions of the evidence, see B. M. Metzger, *A Textual Commentary on the Greek New Testament*, 2d ed. (New York: UBS, 1994), 187–89; D. B. Wallace, "Reconsidering 'The Story of Jesus and the Adulteress Reconsidered,'" *NTS* 39 (1993): 290–96.
229. See Isa. 60:19–22; Zech. 14:5b–8; cf. Rev. 21:23–24.
230. Keener, *BBC*, 285.
231. See Barrett, *John*, 335–37.
232. I owe this comment to Craig Blomberg's forthcoming book on the historicity of John's Gospel, to be published by InterVarsity Press, ad. loc.
233. See 1QS 3:7, 20–21; cf. 1QS 4:11; 1QM 13:12.
234. Jörg Augenstein, "'Euer Gesetz'—Ein Pronomen und die johanneische Haltung zum Gesetz," *ZNW* 88 (1997): 311–13.
235. See Dodd, *Interpretation of the Fourth Gospel* (Cambridge: Cambridge Univ. Press, 1953), 82.
236. Morris, *John*, 393, n. 24, citing Str-B 1:790.
237. Cf. S. Pancaro, *Law in the Fourth Gospel* (NovTSup 42; Leiden: Brill, 1975), 275–78; J. H. Neyrey, "Jesus the Judge: Forensic Process in John 8, 21–59," *Bib* 68 (1987): 512–15; C. Cory, "Wisdom's Rescue: A New Reading of the Tabernacles Discourse (John 7:1–8:59)," *JBL* 116 (1997): 104–5.
238. Morris, *John*, 393, n. 28, quoting Tenney.
239. Cf. A. J. Droge and J. D. Tabor, *A Noble Death: Suicide and Martyrdom among Christians and Jews in Antiquity* (San Francisco: Harper, 1991).
240. Cf. Odeberg, *Fourth Gospel*, 293–94.
241. See esp. 41:4; 43:10, 13, 25; 46:4; 48:12; cf. Deut. 32:39.
242. See Acts 13:22; 1 Sam. 13:14; 16:7; 1 Kings 11:4; cf. Jer. 3:15.
243. E.g. Plato, *Phaedo* 115.A.1; Dio Chrysostom, *Or.* 50.4.9.
244. See *Disc.* 4.1.114; cf. 1.19.9; 4.7.16–17. See Boring, *Hellenistic Commentary*, 282.
245. Cf. Jer. 4:4; 9:25–26; Ezek. 36:26–27.
246. See Gen. 21:9–10; 25:21–34; Rom. 9:6–13; Gal. 4:21–23.
247. On the importance assigned to ancestry in Judaism, see Jeremias, *Jerusalem*, 271–302.
248. See Philo's portrayal of Abraham in *Abr.* 70; *Migr.* 43; 132–33; *Heir* 24–27.
249. See H. Ridderbos, *Paul: An Outline of His Theology* (Grand Rapids: Eerdmans, 1975), 130–35, esp. 131, n. 98.
250. *Gen. Rab.* 22:6, citing Ps. 32:1; attributed to R. Berekiah in R. Simeon's name (c. A.D. 140–165).
251. See also 1QH 12:29–30: "He is in sin from his maternal womb, and in guilty iniquity right to old age."
252. See also Rom. 6:11–18; 7:7–25; see comments on John 13:27.
253. The saying is attributed to R. Nathan b. Abba in the name of Rab (d. A.D. 47).
254. See, e.g., Ezek. 16:15, 32–34; Hos. 1:2; 4:15; for the phrase "children of *porneia*," see Hos. 1:2; 2:6 [4] LXX.

255. Schnackenburg, *John*, 2:212, refers to Origen, *Contra Celsum* I.28; *Acts Pil.* 2.3–4; and later the *Toledoth Jeschu* (the legend of Pandera). Cf. J. P. Meier, *A Marginal Jew* (Garden City, N.Y.: Doubleday, 1991), 222–29, 245–52.
256. R. Joshua b. Ḥananyah (c. A.D. 90–130). The saying is attributed to R. Simeon b. Azzai (c. A.D. 120–140).
257. See J. Schneider, "ἥκω," *TDNT*, 2:926–28.
258. See Köstenberger, *Missions of Jesus and the Disciples*, 121–30.
259. Cf. J. R. Díaz, "Palestinian Targum and New Testament," *NovT* 6 (1963): 75–80; N. A. Dahl, "The Murderer and His Father (8:44)," *NorTT* 64 (1963): 129–62.
260. See Dan. 9:27; 11:31; 12:11; cf. Matt. 24:15 par.
261. See 2 Cor. 5:21; Heb. 4:15; 1 Peter 2:22 (citing Isa. 53:9); 1 John 3:5.
262. See Acts 8:9–11; Justin, *Apol.* 26:1–5; *b. Sanh.* 43a.
263. *b. Soṭah* 22a; the rabbis are R. Eleazar (A.D. 80–120), R. Jannai (c. A.D. 240), and R. Aḥa b. Jacob (c. A.D. 300).
264. B. J. Malina, *The New Testament World* (Atlanta: John Knox, 1981), 25–50.
265. See Ps. 88:48 LXX; Luke 2:26; Heb. 11:5; the close equivalent "will not taste death" is found in John 8:52.
266. See J. Behm, "γεύομαι," *TDNT*, 1:677; B. Chilton, "'Not to Taste Death': A Jewish, Christian, and Gnostic Usage," in *Studia Biblica* 1978, ed. E. A. Livingstone (JSNTSup 3; Sheffield: JSOT, 1980), 2:29–36.
267. Beasley-Murray, *John*, 138, paraphrasing Schlatter.
268. Beasley-Murray, *John*, 139.
269. Cf. M. J. Edwards, "'Not Yet Fifty Years Old': John 8:57," *NTS* 40 (1994): 449–54.
270. Cf. Daube, *The New Testament and Rabbinic Judaism*, 306.
271. See Matt. 9:27–31; 12:22–23; 20:29–34 par.; Mark 8:22–26.
272. Jeremias, *Jerusalem*, 118.
273. See Gen. 25:22; cf. *Gen. Rab.* 63:6, attributed to R. Yoḥanan (d. A.D. 279) and several colleagues.
274. See 6:28; Ps. 64:9; 66:5; 78:7; Jer. 51:10; Tobit 12:6, 7, 11; 2 Macc. 3:36; 1QS 4:4.
275. See Rom. 9:17; cf. Ex. 9:16; 14:4; Ps. 76:10.
276. *Sent. cod. Byz.* 532 = *Sent. Mono.* 1.385.
277. *b. B. Bat.* 126b; dated during the time of R. Ḥanina, who was a student of R. Yehudah ha-Nasi (d. A.D. 217).
278. See Deissmann, *Light from the Ancient East*, 135; K. Rengstorf, "πηλός," *TDNT*, 6:119. According to Boring, *Hellenistic Commentary*, 284, the inscription comes probably from the Asclepius temple on the island in the Tiber in Rome and dates to A.D. 138.
279. E.g., R. Aqiba (c. A.D. 130) in *t. Sanh.* 12:10.
280. Cf. D. Smith, "Jesus and the Pharisees in Socio-Anthropological Perspective," *TrinJ* 6 (1985): 151–56, building on the work of M. Douglas, *Purity and Danger* (London: Ark, 1984).
281. See *J.W.* 2.16.2 §340; 5.4.1 §140; 5.6.1 §252; 5.9.4 §410; 5.12.2 §505; 6.7.2 §363; 6.85 §401.
282. J. Ramsey Michaels, *John: A Good News Commentary* (San Francisco: Harper & Row, 1983), 150.
283. Cf. R. M. Mackowski, *Jerusalem, City of Jesus*, 56–58, 72, 74.
284. See *Gen. Rab.* 98:8; 99:8; *Tg. Onq.*: "till the time that the King, the Meshiha, shall come."
285. See Jeremias, *Jerusalem*, 116–19.
286. P. H. Davids, "Rich and Poor," *DJG*, 704.
287. A. Schlatter, *Der Evangelist Johannes*, 4th ed. (Stuttgart: Calwer, 1975), 227. Incidentally, the second group apparently disregards the fact that Pharaoh's magicians were able to perform miracles as well (Ex. 7:11, 22; 8:7; but cf. 8:18–19).
288. E.g., Acts 9:22; 18:28; Phil. 2:11. Cf. L. W. Hurtado, *One God, One Lord* (London: SCM, 1988), 112–13.
289. Schürer, *HJP*², 2:459–63.
290. See the analysis of the *birkath-ha-minim* in S. C. Mimouni, *Le judéo-christianisme ancien* (Paris: Cerf, 1998), 161–88, who argues that a form of the *birkath* was in use prior to the addition of *noṣrim* to the Palestinian recension (which he dates to around A.D. 90) in order to exclude Jewish Christians.
291. For a survey of the issues and further bibliographic references, see Boring, *Hellenistic Commentary*, 301–2.
292. See Josh. 7:19: "Give glory to the LORD. . . . Tell me what you have done" (see also 2 Chron. 30:8; Jer. 13:16; 1 Esd. 9:8; *m. Sanh.* 6:2).
293. Schnackenburg, *John*, 2:251, and Ridderbos, *John*, 345, n. 287 (referring to K. Rengstorf, "μαθητής," *TDNT*, 4:443), consider this to be a characteristic rabbinic self-designation, while Carson, *John*, 373–74, apparently following Barrett, *John*, 362–63, says this self-designation was not common.
294. See Rengstorf, "μαθητής," 4:443
295. Note also the close parallel to this verse in P. Eg. 2 (c. A.D. 150).
296. See Job 27:9; Ps. 34:15; 66:18; 109:7; Prov. 15:8, 29; 21:27; 28:9; Isa. 1:15; John 14:13–14; 16:23–27; 1 Peter 3:7; 1 John 3:21–22.
297. See similar analysis in Barrett, *John*, 365. For a Hellenistic parallel, see Philostratus, *Life of*

Apollonius 1.12 (after A.D. 217): "If you too really care for uprightness, go boldly up to the god and tender what prayer you will."

298. Plutarch, *Rom.* 22.1; Dionysius of Halicarnassus, *Ant. Rom.* 2.60.4; *Pomp.* 4.2.
299. For Greek parallels, see *aiōn*, MM, 16.
300. See Ps. 146:8; Isa. 29:18; 35:5; 42:7, 18.
301. See Isa. 6:10; 42:19; Jer. 5:21 (cf. Matt. 13:13–15 par.; esp. John 12:40). Cf. J. M. Lieu, "Blindness in the Johannine Tradition," *NTS* 34 (1988): 90.
302. W. Schrage, "τυφλός," *TDNT*, 8:281, 284–86.
303. For a general survey, see D. H. Johnson, "Shepherd, Sheep," *DJG*, 751–54.
304. Francis J. Maloney, *The Gospel of John* (Collegeville, Minn.: Liturgical, 1998), 307; cited by Blomberg in his forthcoming book on the historicity of John's Gospel, ad. loc.
305. G. Dalman, *Arbeit und Sitte in Palästina* VI (Gütersloh: Bertelsmann, 1939), 284–85.
306. Cf. C. T. Wilson, *Peasant Life in the Holy Land* (London: John Murray, 1906), 165; Dalman, *Arbeit und Sitte* VI, 250–51.
307. Cf. Dalman, *Arbeit und Sitte* VI, 249.
308. God by the hand of Moses and Aaron, Ps. 77:20; Isa. 63:11, 14; cf. Ps. 78:52.
309. Kim E. Dewey, "*Paroimiai* in the Gospel of John," *Semeia* 17 (1980): 81–99.
310. W. Barclay, *The Gospel of John*, rev. ed. (Philadelphia: Westminster, 1975), 2:58. Cf. E. F. Bishop, "The Door of the Sheep—John x.7–9," *ExpTim* 71 (1959–1960): 307–9.
311. See Gen. 28:17; Ps. 78:23; *1 En.* 72–75 (e.g., 72:2); *3 Bar.* 6:13.
312. See Matt. 7:7, 13–14; 18:8–9; 25:10 and par.; Acts 14:22.
313. E.g., Gen. 48:15; 49:24; Ps. 23:1; 28:9; 77:20; 78:52; 80:1; Isa. 40:11; Jer. 31:9; Ezek. 34:11–31. See J. G. S. S. Thomson, "The Shepherd-Ruler Concept in the Old Testament and its Application in the New Testament," *SJT* 8 (1955): 406–18.
314. E.g., Ps. 74:1; 78:52; 79:13; 95:7; 100:3.
315. Jer. 23:1–4; cf. 3:15; Ezek. 34; Zech. 11:4–17.
316. 2 Sam. 5:2; Ps. 78:70–72; Ezek. 37:24; Mic. 5:4; cf. *Pss. Sol.* 17:40–41; *Midr. Rab.* 2:2 on Ex. 3:1.
317. Isa. 63:11; cf. Ps. 77:20; *Midr. Rab.* 2:2 on Ex. 3:1.
318. See references in Barrett, *John*, 374.
319. E.g., Jer. 10:21; 12:10; 23:1–4; Ezek. 34; Zeph. 3:3; Zech. 10:2–3; 11:4–17; *1 En.* 89:12–76; 90:22–31; *T. Gad* 1:2–4.
320. Cf. Dalman, *Arbeit und Sitte* VI, 233–35.
321. See Ex. 3:7; 33:12, 17; Jer. 31:34; Hos. 6:6; 13:5; Nah. 1:7.
322. Boring, *Hellenistic Commentary*, 288, identifying the above quotation as a proverb in the *Corpus Paroemiographorum Graecorum*; no date is provided.
323. Jer. 3:15; 23:4–6; Ezek. 34:23–24; 37:15–28; Mic. 2:12; 5:3–5; For a detailed discussion of the Old Testament background to 10:16, cf. Köstenberger, "Jesus the Good Shepherd Who Will Also Bring Other Sheep (John 10:16)," *Faith and Mission* 19/1 (Fall 2001), forthcoming.
324. See *Pss. Sol.* 17:40; *2 Bar.* 77:13–17; CD 13:7–9.
325. Cited in Boring, *Hellenistic Commentary*, 288.
326. See Köstenberger, *Missions of Jesus and the Disciples*, 162, n. 83, with reference to J. W. Pryor, *John: Evangelist of the Covenant People* (Downers Grove, Ill.: InterVarsity, 1992).
327. For a comparison of Luke's travel narrative (Luke 9:51–18:14) with John 10:22–11:57, see Blomberg in his forthcoming book on the historicity of John's Gospel, at 10:22.
328. Cf. Hengel, "Johannesevangelium als Quelle," 317.
329. 1 Macc. 1:59; cf. Dan. 11:31; Josephus, *Ant.* 12.7.7 §§320–21.
330. 1 Macc. 4:52–60; cf. 2 Macc. 10:5–8.
331. See further C. K. Barrett, *The New Testament Background: Selected Documents*, rev. ed. (London: SPCK, 1987), 139–41.
332. Cf. Hengel, "Johannesevangelium als Quelle," 318.
333. So ibid., 318.
334. See esp. D. L. Bock, *Blasphemy and Exaltation in Judaism and the Final Examination of Jesus* (WUNT 2/106; Tübingen: Mohr-Siebeck, 1998), esp. the six conclusions on 234–37.
335. The expression "Law" also covered the Psalter (for a broader conception of the term "the Law," see 12:34; 15:25; Rom. 3:10–19; 1 Cor. 14:21), just as "Torah" in rabbinic literature sometimes covers the Hebrew Scriptures in their entirety. Regarding this "generic sense" of Law, see S. Pancaro, *Law in the Fourth Gospel*, esp. 175–92.
336. See *b. ʿAbod. Zar.* 5a; sayings to this effect are attributed to R. Yose (c. A.D. 150) and Resh Laqish (third century A.D.). For a variation of the first view, see R. Jungkuntz, "Approach to the Exegesis of John 10:34–36," *CTM* 35 (1964): 556–65. The second position is held by J. A. Emerton, "Interpretation of Psalm 82 in John 10," *JTS* 11 (1960): 329–32, and idem, "Melchizedek and the Gods: Fresh Evidence for the Jewish Background of John 10:34–36," *JTS* 17 (1966): 399–401. For a variation of the third view, see A. T. Hanson, "John's Interpretation of Psalm 82," *NTS* 11 (1964–65): 158–62, and idem, "John's Interpretation of Psalm 82 Reconsidered," *NTS* 13 (1967): 363–67. See

further W. Gutbrod, "νόμος," *TDNT,* 4:1022–32, 1054–55.

337. For the charge of blasphemy against Jesus, see now the recent article by L. W. Hurtado, "Pre–70 C.E. Jewish Opposition to Christ-Devotion," *JTS* 50 (1999): 35–58, esp. 36–37.

338. See Ex. 28:41; 40:13; Lev. 8:30; 2 Chron. 5:11; 26:18.

339. The saying is attributed to R. Aḥa (d. A.D. 510) in the name of R. Jonathan (c. A.D. 200).

340. Cf. J. C. VanderKam, "John 10 and the Feast of the Dedication," in *Of Scribes and Scrolls,* ed. J. J. Collins and T. H. Tobin (Lanham, Md.: Univ. Press of America, 1990), 211–14.

341. Cf. E. Bammel, "John Did No Miracles: John 10:41," in *Miracles,* ed. C. F. D. Moule (London: Mowbrays, 1965), 197–202.

342. On the relationship between the two Bethanys referred to in John's Gospel, see W. H. Brownlee, "Whence the Gospel According to John?" in *John and Qumran,* ed. J. H. Charlesworth (London: G. Chapman, 1972), 167–74.

343. The name "Bethany" arose from a combination of the Hebrew word for "house," *beth,* and *ananyah,* whereby one of the two "an's" dropped out, a phenomenon known among linguists as syllabic haplology. Cf. W. F. Albright, "New Identifications of Ancient Towns: Bethany in the Old Testament," *BASOR* 9 (1923): 8–10.

344. Cf. C. S. Clermont-Ganneau, "Sarcophagi," *PEQ* 6 (1874): 7–10; C. H. Kraeling, "Christian Burial Urns," *BA* 9 (1946): 18, cited in F. F. Bruce, *The Gospel of John* (Grand Rapids: Eerdmans, 1983), 253; and Avi-Yonah, *World of the Bible,* 146.

345. Cf. Riesner, "Bethany Beyond the Jordan (John 1:28)," 44–45.

346. See H. Balz, "ὕπνος," *TDNT,* 8:552. Further references are provided by Gerald L. Borchert, *John,* vol. 1 (Nashville: Broadman & Holman, 1996), 352, and Barnabas Lindars, *The Gospel of John* (Grand Rapids: Eerdmans, 1972), 394.

347. Cf. J. A. Fitzmyer, *Essays on the Semitic Background of the New Testament* (London: G. Chapman, 1971), 369–70.

348. The original collection was compiled in Palestine by R. Eliezer b. Zadok (1st cent. A.D.). Later it was embellished and amplified by R. Ḥiyya (2d cent. A.D.). See also A. T. Hanson, "The Old Testament Background to the Raising of Lazarus," in *SE VI,* ed. E. A. Livingstone (Berlin: Akademie, 1973), 252–55.

349. But see Wisd. Sol. 19:3; *m. Ketub.* 4:4.

350. Brown, *John,* 1:424.

351. Cf. T. E. Pollard, "The Raising of Lazarus (John xi)," in *SE VI,* 434–43.

352. See Richard Bauckham, "Life, Death, and the Afterlife in Second Temple Judaism," in *Life in the Face of Death: The Resurrection Message of the New Testament* (Richard N. Longnecker, ed., Grand Rapids: Eerdmans, 1998), 80–95.

353. See Matt. 22:23–33 par.; Acts 23:8; Josephus, *J.W.* 2.8.14 §165; *Ant.* 18.1.4 §16. See A. Oepke, "ἀνίστημι, ἀνάστασις," *TDNT,* 1:370; F. Lang, "Σαδδουκαῖος," *TDNT,* 7:46–47.

354. See Schürer, *HJP*[2], 2:456.

355. For a discussion of the Jewish doctrine of corporate personality see H. W. Robinson, *Corporate Personality in Ancient Israel* (Philadelphia: Fortress, 1964).

356. See Gen. 50:10; 2 Sam. 3:32; Jer. 38:15 LXX.

357. See G. Stählin, "θρηνέω," *TDNT,* 3:151–52.

358. See Ps. 6:2–3, 7; 18:5; 31:9–13; 38:10; 55:2, 4; 109:22; 143:4.

359. See Job 3:24; Ezek. 27:35; Mic. 2:6; 2 Macc. 4:37; Sir. 12:16; 31:13.

360. See Diodorus Siculus, *B. H.* 17.66.4; 27.6.1; Plutarch, *Cam.* 5.5; *Pyrrh.* 34.4; *Pomp.* 80.5; Josephus, *Ant.* 11.5.6 §162; *J.W.* 5.10.5 §445; 6.5.3 §304.

361. Avi-Yonah, *World of the Bible,* 147. For more information and examples of tombs from this period, see R. M. Mackowski, *Jerusalem: City of Jesus,* 20–21, 157–59.

362. Regarding the stone being laid across the entrance, see *m. ʾOhal.* 2:4.

363. For the use of spices in the burial process, see further J. N. Sanders, *A Commentary on the Gospel According to St John,* ed. and compl. by B. A. Mastin (London: Black, 1968), 274.

364. See W. Bingham Hunter, "Contextual and Genre Implications for the Historicity of John 11:41b–42," *JETS* 28 (1985): 53–70, who argues for a similarity in form with Jewish prayers of thanksgiving (*hodayot*).

365. Cf. H. van der Loos, *The Miracles of Jesus* (NovTSup 9; Leiden: Brill, 1965), 133–38; on the raising of Lazarus, ibid., 576–89.

366. See 12:27–28; 17:1, 5, 21, 24; Luke 11:2; 22:42; 23:34, 46.

367. Morris, *John,* 498.

368. Carson, *John,* 418–19; see also Beasley-Murray, *John,* 195.

369. About A.D. 90; cf. *b. Ketub.* 8b; *b. Moʾed Qaṭ.* 27b.

370. See Prov. 7:16; 31:22; Isa. 19:9; Ezek. 27:7.

371. See E. Lohse, "συνέδριον," *TDNT,* 7:861–62.

372. For further information on the Sanhedrin, see Schürer, *HJP*[2], 2:199–226; Lohse, "συνέδριον," 7:861–71. Hengel, "Johannesevan-

gelium als Quelle," 330, questions whether the Sanhedrin had seventy members in Jesus' day as is frequently alleged; he rather favors the view that the composition of the Council depended on the respective ruling high priest, esp. in the period between A.D. 6 and 41.

373. Note also the absence of the definite article before *synedrion* in the Greek (which may imply "a gathering" rather than "the Sanhedrin"), though not too much should be made of this.
374. See Tobias Nicklas, "Die Prophetie des Kaiaphas: Im Netz johanneischer Ironie," *NTS* 46 (2000): 589–94.
375. See Hengel, "Johannesevangelium als Quelle," 332.
376. Cf. D. Daube, *Collaboration with Tyranny in Rabbinic Law* (London: Oxford Univ. Press, 1966), 18–47. M. Barker, "John 11.50," in *The Trial of Jesus. Fs. C. F. D. Moule*, ed. E. Bammel (SBT 2/13; London: SCM, 1970), 41–46, links Caiaphas's words with current messianic expectations.
377. See further C. H. Dodd, "The Prophecy of Caiaphas: John 11:47–53," in *More New Testament Studies* (Manchester: Manchester Univ. Press, 1968): 58–68.
378. See *J.W.* 1.2.8 §68; idem, *Ant.* 13.10.2 §§282–83; 13.10.7 §299; cf. *t. Soṭah* 13:5, with 13:6 referring to Simeon the Righteous (after 200 B.C.).
379. See Ps. 106:47; 107:3; Isa. 11:12; 43:5–7; 49:5; Jer. 23:3; 31:8–14; Ezek. 34:11–16; 36:24–38; 37:21–28; Mic. 2:12; cf. James 1:1.
380. Cf. J. Beutler, "Two Ways of Gathering: The Plot to Kill Jesus in John 11:47–53," *NTS* 40 (1994): 399–404.
381. R. Riesner, "Archeology and Geography," *DJG*, 49. But see W. F. Albright, AASOR 4 (1922–23): 124–33, who argues that the Ephraim mentioned in John is not Et-Taiyibeh but Ain Samieh, slightly to the northeast and lower in a valley.
382. Hoehner, *Chronological Aspects*, esp. 44, 63, 143.
383. W. Reinhardt, "The Population Size of Jerusalem and the Numerical Growth of the City," in *Palestinian Setting* (BAFCS 4; Grand Rapids: Eerdmans, 1995), 262–63. Josephus (*J.W.* 6.9.3 §422–25) provides the unlikely figure of over 2,500,000, on the basis of a census taken by Cestius in the 60s.
384. See Num. 9:6; 2 Chron. 30:17–18; John 18:28; cf. *m. Pesaḥ.* 9:1.
385. Keener, *BBC*, 294.
386. Keener (ibid.) mentions that a flask would normally contain no more than an ounce.
387. Cf. R. H. Harrison, *Healing Herbs of the Bible* (Leiden: Brill, 1966), 48–49.
388. W. Walker, *All the Plants of the Bible* (London: Lutterworth, 1958), 196.
389. See the illustration in A. Millard, *Discoveries from Bible Times*, 179.
390. Cf. J. Lightfoot, *A Commentary on the New Testament from the Talmud and Hebraica*, 3:376.
391. See the survey in L. A. Losie, "Triumphal Entry," *DJG*, 854–59.
392. Avi-Yonah, *World of the Bible*, 148.
393. W. R. Farmer, "The Palm Branches in John 12:13," *JTS* 3 (1952): 62–66.
394. Lit., "give salvation now," "O save!" (cf. 2 Sam. 14:4: "Help me, O king!"; 2 Kings 6:26).
395. See O. Michel, "ὄνος," *TDNT*, 5:284, n. 7; Ferguson, *Background*, 560–61.
396. This kind of conflation of quotations from the Old Testament is not uncommon in the New Testament (e.g., Matt. 27:9–10; Mark 1:2–3).
397. The saying is attributed to R. Meir (c. A.D. 150). Similarly, *Pirqe R. El.* 33, attributed to R. Eliezer (c. A.D. 90). See also 1 Cor. 15:37.
398. See Gen. 29:31, 33; Deut. 21:15; Matt. 6:24 par.; compare Luke 14:26 with Matt. 10:37.
399. See Köstenberger, "Jesus As Rabbi," 119, esp. n. 90.
400. E.g., Ps. 79:9; Isa. 63:14; 66:5; Ezek. 38:23.
401. Old Testament references to the "voice from heaven" include 1 Sam. 3:4, 6, 8; 1 Kings 19:13; and Dan. 4:31–32. For other examples of a "heavenly voice" in Jewish literature, see *1 En.* 65:4; 2 Esd. 6:13, 17; *2 Bar.* 13:1; 22:1; *T. Levi* 18:6. See also Acts 9:4–6; 11:7, 9–10; Rev. 10:4, 8; 11:12; 14:2, 13; 18:4; 19:5; 21:3.
402. Cf. C. K. Barrett, *The Holy Spirit and the Gospel Tradition*, rev. ed. (London: SPCK, 1970), 39–40; G. H. Dalman, *The Words of Jesus* (Edinburgh: T. & T. Clark, 1902), 204–5.
403. Str-B 1:125, cited in Barrett, *Holy Spirit and the Gospel Tradition*, 39, n. 4. The *Tosafot* date to the twelfth or thirteenth century A.D.
404. Cited in Boring, *Hellenistic Commentary*, 292.
405. Cf. A. F. Segal, "Ruler of This World: Attitudes About Mediator Figures and the Importance of Sociology for Self-Definition," in *Jewish and Christian Self-Definition*, ed. E. P. Sanders (Philadelphia: Fortress, 1981), 2:245–68, 403–13.
406. See 1QS 1:18; 2:5, 19; 1QM 1:5; 4:2; 13:2, 4, 11–12; 14:9; 15:3; CD 12:2.
407. See A. S. van der Woude and M. de Jonge, "χρίω, Χριστός," *TDNT*, 9:509–17.
408. See 8:12; 11:9–10; cf. 1 John 1:6–7; 2:11; see also John 1:4–5, 7–9; 3:19–21; 9:4.
409. E.g., 1QS 1:9; 2:16; 3:13, 24, 25; 1QM 1:1, 3, 9, 11, 13.

410. See 13:18; 15:25; 17:12; 19:24, 36. See C. A. Evans, "On the Quotation Formulas in the Fourth Gospel," *BZ* 26 (1982): 79–83; idem, "Obduracy and the Lord's Servant: Some Observations on the Use of the Old Testament in the Fourth Gospel," in *Early Jewish and Christian Exegesis*, ed. C. A. Evans and W. F. Stinespring (Atlanta: Scholars, 1987), esp. 225–26.
411. See Deut. 5:15; Isa. 40:10; 51:9; 52:10; 63:5; cf. Luke 1:51.
412. For a detailed account of the Jewish legal theory of envoys, see K. Rengstorf, "ἀπόστολος," *TDNT*, 1:414–20.
413. Cf. M. J. O'Connell, "The Concept of Commandment in the Old Testament," *TS* 21 (1960): 352.
414. See Finegan, *Handbook*, 357–58, who sees the Synoptics and John in conflict here and prefers the latter as "historically the more likely."
415. See further commentary on 18:28 and 19:14 below. For a thorough defense of the position taken here, see Carson, *Matthew*, 530–32; C. L. Blomberg, *The Historical Reliability of the Gospels* (Downers Grove, Ill.: InterVarsity, 1987), 175–80.
416. Cited in Keener, *BBC*, 297.
417. First-century B.C. and A.D. references include Plautus, *Most.* 267; Catullus, *Carm.* 12.3; Petronius, *Sat.* 28.4; Martial, *Epigr.* 12.70.1; and Juvenal, *Sat.* 14.22. The word originally referred to a piece of linen cloth and was applied to various specific things made of linen, such as handkerchiefs, towels, or curtains.
418. See Gen. 18:4; 19:2; 24:32; 43:24; Judg. 19:21; 1 Sam. 25:41.
419. See *T. Ab.* 3:7–9; *Jos. Asen.* 7:1. Cf. J. C. Thomas, *Footwashing in John 13 and the Johannine Community* (JSNTSup 61: Sheffield: JSOT, 1991), 35–40, who also cites instances of footwashing as part of hospitality in the Greco-Roman world (46–50).
420. Avi-Yonah, *World of the Bible*, 149, including a picture of fifth-century B.C. Attic pottery depicting this scene.
421. The term *niptēr* (only here in the New Testament) occurs elsewhere only in a Cyprian inscription from Roman times (cf. BAGD, 540). The longer expression *podaniptēr* ("footbath") is found in Herodotus 2.172 (5th cent. B.C.; cf. P[66]).
422. For further references and discussion, see Köstenberger, "Jesus As Rabbi," 122–23.
423. R. Yoḥanan (d. A.D. 279) in the name of R. Simeon b. Yoḥai (c. A.D. 140–165), with reference to Elisha's service of Elijah in 2 Kings 3:11.
424. *b. Ketub.* 96a; attributed to R. Joshua b. Levi (third century A.D.).
425. *Mek. Ex.* 21:2. This work may have been originally compiled on the basis of discussions between A.D. 135–150, with the final redaction taking place in the second half of the third century (G. Stemberger, *Introduction to the Talmud and Midrash*, 2d ed. [Edinburgh: T. & T. Clark, 1996], 255).
426. E.g., 1 Sam. 25:41; *Jos. Asen.* 20:1–5. See also the anecdote involving the mother of R. Ishmael (d. c. A.D. 135) recounted in Str-B 1:707.
427. Cf. Köstenberger, "Jesus As Rabbi," 117.
428. In Lev. 15:11, both terms are found side by side. On the distinctiveness in meaning between *louō* and *niptō*, see Thomas, *Footwashing*, 51, n. 25; A. Oepke, "λούω," *TDNT*, 4:305; F. Hauck, "νίπτω," *TDNT*, 4:947.
429. Barrett, *John*, 441.
430. Cf. *Cat. Min.* 67.1; *Pomp.* 55.6; see also Lucian, *Gallo* 7, 9; *Timon* 54; *Mort. Peregr.* 6.
431. E.g., a prophet's patience: James 5:10; cf. Philo, *Her.* 256.
432. E.g., the disobedience of Israel (Heb. 4:11); godless Sodom and Gomorrah (2 Peter 2:6; cf. Philo, *Conf.* 64).
433. 2 Macc. 6:28, 31; 4 Macc. 17:22–23: "atoning sacrifice"; Sir. 44:16; cf. Josephus, *J.W.* 6.2.1 §§103, 106.
434. Carson, *John*, 470.
435. See 2 Sam. 15:12. Cf. *b. Sanh.* 106b; attributed to R. Yoḥanan (d. A.D. 279).
436. J. H. Bernard, *A Critical and Exegetical Commentary on the Gospel of John* (Edinburgh: T. & T. Clark, 1928), 2:467.
437. Carson, *John*, 471; Morris, *John*, 553; Brown, *John*, 2:554; Barrett, *John*, 445.
438. Ferguson, *Backgrounds*, 338–39.
439. On the "disciple whom Jesus loved," see Köstenberger, *Missions of Jesus and the Disciples*, 154–61 (including further bibliographic references). For the identification of this disciple with John the son of Zebedee, see ch. 1 in Köstenberger, *Encountering John*; for the identification of this disciple with the Fourth Evangelist, see H. M. Jackson, "Ancient Self-Referential Conventions and Their Implications for the Authorship and Integrity of the Gospel of John," *JTS* 50 (1999): 1–34.
440. Cf. Jackson, "Ancient Self-Referential Conventions," 31.
441. Cf. G. H. R. Horsley, *New Documents Illustrating Early Christianity*, vol. 1 (North Sidney: Macquarie Univ. Press, 1981), 9 (= §1); vol. 2 (1982), 75 (= §2).
442. See *b. Pesaḥ.* 108a: "Even the poorest man in Israel must not eat until he reclines."

443. "The senior takes his place first, the second next above him, and then the third one below him" (*b. Ber.* 46b).
444. Morris, *John*, 555–56. See also Jeremias, *Eucharistic Words*, 48–49.
445. See *m. Pesaḥ.* 10:3.
446. Cf. Jeremias, *Eucharistic Words*, 54.
447. On acts of charity, see Jeremias, *Jerusalem*, 126–34. On begging, see ibid., 116–19.
448. The saying is attributed to Mar Zuṭra (d. A.D. 417); cf. Luke 21:2–4 par.
449. E.g., Matt. 8:20 par.; 17:24–27; Luke 8:3.
450. Ex. 12:8; cf. *m. Zebaḥ.* 5:8. Cf. Jeremias, *Eucharistic Words*, 44–46, who also cites *Jub.* 49:1, 12; *t. Pesaḥ.* 1:34 and other references.
451. Brown, *John*, 2:611. See also *T. Reub.* 1:3: "My children, I am dying and I go the way of my fathers."
452. Lev. 19:18; cf. Matt. 5:43. For a general survey, see L. Morris, "Love," *DJG*, 492–95.
453. *T. Gad* 6:1; cf. *T. Zeb.* 5:1, 8:5; *T. Jos.* 17:1–2; *T. Iss.* 7:6–7; *T. Sim.* 4:7; *T. Reu.* 4:5.
454. The rendering "mansions" (rather than "rooms"), which crept into English translations through Tyndale (1526) via the Vulgate, mistakenly suggests luxurious accommodations in modern parlance (Lat. *mansio* referred to a halting place, which was still the meaning of "mansion" in Tyndale's day). See Brown, *John*, 2:619.
455. On "father's house" as designating a (patriarchal) family in the LXX and extrabiblical literature, see J. McCaffrey, *The House with Many Rooms: The Temple Theme of Jn. 14, 2–3* (AnBib 114; Rome: Pontifical Biblical Institute, 1988), 50–51.
456. E.g., *1 En.* 39:4–5; 41:2; 71:16; *2 En.* 61:2. Cf. Luke 16:9, where Jesus speaks of his disciples' being "welcomed into eternal dwellings."
457. *Dreams* 1.256; cf. *Confusion* 78; *Heir* 274; *Moses* 2.288.
458. G. Schrenk, "πατήρ," *TDNT,* 5:997.
459. Walker, *Jesus and the Holy City* (Grand Rapids: Eerdmans, 1996), 186–90, esp. 188.
460. Similar language is used in Mark 10:40; 1 Cor. 2:9; Heb. 11:16; 1 Peter 1:4.
461. For specific rabbinic references and discussion, see Köstenberger, "Jesus As Rabbi," 120–22.
462. 1QS 4:2–17; cf. 2 Peter 2:2, 15, where "the way of truth" or "the straight way" is contrasted with "shameful ways" and "the way of Balaam."
463. Perhaps on the basis of Isa. 40:3; cf. 1QS 8:12–16; 9:19–20.
464. Acts 9:2; 19:9, 23; 22:4; 24:14, 22.
465. See Jer. 24:7; 31:34; Hos. 13:4. Cf. H. B. Huffmon, "The Treaty Background of Hebrew *YĀDA'*," *BASOR* 181 (1966): 31–37.
466. But see Ps. 9:10; 36:10; Dan. 11:32.
467. See 20:21. In another sense, it is the Spirit who is Jesus' "successor" (cf. v. 16). In 15:26–27, it is both the disciples and the Spirit.
468. See Deut. 5:10; 6:5–6; 7:9; 10:12–13; 11:13, 22.
469. See *New Docs* 4 §71.
470. Plato, *Phaed.* 65. A similar phrase is also found in Lucian, *Mort. Peregr.* 6.
471. Bammel, "Farewell Discourse," 108.
472. Cf. esp. Ps.-Plat. *Def.* 413a, cited in W. Foerster, "εἰρήνη," *TDNT,* 2:401.
473. Cf. L. Morris, *The Apostolic Preaching of the Cross*, 3d ed. (London: Tyndale, 1965), 237–44.
474. Beasley-Murray, *John*, 262.
475. On peace, see further W. Foerster, "εἰρήνη," *TDNT,* 2:400–17.
476. See BAGD, 592.
477. Cf. Josephus, *J.W.* 5.5.4 §210; *Ant.* 15.11.3 §395; *m. Mid.* 3:8; Tacitus, *Hist.* 5.5.
478. See 5:1–7; 27:2–6; cf. Ps. 80:8–16; Jer. 2:21; 6:9; 12:10–13; Ezek. 15:1–8; 17:5–10; 19:10–14; Hos. 10:1–2; 14:7; see also Sir. 24:17–23; 2 Esd. 5:23. An extensive allegorical depiction of Israel as a vine is also found in *Lev. Rab.* 36:2 (with reference to Ps. 80:9).
479. Since the Old Testament develops the vine metaphor in predominantly negative terms, the notion of the vine as the source of life for the branches is largely absent (but see Sir. 24:17–21).
480. E. M. Sidebottom, "The Son of Man As Man in the Fourth Gospel," *ExpTim* 68 (1956–57): 234, points to similarities in vocabulary between John 15 and the *mamšal* of the vine in Ezek. 17. Other parallels are adduced by B. Vawter, "Ezekiel and John," *CBQ* 26 (1964): 450–58. A general survey is found in R. A. Whitacre, "Vine, Fruit of the Vine," *DJG*, 867–68.
481. For Palestinian horticultural practice, see G. Dalman, *Arbeit und Sitte in Palästina* IV (Hildesheim: G. Olms, 1964), 312–13.
482. See Horace, *Epod.* 2.13: "cutting off useless branches with the pruning knife."
483. Cf. J. C. Laney, "Abiding Is Believing: The Analogy of the Vine in John 15:1–6," *BibSac* 146 (1989): 55–66, esp. 58–60.
484. See Ex. 25:8; 29:45; Lev. 26:11–12; Ezek. 37:27–28; 43:9. E. Malatesta, *Interiority and Covenant* (Anal. Bib. 69; Rome: Biblical Institute Press, 1978), esp. ch. 8; J. W. Pryor, "Covenant and Community in John's Gospel," *RTR* 47 (1988): 49–50.
485. F. Lang, "πῦρ," *TDNT,* 6:934–47, esp. 936–37 and 942.

486. E.g., Isa. 25:9; 35:10; 51:3; 61:10; 66:10; Zeph. 3:14–17; Zech. 9:9. See H. Conzelmann, "χαίρω, χαρά," *TDNT,* 9:362–63.
487. See G. Delling, "πληρόω," *TDNT,* 6:297–98; Conzelmann, "χαίρω, χαρά," 9:365.
488. For further references, see G. Stählin, "φίλος", *TDNT,* 9:151–54. See also Malina and Rohrbaugh, *Social Science Commentary,* 236.
489. For a study of the concept of friendship in Greco-Roman, Jewish, and early Christian literature with special focus on John's Gospel, see J. M. Ford, *Redeemer-Friend and Mother* (Minneapolis: Fortress, 1997).
490. *Jub.* 19:9; CD 3:2; *Apoc. Ab.* 9:6; 10:5; cf. James 2:23.
491. Philo, *Heir* 21; *Sacrifices* 130; *Cherubim* 49; *Moses* 1.156.
492. A similar contrast (between servants and sons) is found in Gal. 4:1–7 and Heb. 3:5–6.
493. See G. Quell and G. Schrenk, "ἐκλέγομαι," *TDNT,* 4:155–68.
494. See Matt. 10:34–38 par.; 1 Cor. 7:12–16. Cf. W. Barclay, *The Gospel of John,* rev. ed. (Philadelphia: Westminster, 1975), 2:183–85.
495. See 1 Sam. 12:22; 2 Chron. 6:32; Jer. 14:21; cf. Acts 5:41; 1 Peter 4:14; 1 John 2:12; Rev. 2:3.
496. See G. Stählin, "σκάνδαλον," *TDNT,* 7:339–58.
497. E.g., Isa. 39:6; Jer. 7:32; 9:25; 16:14; 31:31, 38; Zech. 14:1; 2 Esd. 5:1; 13:29; cf. Mark 2:20; Luke 19:43; 23:29.
498. See the use of "service to God" (*latreia*) with reference to Jewish worship in Rom. 9:4 and Heb. 9:1, 6. On Roman persecution, see comments on 16:1; see further M. Sordi, *The Christians and the Roman Empire* (London/New York: Routledge, 1994).
499. See Acts 8:1–3; 26:9–12; Gal. 1:13–14.
500. E.g., Acts 5:33–40; cf. *m. Sanh.* 9:6: "But the Sages say: [He shall suffer death] at the hands of Heaven."
501. E.g., Isa. 11:1–10; 32:14–18; 42:1–4; 44:1–5; Jer. 31:31–34; Ezek. 11:17–20; 36:24–27; 37:1–14; Joel 2:28–32; cf. John 3:5; 7:37–39.
502. Cf. F. W. Young, "A Study of the Relation of Isaiah to the Fourth Gospel," *ZNW* 46 (1955): 224–26.
503. See Isa. 13:8; 21:3; 26:17–18; 42:14; 66:7–13; Jer. 4:31; 6:24; 13:21; 22:23; 30:6; 49:22–24; 50:43; Mic. 4:9–10; cf. 2 Esd. 16:38.
504. E.g., *b. Sanh.* 98b; *b. Ketub.* 111a; 1QH 11:8–12; cf. Rev. 12:2–5. Cf. W. H. Brownlee, "Messianic Motifs of Qumran and the New Testament," *NTS* 3 (1956/57): 12–30, esp. 29.
505. E.g., Isa. 53:6; Jer. 23:1; 50:17; Ezek. 34:6, 12, 21.
506. See Wisd. Sol. 10:2; *Odes Sol.* 9:11; 10:4; 1 Esd. 3:12. J. E. Bruns, "A Note on John 16 33 and 1 John 2 13–14," *JBL* 86 (1967): 453, contends that John's portrayal of Jesus as victor echoes the pagan myth of Herakles, the conqueror of death and evil.
507. See Damiano Marzotto, "Giovanni 17 e il Targum di Esodo 19–20," *RivB* 25 (1977): 375–88.
508. Cited in Barrett, *John,* 390; cited also in Boring, *Hellenistic Commentary,* 303, where the source is identified as magical papyrus *PGM,* 7.500–504 (3d cent. A.D.).
509. Other relevant passages include Isa. 49:3; *Odes Sol.* 10:4; Phil. 2:9.
510. See also Matt. 11:27; 28:18; Wisd. Sol. 10:2.
511. See *b. Ber.* 63a, citing Prov. 3:6; *Song Rab.* I.4 §1, citing Hos. 4:6; *b. Makk.* 24a, citing Hab. 2:4.
512. Cf. H. M. Jackson, "Ancient Self-Referential Conventions," 24–31.
513. E.g., Ps. 22:22; Isa. 52:6; Ezek. 39:7.
514. E.g., Heb. "children of unrighteousness" becomes "children of perdition" in Isa. 57:4 LXX; the same phrase is found in *Jub.* 10:3.
515. Heb. "the people I have totally destroyed" becomes "the people of perdition" in Isa. 34:5 LXX.
516. See Matt. 23:15: "son of hell"; Eph. 5:6 = Col. 3:6 (textual variant): "those who are disobedient" = "sons of disobedience."
517. Cf. F. W. Danker, "The *huios* Phrases in the New Testament," *NTS* 7 (1960–61): 94, who cites a passage in Menander's *Dyscolos* (published as part of Papyrus Bodmer IV) that contains the word "madman" (lit., "son of madness," *odynēs huios*).
518. 1QS 9:16 and 10:19: "men of the pit"; CD 6:15 and 13:14: "sons of the pit."
519. *y. Ber.* 2:7: "God knows when it is the right time to take the righteous from the world."
520. *y. Pe'ah* 1:1: "If a person guards himself from transgression once, twice, three times, thereafter, the Holy One, blessed be he, will guard him"; *Deut. Rab.* 4:4: "If you will keep the words of the law, I will guard you from the demons" (cf. Ps. 140:1; Matt. 6:13).
521. For a further discussion of Qumran parallels to the notion of unity in John 17, see Brown, *John,* 2:777.
522. *Gen. Rab.* 1:10; 2:5; *Lev. Rab.* 25:3; *Num. Rab.* 12:6; *Deut. Rab.* 10:2; *As. Mos.* 1:13–14. For further Jewish references, see F. Hauck, "καταβολή," *TDNT,* 3:620–21.
523. E.g., Ps. 116:5; 119:137; Jer. 12:1; cf. Rom. 3:26; 1 John 1:9; Rev. 16:5.
524. See the studies in *The Trial of Jesus,* ed. E. Bammel (SBT 2/13; London: SCM, 1970); B. Corley, "Trial of Jesus," *DJG,* 841–54.

525. On Roman and Jewish administrative policies in first-century A.D. Palestine, see now esp. P. Egger, *"Crucifixus sub Pontio Pilato"* (NTAbh NF 32; Münster: Aschendorff, 1997).
526. See 2 Sam. 15:23; 1 Kings 2:37; 15:13; 2 Kings 23:4, 6, 12; 2 Chron. 29:16; 30:14; Jer. 31:40; 1 Macc. 15:39, 41; cf. Neh. 2:15.
527. See Matt. 26:36; Mark 14:32. See J. B. Green, "Gethsemane," *DJG*, 265–68, esp. 267–68.
528. See Jeremias, *Eucharistic Words*, 55.
529. See Blomberg in his forthcoming book on the historicity of John's Gospel, ad. loc.
530. *Chiliarchos* was used to translate Latin *tribunus militum*, a commander of a cohort of 600 or even as few as 200 men (e.g., Polybius, *Hist.* 11.23; the LXX features twenty-nine instances of *chiliarchos* for civil or military officials).
531. Various versions circulated, depending on the high priests targeted: cf. *b. Pesaḥ.* 57a; *t. Menaḥ.* 13:21. The version cited is found in J. Klausner, *Jesus of Nazareth* (London: G. Allen & Unwin, 1925), 337. Ishmael b. Phabi was Annas's successor.
532. See Schürer, *HJP*², 2:203–6.
533. See the discussions in R. H. Smith, "The Household Lamps of Palestine in New Testament Times," *BA* 29 (Feb. 1966): 2–27; J. Jeremias, "*Lampades* in Matthew 25:1–13," in *Soli Deo Gloria*, ed. J. M. Richards (Richmond: John Knox, 1968), 83–87.
534. Cf. Smith, "Household Lamps," 7.
535. Cf. Dion. Hal., *Ant. Rom.* 11.40.2: "carrying torches [*phanous*] and lamps [*lampadas*]."
536. Cf. Josephus, *J.W.* 4.4.6 §293: "the majority were unarmed."
537. See Ezek. 1:28; 44:4; Dan. 2:46; 8:18; 10:9; Acts 9:4; 22:7; 26:14; Rev. 1:17; 19:10; 22:8.
538. Eusebius, *Praep. ev.* 9.27: "the king . . . bade Moses tell him the name of the God who sent him, scoffing at him: but Moses bent down and whispered in his ear, and when the king heard it he fell speechless." The legend is attributed to Artapanus, *Concerning the Jews* (prior to first century B.C.?). Cf. R. G. Bury, "Two Notes on the Fourth Gospel," *ExpTim* 24 (1912–13): 233.
539. See Ps. 27:2; 35:4; cf. 56:9; see also Elijah's experience, 2 Kings 1:9–14.
540. See *Ant.* 1.15 §240; 13.5.1 §131; 14.14.6 §390; 15.6.2–3 §§167–175; *J.W.* 1.14.1 §276; 1.15.1 §287; 1.18.4 §360.
541. Hence the suggestion that Malchus was an Arab; cf. 1 Macc. 11:39: "Imalkue the Arab"; Josephus, *Ant.* 13.5.1 §131: "Malchus the Arab," referring to an earlier namesake. See Brown, *John*, 2:812; BAGD, 489–90.
542. Cf. BAGD, 174.
543. E.g., Ps. 75:8; Isa. 51:17, 22; Jer. 25:15–17; Ezek. 23:31–34; Hab. 2:16.
544. See 1QpHab 11:10–15: "cup of YHWH's right hand," "cup of God's anger"; Rev. 14:10; 16:19; 18:6.
545. Cf. G. Delling, "*Baptisma Baptisthēnai*," *NovT* 2 (1957): 92–115, esp. 110–15; L. Goppelt, "πίνω, ποτήριον," *TDNT*, 6:149–53.
546. Cf. E. M. Smallwood, "High Priests and Politics in Roman Palestine," *JTS* 13 (1962): 14–34.
547. See note on 13:23 and Köstenberger, *Encountering John*, ch. 1.
548. See Morris, *John*, 666, n. 37.
549. E.g., 2 Kings 10:11; Ps. 55:13; cf. Luke 2:44: "relatives and *friends*"; see also *New Docs* 4.44; Homer, *Iliad* 15.350: "kinsmen."
550. MM 295 cite inscriptions dating from 14 B.C. and A.D. 34.
551. Cf. Lady W. M. Ramsay, "Her That Kept the Door," *ExpTim* 27 (1915–16): 217–18, 314–16 and the supplement by J. Mann, pp. 424–25, pertaining to Talmudic literature.
552. Cf. A. N. Sherwin-White, *Roman Society and Roman Law in the New Testament* (Oxford: Oxford Univ. Press, 1963), 45.
553. The charge that Jesus leads the people astray surfaces earlier in John's Gospel: e.g., 7:12, 47.
554. Morris, *John*, 670; Keener, *BBC*, 307.
555. See P. S. Alexander, "Jewish Law in the Time of Jesus: Towards a Clarification of the Problem," in *Law and Religion*, ed. B. Lindars (Cambridge: J. Clarke, 1988), 44–58, esp. 46–49; Schürer, *HJP*², 2:199–226.
556. See the discussion in J. Blinzler, *The Trial of Jesus* (Cork: Mercier, 1959), 112–14.
557. *b. Šabb.* 15a; *b. Sanh.* 41b; *b. ʿAbod. Zar.* 8b.
558. Jeremias, *Jerusalem*, 47–48.
559. Cf. J. H. Bernard, *A Critical and Exegetical Commentary on the Gospel According to St. John* (Edinburgh: T. & T. Clark, 1928), 2:604.
560. Acts 21:35, 40; see the extensive description in Josephus, *J.W.* 5.5.8 §§238–46; both locations are mentioned in *Ant.* 15.8.5 §292. Cf. the discussion in Brown, *John*, 2:845.
561. *Embassy* 306: "the house of the governors"; see also the incident involving Pilate taking place in that location recounted in *Embassy* 299–305.
562. Cf. L. H. Vincent, "L'Antonia, palais primitif d'Hérode," *RB* 61 (1954): 87–107.
563. Cf. C. Kopp, *The Holy Places of the Gospels* (Edinburgh/London: Nelson, n.d. [1963]), 368–39. Brown, *John*, 2:845, also notes that the term *aulem*, used in Mark 15:16 to describe the Praetorium, occurs frequently in Josephus with reference to the Herodian

Palace but never with regard to the Fortress of Antonia.

564. See also Seneca, *De ira* 2.7.3: "All these thousands hurrying to the forum at break of day." Cf. Sherwin-White, *Roman Society*, 45, with primary references.
565. *m.* ᵓ*Ohal.* 18:7: "The dwelling-places of Gentiles are unclean"; cf. Num. 9:7–14; 31:19.
566. See Luke 22:1: "the Feast of Unleavened Bread, called the Passover"; see further notes on 19:14, 31.
567. Cf. C. C. Torrey, "The Date of the Crucifixion According to the Fourth Gospel," *JBL* 50 (1931): 239–40. Contra Keener, *BBC*, 307–8, who says different calendars or John's "making a symbolic point" account for the apparent discrepancy between John and the Synoptics.
568. See the discussion in Barrett, *John*, 533–35; Hengel, "Johannesevangelium als Quelle," 330; and Paul Winter, *On the Trial of Jesus* (Berlin: de Gruyter, 1974).
569. *y. Sanh.* 1:1; 7:2; on "forty years," see note on v. 24 above; this probably refers to A.D. 6. See also Simon Legasse, *The Trial of Jesus* (London: SCM, 1997), 54–56.
570. Cf. Sherwin-White, *Roman Society*, 24–47, esp. 36.
571. A. N. Sherwin-White, "The Trial of Christ," in *Historicity and Chronology in the New Testament* (London: SPCK, 1965), 99, summarized by Brown, *John*, 2:848.
572. Josephus, *J.W.* 1.4.6 §97; 4QpNahum 1:6–8: "the Angry Lion [who filled his den with a mass of corpses, carrying out rev]enge . . . , who hanged living men [from the tree, committing an atrocity which had not been committed] in Israel since ancient times, for it is horrible for the one hanged alive from the tree."
573. Lev. 24:16; cf. John 10:33; Acts 7:57–58; *m. Sanh.* 7:4; 9:3.
574. Cf. Sherwin-White, *Roman Society*, 13–23.
575. Cf. E. Bammel, "The Trial before Pilate," in *Jesus and the Politics of His Day*, ed. E. Bammel and C. F. D. Moule (Cambridge: CUP, 1984), 417–19.
576. Cf. E. E. Jensen, "The First Century Controversy Over Jesus as a Revolutionary Figure," *JBL* 60 (1941): 261–72, esp. 261–62.
577. The expression refers to the entire festival in Deut. 16:1–2; Ezek. 45:21; Luke 2:41; 22:1; John 2:13, 23; 6:4; 11:55; Acts 12:4; Josephus, *Ant.* 17.9.3 §213; cf. *y. Pesaḥ.* 9:5: "and [the first Passover in Egypt was observed for] one night [only], whereas the Passover of [successive] generations is observed for the entire seven [days]."
578. Cf. Josephus, *Ant.* 20.209; Livy, *History* 5.13; *b. Pesaḥ* 91a. See Josef Blinzler, *The Trial of Jesus* (Westminster: Newman, 1959), 218–21.
579. C. B. Chavel, "The Releasing of a Prisoner of the Eve of Passover in Ancient Jerusalem," *JBL* 60 (1941): 273–78 (the quotation is from p. 277).
580. Keener, *BBC*, 309.
581. Cf. J. J. Twomey, "'Barabbas Was a Robber,'" *Scr.* 8 (1956): 115–19.
582. G. Bornkamm, "λῃστής," *TDNT*, 4:257–62.
583. Humphreys and Waddington, "The Jewish Calendar, a Lunar Eclipse and the Date of Christ's Crucifixion," 331–51, with particular reference to the lunar eclipse occurring on that day (cf. Mark 15:33).
584. For ancient references on flogging and torture, see Malina and Rohrbaugh, *Social-Science Commentary*, 263.
585. Sherwin-White, *Roman Society*, 27–28.
586. Similar floggings are recorded in Acts 22:24 (cf. 16:22) and in Josephus, *J.W.* 2.306.
587. The former is favored by E. Ha-Reubéni, "Recherches sur les plantes de l'évangile," *RB* 42 (1933): 230–34; the latter by H. J. Hart, "Crown of Thorns in John 19:2–5," *JTS* 3 (1952): 66–75; E. R. Goodenough and C. B. Welles, "The Crown of Acanthus?" *HTR* 46 (1953): 241–42; and Avi–Yonah, *World of the Bible*, 151, suggest acanthus.
588. C. Bonner, "The Crown of Thorns," *HTR* 46 (1953): 47–48.
589. Hart, "Crown of Thorns," 66–75, esp. 71–74.
590. Carson, *Matthew*, 573.
591. Cf. P. Winter, *On the Trial of Jesus*, 2d ed. (Berlin/New York: de Gruyter, 1974), 148–49.
592. Cf. W. A. Meeks, *The Prophet-King* (NovTSup 14; Leiden: Brill, 1967), 70–71.
593. Demosthenes, *Mid.* 91; *De Falsa Leg.* 198; 4th cent. B.C.
594. O. Michel, "Son," *NIDNTT*, 3:637.
595. A. Deissmann, *Bible Studies* (Edinburgh: T. & T. Clark, 1901), 167.
596. *Life Apollonii* 1.21: "'By the gods,' he asked, 'who are you?' this time altering his tone to a whine of entreaty"; 4.44: "careful not to fight with a god."
597. Yet see P. L. Maier, "Episode of the Golden Roman Shields at Jerusalem," *HTR* 62 (1969): 109–21.
598. See H. W. Hoehner, "Chronology," *DJG*, 121. Contra Keener, *BBC*, 311; Brown, *John*, 2:891, who conjectures that "perhaps the tremors that presaged the fall of Sejanus were already felt by sensitive political observers, and Pilate feared that soon he would have no protector at court," thus placing Jesus' trial and crucifixion prior to Sejanus's demise in October, A.D. 31.

599. See Avi-Yonah, *World of the Bible*, 152.
600. C. C. Torrey, "The Date of the Crucifixion According to the Fourth Gospel," *JBL* 50 (1931): 227–41 (including his critique of Str-B 2:834–85 on 235–36); A. J. B. Higgins, "Origins of the Eucharist," *NTS* 1 (1954–55): 206–9; Cullen I. K. Storey, "The Mental Attitude of Jesus at Bethany: John 11.33,38," *NTS* 37 (1989): 51–66; Blomberg, *The Historical Reliability of the Gospels*, 177–78; Morris, *John*, 708; Ridderbos, *John*, 606.
601. Cf. Josephus, *Ant.* 14.2.1 §21; 17.9.3 §213; *J.W.* 2.1.3 §10; Luke 22:1; see comments on 18:28.
602. See Craig Blomberg, *The Historical Reliability of the Gospels*, 180; Morris, *John*, 708; see also comments on John 1:39.
603. Cf. Sherwin-White, *Roman Society*, 27.
604. Carson, *John*, 597.
605. The upper palm of the hand is considered most likely by F. T. Zugibe, "Two Questions About Crucifixion," *BRev* 5/2 (1989): 41–43.
606. See Lev. 24:14, 23; Num. 15:35–36; Deut. 17:5; 21:19–21; 22:24; Acts 7:58; cf. Luke 4:29.
607. See R. Riesner, "Archeology and Geography," *DJG*, 43; J. E. Taylor, "Golgotha: A Reconsideration of the Evidence for the Sites of Jesus' Crucifixion and Burial," *NTS* 44 (1998): 180–203. Gordon's Calvary is ruled out by A. Parrot, *Golgotha and the Church of the Holy Sepulchre* (London: SCM, 1957), 59–65.
608. Cf. M. Hengel, *Crucifixion* (Philadelphia: Fortress, 1977); J. B. Green, "Death of Jesus," *DJG*, 147–48; Malina and Rohrbaugh, *Social-Science Commentary*, 263–64; David W. Chapman, "Perceptions of Crucifixion among Jews and Christians in the Ancient World" (Ph.D. diss., University of Cambridge, 2000).
609. Seneca, *Consol. ad Marciam* 20.3 (A.D. 37–41); Pliny, *Hist. Nat.* 36.107–18; Josephus, *J.W.* 5.11.1 §451; Philo, *Dreams* 2.213.
610. The latter (shock) is strongly argued by Zugibe, "Two Questions," 41: "Shock is unquestionably the cause of Jesus' death on the cross," referring also to a surgeon's opinion, who contends, "there is overwhelming evidence that Christ died from heart failure due to extreme shock caused by exhaustion, pain and loss of blood."
611. The man's name is incribed on his bone ossuary as Yehoḥanan ben Hagkol. See J. H. Charlesworth, "Jesus and Jehoḥanan: An Archaeological Note on Crucifixion," *ExpTim* 84 (1972–73): 147–50.
612. Cf. Str-B 1:835, with primary references.
613. For a reconstruction of the sign, see Avi-Yonah, *World of the Bible*, 153.
614. Cf. Riesner, *Jesus als Lehrer*, 199.
615. Inscriptions warning Gentiles against entering the inner temple were written mainly in Greek (see comments on 2:14).
616. Polyglot notices were common in the Hellenistic era. Examples include those cited by Josephus (*Ant.* 14.10.2 §191: "both Greek and Latin" [47 B.C.]; *J.W.* 6.2.4 §125: "in Greek characters and in your own" [Hebrew]), and the *Res Gestae Divi Augusti* (prior to A.D. 13), which existed not only in Latin but also in Greek. See also Est. 8:9. Blinzler, *Trial of Jesus*, 254–55, also refers to Roman tombstones still extant today.
617. Keener, *BBC*, 313.
618. Cicero, *Epist. Quint. Fratr.* 1.2.2; 1.2.13: *scripsi, scripsi* (59 B.C.).
619. The ruling is attributed to the "deified Hadrian" (A.D. 117–38).
620. Cf. H. Daniel-Rops, *Daily Life in Palestine at the Time of Christ* (London: Weidenfeld & Nicolson, 1962), 211–18.
621. Cf. Keener, *BBC*, 313.
622. For the use of Ps. 22 in ancient Jewish writings, see Str-B 2:574–80.
623. Cf. E. Stauffer, *Jesus and His Story* (London: SCM, 1960), 111–12 and 179, n. 1.
624. See Ps. 2:7: "You are my Son; today I have become your Father"; Tobit 7:12: "you are her brother, and she is your sister." On the Code of Hammurabi, see R. de Vaux, *Ancient Israel* (New York: McGraw-Hill, 1961), 112–13.
625. M.-J. Lagrange, *Évangile selon Saint Jean*, 2d ed. (Paris: J. Gabalda, 1925), 494, cited in Brown, *John*, 2:907.
626. Brown, *John*, 2:909. There is some uncertainty as to the exact species of hyssop referred to here: see the discussion in J. Wilkinson, "Seven Words from the Cross," *SJT* 17 (1964): 77; W. E. Shewell-Cooper, *Plants and Fruits of the Bible* (London: Darton, Longman & Todd, 1962), 75–76; and F. G. and P. A. Beetham, "A Note on John 19:29," *JTS* 44 (1993): 163–69.
627. Cf. Str-B 2:582.
628. Cf. N. Haas, "Anthropological Observations on the Skeletal Remains from Giv'at ha-Mivtar," *IEJ* 20 (1970): 38–59; J. Zias and E. Sekeles, "The Crucified Man from Giv'at ha-Mivtar," *IEJ* 35 (1985): 22–27; H. Shanks, "New Analysis of the Crucified Man," *BAR* 11 (Nov./Dec. 1985): 20–21.
629. Cf. J. Wilkinson, "The Incident of the Blood and Water in John 19.34," *SJT* 28 (1975): 149–72.
630. See the summary in Carson, *John*, 623–24, and the fuller treatment in Beasley-Murray, *John*, 355–58. For further discussion, see P. Barbet, *A Doctor at Calvary* (New York: P. J.

Kennedy, 1953); W. D. Edwards et al., *Journal of the American Medical Assocation* 255 (1986): 1455–63; A. F. Sava, "Wound in the Side of Christ," *CBQ* 19 (1960): 343–46.

631. See *Lev. Rab.* 15:2 on Lev. 13:2: "Man is evenly balanced, half of him is water, and the other half is blood."
632. *m. Pesaḥ.* 5:5–8; cf. *m. ᵓOhal.* 3:5.
633. Cf. J. M. Ford, "Mingled Blood from the Side of Christ, John 19:34," *NTS* 15 (1969): 337–38.
634. Avi-Yonah, *World of the Bible*, 154.
635. Cf. D. Daube, *The New Testament and Rabbinic Judaism*, 325–29.
636. For a survey of funerary customs in antiquity and a discussion of the likely location of Jesus' burial site, see J. B. Green, "Burial of Jesus," *DJG*, 88–92.
637. One possibility is the Judean village Ramathaim-Zephim (cf. 1 Sam. 1:1).
638. See Josephus, *Ant.* 5.1.14 §44: Achan "given the ignominious burial proper to the condemned." Cf. *m. Sanh.* 6:5.
639. See further F. N. Hepper, "Flax and Linen in Biblical Times," *Buried History* 25 (December 1989): 105–16.
640. Cf. Taylor, "Golgotha," 180, referring also to G. Barkay, "The Garden Tomb—Was Jesus Buried Here?" *BAR* 12/2 (March/April 1986): 40–53, 56–57.
641. In emergency situations it was probably permissible to wash and anoint a dead person's body even after sundown; cf. the cases adjudicated in *m. Šabb.* 23:4–5.
642. See Brown, *John*, 2:982–83.
643. Text in Barrett, *New Testament Background*, 15.
644. Morris, *John*, 734.
645. Judg. 5:28; Prov. 7:6; Song 2:9; Sir. 14:23; 21:23.
646. Dan. 10:5–6; Ezek. 9:2; Rev. 15:6; cf. *1 En.* 87:2.
647. E.g., in 2 Macc. 3:26, where two "splendidly dressed" young men appear to Heliodorus; cf. Acts 1:10: "two men (i.e., angels) dressed in white."
648. Cf. R. G. Maccini, *Her Testimony Is True* (JSNTSup 125; Sheffield: Sheffield Academic Press, 1996), 207–33.
649. C. S. Keener, *BBC*, 317.
650. See also 1 Kings 17:21; Ezek. 37:9; Wisd. Sol. 15:11; cf. Philo, *Opif.* 135.
651. The Greek words used for "binding and loosing" in Matthew are *deō* and *lyō*; John has *aphiēmi* for "forgive" and *krateō* for "retain."
652. J. A. Emerton, "Binding and Loosing—Forgiving and Retaining," *JTS* 13 (1962): 325–31.
653. A. Schlatter, *Der Evangelist Matthäus*, 5th ed. (Stuttgart: Calwer, 1959), 511.
654. Cf. Str-B 1:738–41; H. Büchsel, "δέω," *TDNT*, 2:60–61; Lightfoot, *A Commentary on the New Testament from the Talmud and Hebraica*, 2:237–41; G. Dalman, *The Words of Jesus*, 213–17.
655. Cf. Deissmann, *Light from the Ancient Near East*, 361–62.
656. Cited in Barrett, *John*, 574.
657. See Bultmann, *John*, 697–98, n. 2.
658. Cf. C. F. D. Moule, "The Post-Resurrection Appearances in the Light of Festival Pilgrimages," *NTS* 4 (1957–58): 58–61.
659. G. Dalman, *Arbeit und Sitte in Palästina VI* (Hildesheim: G. Olms, 1964 [1939]), 346–51, esp. 349. See also Keener, *BBC*, 318.
660. Avi-Yonah, *World of the Bible*, 155.
661. See *t. Ber.* 2:20: "where people stand naked, he may not greet [his fellows] there."
662. *T. Zeb.* 6:6: "Therefore the Lord made my catch to be an abundance of fish; for whoever shares with his neighbor receives multifold from the Lord."
663. See Beasley-Murray, *John*, 408–409; Hengel, *Crucifixion*, esp. ch. 4.
664. *Barn.* 12; Justin, *Apol.* 1.35; Irenaeus, *Dem.* 79.
665. 1 Peter 5:13 places Peter in Rome not much earlier.
666. *Scorpiace* 15: "Peter is struck [i.e., his legs are broken to hasten the crucified's death]. . . . At Rome Nero was the first who stained with blood the rising faith. Then is Peter girt by another, when he is made fast to the cross." Blomberg in his forthcoming book on the historicity of John's Gospel also cites *Acts Pet.* 37–39 and Eusebius, *Eccl. Hist.* 3.1.
667. Cf. Jackson, "Ancient Self-Referential Conventions," to whom I am indebted also in my note on 21:24. On the present verse, Jackson writes, "Verse 23 . . . makes perfectly good sense as a corrective from a living Beloved Disciple anxious to dispel what he feels are overly enthusiastic eschatological inferences being drawn by some from Jesus' words" (21–22).
668. See Gal. 6:11; Col. 4:18; 2 Thess. 3:17; Philem. 19.
669. "This is the disciple," "his testimony." Compare the high-priestly prayer, where Jesus refers to himself as "Jesus Christ" (17:3) and Thucydides's practice of introducing himself in the third person (1.1.1 and 5.26.1) and of referring to himself as "Thucydides" (4.104–7: "Thucydides, the son of Oloros, who composed this history"). Cf. Jackson, "Ancient Self-Referential Conventions," 27; see also 28–30 on Josephus.
670. An "associative collective," where the "you" subsumed under the "we" are the book's

Christian readers but where the "I" included in the "we" is the author (ibid., 23–24).

671. Other later examples are cited in Boring, *Hellenistic Commentary*, 308.

Sidebar and Chart Notes

A-1. See esp. Henry Mowvley, "John 1[14–18] in the Light of Exodus 33[7]–34[35]," *ExpTim* 95 (1984): 135–37.

A-2. There are two major possibilities for the dating of Jesus' ministry, A.D. 26–30 or 29–33, with the latter set of dates to be preferred. See H. W. Hoehner, *Chronological Aspects of the Life of Christ* (Grand Rapids: Zondervan, 1977); idem., "Chronology," *DJG*, 118–22. A less detailed but congruent chronology is found in J. Finegan, *Handbook of Biblical Chronology* (rev. ed.; Peabody, Mass.: Hendrickson, 1998), 352.

A-3. For the dating of the four Passovers between A.D. 29 and 33 mentioned above, see Humphreys and Waddington, "Jewish Calendar," 368, likewise settles on Friday, April 3, A.D. 33, as the most likely date of Jesus' crucifixion, with reference to Hoener, *Chronological Aspects*, 44, 114, and P. Maier, "The Dates of the Nativity and the Chronology of Jesus' Life," in J. Vardaman and E. M. Yamauchi, eds., *Chronos, Kairos, Christos; FS Finegan* (Winona Lake, Ind.: Eisenbrauns, 1989), 125 and Table 1.

A-4. For a defense of the temple cleansing as a sign in John's Gospel, see Köstenberger, "The Seventh Johannine Sign: A Study in John's Christology," *BBR* 5 (1995): 87–103.

A-5. Cf. S. Safrai, "Home and Family," in *The Jewish People in the First Century*, vol. 2, eds. S. Safrai and M. Stern (Philadelphia: Fortress, 1987), 728–92; J. D. M. Derrett, *Law in the New Testament* (London: Darton, Longman & Todd, 1970), 227–38; E. Ferguson, *Backgrounds of Early Christianity*, 2d ed. (Grand Rapids: Eerdmans, 1993), 68–69; D. J. Williams, "Bride, Bridegroom," *DJG*, 86–88.

A-6. On Jesus' "natural family," see esp. R. Bauckham, *Jude and the Relatives of Jesus in the Early Church* (Edinburgh: T. & T. Clark, 1990), 5–44.

A-7. Epiphanius suggests Jesus' brothers were sons of Joseph by a previous marriage; Jerome conjectures they were cousins; but the most likely explanation (already suggested by Helvidius) is that they were the sons of Joseph and Mary, younger half-brothers of Jesus.

A-8. See D. F. Watson, "Wine," *DJG*, 870–73.

A-9. See Gen. 27:28, 37; Deut. 7:13; Judg. 9:13; Ps. 104:15; Prov. 3:10; Song 7:9; Isa. 55:1; 65:8; Joel 3:18; Zech. 9:17; cf. Matt. 26:27–29 par.

A-10. See Deut. 32:32–33; Ps. 60:3; 75:8; Prov. 4:17; 23:29–35; Isa. 5:22; 51:17; Jer. 25:15; Hos. 7:5; Rev. 14:10.

A-11. For a general survey, see M. O. Wise, "Feasts," *DJG*, 234–41.

A-12. On the New Testament characterization of the Jerusalem temple, see esp. P. W. L. Walker, *Jesus and the Holy City* (Grand Rapids: Eerdmans, 1996). A general survey is found in M. O. Wise, "Temple," *DJG*, 811–17.

A-13. Cf. M. Goodman, "A Note on Josephus, the Pharisees and Ancestral Tradition," *JJS* 50 (1999): 17–20.

A-14. See S. Westerholm, "Pharisees," *DJG*, 609–14.

A-15. The considerable literature on Samaritans includes: A. D. Crown, ed., *The Samaritans* (Tübingen: Mohr-Siebeck, 1989); J. Jeremias, "The Samaritans," in *Jerusalem in the Time of Jesus* (London: SCM, 1969), 352–58; J. A. Montgomery, *The Samaritans* (New York: Ktav, 1907; repr. 1968); H. G. M. Williamson, "Samaritans," *DJG*, 724–28. See also H. K. Bond, *Pontius Pilate in History and Interpretation* (SNTSMS 100; Cambridge: Cambridge Univ. Press, 1998), 71–73, 89–93 (esp. 71, n. 69).

A-16. The saying is attributed to the later R. Yannai (c. A.D. 240); the insult "Samaritan" is listed together with "people of the land" (Jews ignorant of the law), "a boor," and "a magician."

A-17. This listing does not imply endorsement as the likely site of Jesus' tomb. The Garden tomb rather provides a setting not dissimilar to the kind of tomb Jesus would have been laid in.

A-18. See, e.g., 5:16, 18; 7:1; 8:48; 10:31, 33; 11:8; 19:12.

A-19. Cf. E. Stern, ed., *The New Encyclopedia of Archaeological Excavations in the Holy Land*, 1:291–96, esp. 292–95, with extensive bibliography; J. C. H. Laughlin, "Capernaum: From Jesus' Time and After," *BAR* 19 (September/October 1993): 55–61, 90, with other helpful bibliographic references.

A-20. For a complete list of high priests from 200 B.C. to A.D. 70, see Jeremias, *Jerusalem*, 377–78. For a list of high priests from 37 B.C. to A.D. 68, see E. M. Smallwood, "High Priests and Politics in Roman Palestine," *JTS* 13 (1962): 31–32.

A-21. Cf. Hengel, "Johannesevangelium als Quelle," 327.

A-22. On these excavations, see esp. W. Horbury, "The 'Caiaphas' Ossuaries and Joseph Caiaphas," *PEQ* 126 (1994): 33–48; E. Stern, ed., *The New Encyclopedia of Archaeological Excavations in the Holy Land*, 2:756. On John's portrayal of Caiaphas and Annas his father-in-law, see now esp. Hengel, "Johannesevangelium als Quelle," 322–34.

A-23. The following is adapted from F. J. Moloney, *The Gospel of John* (Collegeville, Minn.: Liturgical, 1998), 377–78 (for further bibliography, see 389–91). See also E. Bammel, "The Farewell Discourse of the Evangelist John and Its Jewish Heritage," *TynBul* 44 (1993): 103–16; W. S. Kurz, "Luke 22:14–38 and Greco-Roman and Biblical Farewell Addresses," *JBL* 104 (1985): 251–68; idem, *Farewell Addresses in the New Testament* (Collegeville, Minn.: Liturgical, 1990); A. Lacomara, "Deuteronomy and the Farewell Discourse (Jn 13:31–16:33)," *CBQ* 36 (1974): 65–84; R. W. Paschal Jr., "Farewell Discourse," *DJG*, 229–33, esp. 232.

A-24. E.g., Gen. 49; Josh. 23–24; 1 Sam. 12; 1 Kings 2:1–12; 1 Chron. 28–29.

A-25. E.g., *T. 12 Patr.*; *As. Mos.*; cf. *Jub.* 22:10–30; 1 Macc. 2:49–70; Josephus, *Ant.* 12.6.3 §§279–84. For Greco-Roman farewell passages, see Malina and Rohrbaugh, *Social Science Commentary*, 221–22.

A-26. *m. Hor.* 3:4; cf. *m. Meg.* 1:9; *m. Mak.* 2:6; *t. Yoma* 1:4.

A-27. *b. Pesaḥ.* 57a; *t. Menaḥ.* 13:18 "the powerful men of the priesthood."

A-28. See H. W. Hoehner, "Pontius Pilate," *DJG*, 615–17.

A-29. Cf. J. Vardaman, "A New Inscription which Mentions Pilate as 'Prefect,'" *JBL* 81 (1962): 70–71.

A-30. E.g. Josephus, *J.W.* 2.9.2 §§169–74; *Ant.* 18.3.1 §§55–62; Luke 13:1 (?).

A-31. Cf. E. M. Smallwood, "The Date of the Dismissal of Pontius Pilate from Judaea," *JJS* 5 (1954): 12–21.

A-32. Cf. Suetonius, *Tiberius* 58; Tacitus, *Ann.* 3.38.

A-33. Cf. E. Bammel, "*Philos tou Kaisaros*," *TLZ* 77 (1952): 205–10, who consequently insists on a post-A.D. 31 crucifixion date for Jesus.

A-34. See comments on 19:8 above; on Sejanus's anti-Semitism, see Philo, *Embassy* 159–61.

A-35. 1 Macc. 2:18; 3:38; 10:65; 11:27; 3 Macc. 6:23; Josephus, *Ant.* 12.7.3 §298.

CREDITS FOR PHOTOS AND MAPS

Arnold, Clinton E. . . . . p. 4
Claycombe, Hugh . . . . pp. 31, 184–185
Dunn, Cheryl (for Talbot Bible Lands) . . . . pp. 100, 142
Franz, Gordon . . . . p. 40
Haradine, Jane (public domain photos) . . . . pp. 17, 125
Isachar, Hanan . . . . pp. 2–3, 20, 21, 49, 64, 107, 193
King, Jay . . . . pp. 158, 180
Kohlenberger, John R. III . . . . pp. 13, 21, 28, 39, 42, 63, 107, 115, 191
Radovan, Zev . . . . pp. 16, 18, 24, 26, 27, 29, 32, 42, 50, 54, 65, 66, 68, 69, 79, 98, 111, 116, 120, 122, 125, 127, 128, 134, 165, 170, 172, 173(2), 174, 177, 178, 181, 187, 190
Ritmeyer, Leen . . . . pp. 29, 55, 93, 144, 164
Tabernacle . . . . pp. 7, 10
Zondervan Image Archive (Neal Bierling) . . . . . . pp. 4, 8, 15, 22, 30, 43(2), 47, 54, 61, 71(2), 80, 93, 104, 109(2), 122, 123(2), 135, 143, 151, 156, 163, 169, 175, 182, 186, 192, 193

ALSO AVAILABLE

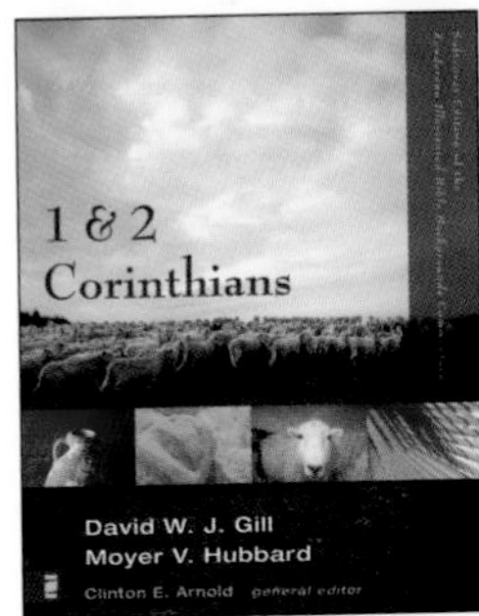

We want to hear from you. Please send your comments about this book to us in care of zreview@zondervan.com. Thank you.

ZONDERVAN.com/
AUTHORTRACKER
follow your favorite authors